D*U*T*C*H

T*I*L*E*S

This exhibition and catalogue are made possible by a grant from Mobil Corporation.

Also generously supported by the National Endowment for the Humanities, a Federal agency; and The Pew Memorial Trust.

Initial funding was provided by the National Endowment for the Arts, a Federal agency; the Women's Committee of the Philadelphia Museum of Art; and generous individuals.

D · U · T · C · H
T · I · L · E · S

IN THE PHILADELPHIA MUSEUM OF ART

Essays by
Jan Daniel van Dam
and Pieter Jan Tichelaar

Catalogue by Ella Schaap
with Robert L. H. Chambers,
Marjorie Lee Hendrix,
and Joan Pierpoline

Technical notes
by P. Andrew Lins

Philadelphia Museum of Art
1984

*Distributed by the University
of Pennsylvania Press*

Cover: Star Tulips (no. 19)

Design: Laurence Channing
Assistant: Mark La Riviere
Photography: Eric Mitchell
Composition: Monotype Composition Company, Baltimore
Printed by Eastern Press, Inc., New Haven

Distributed by the University of Pennsylvania Press
Blockley Hall, 418 Service Drive
Philadelphia, PA 19104

Library of Congress Cataloging in Publication Data

Philadelphia Museum of Art.
    Dutch tiles in the Philadelphia Museum of Art.

    Bibliography: p.
    1. Tiles—Netherlands—History—17th century—Exhi-
bitions. 2. Philadelphia Museum of Art—Exhibitions.
1. Dam, Jan Daniel van, 1950-   . 11. Tichelaar,
Pieter Jan. 111. Schaap, Ella, 1913-   . iv. Lins,
P. Andrew, 1945-   . v. Title.
NK4670.7.N4P48 1984   738.6'09492'0740148ll 84-4854
ISBN 0-87633-058-8 (pbk.)
ISBN 0-8122-7950-6 (Univ. of Penn.)

Contents

Preface

In 1897, when the Philadelphia Museum of Art received the bequest of fifteen eighteenth-century Dutch tiles depicting biblical subjects from the estate of Mrs. Frederick Graff, it was scarcely to be predicted that this small group of objects would prove in time to have been the modest beginning of what is now one of the largest and most comprehensive collections of tiles in this country. This Museum's dedication to the exhibition and acquisition of the decorative arts dates to its founding in 1876. The collection of Dutch furniture and objects grew steadily, emphasized by the purchase in 1928 of a fine seventeenth-century period room from a house in Haarlem, complete with a tiled fireplace, made possible by a gift of funds from Edward W. Bok. The impetus for this exhibition and its accompanying catalogue came from a wonderfully generous succession of gifts, beginning in 1979, from Mrs. Francis P. Garvan and her son Dr. Anthony N. B. Garvan, of the large and important collection of tiles acquired by Francis P. Garvan during the 1920s. Anthony Garvan's concern that the collection become available to the public and scholars for examination, research, and sheer pleasure has greatly enriched this Museum.

Small and practical in format, lending themselves equally well to the bold repetition of a motif (tulips, for example) or the charming variation upon a theme such as children's games, Dutch tiles decorated and protected houses from Amsterdam to Djakarta. In the study of their imagery, later generations find much to learn about the tastes, beliefs, fantasies, and amusements of those resourceful citizens of a young and enterprising republic. Influences from Italy, China, and France are evident in the choice of colors or motifs in many Dutch tiles: in turn, they were exported around the world and widely copied or adapted by craftsmen of other cultures.

It is a source of particular pleasure when an exhibition and its catalogue can focus attention on a little-known aspect of the Museum's permanent collections. Initiated under the directorship of Jean Sutherland Boggs, this project was warmly supported by David DuBon, Curator of Medieval and Renaissance Decorative Arts. It has been conceived and carried out with devotion, energy, and painstaking attention to detail by Ella Schaap as Curatorial Associate, whose years of thoughtful work for this Museum, both on this exhibition and on previous projects, deserve our heartfelt thanks. An important part of this endeavor has been the careful investigation and treatment of the physical condition of the tiles, complementing the study of their iconography and style. Andrew Lins, the Museum's Conservator of Decorative Arts, has conducted a thorough analysis of the collection, and his observations form a valuable addition to this catalogue while the results of the treatment enable the tiles to be presented in both handsome and sturdy condition. It is not possible to mention here all those members of the Museum staff, both temporary and permanent, whose hard work deserves praise, but the Publications and Special Exhibitions departments, as well as the many project assistants working with Andrew Lins and Ella Schaap, made this a truly collaborative effort. The participation of scholars and colleagues both in the United States and in the Netherlands has been essential to the exhibition, and we are particularly grateful to Jan Daniel van Dam, Curator of European Ceramics of the Museum het Princessehof in Leeuwarden, and Pieter Jan Tichelaar for their contributions to this catalogue. Dr. James Tanis, Director of Libraries and Professor of History at Bryn

8

Mawr College, has been of great assistance in his thoughtful review of the project at several stages.

One important aspect of the exhibition is the presentation of the tiles in context, both iconographic and domestic, and we owe our warm thanks to the lenders of comparative objects: prints which provided models for tile images, a tile order book and tools for their making, and handsome examples of the furniture which might have occupied the rooms they decorated.

The Museum is enormously grateful to the remarkable combination of resources which brought this project to realization. As it has done for a sequence of our most significant exhibitions, The Pew Memorial Trust provided substantial funding, particularly in the crucial initial phases. The National Endowment for the Arts, generous private donors, and a gift from the Women's Committee of the Museum helped to support the time-consuming conservation and research. A grant from the National Endowment for the Humanities assured that both exhibition and catalogue could be carried out on the scale and with the detail warranted by the material, so much of it previously unpublished. This exhibition coincides with another Museum project, "Masters of Seventeenth-Century Dutch Genre Painting," and together they offer a unique view of two profoundly characteristic aspects of the history and culture of the Netherlands in its proverbial Golden Age. Without the extremely generous support of Mobil Corporation, with a major grant to both exhibitions, their simultaneous presentation would not have been possible.

Anne d'Harnoncourt
The George D. Widener Director

Foreword

If collecting is a disease, my father, Francis P. Garvan, had contracted it by the time he entered Yale College in 1893. A photograph of his college room shows it filled with furniture, artifacts, and curiously, a large chromolithograph of the German emperor. These acquisitions had been made at the cost of having his East Hartford (Connecticut) cache of personal boyhood memorabilia "cleaned up" by his sister Genevieve, an affront he recalled often in later life.

After the completion of his legal studies, he entered the practice of law in New York. He was proficient at criminal prosecution, and he gained a reputation for it. His prosecution of Harry K. Thaw for the murder of the architect Stanford White was perhaps his most notorious case before World War I; his defense of the Chemical Foundation, his most notable achievement after the war. In 1900 he became an assistant district attorney, and from 1902 he served under William Travers Jerome. An energetic patrician some twenty years my father's senior, Jerome had been elected on a reform platform. Although almost forgotten today, he was a highly regarded leader, not only by the popular press but also by a select group of wealthy and gifted men, including Harry Whitney, his brother Payne Whitney, the writer Finley Peter Dunne (Mr. Dooley), architects Thomas Hastings and Stanford White, the publisher Robert Collier, and the artist Charles Dana Gibson. Jerome introduced my father into this illustrious circle. Together with some others, less well known, the group founded a luncheon club called the Meeting House, which met in a brownstone house at 139 East Forty-fifth Street in New York.

Unlike the University Club and most other social clubs in New York at that time, the Meeting House brought together an interesting and diverse group of men who were actively involved in the arts. Some were creators, some were collectors, and all were committed to encouraging patronage. Their definition of the arts was broad and included the varied work of many of their contemporaries, such artists as John Sloan and Jerome Meyers and illustrators as James Montgomery Flagg, N. C. Wyeth, Howard Pyle, and Maxfield Parrish. The literati were also included, and many of the club's members, like Finley Peter Dunne and Thomas Hastings, well-known leaders in their professions, were also extraordinarily well-read and witty figures.

My father quickly became one of this circle and was their equal in enthusiasm for the arts and for wit at table; his associations with the Meeting House surely influenced the course of his life and inspired his collecting. He and Peter Dunne became lifelong friends—my father named his third son after him. Our family life was centered on Long Island, where my father purchased a large, rambling house on property neighboring his great friend Payne Whitney. He visited Robert Collier in the Adirondacks at Raquette Lake and shortly thereafter purchased Kamp Kill Kare from Timothy Woodruff, the former lieutenant governor of New York.

In the mid 1930s, when all the members were aging and the decision was made to disband the club, Francis Garvan pensioned the steward and removed the mantelpiece from the main room to his office at 640 Madison Avenue. The importance of his association with the Meeting House group and their influence on him as a patron of the arts can be seen in his portrait painted in 1936 by Augustus Vincent Tack (now at Yale), which shows him leaning on that mantelpiece, which held a two-handled silver cup made in early New England (now also at Yale). At the time of his marriage in 1910, the Meeting House group commissioned, inscribed with their signatures, and presented to him a similar grand silver cup. Maxfield Parrish's painting *Pirates in the Inn,* bearing the motto "Quod et demonstrandum," which hung in the Meeting House over that mantel, was installed in his office in the same position and appears prominently in his three-quarter length portrait.

The Meeting House luncheons certainly must have sharpened, if not directed, my father's tendencies toward collecting, and his work in the law, especially as district attorney, definitely shaped his method of collecting. Beginning with a George I mahogany-framed settee, he proceeded to delve deeply and widely into the fields of American and English furniture, English, Irish, and American silver, pewter, portrait prints, coins, sporting art, Dutch tiles, hand tools, illustrated English books, the works of Irish painters and authors, American and Oriental textiles, and porcelain and ceramics from England and America. Like a detective, he defined at the outset the narrow boundaries of the evidence. Next, within those limits, he bought extensively, preferably at public auction and, where possible, whole collections. In this way he avoided or reduced his personal bias and preferences. His purchases were promptly catalogued, photographed, and reviewed for authenticity. The result was that an extensive curatorial-type archive developed for his complete holdings. In addition, and unusual for collectors active at the time, he kept all correlative information about the collections and objects, including correspondence with owners and dealers. Thus, most objects were documented, and his collections were surrounded with evidence forming a "dossier"—better known as a legal method than an art-historical one.

Thus, when in 1927–28 Francis Garvan was beset with diabetes and tuberculosis, he was able to review his collections systematically: silver with Edward Alfred Jones, the leading English silver and furniture authority at the time; American furniture with Richard T. H. Halsey, collector and author of the first handbook of the American Wing at the Metropolitan Museum of Art; and all holdings with John Marshall Phillips, who later became curator of the collections given to Yale University in 1931 in honor of his wife Mabel Brady Garvan.

Parts of the Garvan Dutch tile collection were probably purchased first for decorative use. By 1925 my father had plans to install Dutch and Flemish tiles extensively for fireplace surrounds in his Long Island and Mill Brook houses. Then, in 1927, obviously intrigued by the pictorial variations and charming painted subject matter, such as the sets of children's games, fanciful sea creatures, and soldiers bearing arms, he began to collect tiles more seriously, purchasing widely at auctions. When the enormous Eelco M. Vis collection partially failed to make its reserves at the sale in New York in 1927, he purchased many lots after the sale. Thus the Vis collection became the core for what eventually developed into an encyclopedic assemblage of Dutch tiles. It contained both a broad representation of types and specialized groupings of the highest quality. This purchase gave him the artistic equivalent of a legal dossier. Although he may have first been interested in the quantity of tiles offered in the Vis collection because he was planning to build a new house on Long Island, by this time his interest in the individual and groups of objects that he had collected had sharpened, and the preservation of whole units of material became a primary goal.

The conservation, exhibition, and publication of these little works of art on ceramic tiles by the Philadelphia Museum of Art are very welcome. Standing directly on the boundary between vernacular and stylish art, handcrafted but produced in great numbers, tiles have been generally neglected as serious works of art except in the regions of their origin. It has been my privilege for many years to use part of this collection for teaching and artifact analysis. Dutch tiles not only record the games, emblems, and crafts of the countryside, they also reflect major schools of painting, drawing, and engraving. Now a measure of certainty is being introduced into what has been largely a random and intuitive area of study. Like an unused dossier, Francis P. Garvan's Dutch tile collection has remained complete but relatively unexplored. As a recent accession into the collections of the Philadelphia Museum of Art, his long-term objectives for this collection have been reached. It is finally available to be enjoyed and studied as an entity or in small units; it is evidence and it is art.

Anthony N. B. Garvan
University of Pennsylvania
1984

Author's Note and Acknowledgments

The high standard of craftsmanship attained in the Low Countries in the seventeenth century is reflected in the extensive development of tiles made for interior decoration. Because the excellent and valuable books on Dutch tiles written by a previous generation of museum curators and collectors have been long out of print, the time has come to describe the subject anew. We have chosen to approach the topic from both a thematic and a chronological viewpoint. This grouping reflects, however, the twentieth-century art historian's predilection toward classification, and bears little resemblance to the seventeenth-century disposition of tiles, which made no attempt to match subjects. Mere chronological grouping is pointless in this case, where the sequential adoption of the successes of one workshop by another was so widespread that dating of tiles within decades becomes hazardous. Similarly, it is very difficult to ascribe tiles to a specific workshop. Tiles with similar decorative ornaments were made in more than one workshop in numerous towns, and may have remained in production for a decade or two until a change in fashion dictated the adoption of new patterns. As the town of Delft was neither the oldest production center nor the most prolific, the term "Delft tiles"—so often heard—is a misnomer, and has not been used in these pages. Towns other than Delft, such as Haarlem, Rotterdam, Dordrecht, Hoorn, Amsterdam, Gouda, Enkhuizen, Harlingen, and Makkum, had active tileworks. All except the last two are situated in such close proximity that the distance between the most northerly and the most southerly is no more than seventy miles.

Tiles, a mass-produced folk art, are decorated with simple lines and a few strong colors—yellow, orange, blue, green, or purple. The number of variations, however, is extensive, which can be explained by the large number of competitive workshops who created distinct versions of fashionable designs, and the minute differences of the work of each craftsman in a tileworks, which continued selling a popular pattern. These variations cause difficulties for a museum in composing panels of tiles for exhibition; originally, the tiles would have been produced as a unit without variation, but in this collection, which has been assembled over a period of almost a century from a dozen separate sources, tiles from different workshops and dates have been combined to form meaningful overall design units.

Depictions in woodcuts and engravings and on tiles are closely related. Subjects displayed on tiles, such as animals, flowers, biblical scenes, tradesmen, and ships, were adapted from prints, which were ubiquitous in the seventeenth century. A design from a print could often serve for a series of tiles, and be used thousands of times without the fear of repetitiousness that twentieth-century artists might experience. As far as we have been able to ascertain, ornamental books like those used by craftsmen in such other trades as furniture carving, textiles, and silver did not play a role in tile decoration, nor were pictures taken directly from nature, except by a very few, most skillful, tile painters. More often, motifs were handed down through family members or adopted from other tiles. The same pictures occur repeatedly surrounded by different frames or corner motifs.

As a rule, tiles bear no signatures. Those that when conjoined, constitute a tile picture are numbered on the back to facilitate the composing of a picture consisting of multiple rows of tiles. Some tiles, however, bear an initial of sorts, whose importance has not yet become clear, but one supposition is that these may relate to factory orders. Where the back of a tile is other than blank, a photograph has been included to facilitate further research. Similarly, the results of the extensive analyses performed by the Conservation Department under Andrew Lins appear with his technical note.

An example of virtually all of the early Dutch tiles discussed in the following pages can also be found in the fireplace of the Museum's seventeenth-century room from a house in Het Scheepje, a brewery complex in Haarlem. Only some rare types, such as the Roman soldiers or the ships firing guns simultaneously from port and starboard, are not represented there. The collection of the Philadelphia Museum of Art is quite representative of Dutch tiles, and particularly strong for those made between 1580 and 1680. Insofar as tiles function as a mass-produced art, it is our hope that this volume can serve as a general reference tool for use by other collectors.

During the four and a half years in which this catalogue grew from an intimidating job of documentation into a major publication and exhibition, I have received extensive support and assistance, which transformed what could have been a formidable effort into a fascinating and satisfying challenge. Therefore, I must thank Jean Sutherland Boggs, whose initial support made this exhibition possible, Anne d'Harnoncourt, whose continuing encouragement has seen this project realized, and David DuBon, who suggested I take on this project.

I owe a great debt of gratitude to the co-authors in the Netherlands, Jan Daniel van Dam and Pieter Jan Tichelaar, for their essays, guidance, and insights. Jan Pluis, the foremost expert on biblical tiles and the first person to relate the tiles depicting animals and games to their print sources, deserves my heartfelt thanks for generously sharing his knowledge with me. For their invaluable research, writing, and editorial assistance, I wish to acknowledge the late Robert Chambers, Marjorie Lee Hendrix, Judith Maslin, Joan Pierpoline, and Ana Troncoso. I am deeply grateful to James Tanis for his constructive criticisms and for insuring the historical accuracy of the manuscript. Gary Schwartz is gratefully acknowledged for the translation of Mr. van Dam's essay.

The following people made enthusiastic and versatile efforts in the daily requirements of exhibition planning. Mary Anne Dutt Justice, with infinite patience, arranged and rearranged all the tile panels, coordinated photography, and also generously lent her expertise in selecting decorative arts and furniture for the exhibition. While handling the organizational details of the exhibition, Martha Small expertly coordinated all correspondence involved in securing the loans of prints, furniture, and illustrations for the catalogue. In the Museum library, Barbara Sevy and Carol Homan secured the many publications available only in the Netherlands, without which research would have been severely hampered. Katherine Butler wrote and organized the myriad labels for the exhibition and Tara Robinson designed the handsome installation.

14

Exhibition of the tiles would not have been possible without the unflagging efforts of the following members of the Conservation Department, who under the supervision of Marigene Butler and the skillful guidance of Andrew Lins, cleaned, repaired, analyzed, and mounted the seemingly never-ending supply of tiles and provided their expertise concerning prints and furniture used in the exhibition: Steven Erisoty, Nancy Hughes, Richard Kerschner, Suzanne Maguire-Negus, Melissa Meighan, Marie von Möller, Steven Pine, Thomas Robinson, Susan Schussler, John Scott, Wendy Stayman, Carol Stringari, Yoonjoo Strumfels, and Denise Thomas.

George Marcus, Theodore Lewis, Sherry Babbitt, Mark La Riviere, Jane Watkins, and Larry Channing receive my thanks for making this book a physical reality. The heroic task of photographing all the tiles was admirably undertaken by Eric Mitchell with the assistance of Joan Broderick. Orly Zeewy and Phillip Unetic provided line illustrations and charts.

Others on the Museum staff helped to see this project through: Cynthia von Bogendorf-Rupprath, Elizabeth Drazen, Grace Eleazer, Victoria Ellison, Beatrice Garvan, Anne Havinga, Gary Hiatt, Ellen Jacobowitz, Donald LaRocca, Bernard McNellis, Kimberly Parsons, Susanna Roberts, Donald Lee Savary, Anne Schuster, Gary Smith, Lawrence Snyder, Ann Stebbins, Susan Stuchlak, Peter Sutton, Irene Taurins, Gail Tomlinson, Suzanne Wells, and Regina Zienowicz. I am also indebted to those volunteers who donated their time: Joan Irving, Ann McPhail, Anne Nimick, Susan Pumillio.

In the course of research, many scholars have graciously supplied information, references, and photographs, and I would like to especially thank A. L. den Blaauwen, J. A. Bosmans, Conny Felius, Charles E. Greene, I. M. de Groot, J. F. Heijbroek, Edward Lee Holt, Alison Kettering, J. H. Kluiver, D. V. Kuyken-Schneider, B. N. Leverland, J.V.G. Mallet, Mr. Martin-Demezil, A. M. Meyerman, J. C. Nix, A. E. Piekema-van Berg, Anthony Ray, R.A.D. Renting, D. F. Lunsingh Scheurleer, James E. Walsh, and Phelps Warren.

In conclusion, I would like to thank Anthony N. B. Garvan for his unbounded generosity, without which we would not have had the opportunity to undertake this catalogue and exhibition. I also extend my grateful appreciation to all the generous lenders of prints and furniture, which so enhance the installation of the tiles. Last but assuredly not least, I want to thank my family, who with patience and forbearance made it possible for me to devote my time and energy to this publication and exhibition.

E.S.

The Netherlands

North Sea

Zuider Zee

Leeuwarden

Harlingen

Makkum

FRIESLAND

NORTH
HOLLAND

Enkhuizen

Hoorn

Alkmaar

Zaandam

Amsterdam

Haarlem

GELDERLAND

Leiden

Utrecht

Otterlo

The Hague

UTRECHT

Arnhem

Delft

Gouda

Rotterdam

SOUTH HOLLAND

GERMANY

Maas River

Rhine River

ZEELAND

Antwerp

BELGIUM

Brussels

FRANCE

Tournai

Ramillies

Liège

A Survey of Dutch Tiles

Dutch ornamental tile craft and the Dutch nation itself were creations of the sixteenth century. Both flowered as a result of the extraordinary wealth of the province of Flanders and the interplay of its great cities—first Bruges and, after 1500, Antwerp—with the leading cities of southern Europe. Italian émigrés were attracted to Antwerp, not only to serve as bankers and merchants but also to establish in the north the immensely popular majolica trade of the south.

The Netherlands, comprising by the mid-sixteenth century the present-day Benelux nations, was the creation of the Holy Roman Emperor Charles V. The foundations of the state had been laid in the fifteenth century by the military and political maneuvers of Philip the Good of Burgundy. By the time of his death in 1467, Philip had solidified the core of the hitherto independent southern provinces, as well as some of the northern regions. It was Charles, however, born in 1500 and at the height of his power in the 1530s and 1540s, who completed the unification of the Low Countries.

Charles's achievement was soon undone by the insensitive and inept machinations of Philip II of Spain, Charles's son and heir to the Netherlands. Charles had been born in Flanders and as a ruler had been considered by the Netherlanders one of their own. Philip, by contrast, had been born in Spain and ruled from there; he thus never gained the allegiance or affection his father had enjoyed. Revolution broke out under Philip in 1568 and continued intermittently under his successors until the Treaty of Münster in 1648. The uprising, known as the Eighty Years' War, was brought on by taxation without representation and by the forceful suppression of the new religious ideas of the Protestants. The war engulfed both north and south and finally led to the dissolution of the state Charles had fought so hard to create. In the south was Belgium, then termed the Spanish Netherlands; in the north were the seven provinces, which took the name of the United Provinces of the Netherlands, now known as the Kingdom of the Netherlands.

In the early sixteenth century all of western Europe was nominally Roman Catholic, its unity marred only here and there by local calls for religious reform. By 1520 these indigenous movements were given expression in increasingly aggressive ways: in Saxony, Luther and his followers had come to an open breach with the papacy; the Reformed movement found leaders in Switzerland and along the North Sea. By 1530 the more radical Anabaptists had taken their place alongside the Lutherans and the Reformed. By 1540 Calvin had become a major voice among the Reformed, a voice that was to become dominant in the Netherlands, for a time overwhelming not only the Roman Catholics and Anabaptists but the indigenous Reformed themselves. These religious conflicts, greatly aggravated by Philip's suppression of the Calvinists, led to vast population movements from the southern provinces, which were in Philip's hands, to the northern provinces, which were held by the Protestants. Many Protestant bankers and merchants moved to the north, bringing the money needed to finance the rising new nation and its burgeoning industries. This migration also included many Flemish tilemakers, who were to play an increasingly important role in the development of the Dutch tile trade.

Ceramics in the Netherlands before 1560

Simple ceramics had already been produced in the Netherlands on a large scale in the late fifteenth and early sixteenth centuries. The craft was practiced wherever there was clay and transportation available to bring in wood for the kilns and carry out the finished products. The ceramic industry in the Netherlands was concentrated in the maritime provinces, from south Flanders to north Friesland.

The production of floor tiles, bricks, and roof tiles received a tremendous impetus in the northern Netherlands with the introduction of regulations requiring the use of stone or brick instead of wood for new construction, measures often enacted in the wake of large fires. In some towns even existing wooden walls had to be replaced with brick in order to lessen the danger of fire. Along the coast and in the north, where stone was expensive, brick proved to be a good substitute. Wherever brickworks arose, there were also ceramic factories for the production of household pottery (fig. 1) and tiles. Because stone floor tiles were prohibitively expensive, clay tiles became a readily available alternative. The manufacture of such tiles required only a few simple steps: shaping, drying, and firing. The finished products, however, were porous and subject to wear. To protect them and make them waterproof, the red clay tiles were coated with a mixture of clay and lead oxide before firing. During the firing, at a temperature of about 950 degrees centigrade (1,750 degrees Fahrenheit), this substance fused into a transparent glaze. Some of the tiles were coated before glazing with the application of a slip, which turned white or light yellow in the kiln. These two methods produced tiles of contrasting colors, which could be laid on the floor in patterns. Tiles were also decorated with designs stamped into the soft clay. The impressed areas were filled with slip, so that the finished tiles would bear a light-colored motif against the red clay body.

In Antwerp the situation was more complex. Utilitarian objects and tiles of lead-glazed earthenware were also made there, but there was in addition a flourishing industry for more luxurious ceramics of tin-glazed pottery, or majolica. This craft was begun early in the sixteenth century by Italians who had immigrated to Antwerp and who were more advanced than the Netherlanders in preparing clay, applying tin glaze, and adding painted decoration. These specialized craftsmen set the style for majolica in the north: the forms, motifs, and colors were all derived from the majolica tiles of the workshops of Venice, Faenza, and Urbino, cities where the Italians had learned their craft. In the first half of the sixteenth century, these Italians enjoyed great success in wealthy Antwerp. Some Flemish families—primarily those in the middle class—gradually began to produce majolica as well, while the production of lead-glazed ceramics remained in the hands of those of a lower social level. Hans Floris, one of the Flemish potters, worked as a master majolica potter in Antwerp between 1525 and 1550, when he left for Spain. He came from a family of architects, sculptors, and painters.

Floors of inlaid, lead-glazed tiles were relatively expensive, and were used only in churches, public buildings, and the houses of the wealthy. This was the same market

FIG. 1 Nicolaes Maes (Dutch, 1632–1693)
Woman Plucking a Duck,
c. 1655–56
Oil on canvas
Philadelphia Museum of Art. Gift of Mrs. Gordon A. Harwick and Mrs. W. Newbold Ely, in memory of Mr. and Mrs. Roland L. Taylor

A Dutch interior displaying folk pottery: an earthenware colander, decorated majolica (on the floor and on top of the chest), seventeenth-century German stoneware (*grès*) (on the window sill and the wall), and a white faience jug (on the table in the room beyond). With the exception of Chinese porcelain, every type of ceramic used in the Netherlands, both native and imported, is depicted here.

FIG. 2 Antwerp-Italian polychrome floor tiles from Anjum in Friesland, 1570

FIG. 3 Flemish reddish-brown floor tile inlaid with contrasting whitish-yellow slip in stylized leaf pattern, c. 1550
Musée des Beaux-Arts, Lille

for which the Italian majolica craftsmen worked, but only the wealthiest patrons could afford entire floors of majolica tiles (fig. 2). Floors of Antwerp majolica have been found only in a few churches and in castles and the country estates of the nobility. The aristocrats who ordered floors of this kind were not only rich but also fashion conscious, embellishing their rooms with majolica tiles as an extravagant novelty.

It must be remembered, however, that most of the population did not have decorated floors. Most Netherlanders lived in houses with floors of packed earth; those with a bit of money would cover the earth with wooden planks or undecorated clay tiles.

Competition and Emigration, 1560–80

Surviving materials indicate that the tile industry underwent major changes around 1560. By then the makers of majolica floor tiles had become such strong competitors of the manufacturers of lead-glazed tiles that a number of the latter had shifted to the imported technique. Until 1560 the majolica floor tiles made in Antwerp were still very Italian in appearance, which is not surprising considering the Italian background of most of the craftsmen and the fact that Italy set the pace for the majolica industry throughout the sixteenth century. Many majolica tiles were painted in a pronouncedly figurative style, with portraits enclosed in roundels, for example; other tiles were purely ornamental, featuring stylized leaf motifs (see nos. 5, 6). The figurative tiles were square; the ornamental ones were generally hexagonal. The usual manner of laying them was to group the hexagonal ornamental tiles around the square figurative ones, forming regular octagons. Painted motifs in blue, yellow, green, and purple were applied to the fine white tin glaze so that the decorations stood out in bright colors against the white background.

The Italian and Flemish craftsmen who had specialized in majolica continued to work in this mode after 1560. Makers of floor tiles who had recently been converted to majolica, however, devised a new approach to decoration, or rather, a new way of using an old technique. These tilemakers were modest craftsmen who practiced a rather primitive sort of folk art. Generally, folk art develops at a slow pace, its makers clinging for long periods to their accustomed decorations. Thus the Flemish tilemakers who shifted from lead to tin glaze continued to use their own decorative repertoire (figs. 3, 4).

The decoration of majolica tiles that this group of craftsmen began to produce about 1560 consisted of highly stylized white leaf motifs set against a dark background, motifs that were very different from the multicolored vines of the Italianate designs because they tried to copy from the inlaid floor tiles. In majolica, which consists of a white tin glaze covering a red clay body, the effect of white decoration against a dark background could only be achieved with negative, or reserve, technique, in which the background rather than the motif was painted; the leaf motif was left as a white reserve and the dark background filled in.

This historical reconstruction is probably more straightforward than were the actual events. A transitional period like the one described often gives rise to various intermediate forms: some tilemakers, for example, attempted to imitate majolica tiles by covering a large area of the tile with white slip. Between 1560 and the beginning of the 1600s, the decoration of majolica tiles exhibited the influence of both the primitive ornamentation in reserve technique and the Italian style. Eventually, a synthesis of the two forms developed.

Prosperity in the North, 1580–1625

In about 1580 the northern provinces, most notably Holland, entered a period of economic prosperity that was to continue virtually without interruption for seventy years. The upper levels of Dutch society grew fabulously wealthy, and a substantial segment of the general population also benefited from the growth. The gap between rich and poor was narrower in the Netherlands of the seventeenth century than in the rest of Europe. The diminishing power of whatever nobility was left in the country allowed a much larger segment of the populace to share in the new prosperity.

The situation of the majolica industry in Holland in 1580 was roughly comparable to what it had been in Antwerp twenty years earlier. A number of potters had shifted fully, or in part, to the manufacture of majolica and were producing majolica floor tiles in the reserve technique on a modest scale. There were also majolica makers, émigrés from Antwerp, who worked solely in tin glazes, concentrating on dishes, bowls, and various kinds of pottery. At first these immigrant specialists probably did not make floor tiles; nonetheless, once they had settled in the north, they had a deep impact on the entire majolica industry. True specialists, they were technically in advance of the native craftsmen. Their tableware, in particular, set the tone, and each new style they introduced became a fashion.

The evidence of tiles surviving from 1580 to 1600 and of documents of the early seventeenth century indicates that between 1580 and 1600 in Haarlem, Amsterdam, Delft, and Rotterdam a synthesis of the products of the native floor-tile makers and the majolica specialists took place. From about 1600 on, all majolica makers produced both tiles and tableware. The two groups merged both for the product and for its decoration.

From Floor Tile to Wall Tile, 1580–90

If the majolica tile floor never became popular enough to command a fair share of the market in the improving economy of Holland, this was largely due to the fact that the tiles were easily damaged, a disadvantage that was augmented by their high price. The inlaid decoration of lead-glazed tiles was thickly laid and remained visible even as the tiles were being worn down in use, whereas majolica tiles, with their thin, vulnerable layer of tin glaze, were totally unfit for flooring. The broad ornamental patterns of common floor tiles could take a lot of wear and tear, but the delicately painted portraits and animals of majolica could be disfigured even by small scratches. Only the very wealthy could afford the extravagance of floors that were relatively short lived.

FIG. 4 Blue majolica floor or wall tiles with contrasting stylized leaf pattern in reserve technique, 1580–1600
Rijksmuseum Huis Lambert van Meerten, Delft

The leaf patterns in figs. 3 and 4 are identical

FIG. 5 Hearth flanked with tile paneling, each side consisting of 120 ornamental polychrome quatrefoil tiles made in Delft or Rotterdam, c. 1600

The side wall is paneled with eighteenth-century tiles added later.

These floors were certainly not intended to appeal to the Dutch middle class, who were well known for their parsimony and the care they bestowed on their possessions. These values were reinforced by the teachings of Calvinism, whose stricter forms were adopted by the same middle class. The Dutch burghers, however, were becoming more and more prosperous, and by 1600 they were more than able to afford some sort of decoration for their houses and hearths (fig. 5). A new solution emerged, devised either by the manufacturers on the basis of their technical knowledge or by their customers, in search of a practical way of decorating their houses. In about 1580 the majolica wall tile made a sudden appearance, in a form indistinguishable in composition and decoration from the floor tile.

A number of factors helped to discourage the use of majolica tiles on floors and stimulated the spread of tiles on walls. Increasing national wealth and improved means of transportation widened the availability of marble and other kinds of stone, which now came into use, alongside fired clay tiles and wooden planks, for flooring. Perhaps the most important single factor in the adoption of majolica wall tiles was the fact that about half the population of the Netherlands lived in the province of Holland, the majority in the cities, all of which were located on water. These cities were crisscrossed by canals, the ground level was low, and the water table high. The houses virtually stood in the water and were always damp. Walls were not insulated, and double walls with a hollow space in between had not yet come into use. Moreover, there was usually only one open fire in a house, which doubled for cooking and heating. This was insufficient to keep the walls dry, and the whitewashed plaster was constantly flaking. Wealthy homeowners covered their walls with oak paneling or leather; for others, glazed tiles provided an alternative solution to the problem of damp walls: the tiles were waterproof and easy to keep clean.

Despite their relative affluence, the modest burghers in the cities of Holland lived in relatively small houses, normally consisting of a two-story-high front section (*voorhuis*), usually used as a shop, with one large room, the inner hearth (*binnenhaard*), behind it. This space, which was lit indirectly through windowpanes in the wall between it and the front section, served as living room and kitchen; often this room also had a built-in wooden bed. The high-manteled hearth was used for both heating and cooking. Frequently, above the living room was a bedroom; the rest of the house usually was composed of lofts providing storage space.

The first use of wall tiles was probably in areas where dampness and dirt were at their worst, such as the joining of wall and floor. The earliest wall tiles were used mainly as baseboards, and until very recently, wooden baseboards in Dutch houses were always thirteen centimeters (five inches) high, the height of one tile. At the same time other wall areas began to be tiled as well. Tiles were placed within the hearth and alongside it to a height of eight tiles; they were also often placed on corridor walls and other places where one was likely to brush against whitewash. Even in the houses of the rich, the area adjoining the sooty great hearth was generally faced to a width of three tiles.

It should be noted that at least half of the population lived in one-room dwellings, and any tiles that could be afforded were restricted to baseboards. Until 1650 it was mainly the burghers of the cities in the province of Holland who tiled their living quarters. This group—independent carpenters, plumbers, small merchants, and the like—began to achieve a measure of prosperity in the first half of the seventeenth century; they vastly expanded in most Dutch cities after 1600. As a result of overpopulation in the rural areas, augmented by immigration, about 1580, people flocked to the cities, particularly to the province of Holland. Between 1510 and 1670 Amsterdam, for example, grew from a town of ten thousand inhabitants to a metropolis of two hundred thousand. The tremendous growth of the tile market was a function of the growing prosperity of these new customers, who began using tiles after 1580. This expansion of the market for relatively expensive tiles brought about spectacular growth in the tile industry; after 1600 hardly a year went by without the opening of a new tileworks.

Haarlem was the main center in Holland for the production of majolica and tiles in the sixteenth century. As early as 1560 the Antwerp majolica maker Adriaan Bogaert settled in Haarlem, and by 1600 seven potteries were located there. Two of the seven Haarlem factories were run by immigrants from Antwerp; these apparently set the style for the rest. In about 1600 two of the other workshops switched from lead-glazed to majolica pots and wall tiles, but the scarcity of archival documents makes it difficult to determine who was producing tiles before 1600.

The second-largest center for majolica production in the northern Netherlands was Amsterdam. Here too the manufacture of majolica and tin-glazed tiles flourished after 1580, thanks in part to immigrants from Antwerp. Rotterdam and Delft also were to become important centers for majolica production, and by 1620 a rough parity was reached among these four cities as sources for majolica. Extant inventories from this period show that all workshops produced both tableware and tiles. In 1627 at the death of Jacob van den Heuvel in Rotterdam, the inventory of his majolica workshop listed more than thirty thousand tiles of different types and thousands of dishes, bowls, pitchers, and pots in all sizes. There were also shops for majolica and tiles in a number of other locales in the provinces of Holland, Utrecht, and Friesland, but until 1620 they were eclipsed by those in Haarlem, Amsterdam, Delft, and Rotterdam.

The houses of pottery owners usually had a room set aside for receiving clients. Costs for entertaining clients were always specified in pottery contracts. In this period, when the tiles were produced mainly for customers in the surrounding area, those who did business directly with the shops were usually building contractors. Naturally, buyers first considered items being offered close to home, but because the market for building material was nationwide, customers would buy better or cheaper wares offered elsewhere. Later in the seventeenth century and in the eighteenth, tile production became concentrated in a few places. Perhaps the role of the middleman was to some extent taken over by small tilemakers outside the main centers. Every variety of tile by then had a name and a quality grade; contractors could place orders by mail at any of the plants. Printed price lists were in use by the late eighteenth century, and in the mid-nineteenth, illustrated catalogues began to appear.

When, in 1611, Jan Jansz Vullens wished to enter the employment of Egbert Huygensz Sas, one of the important majolica and tile potters in Delft, he contracted to decorate tiles and be paid the following: *blompotten* (flowerpots), thirteen *stuyvers* (nickels) for one hundred; one hundred round flowerpots, twenty-six *stuyvers;* single *goutsblomkens* (marigolds), sixteen *stuyvers* for one hundred (see no. 19). During those years the price from the tileworks was from three guilders to five guilders per hundred for decorated tiles and two guilders for undecorated white tiles. Two hundred years later, the cost of simply decorated tiles was three guilders, and fully decorated ones, five guilders, per hundred, while the Tichelaar workshop delivered one hundred white tiles for two guilders. Considering inflation, tiles had become cheaper during those two hundred years. Furthermore, tiles were of different grades, and every inventory lists *wrakke tegels* (wretched tiles), those of second or third grade.

The major changes in the manufacture of tiles between 1550 and 1590—the transition from lead glaze to tin glaze and from majolica floor tiles to majolica wall tiles—had far-reaching consequences for tile decoration. Both changes tended to discourage purely ornamental decoration. A floor-tile maker who converted to majolica would at first continue to use his old repertoire of designs, but once accustomed to the new technique, he would begin to explore the wider technical possibilities. Tiles inlaid with slip or pipe clay could be decorated only with broad, highly stylized ornamentation, but majolica could illustrate a wide variety of highly refined patterns or figures.

Tiled floor areas were often large and required patterns that were not restricted to the standard square tile size. Late medieval ornamental floor tiles and the majolica copies had been designed so that sixteen identical tiles could be laid to look like one large block of twenty inches square. Floors of Italian majolica from Antwerp were usually patterned in blocks of five tiles: four hexagons surrounded a square tile, giving rise to a regular octagon (fig. 2). Wall surfaces covered by tiling were generally smaller than those of floors. With the shift to wall tiles, a synthesis took place between the early ornamental tile and the figurative Italian tile from Antwerp. This was the first step; next patternmakers began thinking in terms of single tiles rather than blocks. These developments led to a reduction in the ornamentation of tiles in favor of figurative ones. When this trend culminated in about 1650, tile decoration had come to consist of a single figurative element per tile, combined with a minuscule corner ornament. Dutch tilemakers, shifting to figuration, left the Middle Ages and the floor behind and began to exploit fully the potential of the majolica technique. The early ornamental tile, with its entire surface decorated in reserve, stayed in production with only minor changes until 1600. The Antwerp-Italian style also survived for about twenty more years, but with the transition from floor to wall tiles, the hexagonal tile with its floral motifs was no longer produced.

The two most popular designs between 1580 and 1625 combined reserve ornamentation with the figurative designs of the Antwerp-Italian floor tile: the diamond tile (no. 19) and the quatrefoil with pomegranates (no. 9). One half of the tile was painted in reserve, the other half with positive decoration. The ornamentation of the quatrefoil tile usually consisted of a simplified version of the motif in fig. 4, with a typical Gothic quatrefoil. The quatrefoil, a geometric ornament consisting of four conjoined half-circles, is filled with pomegranates, marigolds, and oak leaves. Decorations with pomegranates originated in Venice, where they adorned large apothecary jars from the mid-sixteenth century on. In the Netherlands in the seventeenth century, they were sometimes called orange apples, a reference to the popular House of Orange, then the country's most important noble family (now the royal family). The ornamental and figurative scheme of this design was complete in a block of sixteen tiles. With diamond (*kwadraat*) tiles, the ornamental scheme comprises four repetitions of one quarter of the central section of tile panel no. 46. A complete pattern consists of four adjoining tiles. This is the first step toward reducing the ornament to a corner motif and the beginning of the evolution toward the single tile as the unit of decoration.

During the Middle Ages, square floor tiles had sometimes been laid diagonally. The disadvantage of this system was that the edges of a floor had to be lined with half tiles. With majolica tiles, the effect of the diagonal floor pattern was achieved by painting a diamond on each tile; the floor's edges could thus be lined with whole tiles. The ornamental scheme, of course, remained incomplete at the edges, but that was then apparently a matter of lesser concern. Animals and people painted within the diamonds were entirely in the style of Antwerp-Italian floor tiles (no. 46). This design provided a synthesis between Renaissance motifs from Italy, such as animals against a solid ground, and Gothic ornamental motifs from northern Europe. The animals on these tiles were often copied from popular engravings sold widely in the Netherlands as separate prints or in books. In the course of the seventeenth and eighteenth centuries, as the central image came to occupy the major part of the tile, tilemakers began to develop original series of figurative motifs in addition to those copied from engravings.

Until 1625 new tile designs were usually adaptations of existing ones. Characteristic of this was the so-called pompadour tile (no. 13), on which the quatrefoil motif usually encompassing four tiles (no. 12) was reduced to single-tile format. These tiles are instantly recognizable as variations with a limited number of motifs. Tiles showing flower vases in diamonds (no. 19) always had a different leaf motif, in the reserve technique, from tiles with animals or human figures in diamonds. Some new tile designs were variants of well-known themes; others grafted elements from one type onto another or combined motifs in different patterns. Ornamentation occupied increasingly less tile space, and shortly before 1625 the laborious filling-in and reserve technique was abandoned as superfluous, sixty-five years after being devised as a way of imitating the inlaid floor tile. The stage had not yet been reached, however, at which the ornament as a unifying element could be dropped altogether.

The first positive corner motif was easy to paint either negatively or positively: the heraldic fleur-de-lis. Tiles with grapes and pomegranates, introduced shortly after 1600, were the first to have positive fleurs-de-lis as corner ornaments (no. 34).

One early seventeenth-century tile differs from all others described in that it lacks corner motifs. This type, which has a place of its own in the stylistic development of tile decoration, was designed exclusively for use on baseboards, where there was no

FIG. 6 Gonzalès Coques (Flemish, 1614–1684)
The Visit, c. 1630
Oil on panel
Musée d'Art et d'Histoire, Geneva

Front section (*voorhuis*) of a house in a prominent part of a town, with, on the left, a built-in bed (*bedstede*). The hearth is flanked by three rows of polychrome tulip tiles. The baseboard consists of three-quarter-sized tiles decorated with jumping animals. Above the hearth and the oak paneling is imported Chinese porcelain from the period of the Wan Li Emperor. The floor is covered in a pattern of alternating marble and stone tiles.

need for a unifying motif. In the single row of tiles along a baseboard, the elaborate ornamentation of sixteenth- and early seventeenth-century tiles would remain incomplete and therefore appear strange. It is believed that this kind of tile was made only in Rotterdam, probably in a single tileworks, among the few to break decisively with the tradition of ornamental decoration.

Changing Fashions, 1625–40

During this period the Netherlands was a major economic power. The battlefield of the Eighty Years' War had moved south and could safely be disregarded as an immediate threat, certainly in the province of Holland. The enormous prosperity and accompanying population growth—first swelled with refugees from the southern Netherlands, then with Germans attracted by Dutch prosperity—led to constant urban expansion.

In the newly constructed houses, especially those built for the middle classes, tiles were used in large quantities. The buyers and uses of tiles varied little between 1600 and 1640. What did change in about 1625, however, was the color of the tiles, in response to a general shift in fashion toward subdued colors. Clothing had become simpler and primarily black; painters such as Rembrandt and Van Goyen had adopted a more monochromatic palette. This change in taste naturally affected tile decoration.

After 1625 most tiles were painted in a single color, blue. Gradually, the area painted also was reduced. Blue was chosen for several reasons. As a neutral color, it went well with the new sober fashion, and moreover, it was easy to handle in the kiln, seldom causing problems such as running of the glaze. Also, from the beginning of the seventeenth century, the United Dutch East India Company (Verenigde Oost Indische Compagnie, popularly known as VOC)—a trading corporation run mainly by Amsterdam merchants as a private shareholding company—had been importing large quantities of blue-and-white porcelain from China. From their warehouses on Taiwan and in Batavia (now Djakarta), the company shipped porcelain to the Netherlands (fig. 6). The product sold very well, and soon not only the Netherlands but all of Europe was flooded with Chinese blue-and-white porcelain. This was undoubtedly also the major factor in the choice of blue as the color for decorated tiles. Until 1620 or 1625 the motifs used had been derived from the Antwerp-Italian or the early ornamental tiles, but now Chinese motifs began to appear as well. With such motifs as mock-fret borders formed by short perpendicular lines, the monochrome blue coloring, and the minimal decoration and the diminishing ornamentation, the tiles of the post-1625 period looked very different from their predecessors (see no. 50).

The importation of Chinese porcelain, which developed on a large scale in about 1620, also influenced the Dutch ceramic industry in other ways. Tile manufacturers who also produced tableware were hard hit by the competition from imported porcelain, which brought about a decline in the majolica industry between 1620 and 1650. This competition, coupled with the constant growth of the home economy, led to specialization in the manufacture of fine ceramics. Some of the products made before 1620 were relatively impervious to competition from China, for example, apothecary jars; tiles also suffered little because they were not imported from China at all. An increasing number of majolica potteries therefore began concentrating on the production of tiles. The general decline in the majolica trade nearly resulted in the disappearance of mixed tile and majolica potteries in Haarlem and Amsterdam. Following this reorganization within the industry, there were only two workshops in all of Amsterdam that specialized in tiles.

In Rotterdam, however, the shops nearly all began to specialize in tiles. Tableware declined until finally it was eliminated from most of the lines. In contrast to developments in Haarlem and Amsterdam, however, very few Rotterdam workshops closed down. In Delft a few workshops continued to make tableware on a small scale while turning increasingly to tile manufacture. However, two majolica plants took the opposite approach and began concentrating on a more refined line of majolica tableware. They attempted to reduce the thickness of the clay body and to equal the whiteness and smoothness of Chinese porcelain.

The clay that had been used until about 1620—which turned red in the kiln—had many disadvantages. Most varieties were quite heavy, making the clay easy to model but leading to shrinking and warping in the drying process. This problem was counteracted by adding a mixture of a chalkier clay called marl (*mergel*) in order to raise the chalk content of the body to about twenty-five percent. The two materials were first combined by kneading, but the resulting mixture was not sufficiently homogeneous. To overcome this problem, manufacturers began to wet the clay before mixing it, a process called "washing the clay." This technical innovation enhanced the quality of Dutch majolica to the point at which it began to resemble Chinese porcelain.

This improvement in clay preparation was first used only for tableware but was also introduced into tile manufacture before 1650. Early majolica floor tiles were almost 2 centimeters (¾ inch) thick, a thickness necessary to withstand being walked on. With the shift from floor tiles to wall tiles in about 1580, it was no longer necessary to make the tiles thick enough to withstand heavy pressure, but the technical problems of shrinking and warping prevented manufacturers from reducing tile thickness to less than 1½ centimeters (⅝ inch). Continuing improvements in clay preparation enabled a few firms at the turn of the eighteenth century to reduce the thickness of their tiles to scarcely more than ½ centimeter (³⁄₁₆ inch). Reducing tile thickness resulted in savings not only in material and labor but also in transportation and, most important, made it possible to put at least twice as many tiles in the kiln for each firing. This resulted in a great reduction in fuel costs and allowed plants to increase production without building additional kilns.

With the constant improvements throughout the second half of the seventeenth century, the clay body became light yellow and rather brittle. The technical advances had a number of attendant advantages. There was less craquelure in the glaze, and it was no longer necessary to cover the tin glaze with a layer of transparent lead glaze. This in turn enabled decorators to paint in greater detail without the danger of glazes running during firing, although they did not begin to take advantage of this until after 1690. The new tiles were also much flatter and their surface smoother; these improvements appealed to Dutch customers spoiled by the high quality of available goods.

Marl was imported from Tournai in southern Flanders, but when the truce with Spain ended in 1621, the Dutch turned to a source in Norwich, England. The extra cost of transporting marl from England and of "washing the clay" was probably fully compensated by savings achieved by the thinner tiles. Many tiles made between about 1615 and 1640 have yellow strains or layers in the red clay body; such tiles consist of a combination of red clay and marl which had not been wet when mixed.

Fashion, which dictated a gradual adaptation of traditional decoration, and the influence of Chinese porcelain combined after 1625 to make tile decoration less exuberant, mainly monochrome blue, and positively painted. In addition, greater emphasis was placed on the figurative element than on the ornamentation. The roundel, diamond, or quatrefoil that framed the image on pre-1625 tiles was now sometimes omitted; if a frame was used, it was apt to be formed by bracketed roundels. The corners were filled with leaf motifs or with the Chinese mock-fret, which had become very popular. One common corner element of post-1625 tiles has entered the jargon of tile literature as the ox-head motif. Actually unrelated to oxen, it is a positive remnant of leaf motifs painted in reserve on earlier tiles. In addition to the ox-head, leaf motifs and fleurs-de-lis were also simplified between 1625 and 1650.

Until 1625, as has been seen, figurative motifs on tiles were primarily derived from traditional Italian majolica. After 1625 there was an increase in the use of motifs from daily life and the surroundings. Until about 1650 tile panels were composed of a mixture of subjects: trades, children's games, elegant couples, ships, and landscapes. The shift toward subjects from daily life was probably reinforced by the fact that the urban middle classes, the main customers for tiles, tended to be puritanical Calvinists, who regarded trade and zestful work as religious service and a boon to society.

From Town to Country, 1640–60

In about 1640 the tile industry entered a period of growth despite the depression of the majolica market. In Delft two large, specialized tileworks were founded, and in Rotterdam, where seven plants already existed, seven new ones were built. The demand for tiles must have been tremendous to justify such an explosion of activity.

Part of the boom was due to new urban construction, but a more important factor was the adoption of tiles by a segment of the population that had not used them before. In the preceding hundred years, the population of the "wet" provinces of Zeeland, Holland, western Utrecht, and Friesland had developed from small farmers producing for local consumption into agrarian businessmen with a wider market. Farmers became fuller participants in the Dutch economy; they rose to new heights of prosperity and they came into closer contact with the cities. By 1640 many farmers had begun to indulge in various luxuries, including tiles.

New uses were found for tiles in the cities. Housing was becoming larger—the middle-class house built after 1650 had a separate kitchen; the living room now came into its own. The urban middle classes, who had long favored tiles, began to imitate the wealthy elite by covering their walls with fabric and leather. Without the necessity of cooking in the living room, tiles, so easy to keep clean, were no longer essential and after fifty years lost their appeal for the burghers. The new, separate kitchens were lined with tiles, but with a cheaper variety—either plain white or with minuscule motifs, such as children's games. The extent of decoration on a tile was not only a matter of fashion but also price; in general, the more decoration a tile had, the more expensive it was.

Between 1640 and 1660, therefore, the market for tiles, particularly the more luxurious ones, declined in relative and absolute importance in the cities and rose in the country. There was considerable difference between city and countryside. Cities were fortifications where relatively large numbers of people lived in close proximity, including a middle class with a fairly high cultural standard. The villages in rural areas were spread far and wide, and interspersed with a few farms. There was not much incentive nor many possibilities for travel from farm or village to town, and the towns were islands in the midst of these rural areas. This tendency continued through the second half of the seventeenth century, helping to shift the geographical location of the tile industry.

The importation of Chinese porcelain, so damaging to the sales of Netherlandish majolica, came to an abrupt end in about 1650 with the outbreak of civil war in China. The two workshops in Delft that had been working on the technical improvement of majolica filled the gap with greatly expanded production of imitation porcelain. Others in Delft followed their example as soon as possible.

The decline of the urban tile market and the near monopoly of Delft in the manufacture of the quality product known as faience led to the disappearance of the last small firms devoted to the old-fashioned mixture of tiles and majolica in Haarlem, Leiden, Amsterdam, and other places. The entire majolica, tile, and faience industry underwent a process of purging, concentration, and specialization. From 1660 on, the production of faience was centered in Delft; tiles were produced in Rotterdam and the towns of Harlingen and Makkum in Friesland. Harlingen had been the site of some small mixed majolica and tile works since about 1600. The new demand from rural areas, also evident in Friesland, led to a sharp increase in tile production in that city. Small centers in Amsterdam, Gouda, and Utrecht renowned for particular specialties remained in existence, but after 1660 most Dutch tiles were made in Rotterdam, Harlingen, and Makkum.

In the early years of the tile and majolica industry, most plants were relatively small, although large in comparison with most other craft shops. Inventories about 1570 listed some fifteen hundred objects for any pottery; this number increased to over ten thousand by the 1650s. The number of employees increased from less than ten in 1570 to about sixty in the largest faience workshop in Delft by 1660. Because the manufacture of fine ceramics demanded specialized technical knowledge, the field was dominated by a small group of people. New ceramic works were generally founded by relatives of other plant owners, although occasionally a foreman with fifteen years of experience might start off on his own. When the market called for an

FIG. 7 Pieter de Hooch (Dutch, 1629–1684)
Woman Delousing Her Child's Hair, 1658–60
Oil on canvas
Rijksmuseum, Amsterdam

Interior of a simple dwelling in the third quarter of the seventeenth century. The wall next to the door and the baseboard are paneled with blue tiles depicting children's games; the floor is covered with lead-glazed floor tiles.

increased number of specialized tileworks in about 1640, various businessmen in other fields began investing in this prospering industry. Vast capital was sunk into large workshops, which hired technical personnel from other plants, workers who had begun at a very young age and served many years of apprenticeship.

The stylistic evolution of tile decoration—the steady shrinking of the painted area, the decreased importance of ornamentation, and the abandonment of the frame—continued throughout this period. This development was furthered by the demand of the urban burghers for a cheaper product. The wishes of rural customers, however, were also increasingly considered. The influence of these two groups of customers brought about a noticeable change in tile decoration over a period of twenty years.

Most tiles made between 1640 and 1660 lacked frames and had very little ornamentation. Figurative representation was stressed, with a strong preference for unity of subject. For wealthy farmers who began buying tiles after 1640, wall tiles were new, and accepted. Generally, the countryside lagged behind the city in matters of fashion. Colorful decoration remained popular there long after 1625. Tiles with old-fashioned polychrome birds and flowers made in this period were probably intended specifically for these customers (no. 65). It is no accident that these two types of tile were the traditional specialties of Gouda and Harlingen, whose surroundings were among the wealthiest rural areas in the Netherlands. However, tiles of this kind were also made in large quantities in such centers as Rotterdam.

The Tile in the Countryside, 1660–1700

The Treaty of Münster in 1648 put an end to the war with Spain and the southern Netherlands. The Republic of the United Netherlands was recognized as a federation of seven provinces functioning as a unit in foreign affairs. This political form was nearly unique in Europe; only the city-state of Venice also called itself a republic. The government of the Netherlands had definitely oligarchic features. The entire country prospered, but the steady rise in the standard of living that had marked the preceding seventy years leveled off. Thanks to acquired wealth and to the technical and economic leadership of the Netherlands over the rest of Europe, the per capita income remained the highest in Europe until the end of the eighteenth century. The difference between rich and poor was smaller than in other countries, and there was a broad, prosperous middle class that could afford luxury, a phenomenon unique in Europe.

Tile production in this period was largely restricted to Rotterdam, Harlingen, and Makkum. Rotterdam tiles were sold in South Holland, Zeeland, and Flanders; those made in the Frisian centers found buyers primarily in the northern provinces and along the shores of the Zuider Zee. The tileworks of Harlingen and Makkum succeeded for the first time in exporting tiles on a large scale to the coastal areas of northern Germany and Denmark, countries with which these towns maintained lively sea trade. The smaller centers of tile production in Utrecht and Amsterdam mainly supplied the surrounding rural areas (fig. 7).

Tiles made for city dwellers were usually decorated simply or not at all. Plain white tiles were used for kitchens, basements, cellars, and occasionally baseboards (fig. 8). In the second half of the seventeenth century, fireplace mantels were still quite high, and the panels adjoining the fireback were often tiled plainly. Occasionally, a polychrome or blue flower picture would be tiled into a hearth as a kind of perennial substitute for the fresh flowers put by the fireplace in the summer. When the living-room mantels in urban homes were lowered in about 1700, the tile disappeared also from the hearth. In kitchens and in country living rooms the high mantel was maintained until well into the nineteenth century, and with it the traditional tile decoration.

Rural customers generally preferred a tile more richly decorated than the tiles for the cellar and the kitchen in the cities with minimal design. Polychrome tiles with birds and flowers, however, went out of fashion in this period and gradually disappeared. The abandonment of the roundel and other framing elements probably left many people with the feeling that the figured representations on tiles were adrift in a white sea. From the beginning, depictions of scenes from daily life had been underlined with a single stroke of the brush (no. 110), and with the popularization of ships, sea monsters, landscapes, and secular and biblical pastorals, the entire breadth of the tile was used for the horizon (see nos. 134, 145, 169, 178, and 182). Small landscapes and ships were found occasionally before 1640 in larger series depicting the trades and other subjects, but walls of tiles devoted to one specific theme were mainly characteristic of the period after 1660, when the tile had become an indispensable adornment to the farmhouse. Because much of the rural population also lived along the coast, it is not surprising that they preferred both seascapes and landscapes.

Rural customers were also the first to use biblical tiles. Subjects from the Bible did not appear on tiles before 1640 and did not rival the popularity of ships and sea monsters until about 1690. Most biblical tiles depicted a scene in a landscape covering the entire breadth of the tile, although there were tiles in which the landscape was placed within a roundel. Although the frame remained a feature of the biblical tile, a new form appeared in about 1660 in which the space beyond the roundel was decorated with spatter, a semi-mechanical technique. The central scene would be covered and the remaining area to be decorated spattered with a fine spray of purple paint, giving these sections a light-purple tone. The spatter technique surged in popularity in about 1680, when it began to be used in landscapes and pastoral scenes (see nos. 136, 167, 168). The central roundel was reduced in size and the spattered section enlarged. Other ornamental effects were achieved by covering different parts of the tile during the spattering.

The Rural Market and Export, 1700–1850

After 1700 the market for tiles within the Netherlands was exclusively rural. Sales in the cities were negligible; the high mantelpiece was replaced by a low one around 1700, and tiles—plain white ones at that—were relegated to the kitchen and cellar. In

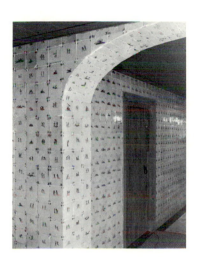

FIG. 8 Basement of a house at Kneuterdijk 6, The Hague, paneled with blue tiles depicting children's games and landscapes, 1675–1725

FIG. 9 Room in the Wilanów palace near Warsaw tiled entirely with pictures of flower vases in oval wreaths, alternated with rows of blue landscape tiles, 1725–50

the countryside, however, the market for tiles continued to grow throughout the eighteenth century; the reduced number of workshops in Rotterdam, Harlingen, and Makkum, and to a lesser degree those in Amsterdam and Utrecht, entered a new period of prosperity.

In addition to the home market, a widely varied export market developed for the Dutch tile between 1670 and 1800. This trade began when the inhabitants of the rural areas bordering the Netherlands began to imitate the way Dutch and Frisian farmers used tiles to decorate their farmhouses. Harlingen and Makkum tiles were particularly popular along the coasts of northern Germany and Denmark, and Rotterdam tiles were used widely in Flanders and northern France. These areas, with which the Netherlands had intensive shipping trade, favored the simple kind of decorated tile most popular in rural areas of the Netherlands.

Although northern Germany, Denmark, and northern France had industries of their own for Dutch-style wall tiles, they lagged so far behind the Netherlands in technical and commercial expertise that they were unable to compete effectively; this production never had more than a marginal importance. Even in Spain and Portugal, where the tile industries were well organized and served the home market adequately, the Dutch were able to make inroads. Despite the extra transportation costs, the Dutch tile was able to conquer part of this market due to its superior quality.

Technical improvements in the manufacturing process had made the Dutch tile thinner, flatter, and more finely decorated. These improvements helped to keep the cost low, making it possible for the Dutch to compete aggressively abroad. In France, Germany, and Poland, some noblemen used the best tiles Holland had to offer for their new summer houses (fig. 9). These customers were not interested in price but in the unparalleled technical refinement achieved toward 1700 by Dutch tilemakers, particularly those of Rotterdam. In England and the area surrounding Liège, this expensive, refined, fully decorated tile was used to line the inner walls of stone fireplaces.

It is not known to what degree Dutch tilemakers themselves cultivated the foreign market. Signs of their adapting the product to local tastes are found only in large, important commissions and in places where they encountered some competition. For the Spanish and Portuguese markets, for example, Dutch tilemakers produced colossal tile pictures for palaces; tiles with Catholic saints were made for churches and monasteries.

The final proof of the preeminence of the Dutch tile industry in Europe is found in the fact that tileworks in northern Germany, Denmark, and northern France produced imitations of Dutch tiles. The English tile industry, which developed gradually after 1725, was also primarily devoted to imitating the Dutch product.

Nearly all of the tiles that became fashionable after 1660 remained in production with only minor changes well into the nineteenth century. Ships, sea monsters, landscapes, and shepherds in tile-wide landscapes remained popular, with a shift occurring in the eighteenth century toward more landscapes and pastorals and fewer ships and sea monsters. Biblical subjects in circular frames were produced in the eighteenth century in incalculable quantities and variations. These tiles were generally destined for the rural markets in the Netherlands and in northern Germany and Denmark; they

FIG. 10 Wall of a farmhouse in Bergambacht, near Rotterdam, paneled with purple landscape tiles and tile pictures made in Rotterdam, c. 1800

were made in a wide extent of decoration. They were not of the best workmanship, as was reflected by their low selling price.

Not until after 1690 was full use made of the technical advances that evolved in the seventeenth century. Simpler tiles were then joined by types painted with great precision and refinement. The strong French influence on Dutch decorative arts after 1680 left its mark on tile design. The more refined tiles of this era often had borders in Louis XIV (see no. 170), Regency, or Louis XV style (see no. 171). In addition to landscapes and biblical scenes, new motifs were adopted for tiles of this quality: genre subjects, mythological themes from Ovid, and acrobats and other performers (see no. 121). The influence of French fashion led to the reintroduction shortly after 1700 of purely ornamental tiles, usually variations on standard eighteenth-century ornamentation found on silver, furniture, leather wall coverings, damask, and stucco decoration.

Tiles of this quality, both the refined figurative type and the precisely painted ornamental ones, were exported in large quantities. Generally, they were too expensive for the home market. In only one area of the Netherlands were expensive tiles of this kind used in great quantity: along the Zaan River, north of Amsterdam. The inhabitants of this part of the country, the seat of large industry and extensive shipbuilding in the eighteenth century, retained the country custom of decorating their living rooms with tiles. With their considerable wealth and exposure to the sophisticated style of Amsterdam, these buyers preferred the stylish, expensive variety of tiles.

The Rotterdam workshop De Blompot (The Flowerpot), which was the source of a steady stream of new designs throughout the eighteenth century, was probably responsible for introducing these luxury tiles. The shop was acquired by the Aelmis family in 1691. De Blompot remained the major producer of such tiles for the duration of the eighteenth century (see no. 167), although it sparked some competition from Amsterdam and Harlingen.

In addition to the traditional wall of fully or partly decorated tiles, there were examples in the eighteenth century of tile paintings or groups of decorative tiles applied to walls tiled predominantly in white. Nearly all the tile paintings that collectors now display as independent panels probably were originally embedded in walls of white tiles or in combination with ornamental or floral tiles (fig. 10).

In the nineteenth century the hand-decorated tile increasingly lost ground. The last group of customers were the inhabitants of the remote areas of the Dutch and German countryside, who, conservative as they were, remained loyal to old traditions. A number of circumstances contributed to the decline of the Dutch tile industry in the nineteenth century. The manufacture of wallpaper was mechanized and grew increasingly cheap, a great advantage over other wall coverings, including tiles. In addition, the introduction of the double wall in about 1920 eliminated the need to camouflage mildewed walls.

Until about 1690 the Dutch tile was constantly being improved by new techniques of manufacture and decoration, assuring its leading position in the European market. After 1750, however, this pioneering role was assumed by England, which retained its lead for about a century and a half. Tiles incorporated into European houses in the nineteenth century were primarily English machine-made products. The Dutch tile industry enjoyed a brief revival between 1890 and 1910. With the advent of the Art Nouveau style, elaborate and colorful household decoration came back into fashion, including specially designed hand-painted tiles.

The Last Customer: The Collector, after 1880

The first collectors of decorative arts in the nineteenth century sought out fine objects from the distant past. When one area of collecting had been exhausted or had become too expensive, collectors instinctively developed new interests. The tile, simultaneously a structural ornament and an example of a folk art, was less luxurious than silver or fine furniture, and it is not surprising that it did not attract collectors' interest until more precious objects began to grow scarce. Also, relatively few old tiles came on the market before the turn of the century.

The first large tile collections came into being in about 1905, assembled from the flood of old tiles that suddenly became available as a result of the passage of a Dutch housing act in 1901 which regulated new construction in the environs of Amsterdam and Rotterdam and allowed for the rehabilitation of the inner cities, many parts of which had fallen into disrepair. Houses generally require renovation every eighty or one hundred years; those built between 1600 and 1650 thus underwent their first renovations between 1700 and 1750, at which time the tiles in the living room, with its stove or fireplace, were often covered with wall hangings. In the eighteenth century there was a tendency to add separate kitchens onto existing houses, and nineteenth-century heirs of original homeowners often found these houses too small and left for larger dwellings. Such areas gradually turned into slums. This was particularly true of houses constructed for modest burghers between 1600 and 1650 in the then newly expanding towns. When these impoverished sections were developed and the old houses demolished after 1901, many tiles came to light.

Private tile collectors between 1905 and 1940 fall into two categories. The first includes the handful of important collectors who attempted to assemble complete representations of Dutch tile production, among them Eelco M. Vis, many of whose tiles now form part of the Philadelphia Museum of Art collection. They tended to concentrate mainly on early tiles—those before 1650—partly because the first generation of collectors tends to be most interested in the oldest examples, and partly because the supply of tiles from this period was greatest in the years after 1900. Whenever they could, these collectors bought tiles in large lots in order to assemble panels of sixteen, thirty, or forty-eight tiles of one type. Tiles are small architectural ornaments, and as such entire walls were originally lined with hundreds of tiles of the same kind. Major collectors attempted to evoke the effect of such walls because, of course, a single tile is an object removed from its context.

The second group of collectors was much larger, individuals who liked to surround themselves with precious objects and conversation pieces, including tiles. This group usually collected tiles as objects independent of their original function. The current terminology of tile collecting—the names of corner motifs, for example—was developed by collectors of this ilk and by the antique dealers who sold to them. These collectors did not work their way down from early to late periods of tile manufacture but instead tended to specialize in one or more pictorial themes, although such tiles had not entered large-scale production until after 1640. Of course, a few small collectors tried to bring together a representative sample of tile production.

The tiled walls from houses demolished or rebuilt between 1910 and 1940 usually went to antique dealers as a unit, to be resold individually or in lots of four. Occasionally a large collector would be able to buy an entire wall in order to assemble panels of similar tiles. One notable fact concerning the important collectors of the pre-1940 period is that nearly all were architects or building contractors or worked with the advice of those professions. Because architects and builders viewed the tile as architectural ornaments, they were invariably interested in tile panels.

After 1945 the tile collectors' interest shifted. Large panels of early tiles from before 1650 were no longer available, yet a number of collectors were nonetheless able to assemble good surveys of the range of Dutch tile production. That generation saw the tile less as an architectural ornament than as a miniature painting, a *plaatje*, or picture. Moreover, the scarcity and high price of early tiles led to a new interest in tiles of the late seventeenth and eighteenth centuries. A number of collectors limited themselves even further to a single subject, such as the Bible, ships, or animals.

Major tile collections in museums—not only in the Netherlands but also elsewhere, including the Philadelphia Museum of Art—were assembled by the major Dutch collectors before 1940. They therefore tend to consist primarily of pre-1650 tiles, with the most common varieties represented in large panels.

For more than three hundred years, constantly shifting segments of the population favored Dutch majolica tiles as home decoration. During that period there was a generally steady descent in the social status of tile customers; they became increasingly removed from the few who dictated fashion. The Dutch tile industry, however, was skilled in accommodating itself, through technical innovations, to new demands and new groups of customers.

The interplay between industry and consumer during these three centuries was so successful that the Dutch majolica tile became an important expression of Dutch culture. This characteristically Dutch product eventually became a popular collectors' item in the Netherlands and abroad as well. Living proof of this is found in the hundreds of private and public collections of Dutch tiles in all parts of the world.

The Literature and Dating of Tiles

Since the late nineteenth century, when the serious study of tiles began, authors have approached the subject in various ways. Paul F. Knochenhauer (1886), the first writer on tiles of the Lowlands, was particularly interested in their ornamentation. Using them as examples, he sought to enrich nineteenth-century concepts of style. In 1926 Eelco M. Vis and Commer de Geus, men interested in tiles both as collectors and as dealers, put together a "coffee table" book with a brief introduction and very broad dating. Their information about dating may have come from Hein Hamer, brother-in-law of De Geus. During the years between 1910 and 1940, Hamer bought, on a large scale, tiles that were still on walls in their original locations. He approximated the dates of the various types of tiles from his knowledge of the ages of the houses in which they were found. A second volume by Vis and De Geus appeared in 1933, with an extensive introduction by Ferrand W. Hudig, giving a history of tileworks, city by city. This was based on long and intensive archival research, but the production information could not be tied to specific tiles and there was no attempt to attribute particular tiles to specific tileworks.

In 1959 Dingeman Korf bypassed the archival information and proceeded very systematically to arrange the existing tile types according to their decorations. He organized groups and developed a chronology on the basis of this material, emphasizing majolica tiles made before 1675. Since seventeenth-century tilemakers did not create their tiles so that twentieth-century art historians could make groups, the systematization according to decoration ended up with the faults of a system made after the fact. One had leftover groups, overlapping groups, and groups with tiles that were not exactly comparable. Thanks to Korf, however, one gained a rather complete overview and a very useful, although broad, dating of tiles into periods of at best a quarter, or at worst, a half, century.

Jan Pluis continued the work of organizing. By grouping tiles with the same subjects (for example, animals or children's games), it became possible, with the aid of graphic material that had served as sources, to begin to establish quite exact dating. Thanks to his inventories, one now has reasonably precise dating to the nearest quarter century for a good number of tile types.

Until 1650 there were so many tileworks producing such similar wares that attributing a certain type of tile to a specific city cannot be done reliably. Knowing that between 1625 and 1660 half of all the tileworks were in Rotterdam, one can estimate with great assurance that half of the surviving tiles of the period were made in Rotterdam. Attributing certain types of tiles to a particular city often rests on traditions dating to the beginning of this century, when early collectors first encountered specific types in certain cities. For example, the Roman soldiers (no. 153) were found predominantly in Rotterdam and surrounding towns; on that basis exclusively, these tiles were ascribed to Rotterdam. With the reorganization and concentration of the tile industry in the middle of the seventeenth century, specific types of tiles became associated with various cities. Since 1960 Pluis has photographed and documented thousands of tiles from the period after 1660, predominantly with tiles still *in situ*. In this way he has provided an overview linking types of tiles to specific areas during this time.

Using surviving transfer patterns (*sponsen*), which are known to have come from certain tileworks after 1680, attributions can now be made with great certainty. For example, the archives of Tichelaar pottery and tileworks in Makkum includes *sponsen* from Makkum and Utrecht; the Gemeentemuseum Hannemahuis in Harlingen, *sponsen* from the firm J. van Hulst and its predecessors in Harlingen and Utrecht; the Fries Museum in Leeuwarden, *sponsen* from the firm Tjalling and its predecessors in Harlingen; the Gemeentelijke Archiefdienst in Rotterdam, *sponsen* of the firm De Blompot in Rotterdam, owned by the Aelmis family and their successors.

Summarizing the dating of Dutch wall tiles made before 1650, one can say that the combination of large-scale production, numerous firms, and well-to-do, style-conscious city dwellers led to a succession of rapid changes, even though there was some overlapping between the various types of tiles. Certain kinds of tiles were probably made for a limited time, for example, ten to fifteen years. The dating of tiles before 1650 is sometimes based on archival information in which tiles are named and on tiles still found in houses for which building or rebuilding data are known, but it is most often determined by the chronological ordering of the decoration on certain types of tiles combined with an evaluation of the differences in measurements and materials.

After 1650, when tile production became concentrated in a few centers and tileworks had greater continuity—and when the tile consumer was less style conscious—various types of tiles remained in production longer, making it more difficult to provide precise dating.

On the basis of the number of tileworks per city in any one period, the early tiles (before 1600) must come predominantly from Haarlem and Amsterdam; for the period 1625 to 1660, about half should be from Rotterdam. After 1650, with production concentrated in Rotterdam and Friesland (Harlingen and Makkum), the largest part must have been made in these two centers. Using the detailed inventories of Pluis, a division can be made between these two areas of production. However, attributions to Amsterdam, Gouda, and Utrecht, cities with smaller production, remain based largely on tradition.

An attempt has been made here to add some new information to that of Korf's and Pluis's systematically organized tile data and, in so doing, to answer the questions of how and why the tile industry developed in the Netherlands, how the use of tiles continuously changed in the course of three hundred years, and how and why the appearance of the tiles (their decoration as well as their thickness and the color of their clay body) was continually subject to change.

By looking at the tile not as a twentieth-century art historian but, as it were, as a seventeenth-century producer and consumer, and by combining this with knowledge of the technical development of the ceramic and tile industry and the prosperity of the various population groups, the tile can be removed from its isolation and can answer many of the questions initially raised above.

The Production of Tiles

The tiles in this collection are primarily faience, or majolica, a term designating the use of a white, opaque tin glaze or tin enamel, which originated in the Near East and was first described in an account by Abulqasim in 1301.[1] Tin glaze probably was used earlier, but whether it was also applied to tiles has not been determined. For some four centuries the faience technique has been applied to both plain white and decorated Dutch tiles, but recently tile manufacture has given way almost completely to modern procedures, and only in one or two workshops is the traditional method still used.

Tiles were made long before the development of tin glaze for pottery, which probably occurred in the Middle East around A.D. 1000. The earliest tiles were made of clay found along the floodplains of riverbeds. The clay was a mixture of eroded rock fragments that had been carried long distances and deposited by rivers and seas. The finer material, the actual clay minerals, had a laminated structure that tended to attract other minerals and organic matter, with which it was greatly infused. Iron invariably appeared in the clay and greatly influenced its color after firing; calcium and magnesium compounds were also present. This clay is no longer considered a good, reliable material for wall and floor tiles, but early craftsmen had to use what was available, and what they accomplished through accumulated experience and inventiveness is astounding.

The earliest potter made tiles and bricks, but did not fire them; he simply dried them in the open air. If they dried too quickly and began to crack, the craftsman improved the drying properties of the clay by adding straw or manure to it. Succeeding generations of potters used fire to bake the dried tiles, thus producing terra cotta, which made it more durable and opened up possibilities for decoration. Early tiles were neither painted nor glazed, and decoration was restricted to relief, achieved by incising or impressing a design into the leather-hard clay. The need for production of greater quantities led to the use of wooden or fired-clay molds, into which clay was pressed to achieve the desired relief decoration. Another method of decorating this still-simple ware took advantage of color differences. The natural color of fired clay containing iron is brick red, which may be darkened by adding oxides with dyeing properties, such as manganese or cobalt. These oxides, in the form of mineral earths, were added to a thin slip of clay to obtain a colored substance that could be used to decorate tiles. Through skillful variations of this technique, handsome contrasts were created on earthenware pottery, as well as on tiles, although examples of these are very rare.

The application of glaze was a major innovation in the development of tilemaking. The earliest glazes were clear—blue, green, and turquoise in color; they appeared in Egypt, about the fourth millenium B.C. At first, the glaze covered the tile completely; later, it was applied to sections, creating fields that were separated by their differences in thickness. In this way, several colors could be applied side-by-side on one tile, and very rich and imaginative effects could be achieved on large surfaces.

The search for other shades and colors, and especially for a pure white glaze, continued for many years. Around A.D. 1000, when Western travel to and commerce with China began, Persians discovered Chinese porcelain with painted decoration on a

1. For a German translation, with notes, of Abulqasim's text see H. Ritter et al., "Orientalische Steinbücher und persische Fayencetechnik," in *Istanbuler Mitteilungen des Archäologischen Instituts des Deutschen Reiches,* vol. 3 (1935).

white background. Potters had been searching for a white glaze that would hide the red, brown, or buff color of the fired clay—unlike porcelain, which has a white clay body—and serve as a ground for a blue or multicolored decoration. Potters in Persia are credited with this accomplishment, although the exact date of this discovery is unknown. The white glaze, which in addition to the usual melting ingredients contained a considerable amount of tin oxide, was a ground onto which the decorator could apply other colors. This technique from the East was rapidly adopted throughout the Western world and became significant in European tile manufacture. It was first applied to European tiles in simple glazes of blue, black, green, white, or red. Later, square tiles were divided into several sections separated by thin threads of clay and glazes were applied. Around 1500 the flat majolica, or faience, tile was produced with a painted decoration in one or more colors.

The development of techniques for the production of earthenware tiles also continued over these years. At first, locally found clay had been used, but later the clays and minerals needed for the body were brought from afar and carefully selected. The pursuit of materials containing very little iron for ceramic products in order to obtain a body as lightly colored as possible was begun in Europe in the seventeenth century. In England Josiah Twyford and John Astbury in 1710 replaced the local red clay of Stoke on Trent with clay brought from Dorset and Devon. In the second half of the eighteenth century, Josiah Wedgwood, with much flair and vision, exploited the potentials of this new material and developed the ancient craft of ceramics into a prosperous industry. His ideas greatly contributed to the development of the tile industry, which today provides a versatile assortment of earthenware wall tiles of excellent quality.

The Production of Tin-glazed Tiles

It may be assumed that toward the end of the sixteenth century, when tin-glazed floor and wall tiles began to be produced, this was done in potteries that had considerable know-how and experience in making ceramic products. To fire a kiln successfully, for example, takes years of training. Clay is difficult to work, requiring great skill, while it takes much experience to develop the formulas needed for making paints and glazes. There is little doubt, therefore, that the early tin-glazed tiles were manufactured in floor-tile workshops, where the "upgrading" or "refinement" of lead-glazed into tin-glazed tiles took place with great ingenuity and perseverance.

Raw Materials and Body Preparation

The clay from which tin-glazed tiles were made was the same as that used for red floor tiles: medium "fat," or plastic, red-firing river or sea clay, abundant even to this day in the delta area of the Schelde, Maas, and Rhine rivers. The biscuit of early majolica wall tiles has the same composition as that of red floor tiles; they are equally thick, almost 2.5 centimeters (1 inch), with a surface of 13 centimeters (5 inches) square. Later they became somewhat thinner, but the material continued to be the same impure, natural clay used without much advance preparation.

Around 1625 attempts were made to improve the body in order to produce a thinner tile. The addition of marl, a secondary clay containing a naturally blended proportion of calcium in the form of chalk, greatly strengthened the body because of its high flux content. At first, however, the method of blending and kneading the materials was tried with little success: after firing, layers of different colors appeared in the biscuit as a result of incomplete blending, and the body became weaker rather than stronger. Later, around 1650, a perfect mixture was achieved by the introduction of liquid slip blending, which produced a strong, uniformly colored body that was less liable to crack. Marl gave the body a buff color because of the interaction between iron and chalk during firing. Over the years the thickness of tiles was gradually reduced to as little as 7 millimeters (¼ inch).

The process of liquid slip blending of the body was described by Gerrit Paape, who in 1794 conveyed many details of earthenware manufacture in Delft.[2] Prescribed quantities of different types of clay, which he enumerated in barrels, were combined with water in a wooden vessel. The stirred slip was subsequently sieved into low settling basins in which sedimentation, decantation, and drying took place. Layers of clay that had sunk to the bottom of the basin were cut into rectangular pieces and stored in a cellar. This so-called washing the clay always took place in the spring, when stock for the year ahead would be prepared. In Makkum this process was used until recently, but it was replaced by mechanical methods not dependent on seasonal changes.

Once a week clay from the cellar was prepared for production by kneading in a pug mill. Clay was put in the top of the mill, kneaded, and squeezed out at the bottom. A pug mill can be seen in a tile picture from 1737 showing a cross section of the Bolsward ceramic factory (fig. 11). On the ground floor at right is a wooden barrel with a clay cutter driven by a blinkered horse; horizontal blades on the vertical axle cut through the clay and stirred it. Paape described this kneading process as done in Delft in 1794 by a clay treader, a man who walked barefoot on the clay body. In Friesland, however, the pug mill, which was patented in 1635, was used by all manufacturers of wall and floor tiles as well as by all potters.

Shaping and Drying

The prepared clay was brought to the tilemaking section, where the tilemaker and his assistant flattened the lumps of clay from the pug mill and cut them roughly into squares, which were then placed in a wooden or iron frame and rolled to their approximate shape and thickness. The tiles were removed by gently lifting the frame and were dried on planks. After a day the tiles were sufficiently dry to be stacked front to back. After a moisture loss of more than 50 percent, tiles were again rolled and flattened to dry slowly and evenly.

The tiles, no longer square after being rolled again, had to be trimmed. They were placed one at a time under a 13 centimeter (5 inch) square wooden block that was pressed down; the tilemaker trimmed three edges with a steel blade, then turned the block and tile to cut the fourth. Copper nails in two or three corners were pressed into the tile to prevent the block from sliding over it. Nail imprints can be found in all tiles

2. Paape, 1794

FIG. 11 Cross section of the Bolsward pottery and tileworks shown in a tile picture of 1737 (replica, 1978)
Tichelaars Koninklijke Makkumer Aardewerk en Tegelfabriek, Makkum

A typical 18th-century pottery and tileworks with a kiln being fired in the center and various production activities taking place. On the ground floor at right, a horse-driven pug mill mixes clay; next to it is a horse-driven glaze grinder, and in the adjacent work space at left is a group of tile decorators. On the second floor, pottery is being made and dried. On the third floor, at each end, tilemakers are forming tiles in frames; after being dried, the tiles are squared and stacked for further drying.

FIG. 12 Interior of a kiln with tiles stacked vertically face to face and back to back, c. 1930

over one hundred years old; the introduction of a four-sided guillotine-like device during the later nineteenth century eliminated these characteristic marks. After tiles were trimmed or cut, the drying process was hastened by stacking them near the kiln, where they would be biscuit fired when thoroughly dry.

Making Glazes and Paints

Red floor tiles and simple red pottery were covered with a transparent glaze. A mixture of galena (lead sulfide) and white firing clay in water was poured over the tiles and turned into glaze when fired in a kiln at 950 degrees centigrade (1,750 degrees Fahrenheit). This unsophisticated method was also used for wall tiles until about 1650. Wall tiles, however, were first biscuit fired, then covered with white, "painted," glazed, and glost fired. The transparent top layer, which sometimes exceeded a millimeter in thickness, tended to become too thin; thus the decoration could run, especially since tiles were placed vertically, face to face, in the kiln during glost firing (see fig. 12).

The development of more refined techniques around the mid-seventeenth century enabled production of a superior material. The liquid body preparation was introduced, and glazing and decorating techniques were improved. Glazes were prepared by melting the glaze materials in a kiln and powdering them to produce a frit which was then mixed with water. This transparent glaze, or *kwaart*, a term derived from the Italian *coperta*, was applied after the tile had been painted, by sprinkling and spraying on a layer a few hundred microns thick. Thus, the brushstrokes were far less affected in the kiln. At a later date—exactly when is unknown—tilemakers began to melt, or frit, all glazing materials together and to use a tin glaze that contained sufficient lead to become glossy (paints had to contain a comparable amount of lead in order to fuse with the glaze). This technique, which generally replaced *kwaarten*, is still used at the Makkum tileworks.

Paints used by the decorator consisted of metal silicates made in the same manner as tin glaze. Instead of tin oxide, however, another metal oxide or compound was used: cobalt for blue, iron for red, copper for green, antimony for yellow, and manganese for purple. Sometimes additional shades were obtained by blending two of these colors. Today, other pigments are available to make a greater range of ceramic colors and shades.

Glazing and Decorating

After being biscuit fired, sorted, and checked for cracks, tiles were glazed. Special skills were required of a good glazer who, using a scoop, could cover one tile with thick, white liquid tin glaze in two splashes. Because tiles are porous, the glaze dried quickly. Excess glaze was removed from the edges, and tiles were glost fired to produce a white finish.

Tiles that were to be decorated were taken to one of the five to ten decorators working for the tileworks. The painter or decorator began by pouncing the tile using a transfer pattern, or *spons:* the outline of a drawing was pricked through a piece of paper the size of the tile, and the *spons* was placed on the tile and dusted with

powdered charcoal. The outline thus produced on the tile was redrawn with a fine
brush (*trekker*) and then deepened with a larger brush dipped in specified colors
(*dieper*). Craftsmanship rather than creativity was required of an accomplished tile
painter, who usually spent about three years as an apprentice acquiring the necessary
skills. Each painter developed a characteristic style; the work of individual tile painters can be recognized by their distinctive personal touch.

Biscuit and Glost Firing

Firing was done in a kiln, which had a chamber of 500 to 1000 cubic feet; clay tiles
were stacked in the bottom, with the glazed and decorated tiles on top. In a picture
showing the inside of a 2 meter (6 foot) high kiln (fig. 12), tiles were placed vertically
in long rows alternating face to face and back to back. Filling the chamber was a
difficult job; it took two or three men several days to fill and ready it for firing.

Wood fuel was fed through a firing gate into the hearth, which was under the
chamber and had draft holes. Similar channels connected the chamber and the chim-
ney, which had a semicircular opening that allowed regulation of draft and observation of fire distribution. In the Bolsward tile picture (fig. 11), a boy watches the fire
distribution. Firing took about thirty-five hours. Controlling the last firing stages was a
precise job requiring sensitivity and experience because no measuring instruments
were available. The kilnmaster held a key position in a tileworks; the final result of
the efforts of the entire staff lay in his hands, and both he and the owner were aware
of this. It took three days to cool the kiln, after which it was opened with great
anticipation. Figures from the past disclose how few tiles produced during this lengthy
process were really firsts—sometimes only 15 percent. Seconds were sold at lower
prices, and the worst ended up as rubble on the path to the clay site where new
material was dug for firing.

Tilemaking has always been an uncertain craft. Despite scientific and technological know-how, there are still failures in tilemaking. Great admiration should be
accorded early tilemakers, who under difficult circumstances succeeded in making
products still cherished today.

Floor Tiles

FIG. 13 Majolica floor tiles from the Belgian abbey of Hercken-rode, near Hasselt, 1552 Museum Boymans–van Beuningen, Rotterdam

Although decorated floor tiles were abundant in Flanders and France from medieval times on, they were not widely used in the Netherlands, except in churches and cloisters, until about 1550. Floor tiles are generally heavy and variable in their shapes and proportions, in contrast to the later wall tiles, which are lighter and vary only slightly from the standard thirteen centimeters (five inches) square. Floor tiles were fashioned of a coarse, red clay—again in contrast to wall tiles, for which the clay underwent a more intensive refining process. A motif was pressed into each tablet with a wooden matrix, and the indented surfaces were filled with white slip or pipe clay, giving a two-colored design. The tile was then leveled, dried, and covered with a transparent lead glaze, which resulted in an overall yellowish tint after firing. Because the inlaid decoration was thick, it remained visible despite surface abrasion.

Unlike the designs of wall tiles, which occur in almost endless variety, only three separate groups of floor tile designs, made up of heraldic, plant, and animal motifs, are known. The designs are repeated on groups of four or sixteen tiles which adjoin so that the ornamentation forms a continuous pattern. Itinerant craftsmen, traveling with their own wooden stamps, made similar tiles from Burgundy to the northern Netherlands; this makes it difficult to pinpoint the place of manufacture of most floor tiles. Tiles inscribed with aphorisms in medieval Dutch (nos. 1, 2), however, unequivo-cally betray their place of origin. Some of the earliest northern Netherlandish exam-ples of such floor tiles were unearthed in cloisters in the northern provinces of Groningen and Friesland, where portions of a floor dating to the thirteenth century were uncovered.

Floor tiles with floral motifs were first introduced by Italian majolica potters who had immigrated to Antwerp during the first quarter of the sixteenth century (see fig. 13). Their technique was quite different from that of most of the local tilemakers, and this resulted in a new product for Flanders and the Netherlands characterized by Italianate designs and by a tile with a uniform, smooth, clay body. When fired, the tile was covered with an opaque white glaze whose essential ingredient was tin oxide.[1] This tin glaze was painted with a polychrome design—blue, orange, yellow, and green—before the second firing (see nos. 5, 6).

1. Lane, 1960, p. 47.

1. FLOOR TILES

1500–1560
Red clay and buff slip
Gift of Mrs. Francis P. Garvan

Within a simple geometric design of light-colored, continuous bands forming interlocked diamonds are large circles divided into quarter segments; each quarter contains a phrase in Gothic script. Together these phrases compose the maxim: *Die tijt is cort—die doot is snel—wacht u va sonde—soe doedi wel* (Time is short—death is swift—beware of sin—so do you well). An extant floor fragment of such size and condition from this early period is quite rare; most remaining examples consist of no more than four tiles.

References: Geus, 1919–21, vol. 4, p. 155, fig. 1; Vis and Geus, 1926, p. 1; Vis coll. sale, 1927, no. 311; Geus, 1931, fig. 1; Vis and Geus, 1933, pp. 2–4.
Similar tiles: Peelen, 1922, fig. 4, p. 27; Renaud, 1958, p. 6; Lane, 1960, p. 34; De Jonge, 1971, ill. 2a.

43

2. FLOOR TILES
1500–1560
Red clay and buff slip
Gift of Mrs. Francis P. Garvan

An inscription in Gothic letters
extends along the sides of a diamond: *Alle dinc—heeft—sijnen—
tijt* (For everything there is a sea-
son). The *i* and the *j* in the word
sijnen on the lower left side
have been transposed, possibly by
an unschooled craftsman. The
emblem in the center of the diamond is the fire steel, the heraldic symbol of the Burgundian
kings.[1] Each corner displays one
quarter of a many-petaled rosette.
References: Geus, 1919–21, vol. 4,
p. 155, fig. 2; Vis and Geus, 1926,
pl. 2b; Vis coll. sale, 1927, no. 300;
Geus, 1931, fig. 1.
Similar tiles: Peelen, 1922, fig. 4,
p. 27; Vis coll. sale, 1927, no. 299
(now Metropolitan Museum of
Art, New York, 27.199.359.69562).

1. Steven V. Grancsay, *The John
Woodman Higgins Armory,
Worcester, Massachusetts, Catalogue of Armor* (Worcester,
1961), p. 50.

3. FLOOR TILE
1500–1560
Red clay and buff slip
Gift of Mrs. Francis P. Garvan

Intertwined lines interspersed
with rosettes and dots, as seen on
this tile, would have contributed
to a pattern of interlocking circles
extending continuously across the
floor. The tile shows traces of
griffins along two edges.

4. FLOOR TILE
1500–1560
Red clay and buff slip
Gift of Mrs. Francis P. Garvan

This tile shows a portion of a design with dots, lines, and foliage.
More tiles would be required to
envision the full extent of the
pattern.

Reverse

5. FLOOR TILE
Antwerp or France
1560–1580
Polychrome
Gift of Mrs. Francis P. Garvan

This tile, with a fine, buff-colored clay body, was part of a very large floor design. The overall decoration consists of curved plant stems and meandering floral designs painted with yellow, brown, blue, purple, and turquoise. One corner shows a section of a brown escutcheon framed by a yellow band, edged with blue.

6. FLOOR BORDER TILE
Antwerp
1560–1580
Polychrome
Gift of Mrs. Francis P. Garvan

This tile, with a very fine, buff-colored clay body, was painted with yellow, brown, blue and green glaze. Stylized leaves are framed by interconnecting blue circles, and yellow bands edged in blue and blue cable motifs extend along the tile's upper and lower borders.
Reference: Vis and Geus, 1926, pl. 11 (erroneously called a wall tile).
Similar tiles: Korf, 1979, fig. 90; Amsterdam, Sotheby, cat. 337, 1981, no. 29.

A   B

7. FLOOR TILES
Flanders
1700–1780
Red clay and buff slip
Gift of Mrs. Francis P. Garvan

Rampant lions facing each other provide the focal points of these tiles from a floor with a lively pattern of circles, diamonds, and dots.

8. FLOOR TILE
Flanders or France
1700–1780
Red clay and buff slip
Gift of Mrs. Francis P. Garvan

A lion rampant, facing left, inscribed within a circle, closely resembles that on the seal of the provinces of Holland.[1] In each corner is one quarter of a circle and an oval shape. Traces of a vine motif are visible along the sides of the tile.
References: Forrer, 1901, p. 51; Vis and Geus, 1926, p. 3.

1. H. Brugmans, *Het huiselijk en maatschappelijk leven onzer voorouders* (Amsterdam, 1931), p. 232.

Ornamental Polychrome

FIG. 14 Adrian Collaert (Flemish, c. 1560–1618)
Natural specimens, plate 6 from *Avium vivae incones* (Antwerp, 1610)
Engraving
Collection of James Tanis, Bryn Mawr

A split pomegranate appears at left.

1. Most of the tiles from Herckenrode are now in the Museum voor Kunst en Geschiedenis in Brussels; a small repository remains in the Museum Boymans–van Beuningen in Rotterdam. A document from 1532 records a commission for tile flooring for an abbey choir issued to Petrus Frans van Venedig. The artisan must have been among the Italian potters who immigrated to the southern Netherlands during the early sixteenth century and who were instrumental in founding the majolica industry there. See Fries Museum, 1971–72, p. 8; Philippen, 1932, pp. 243–57; Henri Nicaise, "Les Carreaux en faïence anversoise de l'ancienne abbaye d'Herckenrode," *Bulletin des Musées Royaux d'Art et d'Histoire,* series 3, vol. 7, nos. 4, 5 (1935), pp. 92–127.
2. De Jonge, 1971, p. 19.

The ornamental wall tiles of the late sixteenth and early seventeenth centuries constitute the chief link between older forms of painted floor tiles decorated with patterns of interwoven vegetation and the more familiar wall tiles. The custom of painting such tiles passed into the Lowlands from Italy. The influence exerted by immigrant potters explains the difference between the polychrome tiles described here and those in the following chapters. Early ornamental tiles were produced in some thirty tileworks situated in towns throughout a relatively small area. Each tileworks made the standard product with some variations. Visually sophisticated and skillfully worked, they directly reflect the sumptuous ornamental tiles used in great numbers in early sixteenth-century Italianate majolica tile floors, such as one formerly in the Belgian abbey of Herckenrode (fig. 13).[1]

Early ornamental tiles are intricately patterned, with complete designs covering large surface areas. The first patterns—the large quatrefoil (see no. 9) and the grape and pomegranate (see no. 34)—encompass sixteen tiles, as does the star tulip (see no. 27). These tiles often present a play of multivalent readings: areas painted in reserve vie for dominance with those on a white ground, for example, in large quatrefoils. Isolated corner decorations, which in later tiles serve as stable, repetitive points of reference, are wholly absent, and in fact, in the star tulip, the four corners of each tile differ entirely from one another. Finally, fruit and flower ornamental tiles present a kind of *horror vacui,* unlike Dutch tiles after the early seventeenth century with their abundance of white space. Secondary motifs, for example, daisies midway along the edges of grape and pomegranate tiles, contribute to the exuberance and intricacy of the overall pattern. Many of the abstract decorative forms in these tiles are also found in earlier tiled floors. The geometric configurations characteristic of star tulip tiles—elements that form squares within octagons—are reminiscent of floors such as that at Herckenrode, which also contains framing tiles decorated with lacy scrolls, forerunners of the small, rectangular border tiles (nos. 25, 26).

Most fruit and flower ornamental tiles feature some of the traditional components of the fruit swag or garland: pomegranates, grapes, flowers, seed pods, and foliage. These elements, which also appear in earlier Netherlandish floor tiles, call to mind the contributions of the immigrant Italian potters. Hexagonal floor tiles forming segments of a wreath of pomegranates, seed pods, and foliage sometimes framed portrait tiles (fig. 2), while other ornamental floor tiles were decorated with split pomegranates and calligraphic flourishes. These were the predecessors of later ornamental tiles depicting pomegranates (see no. 35). The fruit and flower patterns on wall tiles may also have been inspired by other forms of Netherlandish decorative art featuring garlands and fruit festoons. Such motifs occur often in Netherlandish ornamental prints of the late sixteenth and early seventeenth centuries, while the renowned sixteenth-century tapestries of Flanders display magnificent fruit-garland borders. Later, in the seventeenth century, Dutch leatherworkers produced for wealthy clients tooled, gilt wall panels decorated with fruit clusters.

Among the fruits found on early ornamental tiles is a round, orange-colored fruit, possibly a pomegranate but lacking its characteristic grid of seeds (see fig. 14). It was intended to evoke associations with the House of Orange,[2] whose scions had fought for the liberation of the Netherlands from Spanish domination. The fruit appears, for example, in early seventeenth-century inventories of a tileworks, which record stocks of tiles called *appelen van orangen* (orange apples).[3]

Mediterranean produce, however, does not wholly dominate early ornamental tiles. On the flower-vase tile (no. 19), for example, the bouquet of yellow daisies recalls similar motifs on the strapwork cartouches of Northern ornamental prints.[4] Early seventeenth-century contracts and inventories of tile potteries frequently refer to flower-vase tiles, designated as *blompotten, blompotten in de ruyt, ronde blompotten,* and *enckele goutsblomkens* (flowerpots, flowerpots with diamonds, round flowerpots, and single marigolds).[5] Two tile workshops in Delft and one in Rotterdam were also called De Blompot.

Elaborately patterned tile designs, such as the large quatrefoil and the grape and pomegranate, were time-consuming to produce and therefore expensive. As tilemaking procedures were streamlined during the early decades of the seventeenth century, simplified versions of such patterns were compressed onto single tiles (see no. 13). Although fruit and flower ornamental tiles died out about 1625, they fostered an ornamental strain in later Dutch tiles which continued in conjunction with a strong pictorial impulse. Among their progeny are the various types of fruit-dish tiles (for example, no. 100). Flower-vase tiles gave rise to variants in which the unpretentious daisy is replaced by the more fashionable crown imperial and tulip (see no. 96 and fig. 15).

The striking characteristic of star tulip tiles is the decoration of stylized fruits and flowers arranged around a geometric motif. Each set of four tiles forms a central, eight-pointed deep-blue star encircled by four oranges or pomegranates and four tulips interspersed with marigolds, acorns, and berries. In some panels, the central focus is an orange rosette anchored by eight blue petals; this focus is alternated with sets of four tiles, each with an eight-pointed star in the center (no. 27). On other panels of sixteen tiles, tulips and berries forming a square are in the place of the rosette (no. 29). Flowers clearly are not rendered realistically. Tulips are not depicted with ovaries; tulip and other floral leaves bear little resemblance to nature.

The borders of the tiles are decorated with half-bunches of blue grapes, each resting on half of a green leaf; occasionally a small yellow-and-blue rosette is included. Tulips, marigolds, and fruit are either striped or plain. Grape leaves may include tendrils, and bunches of grapes vary in size and composition. There are at least thirty—and possibly forty—variations, differing only in details of star or corner, shape of leaf, size of bunch of grapes, color, or presence of tendrils.[6]

Although each composition is based upon a geometric design, it appears more fluid because of the plant forms and the repeated use of vivid orange, blue, and green balanced by the deep-blue center star. This design is particularly suited to wall wainscoting because, although all the elements of the design are present in each tile, only in a panel of sixteen tiles can the full pattern be seen. (This abstracted floral motif, minus the star, also appears on seventeenth-century dishes.[7]) The star tulip eventually spawned such new tiles as the tulip (no. 73) and the triple tulip (no. 82), among the best known of the legion of Dutch floral tiles.

FIG. 15 Adrian Collaert
Title page of *Florilegium* (Antwerp)
Engraving
Collection of James Tanis,
Bryn Mawr

3. Hoynck, 1920, p. 37.
4. See Rudolf Berliner, *Ornamentale Vorlageblätter* (Leipzig, 1926), p. 54, pl. 196, which cites an illustration from Jacob Floris's series of ornamental prints, *Weelderhande cierlyke compertimenten . . .* (Antwerp, 1564).
5. Vis and Geus, 1933, p. 22, specifically mention two inventories of 1611 and 1620.
6. Geus, 1919–21, vol. 4, pp. 158–60; Korf, 1979, p. 95.
7. Hudig, 1929, figs. 18–20.

9. ORNAMENTAL FRUIT IN QUATREFOILS
1580–1620
Polychrome
Gift of Edward W. Bok; gift of Mrs. Francis P. Garvan

Large, fruit-filled quatrefoils, each formed by four conjoining tiles, are centered around a dark-blue rosette, surrounded by burnt-orange and green foliage; the corners meet the cusps of the quatrefoil. A piece of yellow fruit flanked by clusters of nuts, foliage, and daisies fills each quatrefoil's lobes. Forms within the quatrefoil are outlined in blue, and a pair of blue lines skirts the inner margin of the frame. Each tile is decorated diagonally; half is devoted to blue-and-white foliage in reserve technique, which forms an eight-pointed star when the four tiles constituting the quatrefoil are assembled. This creates an interplay of forms featuring a contrasting figure/ground relationship: quatrefoils contain white grounds filled with colorful figures, and stars are painted in blue-and-white reserve (Corner motif 1).
Reference: Vis coll. sale, 1927, no. 335.
Similar tiles: Hoynck, 1920, fig. 34; Tegelmuseum, 1979, fig. 3.

48

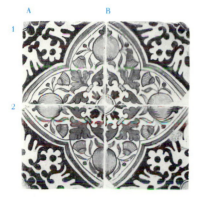

10. ORNAMENTAL FRUIT IN QUATREFOIL
1580–1620
Polychrome
Gift of Mrs. Francis P. Garvan

Several details differ from the previous panel: the frame is composed of a blue band flanked by a pair of white bands. Burnt-orange and green foliate scrolls within the quatrefoil are arranged in spear-shaped triads, their stems conjoined by a yellow rectangle (Corner motif 2). Markings appear on the reverse of tile 2-A. *References:* Geus, 1921, pp. 67, 71; Vis and Geus, 1926, pl. 40; Vis coll. sale, 1927, no. 335; Geus, 1931, fig. 24.

10a. ORNAMENTAL FRUIT IN QUATREFOIL
1580–1620
Polychrome
Gift of Mrs. Francis P. Garvan

Not illustrated.

2-A, reverse

11. ORNAMENTAL FRUIT IN QUATREFOIL
1580–1620
Polychrome
Gift of Mrs. Francis P. Garvan

Running of the copper glaze is apparent on these tiles. *References:* Geus, 1921, pp. 67, 71; Vis and Geus, 1926, pl. 40; Vis coll. sale, 1927, no. 335; Geus, 1931, fig. 24. *Similar tiles:* Korf, 1979, figs. 129, 130.

12. ORNAMENTAL FRUIT IN QUATREFOIL
1620–30
Blue
Gift of Anthony N. B. Garvan

This is an example of a large quatrefoil executed entirely in blue rather than polychrome. Its design is comparable to that of no. 9.

13. ORNAMENTAL FRUIT IN QUATREFOILS (POMPADOUR)
1610–30
Polychrome
Gift of Mrs. Francis P. Garvan

The formal elements found in previous fruit-filled quatrefoils covering four tiles (no. 9) are here compressed onto a single tile, a design referred to as a *pompadour* tile. The lobes of the quatrefoils in this panel are less pronounced, allowing less space for the elements within the frame. The fruit is smaller in relation to the foliage and scrolls than in the larger quatrefoils, and the distinction between primary and secondary design elements within the frame is diminished (Corner motif 3). *Reference:* Vis and Geus, 1926, pl. 41.

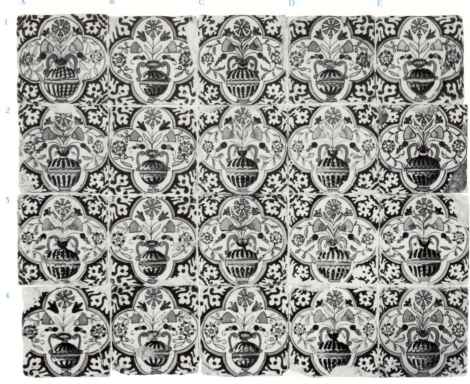

50

**14. ORNAMENTAL FRUIT IN
QUATREFOILS (POMPADOUR)**
1610–30
Polychrome
Gift of Mrs. Francis P. Garvan

Here the quatrefoils are yellow
and display pronounced, rounded
lobes. The brighter colors
heighten the contrast provided by
the dark-blue and white corners.
The foliate scrolls are arranged
so that the central green leaf is
detached from flanking burnt-
orange leaves. The scrolls can
thus be read either as triads composed of a green leaf flanked by
two in burnt-orange or, when
pairing the neighboring scrolls, as
alternating forms in green and
burnt-orange. Rosettes display
yellow centers and stubby blue
petals. A blue dot appears at the
base of each piece of fruit (Corner motif 5).
Similar tiles: Amsterdam, Sotheby,
cat. 337, 1981, no. 201.

**14a. ORNAMENTAL FRUIT IN
QUATREFOILS (POMPADOUR)**
1610–30
Polychrome
Gift of Mrs. Francis P. Garvan

Not illustrated. (Four tiles similar
to no. 14.)

**15. ORNAMENTAL FLOWER VASES
IN QUATREFOILS (POMPADOUR)**
1610–30
Polychrome
Gift of Mrs. Francis P. Garvan

This panel demonstrates the variations within a design as it was
produced by different works and
in different locations. A flower
vase filled with three stylized,
symmetrically arranged daisies
and vines completely fills each
curvilinear frame. The handles of
the rotund, Italianate vase are attached to the lip, which is tipped
forward. One tile (1-A) has yellow
rather than burnt-orange lines
(Corner motif 5). Drawings appear on the reverse of tiles 2-B,
2-C, 3-A, and 4-E.
References: Vis and Geus, 1926, pl.
49; Vis coll. sale, 1927, no. 262.

2-B, reverse   2-C, reverse   3-A, reverse   4-E, reverse

**14b. ORNAMENTAL FRUIT IN
QUATREFOILS (POMPADOUR)**
1610–30
Polychrome
Gift of Mrs. Francis P. Garvan

Not illustrated. (The rosette is
flanked by eight arrows rather
than by eight petals.)

**16. ORNAMENTAL FLOWER VASE
IN QUATREFOIL (POMPADOUR)**
1610–30
Polychrome
Gift of Mrs. Francis P. Garvan

A bulbous, Renaissance-type vase,
lighter blue than those in the preceding panel, fills the quadrilobed
frame. Here, the frame has been
drawn with a triple blue line. As
in the previous panels, corners
are in reserve (Corner motif 2).
References: Vis and Geus, 1926,
pl. 49; Vis coll. sale, 1927, no. 262.

17. ORNAMENTAL FLOWER VASE IN QUATREFOIL (POMPADOUR)
1610–30
Polychrome
Gift of Mrs. Francis P. Garvan

Several details differentiate this tile from the preceding ones. The petals of the crowning flower are curved and slightly drooping; the vase's upper section is decorated with blue and white, and the ribs are formed of alternating blue and brown stripes. The corners are painted with a vine-and-leaf motif (Corner motif 35), which marks a development in tile decoration. Previously, tile corners were painted in the reserve technique.
Similar tiles: Korf, 1979, fig. 137; Amsterdam, Sotheby, cat. 337, 1981, nos. 13, 180.

18. ORNAMENTAL FLOWER VASES WITH ROSETTES
1610–30
Polychrome
Gift of Mrs. Francis P. Garvan

In contrast to the previous panels with vases confined within quatrefoil frames, this design is more open and the curved lines of the vases complement the lines of the corner rosettes (Corner motif 38). The three stylized flowers are or-ange, and the upright stem in the center carries a few berries which vary in color from burnt-orange to yellow to blue; berries are omitted from some tiles (3-A, 4-B, 4-C). The handles and the feet of the vases are burnt-orange; on some, the belt and the line delineating the neck are lighter in color, varying from orange to yellow. Markings appear on the reverse of tile 1-A.

References: Vis and Geus, 1926, pl. 50; Vis coll. sale, 1927, no. 312.
Similar tiles: Hoynck, 1920, fig. 113; Lane, 1960, fig. 32b; Kaufmann, 1973, pl. IV; Korf, 1979, figs. 162, 164, 166; Amsterdam, Sotheby, cat. 337, 1981, no. 199.

1-A, reverse

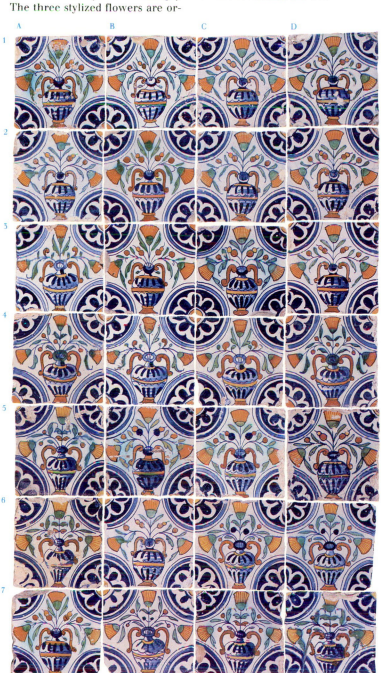

**19. ORNAMENTAL FLOWER VASES
IN DIAMONDS**
1610–30
Polychrome
Gift of Edward W. Bok; gift of
Mrs. Francis P. Garvan

A squat, footed vase containing
a symmetrical arrangement of
marigolds and vines fills the
diamond-shaped frame (called
kwadraattegel). The eight-
petaled, crowning flower is stylized, resembling a pinwheel more
than a flower. The popularity of
this pattern is evidenced by the
fact that it was produced by at
least thirty tileworks. In this
panel, all the diamond frames are
yellow, but because the panel
probably contains tiles from various tilemakers, they are not
identical and the points of some
diamonds are cropped at the
edges. In tiles 1-B and 3-B the
points touch the edges, but in
tiles 1-C and 2-A–C they do not.
The corners are painted in reserve (Corner motif 6).
References: Vis and Geus, 1926, pl.
38; Vis coll. sale, 1927, no. 153.
Similar tiles: Kaufmann, 1973, pl.
IV; Amsterdam, Sotheby, cat. 337,
1981, nos. 9, 183.

52

**20. ORNAMENTAL FLOWER VASES
IN DIAMONDS**
1610–30
Polychrome
Gift of Mrs. Francis P. Garvan

The vases in this panel are somewhat more elongated than in the
previous panel. Both upper and
lower sections are painted burnt-
orange; the blue stripes occurring
on other tiles are absent. The
green leaves are somewhat
lighter in color, and the orange
diamond shapes have cropped
corners at the edges of the tiles.
The corners, in reserve, show
slight variations (Corner motif 1).
Reference: Vis coll. sale, 1927, no.
153.

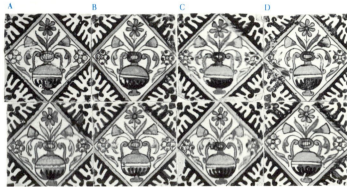

**21. ORNAMENTAL FLOWER VASES
IN DIAMONDS**
1610–30
Polychrome
Gift of Mrs. Francis P. Garvan

The diamond-shaped frames,
flowers, and upper sections of the
vases, which are yellow in no. 19,
are burnt-orange here; the stripe
around the middle of the vases,
white on most other tiles, is deep-
blue. As with all flower vases in
diamond frames, the corners are
in reserve (Corner motif 7).
Reference: Vis coll. sale, 1927, no.
153.

**22. ORNAMENTAL FLOWER VASES
IN DIAMONDS**
1610–30
Polychrome
Gift of Edward W. Bok

This panel of eight tiles is more
uniform in color and in vase
shape than the previous ones, but
it has a sloppier appearance because the glaze on all but three of
the tiles flowed during firing—
these are "seconds." The points
of several of the quadrangular
frames are cut off; this is particularly noticeable in tiles 1-B and
2-B. The colors are deep cobalt-
blue, burnt-orange, and bluish-
green, and the corners are in
reserve (Corner motif 6).

Similar tiles: Vis and Geus, 1926,
pl. 38; Kaufmann, 1973, pl. IV;
Amsterdam, Sotheby, cat. 337,
1981, nos. 9, 183.

2-A, reverse

23. ORNAMENTAL FLOWER VASES IN DIAMONDS
1610–30
Polychrome
Gift of Edward W. Bok

Even these tiles, which look so similar, vary from those on other panels. The points of the yellow diamonds are cropped to the extent that the inner lines of the frames barely touch at the edges. Corners are in reserve technique (Corner motif 6).

24. ORNAMENTAL FLOWER VASE IN DIAMOND
1610–30
Polychrome
Gift of Edward W. Bok

This vase of flowers is drawn with more detail than those on the preceding two panels. It has distinct black stripes on the upper section of the bulbous vase and on the two daisies. The inner lip of the vase is blue, and the outer rim is green. The points of the burnt-orange diamond have been cropped. The corners, painted in reserve, also differ from those of the previous panels (Corner motif 7).

25. ORNAMENTAL FLORAL BORDER TILE
1620–50
Polychrome
Gift of Mrs. Francis P. Garvan

Graceful, curving, intersecting stems connect the foliage on this border tile.
Reference: Vis and Geus, 1926, pl. 58f.
Similar tiles: Korf, 1979, fig. 311.

26. ORNAMENTAL FLORAL BORDER TILE
1620–50
Polychrome
Gift of Mrs. Francis P. Garvan

This border tile was used in conjunction with other tiles similarly decorated with flowers and scrolls (see nos. 15, 18).
Reference: Vis and Geus, 1926, pl. 58e.
Similar tiles: Korf, 1979, fig. 310; Amsterdam, Sotheby, cat. 337, 1981, no. 140.

26a. ORNAMENTAL FLORAL BORDER TILE
1620–50
Polychrome
Gift of Mrs. Francis P. Garvan

Not illustrated.

27. STAR TULIPS

1600–30
Polychrome
Gift of Edward W. Bok; gift of
Mrs. Francis P. Garvan

A deep-blue eight-pointed star,
drawn around an eight-petaled
rosette with an orange heart, is
encircled by four closed pomegranates interspersed with orange
tulips pointing outward. The tulips are supported by the central

stem of eleven short stems
sprouting from a cloverleaf-like
deep-blue shape. The other stems
support marigolds, buds, berries,
and small green leaves. The design's alternate focus is formed by
the eight-petaled orange rosette
immediately surrounded by four
tulips interspersed with bunches
of blue grapes resting on green
vine leaves and ending in blue
tendrils.

Reference: Vis coll. sale, 1927, no.
253.
Similar tiles: De Jonge, 1971, pp.
19–20, ill. 15; Korf, 1979, pl. 11.

54

29. STAR TULIPS
1610–30
Polychrome
Gift of Mrs. Francis P. Garvan

Reminiscent of no. 27, the deep-blue eight-pointed star is here surrounded by four pomegranates interspersed with striped tulips, each borne on the central stem of five short stems emanating from a cloverleaf-like deep-blue shape. The other stems support mari-golds, buds, and small green leaves. The alternate focus of this design is a cluster of berries encircled by four tulips interspersed with bunches of blue grapes resting on green vine leaves. The cluster is composed of alternating blue and orange berries borne on blue stems sprouting from pairs of leaves.
References: Vis and Geus, 1926, pl. 42; Vis coll. sale, 1927, no. 254.

28. STAR TULIPS
1610–30
Polychrome
Gift of Mrs. Francis P. Garvan

This design is similar to the previous panel, but the tulips are a solid burnt-orange rather than striped. A tulip appears on the reverse of tile 1-B.

1-B, reverse

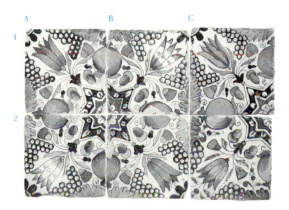

30. STAR TULIPS
1610–30
Polychrome
Gift of Edward W. Bok; gift of Mrs. Francis P. Garvan

The tiles of this panel are similar to the others depicting star tulips. Between each acorn and mari-gold is a stem bearing one blue and one orange berry; the tulips and the fruit are striped. The alternate focus would be formed by a rosette with deep-blue petals surrounding a burnt-orange heart.
Reference: Vis coll. sale, 1927, no. 255.
Similar tiles: Neurdenburg, 1923, *Old Dutch Pottery,* p. 43, fig. 16.

31. STAR TULIPS
1610–30
Polychrome
Gift of Mrs. Francis P. Garvan

The deep-blue eight-pointed star, again drawn around an eight-petaled circle, is surrounded by four closed pomegranates interspersed with tulips striped in blue and orange. Each tulip is supported by the middle of nine stems emanating from a trilobed, deep-blue form; marigolds, seed pods, and acorns radiate from the other stems. The vine leaves and the small leaves which support the pomegranates end in blue tendrils. The alternate focus of the design would be a gold rosette with eight blue petals surrounded by four tulips interspersed with bunches of blue grapes. The blues and the greens are more vivid here than on the other panels.
Reference: Geus, 1931, fig. 25.
Similar tiles: De Jonge, 1971, pp. 19–20, ill. 15.

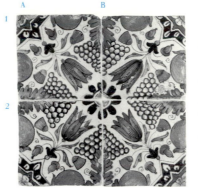

32. STAR TULIPS
1610–30
Polychrome
Gift of Mrs. Francis P. Garvan

The outstanding features of this panel are the blue-and-orange-striped tulips and the relatively well-defined bunches of grapes; it does not contain as much disparate vegetation as most other star tulip panels.
Similar tiles: Korf, 1979, fig. 237.

33. STAR TULIPS
1610–30
Polychrome
Gift of Edward W. Bok

These tiles, which vary slightly from each other, resemble those of the preceding panels, but have slight deviations in detail.
Similar tiles: Korf, 1979, fig. 236.

34. GRAPES AND POMEGRANATES
1620–30
Polychrome
Gift of Mrs. Francis P. Garvan

This panel features an opulent display of fruit and foliage, giving an overall effect of richness and exuberance. The design is formed by four conjoining tiles: a large cluster of grapes appears at the center of two tiles; the remaining two each contain an orange pome-

granate, split open to reveal a grid of blue seeds. The grape clusters and pomegranates are arranged opposite one another along a diagonal axis so that all four elements combine to form a cross axis reinforced at its intersection by a quartet of blue-and-white fleur-de-lis corner motifs (Corner motif 20). Four blue rosettes with orange centers, each appearing midway between a grape cluster and a pomegranate,

form the points of a diamond-like configuration inscribed within the square shape formed by the large fruits. Burnt-orange berries and buds, along with foliate scrolls attached to the fruits, fill the remaining interstices. The grapes and pomegranates contrast with one another as dark and light forms and are visual equivalents. They have a common spatiality, and each displays a cluster or grid of small round forms. The

various elements of the design are outlined in vivid blue.
Similar tiles: Korf, 1979, fig. 239.

A B C D

1

2

34a. GRAPES AND POMEGRANATE
1620–30
Polychrome
Gift of Edward W. Bok; gift of Mrs. Francis P. Garvan

Not illustrated. (Two tiles are decorated with a bunch of grapes, one with a pomegranate.)

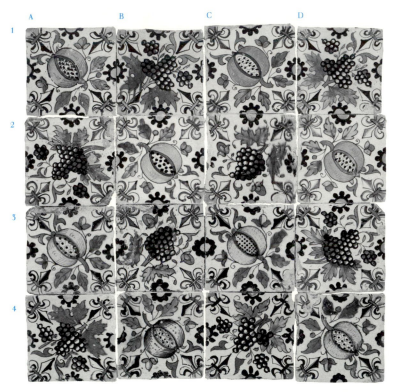

35. GRAPES AND POMEGRANATES
1620–30
Polychrome
Gift of Edward W. Bok; gift of
Mrs. Francis P. Garvan

This design is similar to that of
no. 34, but the treatment is
weaker here. The blue outlines
are somewhat spiky in comparison with those of the other panel,
which are relaxed and curvilinear. The glazes here are carelessly applied. There are also differences in coloration: lemon-
yellow appears on the bases of
the fleurs-de-lis (Corner motif 18)
and on the pomegranates, rosettes, and seed pods. Although
some grape clusters sprout seed
pods similar to those on no. 34,
others give rise to pairs of small
bunches of grapes.
Reference: Vis and Geus, 1926, pl.
47.
Similar tiles: Hoynck, 1920, fig.
163.

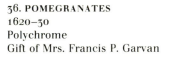

36. POMEGRANATES
1620–30
Polychrome
Gift of Mrs. Francis P. Garvan

This panel is composed exclusively of pomegranates resembling those of no. 35. A slight difference occurs in the inner skin
of each pomegranate, revealed by
the almond-shaped split in its
side. In this panel, the skin is the
same pallid-green that appears in
the foliage (Corner motif 22).
Reference: Vis and Geus, 1926, pl.
47.

37. GRAPES AND POMEGRANATES
1620–30
Polychrome
Gift of Mrs. Francis P. Garvan

Directional emphasis is altered
on this panel: the bands of grapes
and pomegranates are arranged
perpendicularly rather than diagonally. In no. 34, a pomegranate
or a bunch of grapes appears on
each tile, with a fleur-de-lis serving as the link connecting the
tiles; here, all the components
have been compressed onto one
tile, with the fleur-de-lis as the
central element.
Reference: Vis and Geus, 1926, pl.
46.
Similar tiles: Korf, 1979, fig. 247.

38. GRAPES AND POMEGRANATES
1620–30
Polychrome
Gift of Mrs. Francis P. Garvan

The essential features of the design which in the previous panels extends across four tiles are here compressed onto a single tile. Fruit and foliage are so densely packed that individual forms are less pronounced and begin to function as decorative elements within a continuous pattern. Grapes and pomegranates, joined by center motifs and corner decorations, form an interlocking grid of yellow and blue bands silhouetted against a green field. The rosette at the midpoint of each tile, with white petals outlined in blue and a large yellow center, repeats the colors of the bands of grapes and pomegranates. A large, primarily blue flower is formed at the intersection of two bands of grapes. The other corners are filled with burnt-orange and yellow foliate motifs, each constituting one quarter of a flower formed at the intersection of two bands of pomegranates.
References: Vis and Geus, 1926, pl. 45; Vis coll. sale, 1927, no. 101.

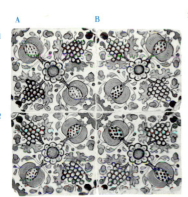

39. GRAPES AND POMEGRANATES
1620–30
Polychrome
Gift of Mrs. Francis P. Garvan

The pomegranates here are burnt-orange, in contrast to those in the previous panel, which are yellow. Each petal of the rosettes is decorated with a blue T reminiscent of those on the square tile in the middle right in fig. 13.
Similar tiles: Korf, 1979, fig. 245.

40. GRAPES AND POMEGRANATE BORDER TILE
1620–30
Polychrome
Gift of Mrs. Francis P. Garvan

The pomegranate and flanking grapes on this border tile are similar in style to those on no. 38.
Reference: Vis and Geus, 1926, pl. 58d.

41. GRAPES AND POMEGRANATES
1620–30
Polychrome
Gift of Mrs. Francis P. Garvan

This panel also resembles no. 38, although it is less carefully executed. The glaze is less luminous and the colors less rich. In place of the decorations with alternating yellow and blue petals are uniform blue petals with yellow centers forming a flower similar to the one at the center of each tile. This demonstrates that the pattern is intended to be uninterrupted; it is not yet composed of tiles with figures and separate corner motifs. Lemon-yellow is used in place of darker yellow and the seeds of the pomegranates are burnt-orange rather than blue. Acorns with dark-blue caps sprout from the bases of the pomegranates.
Reference: Vis coll. sale, 1927, no. 102.

41a. GRAPES AND POMEGRANATES
1620–30
Polychrome
Gift of Mrs. Francis P. Garvan

Not illustrated.

Animals

FIG. 16 Marcus Gheeraerts (Flemish, 1521–c. 1604) *The Old Dog and His Master*, plate 86 from Joost van den Vondel, *Vorstelijke warande der dieren* (Amsterdam, 1617) Engraving Rijksprentenkabinet, Rijksmuseum, Amsterdam

FIG. 17 Adrian Collaert (Flemish, c. 1560–1618) Deer, plate 7 from *Animalium quadrupedum* (Antwerp, 1612?) Engraving Museum Boymans–van Beuningen, Rotterdam

As early as the thirteenth century, beasts from heraldry and the chase appeared on European floor tiles laid in castles and churches.[1] On Netherlandish wall tiles, destined for the domestic interior, this repertoire was extended to include the entire world of fauna, both European and exotic, and even imaginary creatures. In so doing, tile painters borrowed from the many different forms of animal illustration that flourished in the Netherlands during the seventeenth century.

One such source was the illustrations of fables, including those of Joost van den Vondel, the great poet and playwright of the Golden Age. Vondel wrote a series of homely, humorous, and heuristic fables published in a richly illustrated book in 1617 entitled *Vorstelijke warande der dieren* (Princely garden of animals). In the Introduction, Vondel leads the reader through a garden, or menagerie, containing a succession of animated creatures which depict the various stations of human society. These include a "cock who would be king because he has a crown," an aristocratic, "long-necked camel," "a well-heeled horse," and a "baboon, a monkey, and an ape [who] are comedians on stage, playing farces for the prince." The same Dutch burghers who appreciated such fables decorated the walls of their homes with tiled "gardens of animals," which often included creatures copied from the illustrations accompanying Vondel's text. The pursuing hound (no. 52, 2-A), for example, is taken from such an illustration (fig. 16).[2]

More than one hundred species of animals, birds, fish, and insects have been counted on Dutch tiles.[3] Inspired by illustrated natural history treatises, Netherlandish printmakers produced album-sized animal picture books which made art based on nature accessible to a wide audience. Tile painters, in turn, copied from such albums, as exemplified by the stag (no. 46, 1-D) taken from Adrian Collaert's *Animalium quadrupedum* (fig. 17)[4] and the ape (no. 46, 2-B) based on a series of twelve engravings by Abraham de Bruyn (fig. 18).[5] Hunting scenes appear in the background of Collaert's engravings; similarly, the chase functions as an underlying theme in animal tile panels, particularly those dating from the late sixteenth and early seventeenth centuries (nos. 42, 49). Such a panel, called *de groote jacht* (the large hunt), depicts an armed hunter (no. 49, 1-A) and an array of hounds (no. 46), hares (nos. 46, 48), and stags (no. 46).

1. Lane, 1960, pp. 29–31, pls. 18a, c, d.
2. The etchings in Vondel's fable book were designed by Marcus Gheeraerts (Flemish, 1521–c. 1604) and originally appeared in a version of Aesop by Edwaerd de Dene, *De warachtighe fabulen der dieren* (Bruges, 1567), in Hollstein, 1949–, vol. 7, p. 100, no. 108 (Vondel's version is ed. 4 mentioned by Hollstein); see Pluis, Van den Akker, and Muller, 1974, pp. 24–30.

3. Pluis, Van den Akker, and Muller, 1974, p. 2. Pluis illustrates nearly five hundred distinct animal tiles.
4. Adrian Collaert, *Animalium quadrupedum omnis generis verae et artificiosissimae* (Antwerp, 1612?), pls. 1–20, in Hollstein, 1949–, vol. 4, p. 207, nos. 596–615; see Pluis, Van den Akker, and Muller, 1974, pp. 32–35, and Claus Nissen, *Die zoologische Buchillustration*, vol. 2 (Stuttgart, 1973), no. 924.

5. Abraham de Bruyn, "Animals in Landscapes" (1585), pls. 1–12, in Hollstein, 1949–, vol. 4, p. 6, nos. 67–78; see Pluis, Van den Akker, and Muller, 1974, pp. 30–32 (for the most extensive list of animal prints copied on tiles, see pp. 23–49).

Tile painters frequently worked without the aid of print sources, instead using transfer patterns (*sponsen*) containing their own versions of the stock characters which had populated European animal lore and illustration for generations. Such tiles in this collection include a prancing horse (no. 46, 1-A) and a posturing ape (no. 46, 2-B), both of which are reminiscent of Vondel's characterizations.

Although the Dutch have manufactured animal tiles from the very inception of the wall-tile industry in the late sixteenth century until the present day, the most vital stylistic development took place during the seventeenth century. The earliest Netherlandish animal wall tiles employ the yellow frames, dark-blue and white corner motifs in reserve technique, landscape settings, and polychromy characteristic of Italian majolica floor tiles. Animal tiles began to appear in blue between 1620 and 1630, often with frames and corner decorations derived from Chinese porcelain (see no. 51).

Later in the seventeenth century, animal panels became more specialized (no. 55); only animal tiles were combined, and no longer were birds or hunters included. After 1660 small jumping animals began to appear, inspiring in the eighteenth century tiles dubbed *springertjes* (little jumpers), lively creatures emphasizing humor at the expense of anatomical accuracy. A panel of cheerful pups, one sporting a camel-like hump, exemplifies this type (no. 58). Testifying to the enduring appeal of animal tiles, the venerable Tichelaar tileworks in Makkum, Friesland, still utilizes animal *sponsen* containing motifs which have appeared on Dutch tiles continuously since the sixteenth century.

**42. ANIMALS AND HUNTER IN
ROUNDELS**
1600–1625
Polychrome
Gift of Anthony N. B. Garvan

The central scenes in this panel, depicting a dog,[1] a bear, a sheep,[2] and the ubiquitous hunter, are framed by roundels accompanied by rosettes in reserve technique (Corner motif 39). Each elaborate roundel consists of a thick band of yellow and burnt-orange flanked by thinner bands of white. The sunny colors of the animals, which are repeated in the roundels, are shaded in yellow and burnt-orange. Figures resembling those that also appear in animal tiles with diamonds (no. 46) are positioned on convex patches of sparsely foliated meadow and are silhouetted against a striated sky.

1. After Joost van den Vondel, *Vorstelijke warande der dieren* (Amsterdam, 1617; reprint Soest, 1974), fig. 86; see Pluis, Van den Akker, and Muller, 1974, fig. 138, and below, no. 52, 2-A.
2. After Adrian Collaert, *Animalium quadrupedum* (Antwerp, 1612?), pl. 13; see Pluis, Van den Akker, and Muller, 1974, fig. 200, and below, no. 56, 1-B.

62

A   B

1

2

43. ANIMAL BORDER TILES
1610–40
Blue
Gift of Anthony N. B. Garvan

Although normally rectangular, border (or baseboard) tiles are occasionally square, as in this unusual panel. Its decoration features a distinctive striated landscape and turbulent sky. The ground, a striated light-blue mound flanked by two masses of dark-blue, is reminiscent of the waterlogged terrain which constitutes so much of the Dutch countryside. Exotic and familiar animals alike make their ways through the landscape: a lioness [1] proceeds cautiously, while a hound [2] and a fox strike a faster pace (see no. 50). A border composed of white and blue runs along the lower edges of the tiles.

Reference: Vis coll. sale, 1927, no. 295.

1. Pluis, Van den Akker, and Muller, 1974, figs. 168, 169.
2. Ibid., fig. 139.

A

B

C

44. COW BORDER TILE
1610–40
Blue
Gift of Mrs. Francis P. Garvan

This border or baseboard tile depicts a cow reclining in a grassy field.[1] Painted primarily in dark-blue, the creature is silhouetted against an expansive sky. Blue and white stripes extend along the tile's upper and lower margins.

1. After Adrian Collaert, *Animalium quadrupedum* (Antwerp, 1612?), pl. 5.

45. BEAR BORDER TILE
1610–40
Polychrome
Gift of Mrs. Francis P. Garvan

A burnt-orange bear is shown scampering across a patch of turf.[1] The rectangular shape and the absence of corner decorations indicate that this piece functioned as a border tile or filled another space, for example, a baseboard or a narrow windowsill, for which a standard square tile would not suffice.

1. After Joost van den Vondel, *Vorstelijke warande der dieren* (Amsterdam, 1617; reprint Soest, 1974), fig. 107; see Pluis, Van den Akker, and Muller, 1974, fig. 88.

46. ANIMALS IN DIAMONDS
1620–40
Polychrome
Gift of Mrs. Francis P. Garvan

This panel of *kwadraattegels* is largely composed of the stock characters of European animal imagery. Particularly numerous are creatures that hunt or are hunted. Lively hounds chase and growl at unseen prey (3-A–C), a graceful hare flees, casting a glance over its shoulder at its pursuers (2-A). One stag, taken from a Collaert engraving (fig. 17),[1] pauses watchfully (1-D) while a second (2-D) is copied from an engraving in Vondel of a stag staring at its own reflection in the pool of a fountain.[2] The bear (1-B) is also copied from Collaert.[3] An exception is the rigid, scaly crocodile, indicative of the contemporary taste for exotic fauna (2-C). The diamond-shaped frames are burnt-orange. (Corner motif 8.) Markings are found on the reverse of tile 1-C.
References: Geus, 1919–21, vol. 4, p. 260, fig. 14; Vis coll. sale, 1927, no. 283.

1. See Pluis, Van den Akker, and Muller, 1974, figs. 41, 43.
2. Joost van den Vondel, *Vorstelijke warande der dieren* (Amsterdam, 1617; reprint Soest, 1974), fig. 34.
3. Adrian Collaert, *Animalium quadrupedum* (Antwerp, 1612?), pl. 12; see Pluis, Van den Akker, and Muller, 1974, fig. 87.

1-C, reverse

64

47. HOUND IN DIAMOND
1620–40
Polychrome
Gift of Mrs. Francis P. Garvan

This tile is somewhat larger than those in the previous panel. The source of the hound depicted here is plate 10 of Adrian Collaert's *Animalium quadrupedum*. Four hounds in Collaert's illustration, including the one on this tile, were either copied from Al-

brecht Dürer's engraving *Saint Eustace* of c. 1500 (fig. 19) or from a print by Virgil Solis of six dogs, of which five are based on the dogs in *Saint Eustace*.[1] (Corner motif 8.)
Reference: Vis coll. sale, 1927, no. 283.

1. See Pluis, Van den Akker, and Muller, 1974, figs. 20, 21; Ilse O'Dell-Franke, *Kupferstiche und Radierungen aus der Werkstatt des Virgil Solis* (Wiesbaden, 1977), p. 144.

65

48. ANIMALS AND MAN IN DIAMONDS
1620–40
Polychrome
Gift of Karl J. Freund; gift of Mrs. Francis P. Garvan

A menagerie of expressive, colorful beasts appears on this panel, including imaginary and exotic creatures, such as a unicorn stamping its hooves (1-D) and a tawny lion treading a grassy landscape (2-A). Human specimens considered strange or wondrous, such as a Far Eastern type in a pointed cap and loose-fitting suit (3-C), were occasionally exhibited alongside exotic beasts. The everyday world provided tile painters with an equally rich source of subjects, represented here by a frisky hound (1-C), a whiskered gray cat (2-D), a blue crane (3-A), a squirrel (3-B),[1] and three hares (1-A, 1-B, 3-D). Certain animals, such as the ape, were depicted particularly frequently; this panel contains two simians, one consuming a piece of fruit (2-C; see fig. 18), the other glancing pensively over its shoulder (2-B). Each creature appears on a plot of green and orange

turf, silhouetted against a striated blue sky which in most cases is filled with birds. Light-yellow diamond-shaped frames are accompanied by dark-blue and white corners in reserve technique (Corner motif 8).
Reference: Vis coll. sale, 1927, no. 283.

1. Pluis, Van den Akker, and Muller, 1974, fig. 103.

49. ANIMALS AND HUNTER IN DIAMONDS
1620–40
Polychrome
Gift of Mrs. Francis P. Garvan

The tiles in this group are exceptionally small and finely executed. The figures, the abundant foliage, and the frames are delineated crisply, in deep-blue. The animals are depicted from various points of view: a blue unicorn appears in sharp perspective from the rear (1-B),[1] a tan dromedary stands in profile (2-A),[2] and a blue swan flaps its wings with its breast turned toward the viewer (2-B). The spirited hunter, drawn with unusual attention to detail, is poised on the verge of hurling a lance (1-A). The ornamental motifs in reserve are deep-blue; the diamond-shaped frames are burnt-orange (Corner motif 8).

Reference: Vis coll. sale, 1927, no. 283.

1. After Adrian Collaert, *Animalium quadrupedum* (Antwerp, 1612?), pl. 3.
2. After ibid., pl. 5.

50. DOG AND FOX IN ROUNDELS
1625–50
Blue
Gift of Mrs. Francis P. Garvan

These examples of blue animal tiles exhibit a number of features not present in polychrome animal tiles of the period. Mock-fret corner motifs, here used in combination with roundels, indicate the contemporary taste for blue and white Chinese porcelain (Corner motif 9). The ground in each of these examples is composed of three round, stippled patches framing a dark-blue patch. These forms evoke islets of soggy turf surrounded by water. The dog[1] steps gingerly across this terrain, but the fox boldly leaps a hurdle on the central patch. The striated blue sky forms a lively backdrop.
Similar tiles: Korf, 1979, fig. 479.

1. After Roemer Visscher, *Sinnepoppen* (Amsterdam, 1614), p. 80; see Pluis, Van den Akker, and Muller, 1974, fig. 79.

51. ANIMALS AND BIRDS IN SCALLOPED ROUNDELS
1625–50
Blue
Gift of Mrs. Francis P. Garvan

This panel closely resembles no. 52 except for a slight variation in the shape of the scalloped roundels. Animals depicted include hares (2-A, 2-B), stags (4-A, 4-B), a goat (3-A),[1] and a dog (3-B). A pair of sprightly birds appears among the animals (1-A, 1-B). (Corner motif 12.)

1. After Adrian Collaert, *Animalium quadrupedum* (Antwerp, 1612?), pl. 17.

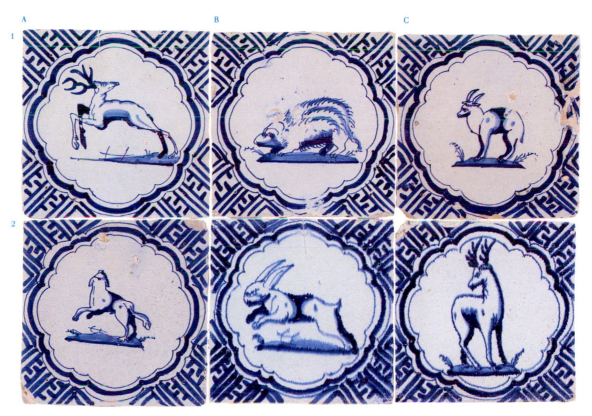

52. ANIMALS IN SCALLOPED ROUNDELS
1625–50
Blue
Gift of Edward W. Bok

This panel features various animals in scalloped roundels with mock-fret corner decorations (Corner motif 14). The creatures appear on abbreviated patches of ground and are large in relation to their frames. The hedgehog with parallel rows of bristles (1-B)[1] and the goat (1-C)[2] are among the more unusual specimens. Predators and prey appear together; the running dog (2-A),[3] pursuing a stag (1-A), is based on an illustration in Vondel (fig. 16), and the stag is similar to one in the same engraving.

1. After Adrian Collaert, *Animalium quadrupedum* (Antwerp, 1612?), pl. 19.

2. After Abraham de Bruyn, "Animals in Landscapes" (1583), pl. 10, in Hollstein, 1949–, vol. 4, p. 6, nos. 67–78.

3. See Pluis, Van den Akker, and Muller, 1974, fig. 138.

A   B   C   D

68

53. CANINE IN SCALLOPED ROUNDEL
1625–50
Blue
Gift of Edward W. Bok

On this tile, a pert dog, or possibly a fox, is framed by a heavy, dark-blue scalloped roundel surrounded by fretwork (Corner motif 10). The craftsman has added some detail to the small canine form, stressing facial features and musculature in dark-blue.

54. ANIMALS
1625–50
Blue
Gift of Edward W. Bok

This composed panel features animals rendered in blue, flanked by blue candelabra framing motifs (Corner motif 24). The specimens, rather lifeless and shown in profile, are a moose (B; see fig. 17),[1] a steer (C),[2] a hare

(A), and a heavy, lumbering creature, probably a bear (D).

1. See Pluis, Van den Akker, and Muller, 1974, figs. 42, 108.
2. Adrian Collaert, *Animalium quadrupedum* (Antwerp, 1612?), pl. 5.

A   B   C   D   E

1

2

55. ANIMALS
1625–50
Polychrome
Gift of Mrs. Francis P. Garvan; gift of Anthony N. B. Garvan

Various animals are set in abbreviated landscapes enlivened with clumps of grass and, occasionally, a fence. Some of the animals, such as the bounding hare (1-A) and the stag (2-E; see fig. 17),[1] are described in previous panels; an exception is the double-humped camel (2-A),[2] shown resting with its legs folded under its body. Other animals pictured are: two dogs (1-B, 1-C), a stag displaying a stiff right leg (2-C), two hares (1-A, 1-D), two horses (2-D, 2-B), and a lion (1-E; face largely repainted).[3] The animals are sketched in dark-blue and often colored in burnt-orange. These specimens appear somewhat flat in comparison with animal tiles from the early seventeenth cen-

tury, whose forms are generally modeled in two tones rather than one. The corners are heavy ox-heads (Corner motif 49). Markings appear on the reverse of tile 2-E.

1. See Pluis, Van den Akker, and Muller, 1974, fig. 45. The glaze ran in the kiln; a cleft appears diagonally across the deer's hindquarters; the corner decoration on the upper right is partially missing.
2. After Adrian Collaert, *Animalium quadrupedum* (Antwerp, 1612?), pl. 5.
3. After Abraham de Bruyn, "Animals in Landscapes" (1585), pl. 1, in Hollstein, 1949–, vol. 4, p. 6, nos. 67–78.

2-E, reverse

56. ANIMALS IN BRACKETED FRAMES
1630–50
Blue
Gift of Edward W. Bok; gift of Mrs. Francis P. Garvan

This panel features diverse animals in bracketed frames (Corner motif 37). Three of the creatures stand on spotted mounds which sprout vegetation. Fable illustrations provided a precedent for the plodding donkey on a somewhat different tile (2-B).[1] The ostrich gripping a horseshoe in its bill (1-A) frequently appears in seventeenth-century emblem books as a symbol of perseverance,[2] and craftsmen often used this emblem on Dutch tiles, as is illustrated twice in this collection (see also no. 67, 1-B). A stag (2-A) and a sheep (1-B)[3] are also pictured. On tile 3-A the head of a giraffe looms high above a farmhouse and haystack. The tile painter, having no opportunity to see such an animal, knew of it only through the stories about its great height.

1. Joost van den Vondel, *Vorstelijke warande der dieren* (Amsterdam, 1617; reprint Soest, 1974), figs. 30 ("The Overloaded Ass and the Horse"), 52 ("The Young Horse and the Ass"), 116 ("The Ass Bearing Food").
2. Lothar Dittrich, "Emblematische Weisheit und naturwissenschaftliche Realität," in Herzog Anton Ulrich-Museum, Brunswick, *Die Sprache der Bilder* (Sept. 6—Nov. 5, 1978), pp. 27–28.
3. After Adrian Collaert, *Animalium quadrupedum* (Antwerp, 1612?), pl. 13; see Pluis, Van den Akker, and Muller, 1974, fig. 200.

57. HORSE
1660–1700
Blue
Gift of Edward W. Bok

A horse with waving mane and tail frolics on a field in front of a farm building. Tiles depicting farm animals were popular in rural areas during this period. A horse in a similar posture is shown on a tile picture (no. 218; see fig. 56).

58. DOGS IN ROUNDELS
1690–1725
Blue
Gift of Mrs. Francis P. Garvan

Four small dogs appear on this panel. They exhibit few distinctive features, except for one dog (2-B), which sports an unusual clump of fur on its back. The others strike lively poses based on those on earlier tiles: one makes its way jauntily, nose in the air (2-A);[1] another leaps a small fence (1-B).[2] All four are framed by roundels; small spider's-heads decorate the corners (Corner motif 58).

1. Pluis, Van den Akker, and Muller, 1974, figs. 141, 142.
2. Ibid., fig. 139.

Birds

Panels of animal tiles dating from the late sixteenth and early seventeenth centuries often contain birds interspersed with quadrupeds (see nos. 48, 3-A, 49, 2-B). During the second quarter of the seventeenth century, however, tilemakers began treating birds as a separate subject matter. The creation of this new category permitted greater expression of nature's variety on decorated tiles. Such panels display a seemingly inexhaustible assortment of birds, both actual and invented.

Like animal tiles, bird tiles reflect the influence of the engravings in natural history treatises, the most frequently consulted being Adrian Collaert's *Avium vivae icones*;[1] one plate in this work (fig. 20) was the source for the greedy parrots in no. 61. Following the schema encountered in Collaert and other natural history illustrations (see fig. 21), tile painters often depicted birds in profile, perched upon a hillock, stump, or leafy branch (see, for example, no. 66).

Many of the identifiable birds on Dutch tiles cannot be traced to specific print sources but rather figure among the animal imagery which by the seventeenth century had become the common property of artists. Such birds are well represented here; they include the owl (no. 66, 1-A), cock (nos. 61, 66, 2-C), and ostrich (nos. 56, 1-A, 67, 1-B). The flamboyant parrot, which appears so often in seventeenth-century Dutch painting, is also among the most frequently depicted species on bird tiles, occurring on five panels in this collection (see nos. 61, 62, 64, 66, 68). Fictitious beasts are relatively rare in animal tiles; bird tiles, however, abound in feathered creatures which do not exist in nature.[2] By mixing stock ornithic traits, tilemakers produced a varied repertoire of peculiar birds, such as a thrushlike specimen with delicate brown breast speckles (no. 66, 1-B).

Bird and flower tiles occasionally were combined, producing an array of colorful and delicate decorative forms. A common format features birds in flight or poised on shadow-ground with calligraphically rendered flowers framed by roundels with curvilinear ox-head corner motifs (no. 65). Birds sometimes appear with insects as well (no. 60).

Although bird tiles are primarily polychrome, they were also manufactured in blue and purple monochrome glazes. Occasionally, tilemakers imitated pictorial motifs found in the center of Ming porcelain dishes (fig. 22), as seen on tiles which feature birds in overgrown, marshy settings (no. 59). One image on blue bird tiles (no. 63, 1-C), based on the motif of a generalized bird, re-occurs a century and a half later on Dutch catchpenny prints, where in one example it is labeled *leeuwerik*, or lark (fig. 23).[3] Inspired by the watery landscape of their native land, Dutch manufacturers also produced a purple tile featuring a swimming swan (no. 71), a design popular during the eighteenth century.

1. Adrian Collaert, *Avium vivae icones* (Antwerp, 1610), pls. 1–32, in Hollstein, 1949–, vol. 4, p. 207, nos. 616–47; Claus Nissen, *Die zoologische Buchillustration*, vol. 2 (Stuttgart, 1973), p. 199. According to Pluis and others, the series was published in two parts, an unnumbered series of sixteen prints (1580) and a numbered series of sixteen prints entitled *Avium iconum, editio secunda* (c. 1600); see Pluis, Van den Akker, and Muller, 1974, pp. 36–38; Holthuis, Muller, and Smeenk, 1971, pp. 3–19.

2. Pluis, Van den Akker, and Muller, 1974, p. 2, state that among animal tiles, those depicting birds contain the greatest number of creatures whose species cannot be determined with certainty.

3. C. F. van Veen, *Dutch Catchpenny Prints* (The Hague, 1971), intro., p. 20.

FIG. 20 Adrian Collaert (Flemish, c. 1560–1618)
Parrots, plate 17 from *Avium vivae icones* (Antwerp, 1610)
Engraving
Collection of James Tanis, Bryn Mawr

FIG. 21 Adrian Collaert
Partridge and eagle, from *Avium vivae icones* (Antwerp, 1610)
Engraving
Collection of James Tanis, Bryn Mawr

FIG. 22 Chinese dish, Ming Dynasty, 16th century. Porcelain with underglaze blue decoration
Philadelphia Museum of Art. Bequest of Emmeline Reed Bedell: The Bradbury Bedell Memorial

FIG. 23 Birds, published by H. Rynders, Amsterdam.
Woodcut, 18th century

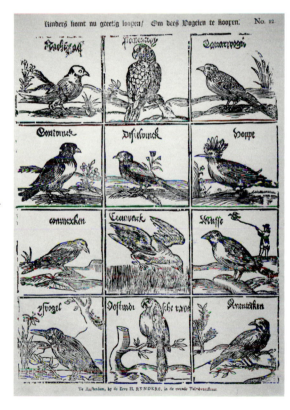

59. BIRDS IN CHINESE GARDENS
1620–40
Blue
Gift of Mrs. Francis P. Garvan

This pair of tiles is referred to as Chinese garden (*Chinese tuin*) tiles. Framing elements consist of bracketed medallions and fretwork corner decorations (Corner motif 14). The central roundels feature birds in rocky, leafy environments suggestive of the shore of a body of water—a thrushlike bird perched in profile on a rock, and a flying fowl with webbed feet and attenuated neck reminiscent of a goose. Birds, rocks, ferns, and large-petaled flowers are executed in dark-blue on a white background covered with light-blue striations. The roundel motifs are derived from a type of decoration appearing frequently in the center of Ming dishes (see fig. 22) and consisting of birds, rocks, and foliage silhouetted by expanses of water and sky.[1]

1. Tegelmuseum, 1979, figs. 6, 7.

60. DUCK AND BUTTERFLY IN ROUNDELS
1625–50
Polychrome
Gift of Anthony N. B. Garvan

This panel features a bright-eyed duck floating on a windswept body of water and a butterfly skimming over a grassy mound. The specimens display similar coloration: light-yellow applied over blue striations appears on the duck's breast, wings, and tail and on the butterfly's wings; details such as the duck's bill and wingtips and the pattern on the butterfly's wings are picked out in burnt-orange. The scenes are framed by roundels accompanied by fretwork corner decorations (Corner motif 9).

61. PARROTS AND ROOSTERS
1625–50
Polychrome
Gift of Anthony N. B. Garvan

This panel pictures pairs of nearly identical roosters and parrots. The brightly colored birds are accompanied by equally exuberant corner decorations: white, yellow, and blue fleurs-de-lis (Corner motif 20). The parrots, rendered in bright-green and yellow with brown scalloped feathers, are copied after the parrot eating cherries in an engraving by Collaert (fig. 20).

72

62. BIRDS

1635–70
Polychrome
Gift of Miss May Audubon Post;
gift of Mrs. Francis P. Garvan; gift
of Anthony N. B. Garvan

The birds, primarily bright-
orange, blue, and green, shown in
profile, perch either directly upon
a hillock or upon a branch or a
bar extending from a grassy
mound. The hillocks, as large and
colorful as the specimens they
support, are outlined in blue and
shaded in green and yellow with
burnt-orange striations. They are
enlivened by fluidly rendered
grass and tubular shrubs. The
birds include a lapwing (2-C),[1] a
parrot (2-B), and a bird resembling a kingfisher (1-B). The birds
are sedentary, but two extend
their wings and arch their necks
to preen their breasts (1-A, 2-A).

The corners are ox-heads (Corner motif 49).
Reference: Vis coll. sale, 1927, no.
319.
Similar tiles: Amsterdam, Sotheby,
cat. 349, 1982, no. 165.

1. Pluis, Van den Akker, and
Muller, 1974, figs. 253, 254.

73

63. BIRDS ON BRANCHES

1635–70
Blue
Gift of Anthony N. B. Garvan

These birds are loosely rendered
and are accompanied by spider's-
head corner decorations (Corner
motif 58). While one duck stands
in a watery habitat, most perch
on truncated, leafy branches. In
addition to the duck and eagles,[1]
there are three imaginary birds;
that on tile 1-C is based on the
motif of a generalized bird which
also appears later on a Dutch
catchpenny print as a *leeuwerik,*
or lark (fig. 23).

1. Pluis, Van den Akker, and
Muller, 1974, figs. 227, 228.

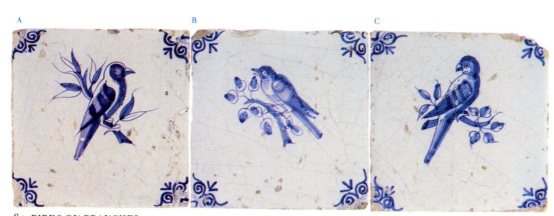

A   B   C

64. BIRDS ON BRANCHES
1625–70
Blue
Gift of Anthony N. B. Garvan

Bird tiles, often polychrome, were also executed in blue. The parrot (C) and the other two birds are outlined and detailed in a crisp dark-blue line and are accompanied by ox-head corners (Corner motif 51).
Similar tiles: Amsterdam, Sotheby, cat. 349, 1982, no. 144.

65. BIRDS AND FLOWERS IN ROUNDELS
1640–70
Polychrome
Gift of Mrs. Francis P. Garvan; gift of Anthony N. B. Garvan

Tiles depicting birds and flowers were often displayed together, as this panel demonstrates. Each tile is framed by a dark-blue roundel with barred ox-head corner decorations (Corner motif 54). The panel is unified by coloration as well as framing devices. The bird tiles are painted primarily in blue, with accents of burnt-orange on the heads, wings, bodies, and tails; the plants are done in green and burnt-orange, with accents of dark-blue on their petals. Lively birds fly (1-C), walk (2-C, 3-B, 4-C), and poise (1-B, 4-B) on a shadow-ground. The only identifiable fowl among them is a pert little hen, which appears here twice (2-B, 3-C).[1] Plants spring from small mounds; their blossoms, stems, and leaves are rendered in a supple blue line. Varieties popular with seventeenth-century Dutch garden enthusiasts are present, including fritillaria (2-A, 2-D; see fig. 24), tulip (1-A, 5-A, 5-D), narcissus (5-B), carnation (4-A), columbine (3-A), and mallow (1-D).
References: Vis and Geus, 1926, pl. 66; Vis coll. sale, 1927, no. 161.

1. Pluis, Van den Akker, and Muller, 1974, fig. 257.

3-C, reverse   5-B, reverse

65a. FLOWER IN ROUNDEL
1640–70
Polychrome
Gift of Anthony N. B. Garvan

Not illustrated.

66. BIRDS
1640–70
Polychrome
Gift of Mrs. Francis P. Garvan

The tiles on this composed panel share similar ox-head corner decorations (Corner motif 50). The birds on tiles 1-A, 1-C, 2-C, and 3-A are yellow, burnt-orange, green, and dark-blue. Their comparatively large perches—stumps, a leafy branch, or a hillock—are outlined in blue and filled in with a flat, green wash enlivened with a few accents of color. Among the birds in this group are a rooster (2-C), a hawk (3-C), a small owl whose dark-blue face contains no features except a pair of watchful eyes (1-A), and a brightly colored parrot perched on a leafy branch (3-A). The generalized bird on tile 2-A is copied from a Collaert engraving of a partridge and an eagle (fig. 21). Tiles 1-B, 3-B, and 3-C are characterized by subdued coloration and delicate handling. The birds on these three tiles are shaded in burnt-orange and blue and are covered with soft brown hatching. Perches are pale-green or a combination of green and brown.
Reference: Vis coll. sale, 1927, nos. 319, 320.

67. BIRDS
1640–70
Polychrome
Gift of Edward W. Bok; gift of Miss May Audubon Post

The tiles in this group lack elaborate landscape appurtenances: the ground, when indicated, appears as a simple blue shadow or mound; a branch consists of a stroke of green glaze. The birds, handled in a similarly cursory fashion, are composed of loosely rendered patches of color, primarily bright yellows, blues, and greens. This freedom of handling is accompanied by a heightened sense of liveliness and movement, with the birds flying (1-C), feeding (2-B), and alighting on a yellow pear (2-A). Only two identifiable birds appear in this panel: a parrot (1-A) and an ostrich (1-B; see no. 56, 1-A). Corner decorations are medium-sized ox-heads (Corner motif 50).

68. PARROT
1630–70
Polychrome
Gift of Miss May Audubon Post

A parti-colored parrot, in yellow, orange, blue, and green glazes, perches upon a leafy branch. The corner decorations derive from the fleur-de-lis (Corner motif 28).

69. SWAN
1650–75
Blue
Gift of Edward W. Bok

This goose, flapping its wings, is the same as that pictured on a polychrome *kwadraat* tile (no. 49, 2-B). The corners are ox-heads (Corner motif 50).

70. BUTTERFLY
1660–1700
Blue
Gift of Edward W. Bok

The butterfly, an insect infrequently depicted on tiles, here rests with folded wings on a stem with three leaves. The corners are spider's-heads (Corner motif 58).

71. SWAN
1750–1800
Purple
Gift of Anthony N. B. Garvan

This tile depicts a swimming swan; the bird's form, shown in profile, is reflected in the water below. The design is executed in thinly applied purple without regard for modeling. The corners are hastily drawn spider's-heads (Corner motif 58). In the eighteenth century, tiles like this were interspersed on walls with seascapes and ships, all colored in purple (see fig. 10).[1]

1. De Jonge, 1971, ill. 114.

Flowers

FIG. 24 Adrian Collaert (Flemish, c. 1560–1618)
Natural specimens, plate 4 from *Avium vivae icones* (Antwerp, 1610)
Engraving
Collection of James Tanis, Bryn Mawr

Fritillaries appear at left and right.

1. The earliest florilegium, produced by Adrian Collaert, was published in Antwerp during the final decades of the sixteenth century. See Wilfred Blunt, *The Art of Botanical Illustration* (London, 1950), p. 87.
2. Ibid., pp. 100–101.
3. The Levantine tulip was introduced in Europe during the sixteenth century. In Holland, its spiritual home (as characterized by Wilfred Blunt), the flower elicited enthusiasm from gardeners, poets, and artists alike. See Wilfred Blunt, *Tulipomania* (London, 1950). According to Regin, 1976, pp. 92, 93: "The farmers invested in paintings; the artists invested in tulip bulbs." Jan van Goyen is the best known among the artists who made this investment.
4. Korf, 1958, "De Drietulp"; Korf, 1979, pp. 127, 128.

Floral tiles transformed Dutch domestic space into a veritable indoor garden. The same ornamental flowers—tulips, fritillaries (fig. 24), crown imperials (fig. 25)—cultivated on the grounds of numerous Dutch houses appeared in tiled interiors as well. Generalized flowers occur as secondary motifs on Italianate tiles produced in the Netherlands during the sixteenth century. Near the beginning of the seventeenth century, however, a wide range of often-identifiable blossoming plants, including the beloved flowering bulbs of the Netherlanders, appeared on tiles, first as stylized motifs and then gradually becoming more naturalistic.

Among the first such motifs were the flower vase (no. 94) and the single flower (no. 76). These were derived from ornamental prints featuring floral species then cultivated by pleasure gardeners. Prints of flower vases by artists such as Claes Jansz Visscher (fig. 26) presented the arranged flowers as examples of nature's artifice, and inspired similar motifs on tiles. Single-flower tiles exhibit the influence of a type of picturebook, the florilegium, which began to be produced in the Netherlands during the final decades of the sixteenth century (fig. 27). A collection of botanically accurate floral engravings, the florilegium served a dual purpose: as a patternbook for craftsmen and as a picturebook for garden enthusiasts.[1] Large tile panels composed of single-flower tiles (for example, no. 77) reflect the florilegium's emphasis on the diversity of nature in their plates illustrating a wide variety of flowers. The Dutch delighted in the brilliant colors of garden flowers. In the Preface to his florilegium, *Hortus floridus,* published in Utrecht in 1614, Crispin van de Passe (c. 1593–after 1670) describes how the viewer should proceed in coloring the illustrations.[2] Similarly, floral tiles styled after florilegium illustrations are overwhelmingly polychrome, with only rare exceptions in blue (nos. 81, 82). In single-flower tiles, a complete plant, rather than an isolated blossom, invariably appears. Tile painters indicated this either summarily, by placing an earthen mound at the plant's base, or more elaborately, by providing an extensive landscape environment, like those found in the rare floral tiles probably produced in Rotterdam during the early seventeenth century (no. 72).

Some of the most original tile designs produced in the Netherlands feature that quintessentially Dutch flower, the tulip.[3] Tulip tiles (no. 74) contain a single large, colorful flower surrounded by an exuberant combination of foliage, volutes, and smaller flowers. The triple tulip, as one of the most popular designs, was produced for a long time, from 1625 to 1850.[4] It appears in different colors and with a variety of frames and corner motifs (nos. 82–85), of which the configuration and coloring of no. 82 occur most often (fig. 28). Triple-tulip tiles are the only floral tiles that appear commonly in blue as well as in polychrome, which attests to their popularity.

Floral tiles are often highly ornamental. Several types display elaborate frames, including ovals (no. 89) and tasseled diamonds (no. 91). Such tiles were usually assembled in large panels (no. 92), which produced a striking decorative effect.

FIG. 25 Adrian Collaert
Flowers, plate 7 from *Florilegium*
(Antwerp)
Engraving
Collection of James Tanis,
Bryn Mawr

A crown imperial appears in the
center.

FIG. 26 Claes Jansz Visscher
(Dutch, 1587–1652)
*Flower Vase with Insects and
Birds,* 1635
Etching and engraving
Herzog Anton Ulrich-Museum,
Brunswick, Germany

FIG. 27 Crispin van de Passe
(Dutch, c. 1593–after 1670)
Narcissus, plate 8 from *Hortus
floridus* (Utrecht, 1614)
Engraving
The New York Public Library.
The Spencer Collection

FIG. 28 Triple tulip, plate from a
tile order book from the Aelmis
family workshop, De Blompot,
Rotterdam, 18th century
Watercolor
Gemeentelijke Archiefdienst,
Rotterdam

72. FLOWERS IN LANDSCAPES
Rotterdam?
1610–40
Polychrome
Gift of Edward W. Bok

A   B

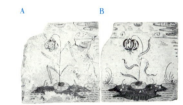

This pair of tiles features flowers
growing in airy landscapes, a lily
with curving petals and prominent stemming, and a nodding,
bell-shaped blossom which resembles a mallow. Each plant's
stem consists of a single line in
deep-blue from which sprout
wispy, green leaves, also outlined
in blue. The landscape, a so-
called Rotterdam type, is composed of concentric rings of dark-
blue and light-blue with dark
striations, suggestive of adjacent
patches of land and water. Over
the turf stretches a sky formed by
blue striations and spirals representing windblown clouds. Lacking corner decorations, tiles of
this type form a continuous landscape when conjoined; this suggests that they functioned as
baseboards.
Similar tiles: Geus, 1931, fig. 49;
De Jonge, 1971, ill. 20a; Amsterdam, Sotheby, cat. 349, 1982, nos.
159–63.

73. TULIPS
1620–30
Polychrome
Gift of Mrs. Francis P. Garvan

The design of this panel consists
of interlocking natural forms
which spill profusely across the
tile's surface. The central element
of each tile is a large, colorful tulip, still very stylized, sprouting
from an orange bulb. The flowers
display various patterns of stripes
and striations in blue, burnt-
orange, and yellow. Each plant
gives rise to a pair of strawberry-
like blossoms which extend to the
tile's lateral margins. Blue tendrils and curvilinear foliage
painted in burnt-orange and
green fill the spaces between the
flowers. A thick, blue volute surrounds the bulb and sprouts
green leaves at either side of its
base. This volute derives from a
motif on floor tiles painted in
reserve (fig. 3). This panel comprises several variants. In the two
bottom rows the tiles are thicker
and heavier; the bar in each
fleur-de-lis is burnt-orange and
the base is yellow, unlike the
other fleurs-de-lis, which have
blue bars and burnt-orange bases.
The tiles in the middle row are
thinner and the painting is stylis-
tically weaker, suggesting a
slightly later date. Markings appear on the reverse of tile 1-D.
References: Vis and Geus, 1926, pl.
48a; Vis coll. sale, 1927, nos. 270,
302.
Similar tiles: Hoynck, 1920, fig.
272; Kaufmann, 1973, fig. 37, pl.
IV; Korf, 1979, fig. 208, pl. 12; Amsterdam, Sotheby, cat. 349, 1982,
no. 134.

1-D, reverse

74. TULIPS
1620–30
Polychrome
Gift of Mrs. Francis P. Garvan

This group of four tiles is similar to the previous panel, except for the rare corners with oak-leaf motifs (Corner motif 41).
Similar tiles: Korf, 1979, fig. 212.

75. FLOWERS AND DRAGONFLY
1625–50
Polychrome
Gift of Edward W. Bok

A tulip (A), fritillaria (B), and Martagon-type lily (C), painted primarily in yellow, brown, and orange, appear on three of these tiles. The fourth features a dragonfly lighting upon a berry-laden bush (D). The insect has been painted with great attention to

detail: brown striations suggest the segments of the abdomen, and lacy wings are rendered in blue and purple (Corner motif 22).
Similar tiles: Amsterdam, Sotheby, cat. 349, 1982, no. 101.

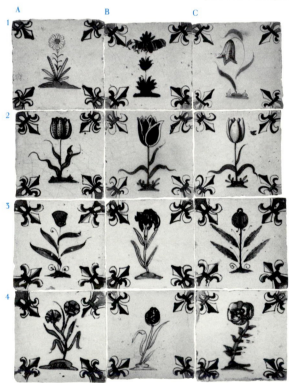

76. FLOWERS
1625–50
Polychrome
Gift of Mrs. Francis P. Garvan

The range of flowers represented here is noteworthy: crown imperial (1-B; fig. 25), iris (3-B), daisy (1-A), fritillaria (1-C, 4-B; fig. 24), lily (3-C), carnation (4-A), marigold (3-A), an unidentifiable flower (4-C), and three examples of the familiar tulip, which differ

in form and coloration (2-A–C). Although details of the corner decorations of this composed panel vary, the basic motif is a large, blue-and-white fleur-de-lis springing from a burnt-orange base (Corner motif 21). The bold color scheme established in the corners is echoed in the blossoms; all but one contain burnt-orange, and the remaining colors include dark-blue, various shades of brown, and mauve.

Similar tiles: Geus, 1931, fig. 59; Lane, 1960, pl. 34e; Berendsen et al., 1967, repro. p. 135; Kaufmann, 1973, pl. IV; Amsterdam, Sotheby, cat. 349, 1982, nos. 85, 89, 90.

77. FLOWERS
1625–50
Polychrome
Gift of Mrs. Francis P. Garvan

This floral panel illustrates three types of ornamental bulbs: tulips (1-A–D, 4-A, 4-D), fritillaries (2-A, 2-C, 2-D, 3-A, 3-D, 4-B, 4-C), and lilies (2-B, 3-B, 3-C). The flowering bulbs display common characteristics: a blossom atop a tall, straight single stem rising from a small mound. Blossoms vary in shape and coloration; the tulips, for example, display petals which are broad (4-A) or slender and lanceolate (1-C), and they range in color from pale purple (1-A, 1-D) to a forceful combination of blue and bright-orange (4-D). Foliage throughout the panel is rendered by a supple, calligraphic blue line. In combination, the flowering bulbs form a lush, colorful decorative pattern. Thin blue bands define the top and bottom edges. The fleur-de-lis corners are bounded laterally by heavy blue-and-white balusters (Corner motif 23). Tile 4-B shows intersecting black lines on the reverse.

Similar tiles: Berendsen et al., 1967, repro. p. 135; Kaufmann, 1973, pl. XII; Korf, 1979, fig. 449; Het Princessehof, Leeuwarden, NO 8318-5X8-V; Amsterdam, Sotheby, cat. 349, 1982, nos. 107, 128.

4-B, reverse

78. FLOWERS
1625–50
Polychrome
Gift of Mrs. Francis P. Garvan

This panel contains a fritillaria (2-A), morning glory (1-A), iris (2-B), and strawberry plant (1-B).The blossoms on tiles 1-A and 2-A are blue and yellow; those on tiles 1-B and 2-B are primarily blue and orange. Particularly attractive is the strawberry plant, with slender, curving stalks laden with ripe berries. Corner decoration consists of large, dark-blue cruciform motifs (Corner motif 47).
Similar tiles: Kaufmann, 1973, fig. 164; Korf, 1979, fig. 450.

84

79. FLOWERS IN SCALLOPED ROUNDELS
1625–70
Polychrome
Gift of Anthony N. B. Garvan

Delicate flowers appear in scalloped frames accompanied by mock-fret corner decorations (Corner motif 14). An attractive carnation (1-A) has serrated petals covered with orange and yellow striations, and an orange-blossomed lily of the valley (2-A) provides a perch for an ethereal dragonfly. The remaining flowers are unidentified.
Similar tiles: De Jonge, 1971, ill. 20b; Amsterdam, Sotheby, cat. 349, 1982, no. 37.

80. FLOWERS
1635–70
Polychrome
Gift of Mrs. Francis P. Garvan

Flowering bulbs—tulips (1-A, 1-B), a Martagon-type lily (2-B), and a fritillaria (2-A)—appear in this panel. The plants grow from small, grassy mounds of earth. Mounds and foliage are painted yellow-green over blue-green. The flowers are outlined by a thin, pale-blue line. Color is applied sparingly, either as striations over a white background glaze, as in the orange and mauve tulips, or as a translucent wash, as in the light-orange fritillaria. Corner decorations, vine leaves sprouting spiraling tendrils (Corner motif 43), are small and precisely executed.
Similar tiles: Korf, 1979, fig. 464; Amsterdam, Sotheby, cat. 349, 1982, no. 87.

81. FLOWERS
1635–70
Polychrome; blue
Gift of Mrs. Francis P. Garvan

Polychrome and blue flower tiles are joined in this composed panel. The tiles are approximately contemporary and display similar stylistic features. Plants spring from small, flat patches of earth and exhibit delicate, curving stems and sparse foliage. An unidentified flower (2-A) and a narcissus (1-B) are depicted in polychrome. The rose (1-A) and fritillaria (2-B) are exceptional: single flower tiles were rarely executed entirely in blue. The corners exhibit small ox-heads (Corner motif 50).
Similar tiles: Amsterdam, Sotheby, cat. 349, 1982, no. 152.

82. TRIPLE TULIPS IN BRACKETED FRAMES
1630–70
Blue
Gift of Edward W. Bok

One of the most common of the triple-tulip motifs appears in this panel. The tulips have three bell-shaped blossoms and a broad clump of leaves at the base of the plant, and a broad ring of white separates it from the frame. The Dutch infatuation with Chinese porcelain is seen in the use of blue monochrome, the frame, composed of segmented brackets, and the mock-fretwork corners, which consist of a web of densely packed lines (Corner motif 13). *Similar tiles:* De Jonge, 1971, ill. 52; Kaufmann, 1973, fig. 160; Korf, 1979, fig. 412.

83. TRIPLE TULIPS IN BRACKETED FRAMES
1630–70
Polychrome
Gift of Mrs. Francis P. Garvan

This panel, contemporary with the previous one, is composed of triple tulips adorned with patterns of stripes and speckles in blue, burnt-orange, and yellow. Stems, tendrils, and foliage curve grace-fully. At the base of each plant is a yellow bulb nestled in a clump of green leaves (Corner motif 13).

86

84. TRIPLE TULIPS IN BRACKETED FRAMES
1640–70
Polychrome
Gift of Mrs. Francis P. Garvan

Polychrome triple tulips here dis-play various combinations of stripes and stipples in yellow, blue, and purple; the tiles were not produced as a unit but were combined later. Deep-blue points wedged between the variegated petals represent background pet-als. Leaves are rounded and lack the attenuation of the foliage in earlier triple-tulip tiles (nos. 82, 83). The bracketed frames are combined with spear-and-tendril corners (Corner motif 37).
Reference: Vis and Geus, 1926, pl. 61.
Similar tiles: Korf, 1979, fig. 415.

85. TRIPLE TULIPS IN BRACKETED FRAMES
1640–70
Blue
Gift of Edward W. Bok; gift of Mrs. Francis P. Garvan

Not illustrated. (Blue triple tulips comparable in style to those of the previous panel but executed somewhat carelessly.)
Similar tiles: Hoynck, 1920, fig. 105.

86. TRIPLE TULIP IN SCALLOPED ROUNDEL
Friesland
1640–70
Blue
Gift of Mrs. Francis P. Garvan

The style of this triple tulip is comparable to those of the pre-ceding panel. This tile, however, is in a scalloped frame with mock-fret corners (Corner motif 14).

87. TRIPLE TULIPS
1635–70
Polychrome
Gift of Mrs. Francis P. Garvan

An assortment of splendidly arrayed striped tulips appears on this panel. Blossoms display various combinations of blue, yellow, orange, and brown striations. Stems are rendered in a thin, wiry line; the cruciform corner decorations (Corner motif 46) are executed in the same style and include forms, such as tendrils, which echo the central motif.
Reference: Vis coll. sale, 1927, no. 239.
Similar tiles: Korf, 1979, fig. 418; Amsterdam, Sotheby, cat. 349, 1982, no. 54.

88. TRIPLE TULIPS
1635–70
Polychrome
Gift of Mrs. Francis P. Garvan

These flowers display a triad of
short orange and white petals.
Their stems spring from yellow
bulbs and give rise to stiff green
and yellow foliage. Corners are
decorated with large cruciform
motifs (Corner motif 46).

Reference: Vis coll. sale, 1927, no.
239.
Similar tiles: Korf, 1979, fig. 418.

88

89. FLOWERS IN OVALS
1640–70
Polychrome
Gift of Mrs. Francis P. Garvan

Among the most festive floral tiles
is the *ovaaltje,* or little oval.[1] In
these examples, an unidentifiable
flower (1-A), fritillaria (1-B; fig.
24), carnation (2-A), and daisy?
(2-B) appear atop stiff blue stems.
Foliage and turf are thinly
painted in burnt-orange and pale-
green. The delicacy of the plants
contrasts with the robustness of
the framing elements and the
corners. Oval frames, consisting
of a thick blue strip flanked by
blue lines, are decorated laterally
and vertically with volutes which
differ in tile 2-A from those in the
other three tiles. Each dark-blue
corner decoration, which fairly
fills the spaces between the volutes, is composed of a cruciform
motif rising from a large volute,
flanked by leafy fronds (Corner
motif 46).
Similar tiles: Berendsen et al.,
1967, repro. p. 150; Korf, 1979, fig.
292, pl. 23.

1. Korf, 1957; Korf, 1979, pp.
103–8.

90. TULIPS IN DIAMONDS
1640–75
Polychrome
Gift of Mrs. Francis P. Garvan

Colorful tulips grow from grassy
mounds of earth lodged in the
lower angles of diamond frames.
At the base of each tulip, under
the ground, is a round bulb. The
blossoms display intricate, inven-
tive coloration; on tile 2-B, the
blossom is covered with a grid of
flecks of blue alternating with
yellow dots with blue centers.
The diamond frames, developed
from those of earlier pictorial
tiles, are each composed of three
straight blue lines with an outer
scalloped line.[1] At each of the diamond's points, a sketchily rendered ox-head appears, whereas
the corner motifs are derivative
of the fleur-de-lis (Corner motif
33).
Similar tiles: Korf, 1979, fig. 437.

1. Korf, 1961; Korf, 1979, pp.
129–32.

91. COMPOSITE FLOWERING BULBS IN DIAMONDS
Makkum
1640–75
Polychrome
Gift of Mrs. Francis P. Garvan

The curious, stylized plant depicted here bears a pair of bell-shaped fritillaria blossoms and a central bud. The shape of the plant conforms to that of the diamond frame. The fritillaries are executed in combinations of blue, yellow, and burnt-orange. The yellow bud, which fits into the topmost angle of the frame, constitutes a formal, coloristic parallel to the bulb at the base of the plant. (Corner motif 33.)
Reference: Vis coll. sale, 1927, no. 309.
Similar tiles: Kaufmann, 1973, pl. IV.

92. FLOWERING BULBS IN DIAMONDS
1640–75
Polychrome
Gift of Mrs. Francis P. Garvan

The design here is a simplified variation of that on the previous panel. The plants represented are primarily flowering bulbs, including fritillaries (1-C, 2-B, 2-C, 3-C, 4-A–D), lilies (1-A, 1-B, 1-D), and tulips (2-A, 2-D). The single exception, a carnation (3-B), which possesses fibrous roots in nature, here displays a bright-yellow bulb in conformity with its neighbors. Blossoms are executed in different combinations of blue and burnt-orange; their shapes and the arrangement of their foliage also vary. The copper glaze used for the turf liquified during firing, producing the blue-green haze in the backgrounds.
Reference: Vis coll. sale, 1927, no. 71.

93. FLOWERING SHRUBS IN DIAMONDS
1640–75
Polychrome
Gift of Mrs. Francis P. Garvan

The tiles in this group display fan-shaped hybrid shrubs in decorated diamond frames. Flowers, such as tulips, and orangelike fruits fill the upper three corners of each frame, and sprays of leaves and seed pods are interspersed among them. Although each tile exhibits touches of polychrome—green and burnt-orange turf and flecks of orange and green in fruit and foliage—deep-blue predominates, appearing in the foliage and the frames and corners (Corner motif 26).
References: Geus, 1922, no. 1; Vis coll. sale, 1927, no. 309.
Similar tiles: Lane, 1960, pl. 34d; Amsterdam, Sotheby, cat. 349, 1982, no. 93.

94. FLOWER VASE
1625–70
Blue
Gift of Edward W. Bok

The central image on this tile is a decorative vase filled with a stiff floral arrangement of a large carnation rising above tiers of nuts, foliage, and a pair of flowers. The flower types and the manner in which the lip of the vase is tipped forward reflect earlier flower-vase tiles (see no. 21). Thin blue bands define the tile's top and bottom edges denoting that these could have been made for baseboards. The fleur-de-lis corners are bounded laterally by heavy blue-and-white balusters (Corner motif 23).
Similar tiles: Korf, 1979, fig. 365.

90

95. FLOWER VASES IN BRACKETED FRAMES
1625–70
Polychrome
Gift of Anthony N. B. Garvan

Vases of flowers are here framed by scalloped roundels and mock-fret corner decorations (Corner motif 13). Each bouquet is composed of foliage, small flowers, and a large crown imperial.

1-A, reverse

96. FLOWER VASES
1625–70
Polychrome
Gift of Miss May Audubon Post;
gift of Mrs. Francis P. Garvan

Various floral arrangements appear on Dutch tiles; this one consists of an ornate, ribbed, blue-and-white flower vase resting on a grassy mound, containing a tall crown imperial flanked by pairs of orange tulips and blue and orange seed pods interspersed with foliage. This group of tiles was not originally produced as a unit. Tiles 4-A, 5-A, and 5-B are inferior to the other tiles in the quality of the clay body and in the dexterity of painting. Corners are decorated with large, thick, ox-heads (Corner motif 49).
Similar tiles: Korf, 1979, fig. 349.

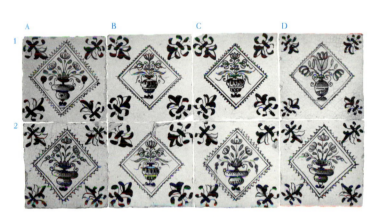

97. FLOWER VASES IN DIAMONDS
1640–75
Polychrome
Gift of Mrs. Francis P. Garvan

The tiles in this panel are decorated with two similar types of vases. Tiles 1-A, 2-A, 2-C, and 2-D contain a squat, blue vase filled with a pyramidal arrangement of nuts, foliage, and flowers. The three orange flowers which fill the upper angle of each diamond probably reflect the arrangement in earlier flower-vase tiles (nos. 15, 18). Stubby leaves are interspersed with the flowers and seed pods. Tiles 1-B–D and 2-B postdate the others in the panel; their central motif is smaller, and the flower vase is more abbreviated. The ribbed blue vase holds a

bouquet of three orange flowers, the topmost of which in tiles 1-B–D and 2-B is probably a tulip, with a lily on either side. Throughout the panel, vases are illuminated from the left, and in six tiles a slight shadow is indicated under the foot of the vase. The frames, called *kussentjes* (little pillows), are composed of two straight lines and a third scalloped line running along the outer edge. Corners are modified fleurs-de-lis (Corner motif 25).

98. FLOWER VASE
1670–1700
Blue
Gift of Edward W. Bok

A tall, top-heavy bouquet stands in a diminutive ornamental vase. The elements of the bouquet are arranged along either side of the stem of a full-blown lily: columbines, lilies, and foliage. Flowers, foliage, and the vase, with its ribs and curvilinear handles, are rendered in a supple, calligraphic style. A shadow extends over the right side of the vase and to the right of its foot. Corners are small ox-heads (Corner motif 50).

Fruit

FIG. 29 Abraham Ortelius
(Belgian, 1527–1598)
Detail of map of Gelderland,
from *Theatrum Orbis Terrarum*
(Antwerp, 1575)
Engraving
Collection Walter G. Arader

Fruit tiles created an atmosphere of bounty and well-being in Dutch interiors. Like early ornamental tiles, of which they are an offshoot, they include grapes and pomegranates, produce of nature's fecundity in the Mediterranean. Fruits are piled symmetrically in ornate standing dishes, or tazzas (see no. 99), which appear in both blue and polychrome. The effect of such tiles approaches what is known in Dutch as *pronk* (rich and ostentatious display), a word used to characterize certain seventeenth-century Netherlandish still-life paintings which also contain elaborate vessels and sumptuous foods. Tile painters were familiar with the motif of the fruit-filled tazza through exposure to Netherlandish ornamental prints, in which it occurred as a component of Italianate grotesque ornament. One such ornamental tazza, which resembles the motif on tiles—not coincidentally perhaps—adorns a sixteenth-century Flemish map of Gelderland, a Netherlandish province noted for its orchards (fig. 29).

During the second half of the seventeenth century, fruit tiles assumed a more homespun appearance, and disheveled heaps of fruit fill ceramic dishes and wicker baskets (see no. 106). Executed in blue, these tiles emphasize the visual effects of lighting and spatiality, which derive from the decoration on Chinese porcelains very much prized in that period.

99. FRUIT COMPOTES
1625–30
Polychrome
Gift of Mrs. Francis P. Garvan

Each of these tiles is decorated with a gilt compote filled with a bunch of grapes flanked by a pair of pomegranates. The ornate Italianate tazza stands on a grassy mound and displays orange scallops along its underside, echoed by the grape leaves and tendrils which surround the fruit arrangement. Corner decoration consists of large ox-heads (Corner motif 50).
References: Vis and Geus, 1926, pl. 56; Geus, 1931, fig. 54.
Similar tiles: De Jonge, 1971, ill. 18b; Korf, 1979, fig. 386.

A   B   C

1   2

100. FRUIT COMPOTES
1625–50
Polychrome
Gift of Edward W. Bok; gift of
Mrs. Francis P. Garvan

The design on this panel consists
of colorful tazzas filled with fruit;
the foot of each tazza is placed at
the base of the tile, and the fruit
extends to the sides. The bowl of
the tazza is decorated with alternating patches of brown and
green, indicating ribbing. Yellow
pomegranates, bunches of blue
grapes, and green foliage compose the mound of fruit. Large,
dark-blue mock-fret motifs fill the
corners (Corner motif 12).
References: Vis and Geus, 1926, pl.
49; Geus, 1931, fig. 53.
Similar tiles: Kaufmann, 1973, pl.
XV; Korf, 1979, figs. 387, 394.

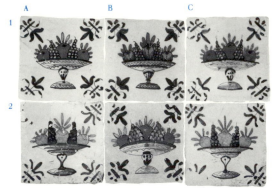

94

101. FRUIT COMPOTES
1625–50
Polychrome
Gift of Edward W. Bok; gift of
Mrs. Francis P. Garvan

The subjects on this panel are
smaller and simpler than those
on the previous panel. Illuminated from the left, the tazzas are
decorated with interlocking dark-
blue lines over a light-blue
ground. Tiles 2-A and 2-C feature
lemons in place of the usual
pomegranates. (Corner motif 28.)
Similar tiles: Korf, 1979, figs. 399,
401.

102. FRUIT COMPOTES
1625–60
Blue; polychrome
Gift of Edward W. Bok; gift of
Mrs. Francis P. Garvan

The design here is a version of
that of no. 100. Tile B which is
painted in polychrome, contains
lemons rather than pomegranates; tiles A and C are painted in
blue. Corners are large ox-heads
(Corner motif 49).
Similar tiles: Korf, 1979, fig. 398.

103. FRUIT COMPOTE
1640–60
Blue
Gift of Mrs. Francis P. Garvan

This tile features a brightly illuminated tazza, which casts a
shadow to the right. The fruit arrangement, which is less stiff
than those of many earlier tiles,
contains curving, leafy fronds,
grapes, and pear-shaped fruit.
Corners are ox-heads (Corner
motif 49).

104. FRUIT AND VEGETABLES
1650–1700
Blue
Gift of Mrs. Francis P. Garvan

This panel is decorated with fruit
and vegetables in graceful disar-
ray. Several tiles (1-D, 3-D,
4-D) feature produce left un-
tended or spilled from containers,
attracting the attention of insects
and birds. In some cases, fruit
and nuts are scattered around the
central arrangement, with each
object casting a distinct shadow
(3-C). The produce is contained in a range of vessels including a box (1-C), a bowl (2-A),
and a cornucopia (4-A).
Similar tiles: Korf, 1979, fig. 407.

105. FRUIT CLUSTERS
1650–1700
Blue
Gift of Mrs. Francis P. Garvan

Pinwheels of leafy fronds and tendrils here surround clusters of fruit and gourds. (Corner motif 50.)
Reference: Vis coll. sale, 1927, no. 221.

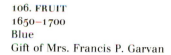

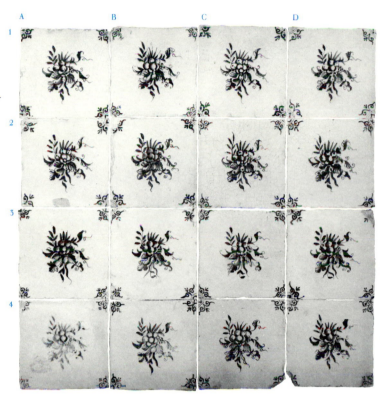

106. FRUIT
1650–1700
Blue
Gift of Mrs. Francis P. Garvan

These tiles feature pears, grapes, and other fruit heaped casually on the ground (1-B) or piled to overflowing in serving vessels, such as baskets (1-A, 2-B) and a bowl (2-A), which cast deep shadows. Vine tendrils, leafy fronds, and alighting birds and insects lend delicacy and grace to the central images. (Corner motif 58.)

107. FRUIT BOWL
1680–1720
Blue and purple
Gift of Mrs. Francis P. Garvan

This is an unusual spattered tile, featuring bold framing and corner motifs in reserve on a field of purple.[1] The frame, an eight-pointed star, encloses a blue bowl overflowing with grapes, pears, and other fruit. White hearts decorate the corners (Corner motif 63).
Similar tiles: Korf, 1979, fig. 407.

1. For other fruit motifs on spattered tiles, see Pluis, 1975, figs. 34–36.

108. FRUIT BASKET
Rotterdam or Friesland
1820–50
Purple
Gift of Mrs. Francis P. Garvan

Reflecting numerous Dutch paintings of still lifes, a basket filled with flowers and fruits is here set at an angle on a marble tabletop. A garland of leaves fastened by a bow completes the composition. Each corner contains a six-petaled, daisylike flower on a stem (Corner motif 67).

Daily Life

FIG. 30 Claes Jansz Visscher
(Dutch, 1587–1652)
Vignette from Abraham Goos,
Comitatus hollandia, c. 1610
Etching
Rijksprentenkabinet,
Rijksmuseum, Amsterdam

FIG. 31 Jacob Matham (Dutch,
1571–1631) after Dirck Hals
(Dutch, 1591–1656)
Fashion print, plate 2 from
*Habitus et cultus matronarum
nobilii et rusticarum apud batavos*
(1615)
Engraving
Rijksprentenkabinet,
Rijksmuseum, Amsterdam

If the kingdom of nature was subject to encyclopedic presentation on Dutch tiles, so too was human society. Tiled hearths, baseboards, and walls were often decorated with distinctively dressed figures, each acting out his or her role in the social order. *Slechte mannekens,* or "ordinary little men," as such tiles were dubbed in an early inventory,[1] were manufactured from the first half of the seventeenth century until its closing decades. Unlike many other forms of subject matter, which were painted in polychrome and purple as well as blue, *mannekens* appeared in blue exclusively.

Such figural tiles drew on the tradition of presenting taxonomies of cultures, classes, and occupations that flourished in prints of the late sixteenth and seventeenth centuries. In such prints, fashion served as the vehicle for the expression of national and regional identity, as well as social position, and the display of fashion was similarly a salient feature of Dutch figural tiles. A woman sporting a pleated skirt, shown from the rear (no. 109, 1-B), was quoted from an etching by Claes Jansz Visscher (fig. 30), where she is one of a group labeled "country folk from North Holland."[2] Burghers, eager to show off wealth and position through costly attire, fairly disappear beneath a surfeit of lace and flounces: such is the case with several gentlemen whose elaborate costumes are matched only by their affected, elegant posture (no. 110, 3-D, 5-A) or a woman copied from a fashion print by Jacob Matham (fig. 31) whose profile is obscured by an oversized ruff (no. 115, 1-A).[3]

While the wealthy and fashionable were marked by style and composure, those populating society's lower ranks participated more actively and less self-consciously in the goings on of life as seen on tiles. Tradesmen and artisans were among the most spirited and picturesque subjects: fishmongers, town criers, and kitchenmaids represent but a few of the occupations culled from the urban life of the seventeenth-century Netherlands. Peasants, too, were represented, often engaging in the village revelries commonly shown in paintings and prints. A peasant bagpiper (no. 112, 2-A), for example, was based on a figure in Nicolaes Clock's engraving *The Peasant Fair* of 1593, after a design by Karel van Mander (fig. 32).

1. See Vis and Geus, 1933, p. 32; De Jonge, 1971, p. 42.
2. This etching was published about 1610 as part of an engraved map; see De Groot and Vorstman, 1980, figs. 30a, 32.
3. This is the second in a series of twelve prints after Dirck Hals entitled *Habitus et cultus matronarum nobilii et rusticarum apud batavos,* in Hollstein, 1949–, vol. 11, p. 233, nos. 331–42. According to Frithjob van Thienen, *Das Kostüm der Blütezeit Hollands, 1600–1660* (Berlin, 1930), p. 37, no. 1, fig. 14, the costume dates from about 1615.

FIG. 32 Nicolaes (Claes Jansz) Clock (Dutch, c. 1570–after 1596) after Karel van Mander (Dutch, 1548–1606)
The Peasant Fair, 1593
Engraving
Ashmolean Museum, Oxford

FIG. 33 Two cavaliers, *spons* for image on no. 117
Fries Museum, Leeuwarden

109. VILLAGERS (PILGRIM TILES)
1625–50
Blue
Gift of Mrs. Francis P. Garvan

Within scalloped roundels accented with open fleur-de-lis corners (Corner motif 34) are various figures: a servant carrying a dead fowl in one hand and a jug under her arm (1-A) repeated on a second tile in reverse, executed by turning the *spons* (1-D); bagpipers (1-C, 2-B), after figures in Clock's engraving of *The Peasant Fair* (fig. 32); a woman carrying a market basket (1-B), after Visscher (fig. 30); a figure wearing tight sleeves and a high collar (2-C), and a town crier (2-D). The woman going to market (1-B) is similar except for corner decorations to other tiles in the collection (nos. 110, 2-A, 2-D). Tiles of this type have become known as "Pilgrim" tiles[1] because of their similarity to a group found in a house in Amsterdam thought earlier in this century to have been the residence of Pilgrims who afterward sailed on the *Mayflower* to Plymouth.[2] There is considerable doubt, however, that this house, which was demolished in 1922, could have been definitely connected with the Pilgrims.
References: Vis and Geus, 1926, pl. 36; Vis coll. sale, 1927, no. 323.

1. Vis and Geus, 1926, pl. 36; Korf, 1979, fig. 529.
2. See affidavit by the architect and building superintendent of Amsterdam in Vis coll. sale, 1927, no. 323.

A   B   C   D

1

2

3

4

5

110. SCENES FROM DAILY LIFE
Rotterdam?
1625–50
Blue
Gift of Mrs. Francis P. Garvan

A variety of occupations and stations in life, as well as two angelic beings, are represented by the relatively large figures painted on these tiles and set among corners decorated with large leaf motifs (Corner motif 42): a journeyman wearing a pack on his back (4-A); jester or juggler (1-B); skater carrying a long pole over his shoulder, used for other skaters to hold on to (1-C); journeyman (1-D), the reverse of tile 4-A, achieved by turning the *spons;* woman carrying a marketing basket on her arm (2-A, 2-D; see fig. 30); archangels (Gabriel?) playing a harp and a lute (2-B, 2-C); gentlemen wearing soft hats decorated with ostrich plumes, flat lace collars, coats with slit sleeves, decorated garters, and high-heeled shoes with tongues (3-A–D); dragoon wearing a high ruff (5-A); figures wearing a wide belt, which was fashionable about 1625 (4-B, 4-C); town crier with his rattle in his belt (5-D); tradesman (1-A); salmon fishermen (5-B, 5-C); workman wearing an apron and holding a tankard (4-D). On the reverse of tile 1-A is a figure 8, and on the reverse of tile 1-B are the initials P. I. A tile from a series from Rotterdam similar to this one also has initials on the reverse (G.G.), suggesting that these tiles, too, were most likely made in Rotterdam.[1]
Reference: Vis coll. sale, 1927, nos. 104, 159, 521.
Similar tiles: Amsterdam, Sotheby, cat. 327, 1981, p. 18, no. 28.

1. Hoynck, 1920, p. 70, figs. 117, 118.

1-A, reverse   1-B, reverse

A   B   C

111. TOWN CRIER, SKATER, AND FISHERMAN
1625–50
Blue
Gift of Mrs. Francis P. Garvan; gift of Anthony N. B. Garvan

An ice skater affects the typical Dutch hands-on-hips skating pose and a town crier declaims from a stepped platform. The smaller size of the fisherman carrying his catch in a bucket suspended from

a pole, the yellow clay body, and the relative thinness of the tile indicate that this one is later in date than its companions. Corners are accented with fleur-de-lis motifs (Corner motif 22).

99

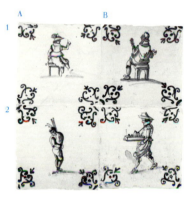

A   B

1

2

112. DRINKER, MUSICIANS, AND PEDDLER
1625–50
Blue
Gift of Edward W. Bok

2-B, reverse

A drinker raising his arm in a toast (1-A), a bagpiper (2-A; see fig. 32) and a seated musician (1-B), and a peddler with his wares on a tray strapped around his neck (2-B)[1] are depicted along with elongated ox-head motifs (Corner motif 48). Initials appear on the reverse of tile 2-B.

1. See Knipping, 1962, fig. 5.

113. FIGURES IN ARCHWAYS
1625–50
Blue
Gift of Mrs. Francis P. Garvan

Tiles decorated with arches springing from columns and with a decorative boss on each keystone are set side by side to create an arcade, their horizontal format suggesting that they were intended for use as baseboards. The area surrounding the arch is filled with mock fretwork (Corner motif 16). Within each arch is a large figure casting a shadow before him. The bending pikeman in a plumed helmet (B) is loosely based on plate 25 of Jacob de Gheyn's *Exercise of Armes* (pike sequence). The other two figures, although carrying swords, wear civilian clothing. The right side of tile C has been cut off.

114. TOWN CRIER
1625–50
Blue
Gift of Mrs. Francis P. Garvan

Set within a bracketed frame a town crier carrying a sword reads from a scroll or pamphlet. The corners are decorated with mock-fret motifs (Corner motif 13).

115. LADIES AND MEN
1625–50
Blue
Gift of Mrs. Francis P. Garvan

Closely allied to the popular series of fashion prints published in Northern Europe at this time, the tiles document with great detail the style consciousness of the prosperous seventeenth-century Netherlanders. The woman holding a fan (1-A) was copied from plate 2 of Jacob Matham's series of Dutch costume prints after Dirck Hals (fig. 31). She, as well as the woman with a well-defined waist that was fashionable before 1625 (2-C), wears millstone ruffs held up by a *porte fraise.* The other tiles depict a woman with a *huik,* or long cloak, attached to a pointed hat, and worn over a long dress (2-B); a gentleman wearing a mantle, a soft-rimmed hat decorated with an ostrich plume, and spurs (2-A); a figure wearing a mantle (1-B), and a bearded man carrying a fishing rod (1-C). The figures, with pronounced shadows, are set within bracketed roundels framed by mock-fret motifs (Corner motif 10).
References: Vis and Geus, 1926, pl. 69; Vis coll. sale, 1927, no. 188.

116. FIGURES
1625–50
Blue
Gift of Edward W. Bok

Large figures of a dancing juggler
(A), a farmer's wife carrying a
milking pail on each arm (B), and
a young man holding an earthenware pitcher (C) cast broad horizontal shadows. Corners are ox-
head motifs (Corner motif 50).

117. ELEGANT PAIRS
Harlingen
Grauda brothers
1660–1700
Blue
Gift of Mrs. Francis P. Garvan

Couples holding hands (1-A) and
strolling (1-B), a long-haired girl
playing a flute and a boy, the violin (2-A), and two gentlemen

wearing swords (2-B; see *spons*,
fig. 33) are represented. The corners are decorated with small
spider's-heads (Corner motif 58).
Transfer patterns (*sponsen*)
marked with the initials P.G. (for
Pieter Grauda of the Grauda
workshop in Harlingen in Friesland) exist for tiles of this type,
and since 1910 have been preserved in Het Hannemahuis in
Harlingen and the Fries Museum
in Leeuwarden.[1]

1. Ottema, 1920, pp. 12, 13; Wassenbergh, 1968, pp. 198–213; sections of this article are quoted in
Ray, 1973, pp. 51, 52. See also
Simões, 1959, pp. 17–20.

118. HUNTER
Harlingen
Grauda brothers
1680–1700
Blue
Gift of Edward W. Bok

This tile shows a lively scene of
hunters with three dogs. Tiles
with several figures that virtually
tell a story are generally attributed to the Grauda workshop.

A   B

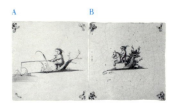

**119. FISHERMAN AND HORSEBACK
RIDER**
1700–1760
Blue
Gift of Edward W. Bok

A fisherman amidst the rushes
along the side of a canal rests on
a willow tree, and a man, wearing a feathered hat, rides a pony.
Both tiles are finely painted with
shadow and highlight details. The
corners have spider's-head motifs
(Corner motif 58).

120. ACROBAT
Rotterdam
De Blompot (owned by the Aelmis
family)
1725–1800
Purple
Gift of Mrs. Francis P. Garvan

An acrobat performs on a cartouche decorated with a face
(symbol for an illusionary stage),
an acanthus leaf, and a shell motif and embellished symmetrically
with long-tailed pheasants and
trailing vines with flowers, leaves,
and tendrils. A well-known and
very large family of comedians
and tightrope dancers named
Magito performed the popular
commedia dell'arte character
plays in Rotterdam and elsewhere
from the second quarter of the
eighteenth century into the nineteenth, and were often depicted
on tiles as well as in other mediums. Each corner shows two sections of an eight-petaled carnation (Corner motif 68).
Similar tiles: De Jonge, 1971, ill.
95b; Kaufmann, 1973, fig. 112.

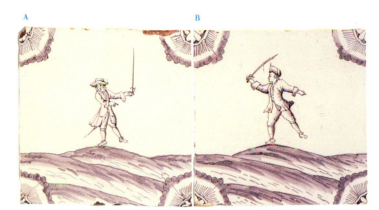

A   B

121. ACROBATS

Rotterdam
De Blompot (owned by the Aelmis
family)
1725–1800
Purple
Gift of Anthony N. B. Garvan

Two acrobats perform a sword
dance in the hills. The figures are
very similar to that on the previous panel, although the surrounding area is different. The
corners form a radiant rosette
(Corner motif 68).

122. PORTRAIT IN OVAL FRAME
Rotterdam
1750–1800
Purple
Gift of Anthony N. B. Garvan

A curious amalgam of subject
matter is presented on this tile. A
female portrait medallion is centered in a cartouche surmounted
by a mixed bouquet in an urn and
flanked by figures representing
Neptune. The fusion of disparate
elements is continued in the corners, which are composed of dia-
per-patterned, leafy shapes which
sprout vinelike tendrils.
References: Geus, 1919–21, vol. 6,
pp. 127–30; Vis coll. sale, 1927,
no. 177.

Diversions

FIG. 34 Johannes Vermeer
(Dutch, 1632–1675)
*Young Woman Standing at a
Virginal*
Oil on canvas
National Gallery, London

1. *Encyclopaedia Britannica*
(1911), vol. 11, p. 446.
2. Meyer, 1962, p. 534.
3. See, e.g., Jacques Stella, *Les
Jeux et plaisirs de l'enfance*
(1657); reprint, *Games and Pastimes of Childhood* (New York,
1970).
4. Pluis, 1979, p. 19.
5. Much has been written about
the symbolism of the cupids and
children's games depicted in
Dutch genre paintings (see, e.g.,
Rijksmuseum, Amsterdam, *Tot
lering en vermaak*, September 16–
December 5, 1976, pp. 44–47, no.
4), but games depicted on tiles
probably had lost any of their emblematic significance.
6. See Sandra Hindman, "Pieter
Bruegel's *Children's Games*, Folly,
and Chance," *The Art Bulletin*,
vol. 63, no. 3 (September 1981),
pp. 447–75.
7. Pluis, 1979, pp. 62, 63.
8. Ibid., p. 14.
9. Meyer, 1962, p. 536; Pluis, 1979,
p. 14.
10. Pluis, 1979, p. 12.

Because houses in the Netherlands were small and spacious gardens were the exception, children played in the streets. The games depicted on seventeenth- and eighteenth-century tiles are therefore usually the outdoor games played by children, although some were also played by adults. Many of these are age-old pastimes, like hoops, rope skipping, kite flying, knucklebones, and hopscotch, games already popular during ancient Greek and Roman times.[1] Children playing with hoops appear along with other games in the border decorations of manuscripts of the fourteenth and fifteenth centuries.[2]

The games in sixteenth- and early seventeenth-century engravings, adapted by tile painters, are invariably played by sportive putti;[3] games on tiles made before the middle of the seventeenth century likewise depict putti[4] as well as cupids[5] at play. In Johannes Vermeer's *Young Woman Standing at a Virginal* (fig. 34), tiles with cupids form the baseboard, and a large painting of a cupid hangs on the wall.

There is no reason to believe that Pieter Brueghel's well-known painting *Children's Games* of 1560 (Kunsthistorisches Museum, Vienna)[6] had a direct influence on the decorators of tiles with scenes of children playing games; other sources were more readily available. Woodblock prints with various subjects, including allegories and moralizing scenes, were used over and over again and frequently reprinted in the seventeenth and eighteenth century as folk and children's prints. They were sold in the form of books, in almanacs, and as catchpenny prints by many publishers. Moreover, prints were sold at fairs and on the streets (see nos. 129, 2-A, 8-H), given as prizes to reward pupils in schools, and became part of a game, playing at dab (*prentje prikken*), shown on tiles (no. 129, 8-D).

Complicated games were not depicted on tiles, and games painted in polychrome are rare. A few tiles of children's games were produced in the first half of the seventeenth century and composed in wainscotting together with scenes of daily life. The majority were produced from the mid-seventeenth century to the first half of the eighteenth, when they were displayed as a separate group.[7] Pluis has counted ninety-six distinct games on tiles,[8] which does not include variants of individual games, for example, the six variations of marbles shown. The games that occur most often on tiles, as well as in prints, are hoop rolling, rope jumping, "horsy," archery, tops, marbles, and *kolf* (see no. 129, 1-F).

It is difficult to tell whether the players of games on tiles are adults, boys, or girls, or to deduce this from the type of game being played—hopscotch and jump rope, to mention only two, were considered boys' games in the seventeenth and eighteenth centuries.[9] Moreover, boys wore skirts until they were six or seven (see no. 129, 1-H), when they switched to short trousers (see no. 131). Figures wearing broad-brimmed hats similar to cavalier hats worn by adults are usually boys, but when they wear caps it is more difficult to differentiate between boys and girls.[10]

123. PUTTI PLAYING A GUESSING GAME
1565–75
Polychrome
Gift of Anthony N. B. Garvan

In the center of this Antwerp-Italianate majolica tile are three putti playing the guessing game today called "buck, buck, stand pat," in which a player has to guess how many fingers another holds up. This is one of several games portrayed in popular emblem books in the sixteenth century;[1] a similar game continues to be played in Italy, where it is known as *morra.*[2] The putti are clearly outlined in blue and framed by a blue band decorated with alternate spirals and circles in sgraffito technique; the band is flanked by narrower blue circles. The corners are decorated in reserve with ragged leaf forms against an originally bright-yellow background in reserve, but some leaf veins and shadows are drawn directly. The remains of a yellow circle banded in brown is discernible in two corners. Vis and Geus[3] dated this tile to the first half of the seventeenth century, but subsequent research has shown it to be earlier. Two fragments of similar tiles dated [15]68 were unearthed under a dike in Haarlem in 1974, described by Korf,[4] and compared to this tile, whose location was unknown at that time.

References: Vis and Geus, 1926, pl. 29d; Vis coll. sale, 1927, no. 506; Korf, 1979, fig. 95.

1. The most detailed study of this game is by P. G. Brewster, "Hoeveel hoornen heeft de bok?" *Volkskunde,* vol. 46 (1944–45), pp. 361–93; see Meyer, 1962, p. 554, n. 3; Iona and Peter Opie, *Children's Games in Street and Playground* (Oxford, 1969), pp. 295–301.
2. *Encyclopaedia Britannica* (1911), vol. 11, p. 446.
3. Vis and Geus, 1926, pl. 29d.
4. Korf, 1976; Korf, 1979, fig. 95.

124. CUPID IN AN ARCHWAY
1625–50
Blue
Gift of Mrs. Francis P. Garvan

A cupid kneels within an archway on a tile probably designed for a baseboard (see no. 113). In a similar pose, a kneeling cupid with a bow appears in an engraving by Jan van de Velde entitled *Menniste Vrijage* (*Mennonites Courting*) published in the second edition of poems by Jan Jansz Starter, *Friesche Lusthof* (Amsterdam, 1620).[1] (Corner motif 15.)

1. See D. P. Snoep, "Een 17de eeuws liedboek met tekeningen van Gerard ter Borch de Oude en Pieter en Roeland van Laer," *Simiolus*, vol. 3, no. 2 (1968–69), p. 119, fig. 31.

125. BACCHUS
1625–50
Blue
Gift of Anthony N. B. Garvan

Sitting astride a barrel is Bacchus, Roman god of wine and revelry, or possibly his follower, the fat, drunken Silenus; both are usually garlanded in vine leaves with grapes. A fully painted tile such as this with very large ox-head corners (Corner motif 49) is extremely rare, as is the subject matter.
References: Geus, 1919–21, vol. 6, repro. p. 129; Vis and Geus, 1926, pl. 76; Vis coll. sale, 1927, no. 179.

126. CUPIDS PLAYING
1625–50
Blue
Gift of Mrs. Francis P. Garvan

This panel is of extremely high quality, seen in the strong blue of the lines, the excellent drawing of the figures, and the distinct shadow at each cupid's feet. Italianate cupids spin a top (2-A), beat a tambour (2-B), and play at archery (1-A, 1-B) within pronounced, barbed roundels embellished with mock-fret corner elements (Corner motif 10).
Reference: Vis coll. sale, 1927, no. 232.

127. PUTTO PLAYING MUSIC
1630–70
Blue
Gift of Anthony N. B. Garvan

A chubby, winged putto with long hair plays a ten-stringed musical instrument while keeping time with his right foot. The figure is outlined in dark *trek*. The corners are large barred ox-heads (Corner motif 50).

128. MUSICAL ANGELS
Harlingen[1]
1650–1700
Blue
Gift of Edward W. Bok

Tiles depicting angels and cupids were made in various versions and sizes.[2] Angels, playing musical instruments, are representative of the various activities in which celestial beings engage on tiles. Here, three chubby angels sit on delicately drawn clouds; the angel on the left plays a trumpet while the middle one, stationed behind the others, holds a book of music. The corners are spider's-heads (Corner motif 58).
Reference: Vis and Geus, 1933, pl. 57b.
Similar tiles: De Jonge, 1947, fig. 131; Korf, 1969, fig. 132; Korf, 1979, fig. 571.

1. This attribution has been made with information kindly supplied by Jan Pluis.
2. Korf, 1969, p. 63.

129. CHILDREN'S GAMES
1675–1750
Blue
Gift of Anthony N. B. Garvan

Many of the activities and games depicted on this panel of sixty-four tiles, such as jump rope, marbles, and spinning pinwheels (1-D)—typically played in a country where the wind is always blowing—are immediately recognizable today; others are now played only regionally or not at all. *Kolf* (1-F), played with a puck and long, curved sticks, had as its antecedent the thirteenth-century game of *colf* and as its successor, today's game of golf.[1] In tipcat (1-G), a player lightly struck a tapered wooden peg with a bat and, as it flew upward, struck it again to drive it as far as possible while fielders tried to catch it.[2] In the somewhat similar game of blowpipe (*blaas pijp*; 7-E), a player blew an object as far away as possible, and another ran to retrieve it before it hit the ground.[3] In a variation on marbles, *negenkuilen* (5-D), nine holes were dug in a square arrangement and each player tried to get his marble into the center hole. One of the toys depicted was a type of suction cup (*zuigertje*; 5-E), a round piece of leather that, when moistened and flattened against the ground, could be used to pick up stones.[4] The game of bird-on-a-perch (5-B)[5] was a favorite in the seventeenth century;[6] a bird, often a goldfinch, was let fly while tied by a cord to a T-shaped support. In playing at dab (*prentje prikken*; 8-D), a child pricked the pages of a book in which prints were hidden and won the print touched by his pin.[7] Spider's-heads are the most frequent corner decorations on tiles depicting children's games[8] (Corner motif 58).
Reference: Vis coll. sale, 1927, no. 51.

1-A boys flying kites
1-B children holding pipes and a bowl and blowing soap bubbles
1-C boy on a swing
1-D children holding pinwheels
1-E boys playing hopscotch
1-F boys playing *kolf*
1-G figures playing tipcat
1-H figures playing[9]

2-A print seller selling a print to a boy
2-B figures playing[9]
2-C boy playing tipcat (see 1-G)
2-D boys jumping rope
2-E boy jumping rope
2-F boy jumping rope
2-G boy rolling a hoop
2-H boys rolling hoops

3-A boys with kites (see 1-A)
3-B young musicians[10]
3-C boy playing a violin
3-D figure smoking an earthenware pipe
3-E boys playing with suction cups
3-F boy spinning a peg top
3-G figure holding a pinwheel
3-H children holding pinwheels (see 1-D)

4-A young musicians
4-B boy playing a violin (see 3-C)
4-C boys playing with suction cups (see 3-E)
4-D children shooting marbles[11]
4-E two men, one smoking a pipe
4-F boy fishing
4-G boys rolling hoops (see 2-H)
4-H boys playing skittles or ninepins[12]

5-A two figures[9]
5-B boys playing with a bird-on-a-perch
5-C boys playing *kolf*
5-D boy playing marbles (*negenkuilen*)
5-E two fishermen
5-F boy fishing
5-G boy playing marbles (see 5-D)
5-H two figures

6-A boys playing marbles
6-B boys playing marbles[13]
6-C boys fighting[14]
6-D boy spinning a peg top (see 3-F)
6-E children blowing soap bubbles (see 1-B)
6-F child blowing soap bubbles
6-G young fishermen (see 5-E)
6-H boys jumping rope (see 2-D)

7-A boys with featherball (*palet en veerbal*) or shuttlecock
7-B possibly a beggar
7-C figure playing (see 2-B)
7-D boys playing hopscotch (see 1-E)
7-E boys playing with a blowpipe
7-F boy with a hobby-horse
7-G boy carrying a vaulting pole
7-H boys rolling hoops (see 2-H)

8-A children blowing soap bubbles (see 1-B)
8-B two fishermen
8-C boys using a suction cup
8-D playing at dab
8-E playing hopscotch (see 1-E)
8-F two figures (see 5-H)
8-G shooting marbles (see 4-D)
8-H print seller (see 2-A)

1. See S. J. H. van Hengel, "Colf-Kolf-Golf," *Spiegel Historiael*, vol. 17, no. 10 (October 1982), pp. 516–21.
2. Pluis, 1979, p. 235.
3. Ibid., pp. 104, 105.
4. Ibid., fig. 822.
5. Ibid., pp. 276–79.
6. See E. de Jongh, *Zinne- en minnebeelden in de schilderkunst van de zeventiende eeuw* (Amsterdam, 1967), p. 44, figs. 31–33.
7. Pluis, 1979, figs. 23, 511.
8. Ibid., fig. 65.
9. Jan Pluis, in a letter of October 1983, stated he had documentation for this game but could not identify it by name.
10. Pluis, 1979, fig. 448.
11. Ibid., fig. 23.
12. Ibid., fig. 402.
13. Ibid., figs. 23, 329.
14. Ibid., fig. 720.

110   **130. BOY SPINNING A PEG TOP**
1650–1725
Blue
Gift of Edward W. Bok

A boy spins a top, the string held
in his right hand. The spider's-
head corners of this tile show
long tentacles (Corner motif 58).

131. BOYS ROMPING
Utrecht
c. 1700
Blue
Gift of Edward W. Bok

Several boys frolic on these tiles:
one steps on the neck of his comrade (1-A),[1] two play horse and
coachman, the "horse" holding
the bit in his mouth (2-A),[2] and
two, back to back, pull at each
other (2-B).[3] The other tiles depict
specific games, as in the previous
panels: bird-on-a-perch (1-B),
blowpipe (1-C), and tops (2-C)—a
whip top on the left, a peg top on
the right.[4] Pluis points out that
tiles with children romping occur
frequently among those made in
Utrecht.[5] Corners are spider's-
heads (Corner motif 58).

1. Pluis, 1979, fig. 409.
2. Ibid., fig. 464.
3. Ibid., fig. 410.
4. Ibid., fig. 645.
5. Ibid., p. 180, and in correspondence, where he pinpoints the origin and date of these tiles.

2-A, reverse

132. BOY URINATING
1800–1825
Blue
Gift of Edward W. Bok

In an image popular from the
second half of the seventeenth
century well into the eighteenth,[1]
but continuing to be used in the
nineteenth century, a boy is urinating, trying to hit a swimming
comrade.

1. Dubbe, 1972, pp. 303–17, figs.
36–40.

Pastoral Scenes

FIG. 35 Salomon Savery (Dutch, 1594–1665)
Célion and Belinde, from Jan Harmens Krul, *Minne-spiegel ter deughden* (Amsterdam, 1639)
Etching
British Museum, London

Happy shepherds and shepherdesses participate in a range of playful and amorous activities common to Dutch pastoral art and literature of the seventeenth and eighteenth centuries. The lush, hilly landscape settings are idealized and Italianate; amid grazing flocks of sheep, figures play serenades on rustic instruments, partake in country games, and exchange tokens of affection in the form of fruit and wreaths of flowers. On one tile (no. 135 B) a couple carries on a lively dalliance behind a makeshift screen, and on another (no. 137, 2-A) a shepherdess reads a poem, a favorite pastime of pastoral figures in Dutch art.[1] On other tiles elegant figures meet at elaborately sculpted garden fountains (no. 134 D); these images were probably inspired by a scene from the most famous of Dutch pastoral dramas, Pieter Cornelisz Hooft's *Granida* (1605).[2] Indeed, the subjects of these tiles often reflect prints illustrating editions of Dutch pastoral dramas, poems, and songs. An illustration of Jan Harmens Krul's play *Célion en Belinde* (1639) showing a shepherdess weaving her companion's gift of flowers into a wreath (fig. 35) strikes particularly close to spirited tile scenes (nos. 133, 2-A, 3-A, 134 E). In an amusing demonstration of the enduring popularity of tile images, tiles from about 1900 show "shepherds" costumed in top hats and trousers (no. 139). One depicts a shepherdess at a well with a shepherd approaching her from behind (no. 139 B), a scene virtually identical to some appearing on tiles dating two centuries earlier (nos. 133, 1-D, 134 A).

Although the Dutch vogue for pastoral subjects began early in the seventeenth century, tiles did not reflect this until the second half of the century. The shop of the Grauda brothers in Harlingen, Friesland, eventually emerged as a center for the production of tiles with pastoral decoration[3] although they were also made in Rotterdam and Utrecht. Pastoral tiles are still referred to as Frisian shepherds (*Friese herders*) by Dutch collectors.

1. See A. M. Kettering, "Rembrandt's *Flute Player:* A Unique Treatment of Pastoral," *Simiolus*, vol. 9, no. 1 (1977), pp. 19–44.
2. Perhaps the most popular subject of Dutch pastoral art is drawn from the first act of Hooft's drama, where the shepherd Dafilo falls in love with the lost princess Granida while offering her spring water from a shell. In later seventeenth-century depictions of this scene, the simple spring of Hooft's play is transformed into an elaborate fountain of love. See S. J. Gudlaugsson, "Representations of *Granida* in Dutch Seventeenth-Century Painting: III," *The Burlington Magazine*, vol. 91, no. 551 (February 1949), pp. 39–43.

3. Gessina ter Borch, sister of the famous painter Gerard, has been linked to the Grauda shop. Although certain Grauda tiles, particularly those with pastoral decoration, are similar in spirit and style to Gessina's work, there is no documentation connecting her with this shop or establishing her as a designer of tile decoration. See Wassenbergh, 1968.

133. SHEPHERDS AND SHEPHERDESSES IN LANDSCAPES
Harlingen?
1660–1725
Blue
Gift of Mrs. Francis P. Garvan

Amid sylvan landscapes, shepherds and shepherdesses engage in a range of pastoral rituals. Questing for the affections of their companions, shepherds proffer gifts of flowers (1-A, 2-A, 3-A). A flute serenade brings particular success, inspiring a maiden with a revealing bodice to lean forward and beckon the rustic musician to sit beside her (1-B); elsewhere a blindfolded shepherd and a shepherdess play a titillating game of blindman's bluff, causing their flocks to flee behind them (1-C). Finally, decorum yields to amorous fervor, and a shepherdess must fend off the too-bold advances of her suitor (4-D). The garden fountain, an essential prop in the pastoral drama, figures in a number of these tiles. Such structures, often highly ornate, provide water which a shepherdess offers her swain from a bowl or shell (3-D, 4-B) or serve merely as charming backdrop for a flower-crowned maid with a herd of sheep (3-C). Corners are decorated with spider's-heads (Corner motif 58).
Reference: Vis coll. sale, 1927, no. 209.

112

A   B   C   D

134. SHEPHERDS AND SHEPHERDESSES IN LANDSCAPES
1660–1725
Blue
Gift of Edward W. Bok; gift of Mrs. Francis P. Garvan

These tiles show shepherds and shepherdesses in rolling landscapes which form a continuous ground line when arranged horizontally. Similarities in graphic style and execution of detail sug-

gest that this panel was decorated by the same painter as the preceding panel: shepherd couples engage in similar rustic pastimes and several tiles (A, C, and D) repeat motifs found there. Corners are small spider's-heads (Corner motif 58).
Similar tiles: Simões, 1959, pp. 20, 44, 113, pl. XXXa; Kaufmann, 1973, figs. 113–15; Korf, 1979, figs. 558, 561.

135. SHEPHERDS AND SHEPHERDESSES IN LANDSCAPES
Harlingen?
1700–1750
Blue
Gift of Edward W. Bok

A shepherd and shepherdess pass beneath a leafy tree in a landscape with a distant church spire on one tile (A); on the other, a shepherd and shepherdess dally, screened by a cloak arranged on a shrub. Corners are decorated with medium-sized spider's-heads (Corner motif 58).

113

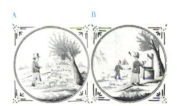

136. SHEPHERDS AND SHEPHERDESSES IN LANDSCAPES
1700–1750
Purple
Gift of Mrs. Francis P. Garvan

These images are paired to form dramatic vignettes: a shepherdess (1-A) is pursued by a piping shepherd (1-B); a gallant pastoral figure (2-A) apparently asks a shepherdess (2-B) to join his company. The backgrounds of these scenes are set with sheep, farm buildings, a church, and a rustic fence. The landscapes are enclosed in roundels delineated by two thin bands of purple. Eight white reserve scallops ring each roundel, and the surrounding area is filled with purple spatter. Corners are decorated with large carnations in reserve (Corner motif 65).

137. SHEPHERDS AND SHEPHERDESSES IN LANDSCAPES
1750–1825
Blue
Gift of Mrs. Francis P. Garvan

These shepherds and shepherdesses are situated in hilly landscapes with cloudy skies, enclosed in roundels of two thin blue bands. A shepherdess watches her flock while reading (2-A); a shepherd walks by a row of fernlike plants holding his staff on his shoulder, while two sheep turn their heads to follow his progress (2-B). A shepherdess standing with outstretched arm holds a staff (1-A); a seated shepherd blows a horn (1-B). Corners are spider's-heads (Corner motif 58).

138. SHEPHERDS IN LANDSCAPES
1750–1840
Purple
Gift of Anthony N. B. Garvan

Two shepherds wearing wide-brimmed hats tend their flocks in landscapes under cloudy skies. The scenes are enclosed by roundels; corners are decorated with small pin-wheel motifs (Corner motif 60).

139. SHEPHERDS AND SHEPHERDESS IN LANDSCAPES
Utrecht
c. 1900
Polychrome
Gift of Mrs. Francis P. Garvan

Dating from around the turn of the century, these polychrome tiles are decorated with pastoral scenes in roundels surrounded by two dark-purple lines. The figures on tile B follow a pastoral motif that first appeared on tiles in the late seventeenth century (see nos. 133, 1-D, 134 A). A shepherdess dressed in a blue smock and long yellow skirt and wearing a derbylike, plumed hat stands on a country path filling a pitcher at a well. She turns to watch a shepherd and his flock approaching. The shepherd wears a blue tunic, green pants, and a top hat. Behind him is a grove of trees indicated by summary strokes of green glaze; to the left are mountains outlined in purple. The other tile (A) shows a solitary shepherd, with an elegant top hat, holding a staff in one hand. Corners are large barred ox-heads (Corner motif 53).

Portraits

Tile portraits of princes and princesses of the House of Orange were in demand from the mid-seventeenth century until the second half of the eighteenth. They were bust length, encircled by roundels, and usually blue. Corner elements included spider's-heads, rosettes, or acanthus in reserve. Especially popular were portraits of Frederik Hendrik, his wife Amalia van Solms, and their four daughters, of whom no less than thirty examples have been published.[1] Portraits of members of the House of Orange decorated houses of dignitaries and of ordinary people, most often in prints and only rarely in tiles, from the beginning of the seventeenth to the early part of the nineteenth century, as evidenced by a portrait medal of Frederik Hendrik, about 1655 (fig. 36) and the portrait of William III as "The Young Prince of Orange" (fig. 37), this time printed in reverse, published as a pennyprint between 1748 and 1761.

FIG. 36 Pieter van Abeele (Dutch, active 1622–77) after Willem Delff (Dutch, 1580–1638)
Portrait medal of Frederik Hendrik, c. 1655
Koninklijk Kabinet van Munten, Penningen es Gesneden Stenen, The Hague

FIG. 37 After Frederik de Wit
The Young Prince of Orange, 1748–61
Woodcut
Rijksprentenkabinet, Rijksmuseum, Amsterdam

1. See Scheurleer, 1969; Amsterdam, Sotheby, cat. 327, 1981, nos. 101–6.

140. PORTRAITS OF FREDERIK HENDRIK AND WILLIAM III
c. 1660
Blue
Gift of Mrs. Francis P. Garvan

These portraits of the princes of Orange, counts of Nassau, are set within roundels composed of blue circles flanked by white circles in reserve. The corners are decorated with white reserve rosettes (Corner motif 40). Both princes are pictured bust length, almost fullface. Frederik Hendrik (1584–1647), stadholder (1625–47), is shown with a moustache and goatee (B). He wears a flat, lace collar on top of a breastplate; on a ribbon around his neck hangs a medal, which Scheurleer identifies as the Order of the Garter, granted to Frederik Hendrik in 1627.[1] Frederik Hendrik's grandson (A), William III (1650–1702), who later became king of England (1689–1702), wears a bonnet tied with ribbons under a beret decorated with ostrich feathers;

he holds a marshall's staff in his right hand. Lace on his collar, cuffs, and cap is indicated by blue dots. Both images are derived from an etching of the members of the House of Orange (fig. 38), published in 1653 in Amsterdam by Frederik de Wit.[2] The print comprises fifteen bust-length oval portraits, copied from prints by various artists.[3] For the portrait of Prince Frederik Hendrik, De Wit utilized a print by Cornelis Visscher (1629–1658) after a painting by Gerrit van Honthorst (1590–1656), who as court painter executed many commissions for the House of Orange.[4] The portrait of William III—who could have been no more than three years old at the time of the engraving—is based on an engraving by Johan van Houten, also published by De Wit, after a painting by Honthorst.[5]

References: Vis and Geus, 1926, pls. 32b, c; Vis coll. sale, 1927, no. 290; Vis and Geus, 1978, vol. 2, p. 50.
Similar tiles: De Jonge, 1971, pp. 37–39, ills. 40c, d.

1. Scheurleer, 1969, p. 331, n. 13.
2. Ibid., p. 329.
3. Scheurleer, ibid., p. 327, mentions Pieter van Sompel, Cornelis Visscher, Jonas Suyderhoef and the publisher Pieter Soutman.
4. G. K. Nagler, *Neues Allgemeines Künstler-Lexicon*, vol. 20 (Munich, 1850), p. 392, lists a series of twelve portraits of princes in ovals painted by Honthorst and engraved by Visscher, published by Pieter Soutman in 1649; see Clifford S. Ackley, *Printmaking in the Age of Rembrandt* (Boston, 1981), p. 201.
5. Hollstein, 1949–, vol. 9, p. 151, no. 3. J. C. Nix of the Museum Atlas van Stolk, Rotterdam, identified the print by Van Houten as the source for William III in the 1653 engraving.

FIG. 38 Frederik de Wit (Dutch, active 1650s)
Portraits of members of the House of Orange, 1653
Etching
Museum Atlas van Stolk, Rotterdam

Religious Scenes

Tiles with biblical scenes served both a decorative and a didactic function in the Dutch home from the middle of the seventeenth century, when they first became plentiful, through the nineteenth century. By their very presence in the domestic interior, they created an air of piety and morality, qualities Dutch families were eager to display. Fireplaces and large wall areas were covered with tiles illustrating both the well-known and the less-familiar stories of the Old and New Testaments and occasionally the Apocrypha. A total of five hundred biblical scenes have been counted on Dutch tiles.[1] Often the tiles include cartouches citing the chapter and verse of the events illustrated.

In most Dutch homes, both urban and rural, a chapter of the Bible would be read each day. In the seventeenth and eighteenth centuries, Netherlandish and Central European artists produced engravings of biblical narratives, which were included in the Bible or were assembled with minimal text in the form of picture Bibles. The prints identified as sources for tiles in this collection were executed by Matthäus Merian (1593–1650), Pieter Hendricksz Schut (1619–1660), and Jan Luyken (1649–1712).[2] Determining the exact print source for a tile is complicated by biblical illustrators' practice of copying one another's images as well as those of other artists. Schut, for example, borrowed freely from Merian and others.[3]

The ways in which prints were utilized for tile designs also varied. Sometimes a print was made into a transfer pattern (spons) in its entirety, as with the tile of Samson carrying the doors of Gaza's gate (no. 148, 3-E), copied directly from Luyken (fig. 39); more often, the designs were adaptations. In some cases, the figures and the backgrounds were based on the same print, as with Moses about to smash the Ten Commandments as the Israelites worship the Golden Calf (no. 146, C), adapted from a copy of Schut or Merian (see fig. 40).[4] In other instances, the backgrounds were modified and superfluous figures eliminated, as in Christ and the centurion (no. 144, 1-B), adapted from Merian (fig. 41). Although scenes and figures vary from tile to tile, the same sponsen were frequently reused for the backgrounds, sometimes in reverse; this indicates that painters often utilized separate sponsen for background and figures. Most outdoor scenes display foreground motifs of two or three mounds topped with tufts of grass (no. 147, 2-A) similar to those in pastoral tiles (for example, no. 137, 2-B). Stories set indoors were often placed in rooms with tiled floors and latticed windows (no. 148, 2-A). Almost all the tiles in this collection are framed by double-banded roundels, but other shapes, such as brackets and octagons, occur as well.

The transfer of the image from print to tile often resulted in an alteration of detail, lending confusion to the narrative. In a tile depicting Jesus and Zacchaeus (no. 149, 1-A), for example, a text from Matthew rather than Luke is cited, as inscribed at the bottom of the print on which the design is based (fig. 42). Another tile painter gave Elisha a head of hair (no. 148, 3-C), which is not in the print by Merian (fig. 43), thereby obscuring the point of the narrative, which is that the children of Bethel were punished for mocking the prophet's baldness.

1. See Tegelmuseum, 1972. This catalogue presents the most comprehensive overview of biblical tiles.

2. Ibid., p. 5. Matthäus Merian, *Historiae sacrae tam Veteris quam Novi Testamenti* (Amsterdam, c. 1700); Pieter Hendricksz Schut, *Toneel ofte vertooch der bybelsche historien . . .* (Amsterdam, 1659); and Jan Luyken, *De schriftuurlyke geschiedenissen en gelykenissen van het Oude en Nieuwe Verbond* (Amsterdam, 1712).

3. Occasionally, one printmaker's ability to reproduce the images of an artist is sufficient to make it impossible to determine whether the model or the copy served as the tile source. This is especially true of Schut's copies of Merian.

4. Schut, *Toneel*, Old Testament, pl. 45; Merian, *Historiae sacrae*, First Section, p. 62. Another obstacle to the identification of print sources is the successive editions of biblical illustrations. For example, Merian's Bible prints appeared in several editions; those that include the fullest range of images utilized on tiles are the *Biblia Strassburger* (1630) and the *Historiae sacrae*; the latter comprises many of the illustrations in the Strassburg Bible, along with images by Nicolaas Visscher the Elder (1550–1612) and the Younger (1587–1652).

FIG. 39 Jan Luyken (Dutch, 1649–1712)
Samson Carrying the Doors of Gaza's Gate, plate 90 from *De schriftuurlyke geschiedenissen en gelykenissen van het Oude en Nieuwe Verbond* (Amsterdam, 1712)
Etching
Rijksprentenkabinet, Rijksmuseum, Amsterdam

FIG. 40 Matthäus Merian the Elder (Swiss, 1593–1650)
Moses About to Smash the Ten Commandments as the Israelites Worship the Golden Calf, page 62 from *Historiae sacrae tam Veteris quam Novi Testamenti* (Amsterdam, c. 1700)
Engraving
Princeton University Library. Department of Rare Books and Special Collections

This is a typical reworked, reversed image from an earlier Merian edition, *Die bilder zur Bibel*, published in 1627 and reprinted in 1630.

FIG. 41 Matthäus Merian the Elder
Christ and the Centurion, page 16 from *Historiae sacrae tam Veteris quam Novi Testamenti* (Amsterdam, c. 1700), Third Section
Engraving
Princeton University Library. Department of Rare Books and Special Collections

FIG. 42 Pieter Hendricksz Schut (Dutch, 1619–1660)
Jesus and Zachaeus, plate 57 from Pieter Hendricksz Schut, *Toneel ofte vertooch der bybelsche historien . . .* (Amsterdam, 1659)
Engraving
Houghton Library, Harvard University, Cambridge, Mass.

FIG. 43 Matthäus Merian the Elder
Elisha and the Bear, from *Biblia Strassburger* (1630)
Engraving
The New York Public Library

141. THE SACRIFICE OF ISAAC
c. 1700[1]
Blue
Gift of Edward W. Bok

Abraham is pictured with Isaac, who carries wood for his own sacrifice (Gen. 22:6). Corners are spider's-heads (Corner motif 58).

1. Biblical tiles are usually 7 to 8 millimeters thick; those made before 1700 are thicker, and can be as much as 11 millimeters.

142. MOSES RECEIVING THE TEN COMMANDMENTS
1700–1750
Purple
Gift of Mrs. Francis P. Garvan

A simply drawn figure of Moses kneels on Mount Sinai, holding the tablets of the Ten Commandments. In deference to the heavenly rays suggesting the presence of God, which appear above Moses, the tile painter eliminated clouds from the sky. The corners are decorated with barred ox-heads (Corner motif 57).
Reference: Vis coll. sale, 1927, no. 327.

143. THE RESURRECTION
1725–75
Blue
Purchased: Joseph E. Temple Fund

In this delicate, graceful rendering, the resurrected Christ holds a banner. This scene appears in numerous paintings and prints of the seventeenth and eighteenth centuries and was popular on tiles, where it occurs in a wide variety of forms.[1] The corners are small spider's-heads (Corner motif 60).

1. See Tegelmuseum, 1972, pp. 33–38; the tile illustrated that is the closest to this one is no. 84b, p. 36, a Frisian tile dating to the first half of the eighteenth century.

144. SCENES FROM THE NEW TESTAMENT
Utrecht
1740–60
Blue
Ozeas, Ramborger, Keehmle Collection; gift of William Seltzen Rice

Blue biblical tiles were produced in Utrecht in the second half of the eighteenth century.[1] *Sponsen* with biblical scenes such as these are preserved in the Museum Hannemahuis in Harlingen. The scenes represented here are Peter remembering Christ's prophecy (Matt. 26:75; 1-A), Christ and the centurion (Matt. 8:5–13; 1-B) after Merian (fig. 41), the Parable of the Good Seed (Matt. 13:24; 2-A) after Merian,[2] and Peter led out of prison (Acts 12:9, 2-B) after Merian.[3] The corners feature barred ox-heads (Corner motif 52).

1. This information was kindly provided by Jan Pluis.
2. *Historiae sacrae*, Third Section, p. 26.
3. Ibid., p. 71.

118

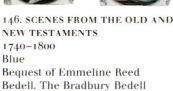

145. SCENES FROM THE OLD TESTAMENT

1740–1800
Purple
Gift of Mrs. Francis P. Garvan

Two Old Testament scenes are depicted: Saul and his servant looking for Saul's jennies (1 Sam. 9:3; A) after Schut,[1] and Samson slaying the lion (Judg. 14:5–6, B) after Merian.[2] Both scenes are coarsely painted in dark-purple. Each landscape is marked by tufted mounds and by a tree with a split trunk that forms a fence along the road. Corners are barred ox-heads (Corner motif 53).
Reference: Vis coll. sale, 1927, no. 328.

1. *Toneel*, Old Testament, pl. 73.
2. *Historiae sacrae*, Second Section, p. 15.

146. SCENES FROM THE OLD AND NEW TESTAMENTS

1740–1800
Blue
Bequest of Emmeline Reed Bedell. The Bradbury Bedell Memorial

These carefully articulated tiles are remarkably faithful to their print sources, reproducing both the figures and the backgrounds from Schut and copies after Merian: Peter denies Christ (Matt. 26:69–74; A) after Schut,[1] the Ascension (Acts 1:9; B) after Schut,[2] Moses about to smash the Ten Commandments as the Israelites worship the Golden Calf (Exod. 32:19; C) after Schut[3] and Merian (fig. 40), and the creation of man (Gen. 2:7; D) after Schut.[4] Corners are carnations (Corner motif 66).

1. *Toneel*, New Testament, pl. 94.
2. Ibid., pl. 112.
3. Ibid., Old Testament, pl. 45.
4. Ibid., pl. 1.

119

147. SCENES FROM THE OLD AND NEW TESTAMENTS

1740–1850
Purple
Bequest of Mrs. Frederick Graff; gift of Mrs. Francis P. Garvan

This panel of ten Old Testament and six New Testament scenes consists of tiles made over a number of years, probably in more than one workshop. Most have been identified with the prints of Schut or Merian. Corners are decorated with barred ox-heads (Corner motif 52).
Reference: Vis coll. sale, 1927, no. 327.

1-A Elisha and the bear (2 Kings 2:23–24) after Merian[1]
1-B Moses about to smash the Ten Commandments (Exod. 32:19) after Schut[2]
1-C Jesus and the woman of Canaan (Matt. 15:22) after Schut[3]
1-D God's covenant with Noah (Gen. 9:13) after Merian and Schut[4]

2-A Christ and the man with the withered hand (Matt. 12:10–13) after Schut[5]
2-B Manoah's offering (Judg. 13:20) after Schut[6]
2-C Peter cutting off the ear of the high priest's servant (Matt. 26:51) after Schut[7]
2-D animals entering Noah's ark (Gen. 7:14–16)

3-A The Annunciation (Luke 1:26–32) after Schut[8]
3-B Jesus in the manger (Luke 2:16)
3-C Pilate washing his hands in guiltlessness (Matt. 27:24)
3-D Christ carrying the Cross (Luke 23:26)

4-A The Prodigal Son (Luke 15:15–17) after Schut[9]
4-B Jonah and the whale (Jon. 2:10)
4-C angel announcing the Resurrection (Matt. 28:5–7) after Schut[10]
4-D Moses on Mount Sinai (Exod. 19:20)

1. *Biblia Strassburger*, opp. p. 203.
2. *Toneel*, Old Testament, pl. 45.
3. Ibid., New Testament, pl. 35.
4. *Historiae sacrae*, First Section, p. 13, and *Toneel*, Old Testament, pl. 8.
5. Ibid., New Testament, pl. 26.
6. Ibid., Old Testament, pl. 63.
7. Ibid., New Testament, pl. 92.
8. Ibid., pl. 6.
9. Ibid., pl. 43.
10. Ibid., pl. 106.

148. SCENES FROM THE OLD AND NEW TESTAMENTS AND THE APOCRYPHA
1740–1850
Purple
Bequest of Mrs. Frederick Graff; gift of Mrs. Francis P. Garvan

Few of the tiles in this panel can be traced to specific print sources. Corners are barred ox-heads (Corner motif 57).
Reference: Vis coll. sale, 1927, nos. 327, 328.

1-A   anointing of Jesus' feet (Luke 7:37–38)
1-B   Esther receiving the king's favor (Esther 8:4)
1-C   Israelites worshiping the Golden Calf (Exod. 32:3–6)
1-D   Christ carrying the Cross (Luke 23:26)
1-E   The Expulsion from Eden (Gen. 3:23–24)

2-A   Salome receiving the head of John the Baptist (Mark 6:28)
2-B   David playing for King Saul (1 Sam. 16:23)
2-C   The Tower of Babel (Gen. 11:4)
2-D   The Ascension (Luke 24:51)
2-E   The Annunciation (Luke 1:26–32)

3-A   Moses about to smash the Ten Commandments (Exod. 32:19) after Schut[1]
3-B   The Flight into Egypt (Matt. 2:14)
3-C   Elisha and the bear (2 Kings 2:23–24) after Merian (fig. 43)

3-D   Abraham and Isaac (Gen. 22:1–3)
3-E   Samson carrying the doors of Gaza's gate (Judg. 16:3) after Luyken (fig. 39)

4-A   Ruth and Boaz (Ruth 3:7) after Schut[2]
4-B   Tobias and the Angel (Tob. 6:2)
4-C   Moses and the Ten Commandments (Exod. 31:18)
4-D   Samson carrying the doors of Gaza's gate (Judg. 16:3) after Merian[3]
4-E   The Resurrection (Matt. 28:2–4)

5-A   Moses about to smash the Ten Commandments (Exod. 32:19) after Schut (see 3-A)
5-B   Christ on the road to Calvary (Luke 23:36)
5-C   Christ on the Cross (John 19:26–27)
5-D   The Last Supper (Matt. 26:20–25)
5-E   The Sacrifice of Isaac (Gen. 22:9–13)

1. *Toneel*, Old Testament, pl. 45.
2. Ibid., pl. 71.
3. *Historiae sacrae*, Second Section, p. 17.

149. SCENES FROM THE NEW TESTAMENT
Makkum
1750–1800
Blue
Gift of Mrs. Francis P. Garvan

These New Testament scenes after Schut—Jesus and Zacchaeus (Luke 19:1–6 [changed by the tile painter to Matt. 12:12]; A, see fig. 42) and the Parable of the Lost Sheep (Luke 15:3; B)[1]—

150. JESUS ON THE ROAD TO EMMAUS
Amsterdam
1800–1850
Purple
Bequest of Mrs. Frederick Graff

This tile sketchily depicts Jesus on the road to Emmaus (Luke 24:13–16). Although most of the small group of so-called carnation tiles *(anjertegels)* (Corner motif 69) on biblical themes are after

151. SCENES FROM THE OLD AND NEW TESTAMENTS
Amsterdam
1800–1850
Purple
Gift of Mrs. Francis P. Garvan

Five of these tiles are based on Jan Luyken's etchings[1]: the watchful servant (Luke 12:35–38; 1-A),[2] Jesus restoring the sight of the blind man (Mark 8:22–26; 1-C),[3] Jesus and the woman of Samaria (John 4:5–14; 2-A),[4] Nathan accusing David (2 Sam. 12:7; 2-B),[5] and God calling Moses to deliver Israel (Exod. 3:5–6; 2-C).[6] The sixth, Jonah and the gourd (Jon. 4:6; 1-B), is after Merian.[7] Corners are coarsely drawn barred ox-heads (Corner motif 53).

contain figures that are well constructed and shaded but are lacking in facial expression. The striking contrast between the dark and light tonalities of blue suggests a Frisian origin for these tiles. Corners consist of barred ox-heads (Corner motif 53).

1. *Toneel*, New Testament, pl. 40.

engravings by Schut, this example is after Jan Luyken.[1]

1. Tegelmuseum, 1972, p. 5. Used here is Luyken, *Schriftuurlyke geschiedenissen*, p. 629, no. 125.

Reference: Vis coll. sale, 1927, nos. 327, 328.

1. This information was kindly provided by Jan Pluis.
2. Luyken, *Schriftuurlyke geschiedenissen*, p. 517, pl. 69.
3. Ibid., p. 489, pl. 55.
4. Ibid., p. 409, pl. 15.
5. Ibid., p. 225, pl. 112.
6. Ibid., p. 95, pl. 47.
7. *Biblia Strassburger*, opp. p. 126.

Soldiers

FIG. 44 Jacob de Gheyn (Dutch, 1565–1620)
Musket sequence, plate 12, from *Wapenhandelinghe van roers, musquetten ende spiessen* (The Hague, 1608)
Engraving
The New York Public Library

Soldiers and militiamen were undoubtedly a common sight in the Netherlands during the first half of the seventeenth century, and Dutch artists frequently included them in their stock of characters. Scenes of swaggering military men were often depicted by painters,[1] and between 1580 and 1650 they became a favored decoration for tiles. After the treaty of Münster in 1648, however, the states were reluctant to provide the funds necessary for the upkeep of an army, and the number of soldiers was drastically reduced; correspondingly, on tiles at that time, soldiers were replaced by horsemen.

The Dutch infantry was formed of soldiers equipped with three different types of weapons. Shots or marksmen (*schutters*) carried a small-bore shoulder arm called a *roer*, or caliver, a weapon that was not used in the Dutch army after the first decade of the seventeenth century and appears only infrequently on tiles.[2] Musketeers were armed with a heavy, large caliber musket, fired from a rest. These matchlock guns, operated with a trigger, discharged when a slow-burning wick, called the "match," was brought into contact with gunpowder in the weapon's firing pan mounted on the side of the barrel. Musketeers were also equipped with a bandolier, from which hung twelve powder charges in leather-covered wooden casings, a small pouch holding bullets, and a flask of gunpowder used in priming the firing pan (see fig. 44). Pikemen (*piekeniers*) were armed with an eighteen-foot, ashwood pike tipped with an iron point. They wore armor consisting of a back and front plate (together forming a cuirass), thigh plates (tasses), and a gorget (see fig. 45). According to a 1599 resolution that standardized the weaponry carried by Dutch infantry, soldiers were required to have helmets,[3] yet many sported fashionable wide-brimmed, plumed hats both in and out of battle. As depicted on tiles, all soldiers carried swords.

Largely mercenaries from other countries, soldiers in the Dutch army wore no specific uniform, but dressed according to the fashion in doublets and knee breeches of various patterns. Outerwear typically consisted of a leather waistcoat, or buff jerkin, and a longer, flaring coat, or cassock. Throughout Europe, military insignia took the form of sashes in national or regimental colors. In the Lowlands these were sometimes orange, symbolizing the ruling House of Orange. Regular infantry wore sashes around the waist, while officers usually wore them diagonally across the chest (nos. 161, 2-A, 164, 2-A).

The depictions of musketeers and pikemen are mostly derived, or copied directly, from Jacob de Gheyn's *Wapenhandelinghe van roers, musquetten ende spiessen (The Exercise of Armes)*, first published in 1607 in The Hague.[4] An illustrated drill manual for the discipline of Dutch infantry, De Gheyn's book became the most popular and imitated manual of its kind in seventeenth-century Europe. Rembrandt referred to *The Exercise of Armes* for several figures for the 1642 portrait of the Amsterdam militia, the *kloveniers*, known as *The Nightwatch* (Rijksmuseum, Amsterdam). *The Exercise of Armes* consists of three separate sequences of "stop action" figures performing a drill with the caliver, musket, and pike, and each plate corresponds to one of a series of commands. The soldier in plate 12 of the musket sequence (fig. 44), used as a model for tile no. 159, 1-A, follows the command *schiet* (shoot!).

Cavalrymen also appear frequently on tiles. After 1660 cavalry troops were formed of mounted soldiers of two types. Heavily armed soldiers, or cuirassiers, carried

1. For a discussion of Dutch artists specializing in the depiction of soldiers, see National Gallery, London, *Dutch Genre Painting* (1978), pp. 38–39.
2. Arne Hoff, *Dutch Firearms* (New York, 1979), p. 10.
3. J. B. Kist, *Jacob de Gheyn, The Exercise of Armes: A Commentary* (New York, 1971), p. 28.
4. Facsimile, *The Exercise of Armes* (New York, 1971). The engraver of De Gheyn's designs is unknown; see Kist's commentary, pp. 20–27.

swords and wheel-lock pistols, and sometimes lances. Light cavalry soldiers, or dragoons, carried swords and light muskets, or pistols, and occasionally, pikes. Series of prints illustrating cavalry exercises and skirmishes were popular in the Netherlands throughout the course of the seventeenth century. The first cavalry soldiers depicted on tiles were copied from Jacob de Gheyn's engravings of *The Exercise of Cavalry*,[5] while images of rearing horses and fighting riders on later tiles were probably inspired by the series of nine cavalry battles etched by Jan Martsz de Jonge (see fig. 46).

FIG. 45 Jacob de Gheyn
Pike sequence, plate 1, from
*Wapenhandelinghe van roers,
musquetten ende spiessen* (The
Hague, 1608)
Engraving
The New York Public Library

FIG. 46 Jan Martsz de Jonge
(Dutch, 1609–1647)
Cavalry Battle, c. 1640
Etching
Rijksprentenkabinet,
Rijksmuseum, Amsterdam

5. Twenty-two plates were engraved, but this series was never published with a text in book form; see ibid., p. 16.

A   B

152. PIKEMAN AND MUSKETEER
1580–1625
Polychrome
Gift of Anthony N. B. Garvan

The pikeman, sporting a beard, moustache, and green plumed helmet, thrusts his weapon; the musketeer, in an orange plumed helmet, points to the left, holds a musket rest, and supports a musket on his shoulder. The soldiers are set in the center of roundels composed of a band of orange flanked on either side by two lines of blue. Corners are decorated with reserve petal designs on a dark-blue ground (Corner motif 39).
Similar tiles: Korf, 1979, fig. 180.

A   B   C   D

**153. ROMAN SOLDIERS AND
SARACEN BOWMEN**
Rotterdam
1600–1625
Polychrome
Gift of Anthony N. B. Garvan

Tiles produced between 1600 and
1625 were decorated in patterns
encompassing sixteen tiles and
repeated over large wall areas.
These exceptional tiles are each
decorated with one large figure,
separate from the others, which
indicates they were made for use

as baseboards (see nos. 175, 183).
Masterfully painted with forceful
details in orange and green. The
archers wear turbans, billowing
scarves, and kaftans, and carry
quivers filled with arrows. The
Romans sport plumed helmets,
cuirasses, and sashes, and carry
modeling and with blue shadows
that create bold chiaroscuro
patterns, they depict Saracen
bowmen and Roman warriors
outlined in blue and black, with
shields, short swords, and lances.
The figures are derived from en-

gravings by the Netherlands' most
significant printmaker of this period, Hendrik Goltzius (1558–
1616). The balletic soldiers are
simplified variations of figures
conceived by Goltzius for his series of eight "Roman Heroes."[1]
The costumes of the Roman soldiers on the tiles closely reflect
this model, but the exotic dress of
the archers is an imaginative departure from Goltzius's example.
References: Vis and Geus, 1926, p.
23, pl. 18; Vis coll. sale, 1927, no.
297.

Similar tiles: Peelen, 1922, p. 40,
fig. 23; Neurdenburg, 1923, *Old
Dutch Pottery,* p. 44, pl. X; Hudig,
1929, fig. 57; De Jonge, 1971, ill.
26; Kaufmann, 1973, pl. V; Korf,
1979, fig. 183; Amsterdam, Sotheby, cat. 327, 1981, nos. 146–48;
Het Princessehof, 1982, repro. p.
13.

1. Walter L. Strauss, ed., *The Illustrated Bartsch,* vol. 3 (New York,
1980), pp. 96–103; Peelen, 1922,
p. 40.

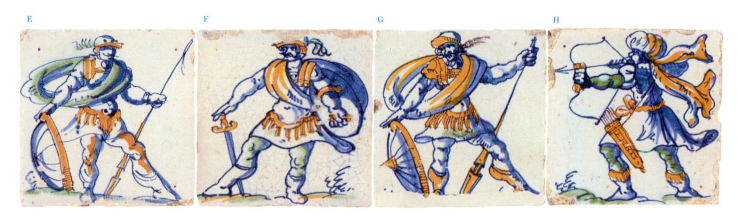

E   F   G   H

153a. ROMAN SOLDIER
Rotterdam
1600–1625
Polychrome
Gift of Anthony N. B. Garvan

Not illustrated. (Similar to tile C.)

154. SOLDIERS
1600–1625
Blue
Gift of Anthony N. B. Garvan

The large figures, almost filling the tiles' surfaces, wear swaggering, broad-brimmed cavalier hats ornamented with ostrich feathers, over shoulder-length hair. One soldier brandishes his sword and holds his pike before him, its end braced against his foot (1-A);[1] another holds up his shield while carrying his pike and sword (1-B); a musketeer withdraws the ramrod from his musket (2-B);[2] and a soldier marches and carries his musket and rest (2-A).[3] Corners are spear-head fleurs-de-lis (Corner motif 22, but with a blue rather than a white bar).

1. Adapted from De Gheyn, *The Exercise of Armes*, pike sequence, pl. 25.
2. After ibid., musket sequence, pl. 27.
3. After ibid., pl. 2.

126

155. PIKEMEN AND MUSKETEERS
1625–50
Blue
Gift of Anthony N. B. Garvan

A soldier performing a drill is set in the center of each tile, casting a shadow to the right. Although the stances of several of the soldiers are similar to those in the previous panel, these tiles must be dated somewhat later; the figures are smaller and do not extend to the edge of the tiles, the shadows are thinner, and the fleur-de-lis motifs are reduced in size (Corner motif 22, but with a blue rather than a white bar). Tile 2-C has markings on the reverse.

1-A helmeted pikeman supports a pike on his shoulder[1]
1-B pikeman in a plumed hat holds a pike horizontally above his head
1-C soldier brandishes his sword and holds his pike before him, braced against his foot[2]

1-D soldier wearing a plumed hat and a sash holds a standard
1-E musketeer wearing a cassock fires his weapon, his left hand supporting the musket rest and holding a smoking "match"
1-F musketeer in a plumed hat supports his weapon on his shoulder, reaching across his chest to grasp its stock
1-G pikeman wearing a plumed hat supports a pike on his shoulder and grasps the hilt of his sword

2-A soldier seen from behind withdraws the ramrod from his musket in order to tamp down a gunpowder charge previously loaded in the barrel[3]
2-B helmeted pikeman seen from behind holds a pike at eye level
2-C soldier withdraws the ramrod from his musket (see 2-A)
2-D soldier in plumed hat plays a side drum

2-E musketeer holds his musket and rest before him with both hands[4]
2-F soldier brandishes his sword and braces a pike against his foot (see 1-C)
2-G pikeman wearing a plumed hat holds a pike before him in a vertical position[5]

1. Adapted from De Gheyn, *The Exercise of Armes*, pike sequence, pl. 16.
2. After ibid., musket sequence, pl. 25.
3. After ibid., pike sequence, pl. 25.
4. After ibid., musket sequence, pl. 21.
5. After ibid., pike sequence, pl. 6.

2-C, reverse

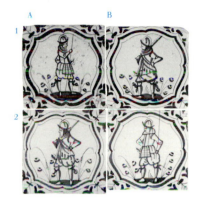

156. PIKEMEN AND MUSKETEERS
1625–50
Blue
Gift of Mrs. Francis P. Garvan

Set within bracketed frames composed of a band of blue flanked by two lines, soldiers drill with pike and musket. Delineated in a distinctive and rather wooden style, these soldiers were clearly all painted by the same hand, and based on the example of Jacob de Gheyn's *The Exercise of Armes*. In 1627 the French Controleur Général des Guerres ordered some six thousand tiles depicting soldiers very much like these to decorate the château de Beauregard, near Blois. Richly documenting the popularity of Dutch tiles outside the Netherlands, these still cover the floor of an entire gallery, where they are arranged to represent a complete army marching in formation.[1] The corners have leaf and tendril motifs (Corner motif 37).

Similar tiles: Korf, 1969, fig. 114; De Jonge, 1971, ills. 43c, d; Korf, 1979, fig. 541.

1. De Jonge, 1966.

156a. PIKEMAN
1625–50
Blue
Gift of Edward W. Bok

Not illustrated.

127

157. PIKEMEN AND SARACEN BOWMAN
1625–50
Blue
Gift of Mrs. Francis P. Garvan

A soldier in a plumed hat and wearing a cassock with slit sleeves carries a halberd on his shoulder (1-A, 2-A). This weapon, essentially a pike with an ax-like blade, was not used by the regular Dutch army, but was often carried by members of town militias. A helmeted pikeman (2-B) supports a pike on his shoulder, while his other hand rests on the hilt of his sword.[1] A mustachioed Saracen bowman dressed in a long kaftan and a turban sets his bow before him and carries a saber at his side (1-B). Such exotic types were of lively interest in the seventeenth-century Netherlands and figure frequently in prints of this period. Corners are deco-rated with spear-head fleurs-de-lis (Corner motif 22) and show evidence of glaze running in an over-hot kiln.
Reference: Vis coll. sale, 1927, no. 220.

1. Adapted from De Gheyn, *The Exercise of Armes*, pike sequence, pl. 11.

158. PIKEMAN
1625–50
Blue
Gift of Mrs. Francis P. Garvan

A helmeted pikeman prepares to repel a cavalry charge. With his left hand he holds a pike before him at a forty-five degree angle, bracing the end of the weapon against his back foot, and with his right, he draws a sword. This figure is based on plate 25 of Jacob de Gheyn's *Exercise of Armes* (pike sequence). The figure is set within a bracketed frame, and the corners are mock-fret (Corner motif 14).

159. PIKEMEN AND MUSKETEERS
1625–50
Blue
Gift of Edward W. Bok; gift of
Mrs. Francis P. Garvan

Swaggering pikemen and musketeers, many wearing plumed hats,
decorate these tiles. (Corner motif 50.)
Reference: Vis and Geus, 1926, pl. 73.
Similar tiles: Hoynck, 1920, p. 92,
fig. 155.

1-A musketeer fires his weapon,
a wisp of smoke issuing from the
powder ignited in the gun's firing
pan (see fig. 44)
1-B pikeman holds a pike at his
side (see fig. 45)
1-C helmeted soldier plays a flute
1-D pikeman in a cassock holds a
pike before him

2-A musketeer primes the firing
pan of his musket with gunpowder held in a small flask[1]

2-B soldier turns his head while
holding a pike, the end of an officer's sash hanging behind him
2-C soldier supports a halberd on
his shoulder
2-D soldier supports a pike on his
shoulder

3-A pikeman supports a pike on
his shoulder, the ends of an officer's sash fluttering behind him
3-B bearded soldier with a sword
at his side, carries a pike in his
left hand

3-C pikeman holds a pike at his
side[2]
3-D pikeman holds his weapon
before him and draws his sword[3]

1. Based on De Gheyn, *The Exercise of Armes,* musket sequence,
pl. 11.
2. Except for the head, which is
turned to the side, this is based
on ibid., pike sequence, pl. 1; see
fig. 45.
3. Based on ibid., pike sequence,
pl. 25.

128

A   B   C   D

159a. PIKEMAN
Rotterdam
1625–50
Blue
Gift of Mrs. Francis P. Garvan

Not illustrated. (Similar to tile 3-A.)

160. MARKSMAN, MUSKETEER, AND PIKEMAN
1625–50
Blue
Gift of Anthony N. B. Garvan

Kneeling, a marksman fires a caliver, smoke issuing from the gun's firing pan and barrel (A); a mustachioed musketeer holds a musket rest and "match" in one hand and a musket in the other (B); a pikeman in a broad-brimmed hat supports a pike on his shoulder (C). The soldiers and the corners, which are decorated with fleurs-de-lis (Corner motif 22), are outlined with purple *trek*.

161. MUSKETEERS AND PIKEMEN
1625–50
Blue
Gift of Mrs. Francis P. Garvan

Two musketeers (1-A, B) support a musket on their shoulders and hold musket rests and "matches" from which issue two wisps of smoke. A mustachioed officer in a plumed hat with a sash billowing out from his shoulder (2-A) supports a pike at his side, while a helmeted pikeman (2-B) holds a pike on his shoulder.[1] The figures are outlined with purple *trek*. Corners are ox-heads. (Corner motif not illustrated.)

1. Adapted from De Gheyn, *The Exercise of Armes,* pike sequence, pl. 11.

130

162. CAVALRY
1640–80
Blue with color accents
Gift of Anthony N. B. Garvan

Light cavalry soldiers and dragoons on rearing horses charge across these tiles; with the exception of the one on tile 1-C, they all wear yellow, red, brown, or orange sashes around their waists. Corners are ox-heads (Corner motif 50).
References: Vis coll. sale, 1927, no. 282; Vis and Geus, 1933, pl. 19a.
Similar tiles: De Jonge, 1971, ills. 44e, f.

1-A dragoon heads to the right, his sash flying behind
1-B dragoon turns on his horse, brandishing a sword in his upraised right arm as if to strike a foe[1]

1-C dragoon wearing an orange-plumed helmet charges, holding a lance in his outstretched hand
1-D dragoon flings up his arms as he is shot and falls from his horse, his hat lying under his mount

2-A dragoon heads to right (see 1-A)
2-B dragoon heads to right (see 1-A)
2-C dragoon thrusts his pike upward as if to salute the spectator
2-D dragoon fires his pistol at an attacker from his rearing charger, smoke issuing from the lock and barrel of his weapon

3-A dragoon charges into battle pointing a large-headed pike before him
3-B dragoon, taken from the same *spons* as tiles 1-A, 2-A, and 2-B but with the position of his right arm changed to

hold a sword at his side (see fig. 46)
3-C dragoon, brandishing his sword, rides a strongly and skillfully foreshortened horse
3-D dragoon wearing orange plumes on his helmet, turns on his mount and thrusts his pike behind him as if to strike at a fallen enemy

4-A dragoon taken from the same *spons* as 3-A rides on a galloping horse
4-B dragoon rides to the right, holding a sword at his side (see 3-B)
4-C dragoon gallops to the right, turning his head toward the viewer
4-D dragoon astride a rearing mount holds his unsheathed sword at his side

1. This figure may be derived from Jan Martsz de Jonge's "Cavalry Battles," pl. 2.

163. DRAGOON
1640–80
Blue
Gift of Edward W. Bok

A dragoon reins in his rearing horse and seems about to draw his sword or pistol. Corners are large ox-heads (Corner motif 49).

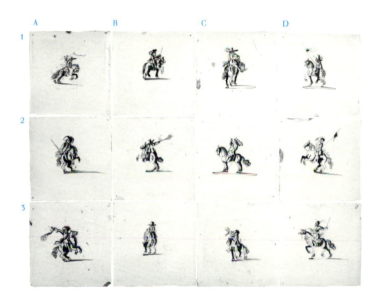

164. CAVALRY
1660–1700
Blue
Gift of Mrs. Francis P. Garvan; gift of Anthony N. B. Garvan

Cavalrymen, several wearing beaver hats ornamented with ostrich feathers,[1] decorate these tiles. A number of strongly foreshortened figures, rare in Dutch tiles, make these tiles particularly noteworthy. The two with extreme foreshortening, showing a dragoon and mount from the rear (1-C, 3-B), suggest that they were excerpted from the print of a large battle scene, although the painter of tile 3-B was less adept at his task, producing a small, quite confused image of horse and rider. The small size of the

figures and absence of corner motifs support a later date for this panel.
Similar tiles: Amsterdam, Sotheby, cat. 327, 1981, no. 13.

1-A rider on a horse at full gallop cracks his whip
1-B rider on a prancing horse
1-C dragoon and his mount seen from behind
1-D rider, holding a banner, reins in his horse

2-A cavalry soldier, with the diagonal sash of an officer, brandishes his sword
2-B dragoon turns and fires his musket
2-C soldier leans back on his mount to quench his thirst,[2] a figure probably understood by con-

temporary Dutch viewers as pausing at his camp canteen
2-D cavalry officer holding a striped banner turns toward the spectator
3-A dragoon on a rearing horse defends himself from an attacker and fires his wheel-lock pistol
3-B dragoon and his mount seen from behind (see 1-C)
3-C falconer on horseback
3-D Saracen bowman, astride a charger, wears a plumed helmet and supports a lance, while a quiver filled with arrows hangs at his side

1. See R. Turner Wilcox, *The Mode in Hats and Headdress* (New York, 1945), p. 113.
2. A similar subject is depicted in Jan Martsz de Jonge's "Cavalry Battles," pl. 1.

165. SARACEN HORSEMAN
1680–1725
Purple
Gift of Mrs. Francis P. Garvan

A Saracen horseman carrying a scimitar raises his shield with one arm while brandishing his weapon in the other hand. The horse and rider are placed within an eight-lobed roundel in reserve and bounded by two thin lines of purple and surrounded by a spattered field. Corners are hearts in reserve (Corner motif 60).
Similar tiles: De Jonge, 1971, ill. 87a.

Landscapes

FIG. 47 Jan van de Velde (Dutch,
1593–1641)
Winter Scene with Skaters, plate
25 from "Playsante lantschappen
ende vermakelike gesichten,"
1617
Etching and engraving
The British Museum, London

FIG. 48 Willem Buytewech
(Dutch, 1591/92–1624)
*Ruins of Eykenduynen Chapel
near The Hague,* 1621
Etching
The British Museum, London

1. David Freedberg, *Dutch Landscape Prints of the Seventeenth
Century* (London, 1980), pp. 9–20.
2. See Stettner, 1982, pp. 12–21;
Reinier Nooms, *Harbor Scene
with Hoisting Tower* from "Sea-
ports," Otto Naumann, ed., *The Illustrated Bartsch,* vol. 6 (New
York, 1980), no. 28, p. 132; Her-
man Saftleven, *The Four Seasons:
Spring,* in Hollstein, 1949–, vol.
23, pp. 120, 121.

The native countryside was a source of ceaseless delight to seventeenth-century Dutchmen. Apparently awakening to its charms at about the turn of the sixteenth century, northern Netherlanders hymned the land in literature, prints, and paintings throughout the Golden Age.[1] The topography, so thoroughly at peace with the presence of man, was further domesticated as decorative motifs on tiles. Tiled hearths and baseboards provided a repertoire of vignettes—windmills, farm huts, and harbors—which eventually became symbolic of the Netherlandish terrain.

Landscape tiles first appeared at the beginning of the seventeenth century, sometimes in panels with scenes from daily life (they were later removed from these panels by collectors and dealers). They became abundant in the eighteenth and nineteenth centuries and were produced without much variation until about 1900. This is underscored by the holdings in this collection, which date primarily to the latter centuries. Landscape tiles were inspired by the pioneering prints of Haarlem artists who celebrated the Dutch town and its outlying fields and byways: Willem Buytewech (1591/92–1624), Esaias van de Velde (c. 1590–1630), and Jan van de Velde (1593–1641). According to their pictorial vision, the characteristic features of the terrain are contributed equally by nature and by man. Human handiwork, such as drawbridges (fig. 47) and ruins (fig. 48), frequently figure as primary subject matter and are sometimes placed at the center of the work. Tile painters singled out such rustic structures for particular attention. In addition to the drawbridge (nos. 166 A, 174, 2-B) and the ruin (no. 166 C), lesser-known sights that marked the Dutch landscape are also depicted, including a dovecote (no. 169 B) and a *wipvuur,* a tall structure from which a basket of smoking coals was suspended to serve as a beacon for ships (nos. 167, 169 A, 172, 3-C).[2]

While some tiles present isolated motifs, others contain elaborate panoramas full of eye-catching detail (no. 172). Such tiles usually include human figures pursuing occupations characteristic of the land they inhabit: fishermen haul their catch from the water (no. 172, 2-B), shepherds tend a flock grazing amid forested hills (no. 172, 1-A), and workers at the mouth of a harbor replenish the coals of the *wipvuur* (no. 172, 3-C). Ample expanses of sky filled with windblown clouds, perhaps the most pervasive aspect of the Dutch outdoors, appear in all panoramic tiles. Water is also present in these and most landscape tiles. It is featured in the abundant harbor scenes (no. 167) or occurs as a blue stripe marked by sailboats behind farmhouses and other structures (no. 169 F), a reminder of the proximity of all Dutch land to the surrounding water.

The Dutchman's hearth depicted the outdoor world he frequented in the course of daily life. Dutch prints tapped the poetry of familiar surroundings; Dutch tiles made charming formulas of the terrain, thus providing lasting images which in the popular imagination continue to encapsulate the Dutch countryside.

166. DRAWBRIDGE, WELL, AND RUIN
1675–1725
Blue
Gift of Edward W. Bok

These three tiles are vignettes of the rural landscape: an open drawbridge, a well, and ruins. The corners are bee's-heads (Corner motif 58).

167. HARBOR SCENE
Rotterdam
De Blompot (owned by the Aelmis family)
1680–1725
Purple and blue
Gift of Mrs. Francis P. Garvan

A crenelated tower on a pier serves as a lighthouse; a smoke signal hangs from the roof to assist sailboats entering the harbor. A ferryman pushes his boat— which carries a man, farm animals, and a dog—away from the bank. Large fleurs-de-lis in reserve form the corners of the purple octagonal frame[1] (Corner motif 34). Each motif is decorated with a blue vein in the center, counterbalancing the blue landscape. Unusually complex in composition and execution, this tile was produced in the Aelmis workshop in Rotterdam, then the only shop capable of producing such high-quality faience.

1. P. J. Tichelaar describes this technique, also demonstrated on no. 168, in Pluis, 1975, pp. 5–9, fig. 2; see Ray, 1973, pp. 47, 94.

168. WATERSCAPE
1680–1725
Purple and blue
Gift of Mrs. Francis P. Garvan

Concentric octagonal bands surround a house on a riverbank set among trees. The central picture is glazed in blue. Corners are purple spatter fields outside the white octagon painted in reserve.

169. WATER SCENES
1690–1750
Blue
Gift of Edward W. Bok; gift of S. Krider Kent; gift of Mrs. Francis P. Garvan

Typical water scenes with buildings and ships decorate this panel. Lighthouses appear on tiles A, D, F; other buildings depicted on the waterfront are a city gate (C), a dovecote on a grassy dune (B), a church (E), and a farmhouse (H). The spider's-heads on tiles A and C are larger and more elaborate than on the others (Corner motif 58).
Similar tiles: Amsterdam, Sotheby, cat. 327, 1981, nos. 16, 192.

G, reverse

170. HARBOR VIEWS
1720–1825
Blue
Gift of Edward W. Bok

Towers and houses bordering the water evoke a mood of placid simplicity. Depicting typical villages, this type of tile is described in old pattern books as a "landscape in an octagon" *(landschap in een achtkant)*. The scenes are surrounded by Louis XIV-style frames with trellis corners (Corner motif 64). Popular from their inception until the end of the nineteenth century (see nos. 171, 174), these tiles were copied repeatedly until they were reduced to schematic essentials. They also achieved great popularity in England, where Dutch tile motifs were assiduously copied.[1] Scenes depicted include harbor views with fishermen and sailboats (1-A, 1-B, 2-A), a view of a village with sailboats and swans (1-C), and a lookout point with guardbox, sailboats, swans, and windmill (1-D).

1. Van Lemmen, 1980; Ray, 1973, pp. 89–91.

171. WATERSCAPES
Utrecht or Rotterdam
1725–1875
Purple
Gift of Mrs. Francis P. Garvan

Figures, a horse-drawn carriage, city gates, and farmhouses are located at the water's edge on these tiles. Characteristic of Dutch landscapes set against the horizon are the numerous church towers, each topped by a large weathervane. Brickwork promontories line the waterfront. Each octagonal scene is set within an elaborate trellis and flower-head frame (Corner motif 64). Scenes depicted are a church with a windmill in the background (1-A), a waterscape with fisherman near a fortification (1-B), sailboats near a lighthouse (1-C), a man walking on a bridge (1-D), a wooden bridge by a village (1-E), country scene with houses and two men (2-A), a church by a dock at the water's edge (2-B), a fisherman (2-C), travelers on a dike (2-D), city gates with drawbridges (2-E, 3-E), a farm on the water's edge with sailboats and a rower (3-A, 3-D), a horse-drawn towing barge with a pipe-smoking passenger (3-C), and a riverscape with a village (3-B).
Reference: Vis coll. sale, 1927, no. 62.

172. LANDSCAPES
1720–1840
Blue
Gift of Mrs. Francis P. Garvan;
gift of Anthony N. B. Garvan

Busy scenes of everyday activity along rivers and canals are depicted on this panel of "open skies" *(open luchtjes),* the common nomenclature for landscapes on tiles not enclosed by frames or corner decorations. The climate of the Netherlands, with its wind-swept, cloudy skies, is reflected on these tiles. Scenes pictured include an imaginary landscape with shepherds, rowboats, and two ships in the distance (1-A); shepherds and shepherdesses tending livestock (1-B); cattle and people crossing a bridge while others swim near the bank (1-C); a meadow with cows and a milkmaid (2-A); a harbor scene (2-B); a castle on a promontory—outside the walls a man is replenishing the embers of a *wipvuur,*[1] which served as a beacon for ships (3-C)[2]; a church topped by a weathervane (3-A); a ferry with people and livestock arriving at the dock (3-B); and a farmer tilling a field (2-C).

1. Stettner, 1982, pp. 14, 15, 27 n. 4, fig. 4.
2. The same castle scene, although framed, as in no. 170, is pictured in Vis and Geus, 1933, pl. 29a.

136

A   B   C

173. COUNTRY SCENES
1720–1840
Blue
Gift of Anthony N. B. Garvan

Sharp lines here delineate *open lucht* landscapes showing country life. The unusual clouds, formed of parallel horizontal strokes combined with closely grouped spirals, suggest that these were executed by a single tile painter. Scenes depicted are a harbor with people unloading baskets from a ferry (A); a river scene near a bridge, with swans, a rower, and an artist sketching (B); and a landscape with figures, a boat, and windmills (C).

174. WATER AND COUNTRY SCENES
1850–1900
Polychrome
Gift of Anthony N. B. Garvan

Traditional "landscape in octagon" motifs were revitalized in the nineteenth century through the use of brilliant polychromy. In contrast to the polychrome tiles of the late sixteenth and early seventeenth centuries, nineteenth-century polychrome tiles are painted in bright colors and have elaborate corners (Corner motif 64). Scenes include a castle moat with swans and a docked sailboat (1-A), sailboats coming into port (1-B), a farmhouse in a meadow with a sower (2-A), and a city gate with a drawbridge (2-B).

Ships and Sea Creatures

FIG. 49 Jacob de Gheyn (Dutch, 1565–1620), after Wilhelm Tetrode (Dutch, active second half 16th century)
Neptune's Kingdom, 1587
Engraving
Philadelphia Museum of Art.
Purchased: Lola Downin Peck Fund

FIG. 50 Jan Muller (Dutch, 1571–1628)
Arion Playing His Lyre, Carried by a Dolphin to Shore at Taenarum
Engraving
The Metropolitan Museum of Art, New York. The Elisha Whittelsey Collection

Artists throughout the Netherlands, from painters to popular printmakers, from cartographers to tile decorators, produced images of the sea, which is so much a part of Dutch daily life and culture. Sailing ships, fantastic sea monsters, mythological creatures, exotic fish—all appear on tiles. Prints of marine subjects served as a major source of inspiration for tile painters. The imagery of sea creatures followed Mannerist traditions that were developed in the graphic medium by Hendrik Goltzius (1558–1616) and his followers.[1] A figure of Triton was borrowed from *Neptune's Kingdom* by Jacob de Gheyn (fig. 49) for a tile (no. 184) as well as a piece of decorative silverware; a companion tile, depicting Arion (no. 183), came from an engraving of *Arion Playing His Lyre* (fig. 50) by Jan Muller. The more realistic rendition of ships and seascapes derived principally from the graphic work of Reinier Nooms. Such prints as *The "Vrijheijt," a Man-of-War, and the "Hasewint," a Spaniarder* (fig. 51), showing a frigate, a man-of-war, and a flute, a trading ship, served as models for the tile painter (no. 177).[2] Another source was Claes Jansz Visscher, whose etching entitled *"Nothing Ventured, Nothing Gained"* (fig. 52) was transposed on a tile showing a herring buss (no. 177, 1-D).

Ships as well as sea creatures can also be found on maps and in emblem books of this period. Images of Fortuna (no. 186 M), for example, come from one of the many well-known Dutch emblem books. Their popularity paralleled quite closely that of maps in the Netherlands, where decorative cartography reached its height in the second half of the sixteenth century and remained important until the eighteenth century.[3] The technical skill of the engravers and the competition of the map trade combined to fill maps with increasingly elaborate ornament and a wealth of pictorial detail. Tile painters borrowed both the weird and fantastical creatures and the natural ones that inhabited the seas on maps—sea turtles, dolphins transporting Nereids, tritons, mermaids, and mermen. Pliny thought that the sea formed an independent state where one could find *mutatis mutandis,* all the creatures that occur on land or in the sky. As such there were sea-oxen, sea-mice, sea-hares, and so forth.[4] Hippocampi (nos. 186 H, 188 C, 193 D) and other mythological creatures, for example, embellish the maps of Willem Blaeu (1571–1638); on his map of Cyprus, Venus rides on a shell throne pulled by swans in a manner similar to that on tile no. 192 A.

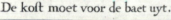

FIG. 51 Reinier Nooms, called
Zeeman (Dutch, 1623–before
1668)
*The "Vrijheijt," a Man-of-War,
and the "Hasewint," a
Spaniarder*
Etching
The Cleveland Museum of Art.
Mr. and Mrs. Lewis B. Williams
Collection

FIG. 52 Claes Jansz Visscher
(Dutch, 1587–1652)
*"Nothing Ventured, Nothing
Gained,"* plate 49 from Roemer
Visscher, *Sinnepoppen*
(Amsterdam, 1614)
Etching
Rijksprentenkabinet,
Rijksmuseum, Amsterdam

During the first decades of the seventeenth century, tiles depicting life at sea were produced in potteries in many locations, Rotterdam, Amsterdam, Delft, Hoorn, and others. After 1650, when they first became a separate subject matter, blue tiles decorated with sea creatures and ships were made in Rotterdam, but were mainly products of Harlingen and Makkum, both important harbor towns on the shores of the Zuider Zee in the province of Friesland. Frisian tile painters display familiarity with the configuration of hulls, masts, sails, rigging, and flags because the consumers of this region, whose livelihood centered upon the construction and operation of ships, delighted in accurate details.

Various types of ships sail the seas on Frisian tiles, among them, men-of-war; flutes (nos. 176 A, 177, 2-A, 3-D; see fig. 51), armed merchant ships,[5] primarily trading vessels, that carried grain from the Baltic and various other products from the Mediterranean; and frigates (no. 177, 2-B, 4-C), three-masted warships used as scouting cruisers and general handmaidens of the fleet. Seagoing ships characteristically display square sails (nos. 176 A, D, 177, 1-C) unlike inland vessels, which plied the lakes, rivers, and canals as well as the Zuider Zee. These are generally rigged with fore-and-aft sails, although occasionally they carry square sails (no. 179).[6] Fishing vessels (no. 177, 1-D; see fig. 52) and yachts also are depicted on tiles.

Ship tiles, when mounted, were frequently interspersed with tiles decorated with sea creatures and fish. When placed side by side along the base of a wall or across the top tier of wainscoting, these tiles created a continuous horizon line (by the banding together of the seas), which united them into an unbroken image of real and fictitious life at sea. The surging, crested waves that encompassed the lower third of the tile's surface on earlier examples, became schematized, rendered only by a few short stripes, after 1700.[7] The transition is illustrated by a comparison of tiles with ships (no. 177, 2-A with no. 181 C) or sea creatures (no. 184 with no. 186 I).

Dutch shipbuilding went into decline at the end of the seventeenth century, when new models were no longer introduced and the flute, for one, became standardized.[8] By the middle of the eighteenth century, Dutch shipbuilders had lost their superiority over foreign competitors. Concurrently, the tile industry became less innovative, and outstanding tiles decorated with ships and sea creatures were no longer made.

1. See Walter Strauss, *Hendrik Goltzius: Complete Engravings, Etchings, Woodcuts* (New York, 1977), pp. 748–55.
2. See De Groot and Vorstman, 1980, pl. 81 (this work has been the primary source consulted for information about Dutch ships).
3. See R. A. Skelton, *Decorative Printed Maps of the Fifteenth to Seventeenth Centuries* (New York, 1952), pp. 58–59.
4. Van de Waal, 1952, vol. 1, p. 290.
5. All ships sailing the high seas were armed with a few cannons for their own protection and thus could be converted to warships by the addition of more guns. See Preston, 1974, pp. 86–87.
6. See Donald Macintyre et al., *The Adventure of Sail: 1520–1914* (New York, 1972), p. 247; Preston, 1974, p. 85; De Groot and Vorstman, 1980, p. 21.
7. For an exhaustive compendium of sea-creature tiles, see Scheurleer, 1970.
8. Regin, 1976, p. 105.

175. SAILBOAT
Rotterdam
1600–1625
Polychrome
Gift of Anthony N. B. Garvan

This exceptional tile depicts two figures seated in a round, flat-bottomed boat floating on a blue-green sea. The boat has a rounded bow with hull planking painted alternately in ocher and purple. The short and heavy single mast is supported by the shrouds and is rigged with one square sail, which is furled on the headstick. The boat is a typical one of the period and can be seen in prints[1] and paintings; this one seems to have been based on the boat depicted in the background of Jan Muller's engraving of Arion (fig. 50). This and tile no. 183 were probably made in the same factory, and it is possible that they were part of a series of baseboard tiles (see nos. 153, 182–84).
References: Vis and Geus, 1926, pl. 16; Vis coll. sale, 1927, no. 247.

1. Arthur Henkel and Albrecht Schöne, *Emblemata: Handbuch zur Sinnbildkunst des XVI. und XVII. Jahrhunderts* (Stuttgart, 1967), p. 686.

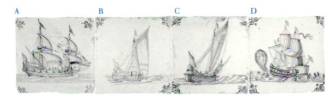

A   B   C   D

176. MEN-OF-WAR AND SLOOPS
1650–1700
Blue
Gift of Mrs. Francis P. Garvan

The painter of this series of tiles took great pains to show accurate details of hull and rigging, which makes these tiles exceptionally beautiful. The foremast and mainmast of the three-masted flute (A; see fig. 51)[1] are square-rigged, while a lateen is carried on the mizzenmast and the sprit-sail is furled on the bowsprit. The movement of the water, the configuration and planking of the hull, the ratlines and blocks of the rigging, and even the bonnets laced to the bottom of the full-blown sails are meticulously shown, in contrast to the crew, who are drawn only in outline. The small, flat-bottomed, broad-beamed cargo vessel (B; see nos. 179 C, 181 F) with a round hull and curved hatches, is under sail in a light breeze. She is running before the wind with the mainsail sheeted out to port and the fore-sail to starboard. The leeboards have been pulled up out of the water as is customary when a ship is sailing before the wind.

The roof and side of the deck cabin are visible behind the curved lines of the deck load. The helmsman, standing near the flag at the stern, holds the tiller in his left hand. The round-hulled yacht (C) is under sail in a light breeze. The main spritsail[2] is clearly visible because the ship is running free with the wind over her port quarter and the sail is let out over starboard, giving a clear view of the entire sail and its lacing to the mast.

The three-masted, square-rigged man-of-war (D) is firing her stern cannon while running before the wind.[3] The sail on the mizzenmast is tightly furled but the large square topsails are fully blown, as is a square spritsail under the bowsprit. In addition to the long, swallow-tailed pennant—which shows her to be a commodore's flagship—the ship flies a flag on the peak of each of her three masts and the tricolor from the end of the bowsprit. The corners are barred ox-heads (Corner motif 50).

Reference: Vis coll. sale, 1927, no. 249.
Similar tiles: De Jonge, 1947, fig. 141; Kaufmann, 1973, fig. 192; Het

Princessehof, 1980, no. 4; Amsterdam, Sotheby, cat. 327, 1981, no. 201.

1. Preston, 1974, p. 87; De Groot and Vorstman, 1980, p. 280. A similar frigate was depicted by Hendrick Cornelisz Vroom (c. 1566–1640) in the painting *The Return to Amsterdam of the Second Expedition to the East Indies, July 19, 1599* (Rijksmuseum, Amsterdam).
2. See De Groot and Vorstman, 1980, p. 20, fig. 81.
3. Ibid., no. 12, mentions a ship firing her guns to announce her departure from the roadstead.

1-A, reverse

177. MEN-OF-WAR, FRIGATES, FLUTES, AND A HERRING BUSS
Harlingen
1650–1700
Blue
Gift of Mrs. Francis P. Garvan;
gift of Anthony N. B. Garvan

This impressive panel consists primarily of two important types of ships, the flute[1] and the frigate,[2] both of which were depicted in an etching by Reinier Nooms (fig. 51). The ships reach to the top edge of each tile and the sea covers the entire lower section, extending from the tile's edge to the horizon. Restless water with crested waves is realistically rendered; on only two tiles (1-A, 4-D) is the sea calm. The two men-of-war shown in a rare foreshortened view (1-A, 4-D)—most ships are depicted in profile and in action—seem identical. The same *spons* was used to delineate these warships hove to with all sails furled on the yardarms and anchors stowed at the catheads. Here, however, the similarity ends: sea and ships were obviously painted by different hands and the colors are different owing to the tiles' having been fired in separate kiln loads. One three-masted frigate (1-C) is similar to that on two other tiles (2-B, 4-C), but the details on tile 1-C are so poorly rendered that either the painter had no knowledge of ships, which would have been very unusual, or was a poor craftsman. A herring buss (1-D), a common Dutch fishing boat with

a high, curved stem, low, rounded transom stern and square sails (fig. 52), is lying to her nets and has lowered two masts while fishing. A fisherman standing at the stern is hauling the net over the port transom, while the tank midships is open to receive the fish. The lantern on the stern, which seems overly large, is an important feature, as fishing was also done at night "to reduce the risk of the fish seeing the nets."[3] A three-masted flute flying the Dutch tricolor from all three masts (2-A) runs on her starboard side in a choppy sea, and throws a large crest wave. She carries square sails on the fore- and mainmasts, and the topsails as well as the lateen on the mizzenmast are furled. The heavily carved aft castle contains the cabin accommodation. Another flute (3-C) similarly has her topsails furled because, judging from the way she heels and the spray shooting across her bow, she too is sailing in a high wind. Corners are ox-heads (Corner motif 50). Markings appear on the reverse of tile 2-A.

References: Geus, 1922, p. 81, no. X; Vis coll. sale, 1927, no. 249.
Similar tiles: Het Princessehof, 1980, nos. 1–120.

1-A man-of-war on a calm sea
1-B man-of-war shooting a cannon from starboard
1-C three-masted frigate displaying her starboard bow
1-D herring buss

2-A three-masted flute with furled topsails
2-B three-masted frigate
2-C merchant man running before the wind
2-D three-masted frigate (compare 1-C, but shows more detail)

3-A flute shooting cannons from both sides[4]
3-B ship shooting
3-C flute heeling in a high wind with furled topsails
3-D three-masted flute

4-A three-masted flute (similar to 3-A)
4-B three-masted vessel shooting stern cannon
4-C three-masted frigate (see 2-B)
4-D man-of-war shooting (see 1-A)

1. Preston, 1974, p. 87; De Groot and Vorstman, 1980, p. 280.
2. Donald Macintyre et al., *The Adventure of Sail: 1520–1914* (New York, 1972), fig. 19, illustrates *De Vergulde Zon,* a warship of Dunkirk, in two views by Willem van der Velde the Elder, c. 1645.
3. Pieter de la Court, 1662, noted: "Emanuel van Meteren says, that in the space of three days, in the year 1601, there sailed out of Holland to the eastward, between eight and nine hundred ships, and 1500 busses a herring fishing . . . that there are yearly taken and spent by the Hollanders more than 300,000 last of herrings, and other salt fish: and that the whale fishing to the northward, takes up above 12,000 men, which sail out of these countries."
4. See no. 176, n. 3.

2-A, reverse

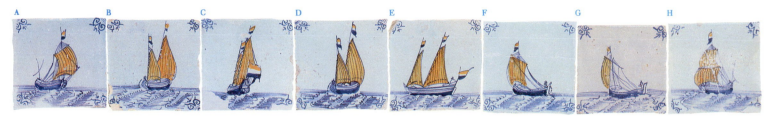

178. SAILING SHIPS
Harlingen
1650–1700
Blue and orange
Gift of Anthony N. B. Garvan

These ships, with their brilliantly colored orange sails, and orange, white, and blue flags waving from each mast,[1] are extremely rare; usually ship tiles are painted in blue only. These small, round-hulled, flat-bottomed ships were used on inland waters as cargo or fishing boats. The mainsail of the boats on tiles A, F, G, and H is a square sail and hinges around the single mast on a horizontal head-stick. The other ships (B–E) carry a mainsail and a foresail, each clearly laced to a mast. Tiles B and D were derived from identical *spons*, even to the detail of the mate urinating over the side.[2] The outlines of tiles G and F were also obviously obtained from the same *spons* but the difference in the skill of the painters is clearly demonstrated. The painter of tile G deleted the color on one half of the mainsail and the blue panel of the flag. The tile's appearance is not white, and shows no gloss; apparently he simply neglected to finish it. Corners are ox-heads (Corner motif 50).
References: Vis and Geus, 1926, pl. 83; Vis coll. sale, 1927, no. 286.
Similar tiles: Het Princessehof, 1980, no. 11; Amsterdam, Christie's, 1981, no. 419.

1. The flag of orange, white, and blue in horizontal bands was adopted by the water-beggars to prevent their being described as pirates. The earlier flag of red, white, and blue had been changed to demonstrate loyalty to the House of Orange. See Preston, 1974, p. 88.
2. Dubbe, 1972, p. 313, fig. 25.

179. PINKS
Harlingen?
1650–1700
Blue
Gift of Mrs. Francis P. Garvan

A group of four pinks,[1] used for fishing or as small coasters carrying goods and passengers on inland rivers and lakes and across the Zuider Zee, appear on these tiles. The two-masted ships on tiles A and D, with a fully blown square sail on each mast, sail on opposite tacks. The hoy on tile C carries a gaff sail on its single mast and a triangular foresail similar to those in nos. 176 B, 181 E, F; here, however, the workmanship is not of the same quality. The corners are ox-heads (Corner motif 50).
Reference: Vis coll. sale, 1927, no. 249.
Similar tiles: Het Princessehof, 1980, nos. 7–8; De Jonge, 1971, ill. 63.

1. Pinks can have from one to three masts, but usually have two and are square rigged. See De Groot and Vorstman, 1980, no. 89.

180. FISHING FLEET
1680–1750
Blue
Gift of Edward W. Bok

A smoke signal[1] on a water gap in the dike guides the herring fleet home. Corners are spider's-heads (Corner motif 58).
Similar tiles: Kaufmann, 1973, fig. 204.

1. Stettner, 1982, fig. 13. Stettner discusses smoke signals as guides for Northern European shipping illustrated by maritime prints and on tiles.

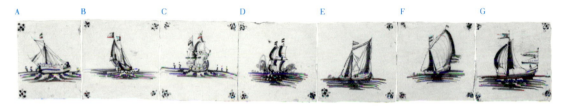

181. COASTAL VESSELS
1700–1800
Blue
Gift of Edward W. Bok

Coastal vessels, drawn carelessly with little attention to detail, are shown on these tiles: a passenger boat with many passengers crowded on the railing (A), moving under bare poles and heeling to port, probably sailing in a heavy storm; a two-masted yacht with a high, carved stern (B); possibly a flute (C); a two-master, foreshortened, seen from her port bow sailing toward the viewer and shooting off cannon from both sides (D); a *kaag* (E) and a galliot (F), two other inland vessels, fitted with leeboards; possibly a hoy (G), with two triangular flags of enormous size at her stern, sailing before the wind. The water, too, is not rendered realistically, and on a number of the tiles, does not extend to the full width of the surface. Corners are spider's-heads (Corner motif 58).

182. SEA CREATURES
Rotterdam
1600–1625
Polychrome
Gift of Anthony N. B. Garvan

These three early polychrome tiles have extremely unusual compositions: a large, blue-green, cresting wave curls along the bottom edge of the tile; behind this wave, the sea extends in a horizontal band marked by continu-

ous lines drawn in a scallop pattern; and above, the sky stretches up and is colored by lines of blue across the top edge of the tile. Against this backdrop swim weapon-wielding tritons with extremely well-defined physiques and curling fish tails, and a large fish. These tiles, comparable to nos. 153 and 175, were inserted as baseboards.

Reference: Vis and Geus, 1926, pls. 17a, b.
Similar tiles: Scheurleer, 1970, figs. 15–19.

146

A

B

C

183. ARION PLAYING THE LYRE
Rotterdam
1600–1625
Polychrome
Gift of Anthony N. B. Garvan

Another early baseboard tile, like nos. 153, 175, 182, and 184, depicts the blue and orange muscular figure of Arion, a mythical creature,[1] riding a blue dolphin in a seascape setting. Arion, a poet thrown overboard by murderous

mariners, was rescued by a dolphin, whom he had charmed with his sweet voice and lyre playing.[2] This image is based on a print of Arion on a dolphin by Jan Muller (fig. 50).
References: Vis and Geus, 1926, pl. 16 (reversed); Vis coll. sale, 1927, no. 245.
Similar tiles: Geus, 1931, fig. 10; Scheurleer, 1970, fig. 7; Korf, 1976, p. 82; Amsterdam, Sotheby, cat. 337, 1981, no. 220.

1. Ovid, *Fasti,* II, pp. 83–118.
2. John Vinycomb, *Fictitious and Symbolic Creatures in Art* (Detroit, 1969), pp. 260–61.

184. TRITON
Rotterdam
1600–1625
Polychrome
Gift of Anthony N. B. Garvan

A triton blows on the tail of a green serpent as if it were a horn, and in response, a cloud of blue smoke issues from the serpent's mouth. Outlined in blue, the triton is inpainted in hues of orange for flesh, purple for genitalia, and green for his seaweed-like hair and fish tails. This fanciful sea creature is drawn from Jacob de Gheyn's *Neptune's Kingdom* (fig. 49) and is one of a series of mythological tiles in the collection (see nos. 182, 183) produced in Rotterdam during the first quarter of the seventeenth century.[1]

References: Vis and Geus, 1926, pl. 16; Vis coll. sale, 1927, no. 245.

Similar tiles: Scheurleer, 1970, fig. 6; De Jonge, 1971, ill. 28e.

1. Scheurleer, 1970, pp. 18, 35.

185. WHALE AND DOLPHIN
Rotterdam
1600–1625
Polychrome
Gift of Anthony N. B. Garvan

A fantastical whale and a dolphin are painted on these early and rare tiles. Like many early polychrome marine tiles, these portray the creatures against a fully developed background of sky and sea, and the horizontal blue stripes in the sky, as well as the green-blue sea, create a strong horizontal composition. By depicting the creatures in profile, the painter was able to emphasize their long, curling, blue and gold tails. Both animals are shown at the same size and with similar detail; only the head and prominent water spout distinguish the whale from the dolphin. Whales were beached on the Dutch North Sea coast in 1520, 1522, and again in 1601. The arrival of these unusual creatures was interpreted as a sign from the heavens, and given prognostic meaning.[1] Crowds assembled to view the spectacle, and artists depicted the events, seen, for example, in Jan Saenredam's engraving *Sperm Whale Stranded at Beverwijk, December 20, 1601* (Rijksmuseum, Amsterdam).

Reference: Vis and Geus, 1926, pl. 17.
Similar tiles: Scheurleer, 1970, fig. 3; Kaufmann, 1973, fig. 77; Amsterdam, Sotheby, cat. 337, 1981, nos. 212–14.

1. Van de Waal, 1952, vol. 1, p. 20.

A, reverse

A, reverse   B, reverse

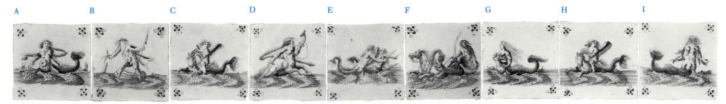

186. SEA CREATURES
1650–1700
Blue
Gift of Mrs. Francis P. Garvan

Characterizing this panel of eighteen tiles is the distinctive V pattern of the waves, which serves as a horizontal device linking the tiles together. The frolicking sea creatures, however, are individual images, which do not relate to one another through their actions or attributes. Several tiles are similar, demonstrating the process of tile duplication with the use of transfer patterns (*sponsen;* see tiles I, L); often, however, certain details are lost or misread in the process. The centaur on tile D, for example, lacks the harpoon that he holds in his outstretched right hand in other representations (no. 193 C). The tile showing Neptune being driven by two hippocampi (F) differs from other images in the collection (nos. 193 D, G); in those he is depicted in an identical pose, but is bearded and is pulled by only one spotted hippocampus. The corners are spider's-heads (Corner motif 58).

A   merman
B   man with a javelin standing on a scallop shell
C   cupid riding a hippocampus
D   leaping centaur
E   mermen fighting with swords
F   Neptune riding the waves
G   mermaid with child
H   cupid riding a hippocampus
I   merman

148

187. MERMAN AND VENUS
1650–1700
Blue
Gift of Mrs. Francis P. Garvan

Although these tiles of a merman holding a small animal aloft and Neptune supporting a nude Venus on his fishtail while stroking her leg (see no. 192 B) appear similar to those in the previous panel, the color of the glaze is considerably lighter and the workmanship is by a different hand. Corners are small spider's-heads (Corner motif 58).
Similar tiles: Amsterdam, Sotheby, cat. 337, 1981, no. 175.

188. SEA CREATURES
1650–1700
Blue
Gift of Mrs. Francis P. Garvan

The creatures disporting themselves on these tiles are a cupid riding a dolphin (A), an armed triton (B), a mounted hippocampus (C), and a merman (D). The merman plays a violin, an image as common on tiles as on seventeenth-century maps and prints, and similar to one depicted on a 1570 map by Ortelius.[1] Coming from another print, one by Ulysses Aldrovandi,[2] is the hippocampus, the half-horse, half-fish mount of Neptune. Cupid, son of Venus as well as the messenger of love, rides the dolphin, the attribute of Venus, and holds a flaming bowl, symbol of sacred love.[3] Corners are spider's-heads (Corner motif 58).
Similar tiles: Scheurleer, 1970, fig. 40t; Amsterdam, Sotheby, cat. 337, 1981, p. 52, no. 175.

1. Gerhart Egger, ed., *Theatrum orbis terrarum* (Vienna, 1970), pl. 13.
2. Ulysses Aldrovandi, *Monstrum historia* (1590?).
3. Knipping, 1961, p. 36.

189. NEPTUNE
1650–1700
Purple
Gift of Anthony N. B. Garvan

Unlike many depictions of Neptune on tiles (see no. 193 D), this tile portrays the god of the seas resplendent with all of his attributes: triton, scallop shell, and a pair of hippocampi. Corners are ox-heads (Corner motif 51).
Similar tiles: Scheurleer, 1970, fig. 39g.

J   man with a javelin standing on
a scallop shell
K   cupid riding a swan chariot
L   merman (see I)
M   Fortuna
N   female figure riding a dolphin
O   Venus with Neptune
P   cupid with a smoking torch
(Eternal Love)
Q   leaping centaur
R   Venus enthroned

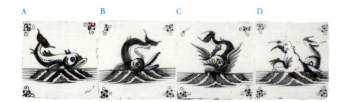

190. FISH
1650–1700
Blue
Gift of Anthony N. B. Garvan

A fantastical fish-tailed walrus (D)
and a dolphin (A), whale (C), and
swordfish (B) are painted with
broad strokes of color and generalized details. Although the three
creatures resemble those found
in the compendiums of fish and
sea life popular in the period,[1]
there are no direct parallels for
these images. The corners are
spider's-heads (Corner motif 58).
Reference: Vis and Geus, 1933, pl.
12b.

1. See, for example, Nicolaus de
Bruyn, *Libellus varia genera
piscium complectens.*

191. MERMAN AND MERMAID
1650–1700
Blue
Gift of Mrs. Francis P. Garvan

The figures of a merman and
mermaid are depicted in profile,
an unusual viewpoint as most sea
creatures on tiles are shown
either frontally or in a three-
quarter pose. The merman holds
a flaming torch; the mermaid,
with a distaff in her hand, en-
gages in the simple chore of spinning thread. This is but one of the
common activities of mermaids
on tiles; they also hold looking
glasses, play instruments, and
blow horns.[1] Although these tiles
are painted in a similar style with
the same white-crested sea, they

are clearly not by the same hand.
The tile with the mermaid is
probably a second; its lower corners, larger than the standard ox-
heads of the upper ones (Corner
motif 50), were distorted during
firing.
Similar tiles: Scheurleer, 1970, fig.
41e.

1. Scheurleer, 1970, p. 27.

A   B

192. FORTUNA AND VENUS
1650–1700
Blue
Gift of Mrs. Francis P. Garvan

Fortuna and Venus are the subjects of these vigorously painted tiles, which display an unusual contrast of patterns created by the overall stippling technique used to depict the waves, floating seaweed, and stag. Corners are ox-head motifs (Corner motif 50).

The pose of the nude figure of Fortuna seated on a scallop-shell throne pulled through the water by a stag (A) is characteristically associated with Venus;[1] here, however, the figure is identified as Fortuna by the ball on which she is seated—her attribute and the symbol of shifting human fortunes.[2] A seductively posed Venus, supported on Neptune's fish-tail, is depicted on the second tile (B). Cestus, the girdle about her

waist that identifies her as Venus, is known to give beauty, grace, and elegance to even the most deformed human, exciting love and rekindling extinguished ardors.[3] Markings appear on the reverse of tile A.

A, reverse

References: Geus, 1931, fig. 73; Vis and Geus, 1933, pl. 11.
Similar tiles: Hoynck, 1920, p. 239, fig. 271; Berendsen, et al., 1967, repro. p. 188; Scheurleer, 1970, fig. 38 (reversed).

1. Scheurleer, 1970, p. 25.
2. Cesare Ripa, *Baroque and Rococo Pictorial Imagery*, reprint of *Iconologia*, 1644 (New York, 1971), p. 152.
3. J. E. Zimmerman, *Dictionary of Classical Mythology* (New York, 1964), pp. 25–26.

A   B   C   D   E   F   G   H

193. SEA CREATURES
1650–1700
Blue
Gift of Mrs. Francis P. Garvan

Four of these tiles depict sea creatures wielding sabers, swords, spears, and daggers as if to strike unseen opponents (A, B, C, E), common figures on period maps[1] and ornamental prints.

Two other tiles depict Neptune (D, G), identified by the half-horse, half-fish creature, the hippocampus, who pulls his shell chariot. These identical images were taken from similar *sponsen*, but the style in which they are rendered is significantly different and they are obviously by different hands. The corners are ox-heads (Corner motif 50). Markings appear on the reverse of tiles B and F.

Similar tiles: Amsterdam, Sotheby, cat. 327, 1981, nos. 175, 176.

1. See Royal Geographical Society, London, *The Map of the World on Mercator's Projection by Jodocus Hondius, Amsterdam, 1608* (London, 1927).

B, reverse   F, reverse

194. SEA CREATURES
1650–1700
Blue
Gift of Anthony N. B. Garvan

Europa (B), Neptune (D), Chastity (A), sea creatures (C, E), and figures who may be Venus and Neptune (F) frolic in the seas. Loosely painted, their curvilinear bodies and exuberant poses are set against a curling pattern of waves. Notable among these classical groups are Europa and the Bull (B); in this representation of the myth, a crowned Europa is being carried off by a fishtailed bull, a somewhat fantastical animal. Corners are ox-heads (Corner motif 50).
Similar tiles: Scheurleer, 1970, figs. 39j, 41r, 43o, 47f; Kaufmann, 1973, fig. 79; Amsterdam, Sotheby, cat. 327, 1981, no. 176.

195. SEA CREATURES
1650–1700
Blue
Gift of Anthony N. B. Garvan

Unlike many earlier representations of sea creatures on tiles, these depictions are generalized and quite awkwardly painted. The seas on which they swim are little more than horizontal lines slashed across the tiles. The figures of a merman with a harpoon (A), hippocampus (B), dolphin (C), and a man riding a dolphin and holding a flaming torch (D) also lack the little details that add visual interest to such subjects. Corners are ox-heads (Corner motif 50).

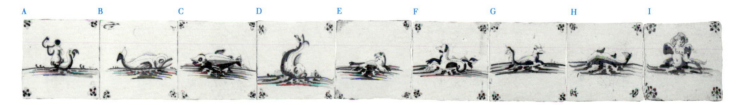

196. SEA CREATURES
1680–1750
Blue
Gift of Edward W. Bok

Painted in a very cursory fashion with little attention to detail, these images of a mermaid blowing a horn (A), dolphins (B, D), a swordfish (C), walrus (E), seadog (F), horned sea animal (G), winged mermaid (I), and a seal (H) seem to be based on the sea creatures that appear in the maps of Jodocus Hondius, for example, his world map of 1611. The unusual rendering of the sea with the waves emanating from the creatures is a convention that was first used on maps and then taken over by the painters of ship tiles. Corners are spider's-heads (Corner motif 58).
Similar tiles: Vis and Geus, 1933, pl. 11a; Scheurleer, 1970, fig. 37l.

"Haarlem" Type

FIG. 53 Italian majolica dish,
probably from Faenza, 1600–1620
Victoria and Albert Museum,
London

FIG. 54 Dutch majolica dish
painted in blue and orange,
1600-1625
Rijksmuseum, Amsterdam

A group of ornamental seventeenth-century tiles with a distinct vocabulary and independent style of decoration has become known to collectors as "Haarlem" tiles. Haarlem had been a thriving town since the twelfth century and became the most important industrial center in Holland before 1600. At least three major potteries were flourishing there before 1570, and seven, before 1620.[1] These had attracted refugee potters from Antwerp in the southern Netherlands, a city in which immigrant Italian potters had settled in the early years of the sixteenth century. Excavations of a dike in Haarlem have unearthed kiln wasters from which it can be deduced that faience workshops there did indeed decorate their wares with the *aigrette* borders[2] characteristic of this production, but whether all the tiles and dishes with this type of decoration were made in Haarlem still remains uncertain.

The characteristics shared by "Haarlem" tiles, which presumably were executed in workshops that specialized in dinnerware, are a tin glaze that is of a purer white than is generally found on tiles; colors that are subtle and used sparingly, lack gloss, feel dull to the touch, and are slightly raised; decoration that is completely symmetrical, with strong accents on horizontal, vertical, and diagonal lines; free-floating center decoration; and spiral flourishes. The *aigrette* border—as this spiral, feathered wreath is commonly called by tile collectors—appeared in the late-sixteenth and early seventeenth centuries in Faenza and Deruta in Italy framing portraits, amorini, and putti on dishes (fig. 53). *Aigrette* wreaths also became quite popular during the 1620s to 1640s in Holland, where they were also used to decorate dishes (fig. 54)[3] and tiles, framing animals and amorini or putti more often than landscapes. These unusual tiles, which cannot be grouped in any specific subject category, are described separately here. It is unusual to find polychrome tiles that were produced after 1625.

1. Van Dam, 1982, *Geleyersgoet,*
p. 6.
2. Korf, 1968.
3. Hudig, 1929, figs. 6, 15, 59.

197. ORNAMENTAL LANDSCAPES, FRUIT, AND FLOWERS WITH AIGRETTE WREATHS
Haarlem?
1625–50
Blue with brown accents
Gift of Anthony N. B. Garvan

Each tile in this panel is decorated with a miniscule blue landscape with such vignettes as an insect (1-B, 1-D), a butterfly (1-E),

a lighthouse on a dike (3-A), a man with a fishing pole on a bridge (3-B, 5-C), a barn (3-C, 5-A), a well (3-E), grass (4-C), a church with ruins of the tower (5-B), a lighthouse (5-D), and fruit and flowers. They are framed by a feathered, or *aigrette*, wreath, providing a striking contrast between the elaborate design of the *aigrette* and the sketchy, free-floating central image.

Reference: Vis coll. sale, 1927, no. 40.
Similar tiles: Hudig, 1929, pp. 159–61, fig. 61; Amsterdam, Sotheby, cat. 327, 1981, no. 62.

197a. ORNAMENTAL WITH AIGRETTE WREATHS
Haarlem?
1625–50
Blue with brown accents
Gift of Anthony N. B. Garvan

Not illustrated. (Two tiles similar to 2-B and 3-D.)

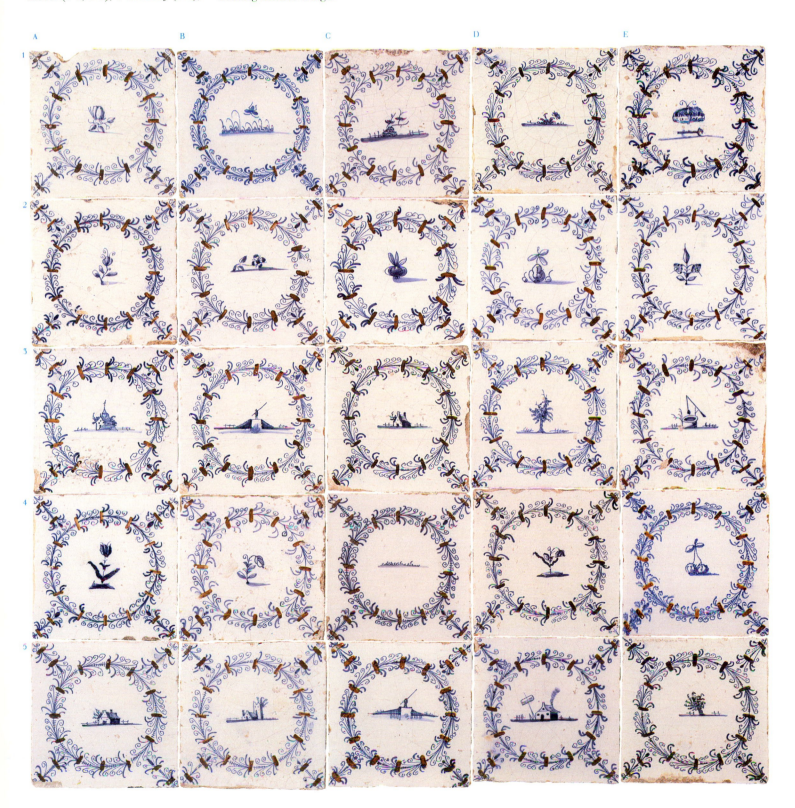

198. ORNAMENTAL STARS, CRUCIFORMS, AND FLEURS-DE-LIS
Haarlem?
1625–50
Polychrome
Gift of Mrs. Francis P. Garvan

In the center of each tile is a green eight-pointed star, embellished with eight blue crosses each showing three blue dots, similar in configuration to the cruciform corner motif (Corner motif 44). Within the star is an eight-petaled rosette filled with alternating burnt-orange and white petals, surrounding a burnt-orange circle. At the center of each of the sides is a blue spiraled flourish, emanating from a blue-accented, brown half circle. The fleur-de-lis corner (Corner motif 27) is burnt-orange with blue bars and dots. A complete pattern is formed when four tiles are joined together. On the reverse of tile 2-B are the initials A. C.
References: Geus, 1921, no. XV; Vis and Geus, 1926, pl. 59; Vis coll. sale, 1927, no. 263.

154

2-B, reverse

199. ORNAMENTAL STARS, CRUCIFORMS, AND FLEURS-DE-LIS
Haarlem?
1625–50
Polychrome
Gift of Mrs. Francis P. Garvan

"Haarlem" ornamental tiles are painted in several, slightly different, color combinations. This panel is quite similar to the previous one, but the petals in the center of the green stars, burnt-orange there, are of a lighter, more yellowish-orange color here.
Reference: Vis coll. sale, 1927, no. 264.

200. ORNAMENTAL
Haarlem?
1625–50
Blue with burnt-orange accents
Gift of Mrs. Francis P. Garvan

The entire design is blue except
for the small circle in the very
center, four center petals, and the
half circles at the sides of each
tile, which are burnt-orange. The
four petals forming part of the
central eight-petaled rosette are
left white in this panel.

201. ORNAMENTAL
Haarlem?
1625–50
Blue with burnt-orange accents
Gift of Mrs. Francis P. Garvan

The tiles are similar to those in
the previous panels, but here the
four petals in the center rosette
are striped and dotted in blue.
Reference: Vis coll. sale, 1927, no.
263.
Similar tiles: Korf, 1979, fig. 255.

202. ORNAMENTAL
Haarlem?
1625–50
Blue with yellow accents
Gift of Mrs. Francis P. Garvan

These tiles resemble closely the
previous panels, but here the
central circle, four petals of the
rosette, and the half circles at the
outer edges of the tiles are yellow.

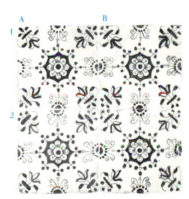

203. ORNAMENTAL
Haarlem?
1625–50
Blue
Gift of Mrs. Francis P. Garvan

The entire design is blue with
four of the center petals striped
rather than colored as in the
other panels.
Similar tiles: Korf, 1979, fig. 255.

Decorative

All tiles are decorative in that they form designs; the tiles included here, however, form geometric or stylized rather than figurative or realistic patterns. Seventeenth-century decorative tiles reflect patterns used earlier in other decorative arts, such as the Burgundian fleurs-de-lis (no. 204); stylized foliage (nos. 205–7), a nonfigurative form used throughout the Islamic world; and the papyrus roll (no. 207, 1-B), an adaptation of a Chinese motif. Their colors are predominantly blue (no. 206) and sometimes include touches of yellow (nos. 204, 205).

Eighteenth- and nineteenth-century tiles are decorated with abstract motifs, and coloration is primarily purple (no. 214). At this time, tiles were no longer in great demand due to competition from other styles of interior decoration. Tile producers tried to adapt designs in vogue in other mediums, such as marble (no. 209), linen damask, and plaster ceiling decoration (no. 210). When applied to ceramic tiles, however, these designs remained stilted and static, and were less than successful.

Marble, which had to be imported and was therefore expensive in the Netherlands, was imitated on tiles from the middle of the seventeenth century to the eighteenth. Such tiles were frequently used in fireplaces or as baseboards. The tortoise-shell effect was obtained with slips of various colors superimposed in layers and then combed to achieve the desired swirls, whereas the marbleized effect was achieved by "painting" covered by a tin glaze. A glossy finish was achieved with the application of clear lead glaze on the tortoise-shell tiles.

Precise dating of decorative tiles is difficult. A purchase agreement of 1787 from the tileworks of Jan Aelmis (see no. 220)[1] includes "tortoise shell and flame-colored" tiles; an inventory from nearly a century later lists 250,000 tiles, including "Jerusalem feathers [no. 210] . . . , imitations of marble . . . , tortoise shell. . . ."[2]

1. Hoynck, 1920, p. 187.
2. Ibid., p. 190.

204. FLEURS-DE-LIS
1550–1600
Blue with yellow accents
Gift of Mrs. Francis P. Garvan

The decoration of fleurs-de-lis, which was used earlier on inlaid floor tiles, forms a continuous pattern on each tile, but the complete design becomes apparent only when four or more tiles are conjoined. The design of circles and polygonal forms is executed in reserve technique with deep-blue painted around the white fleur-de-lis. The same design was used in both blue and poly-chrome,[1] and was the first of the old motifs to be painted in blue after the reserve technique was no longer used. Tile 2-A, on which the glaze ran during firing in the kiln, is considered a rarity today, whereas in the seventeenth century such misfired tiles were mixed with a kiln load of first quality.

1. See Korf, 1979, fig. 105; Peelen, 1922, p. 30, nos. A706 (blue), A431, A583 (polychrome), fig. 7.

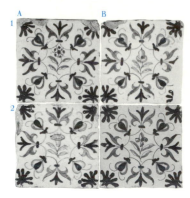

158

205. ACANTHUS LEAVES (PALMETTE)
c. 1620
Blue with yellow accents
Gift of Mrs. Francis P. Garvan

In each tile, a four-sided symmetrical pattern of stylized acanthus-type leaves, called palmettes in the tile trade, is grouped around an eight-petaled flower with a slightly raised blue circle in the center. Half of a similar flower lies along each edge, forming a rosette when two tiles are joined.
Similar tiles: Hoynck, 1920, fig. 265 (nearly identical tiles, from Rotterdam, but with orange accents); Peelen, 1922, p. 36, no. A878, fig. 15; Korf, 1969, fig. 42; Korf, 1979, fig. 194.

206. STYLIZED VINES
1620–25
Blue
Gift of Mrs. Francis P. Garvan

In the center of each tile is a different flower framed by a vine, which connects the symmetrical decoration of alternating leaves and flowers. Each flower is balanced atop a stem with four leaves. The four stylized flowers in the outer ring of each tile are pointed toward the corners and are interspersed with four pairs of leaves, each supporting another abstract flower. The highly stylized design is enlivened by the variation between light and deep dark-blue. The corners are slightly raised and very deep blue.
Reference: Geus, 1931, fig. 41.
Similar tiles: Amsterdam, Sotheby, cat. 337, 1981, no. 204.

207. PLANT FORMS AND CHINESE SCROLL
Haarlem?
1620–40
Blue
Gift of Mrs. Francis P. Garvan

Although these four tiles do not belong to the same series, they do have common characteristics. The design is geometric and symmetrical, accentuating the horizontal, vertical, and diagonal axes. The compositions consist of stylized plant forms, with the exception of tile 1-B, which is reminiscent of Chinese decoration. This design shows the strong influence on tile decoration of Chinese blue-and-white porcelain, imported during the reign of the Wan Li Emperor (1573–1619). The design of tiles 1-A and 2-B consists of a rosette framed by a double-scalloped roundel surrounded by a twelve-pointed star; the star is formed by four holly leaves and eight smooth-rimmed,

pointed leaf shapes. Tile 2-A, an amalgamation of Oriental, Dutch, and Italian motifs, achieves a remarkably harmonious result. Corner motifs, although not identical, are all based on the ox-head embellished with the cruciform (which itself developed from the ox-head). When four corner motifs are joined together, they match the design used in the center of "Haarlem" tiles (see no. 198); likewise, spiral motifs surrounding the center decorations on tiles 2-A and 1-B are similar to those on "Haarlem" tiles (see no. 199).
Similar tiles: Vis and Geus, 1926, pl. 64; Korf, 1969, fig. 43; Korf, 1979, fig. 200; Amsterdam, Sotheby, cat. 337, 1981, no. 97; Het Princessehof, Leeuwarden, 8461-1-6.

208. TORTOISE SHELL
1625–1700
Black, brown, and yellow
Gift of Mrs. Francis P. Garvan

Judging by coloration, clay body, and size, these four tortoise-shell tiles come from different workshops and were made at different times.
Reference: Vis and Geus, 1933, pl. 59.

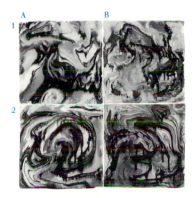

209. MARBLEIZED
1650–1700
Green, brown, and black
Gift of Mrs. Francis P. Garvan

These tiles, which differ from those of the previous panel, are evidently "seconds"; the dark-colored slip matured earlier in the firing than the other colors, liquefying and dripping over them.
Reference: Vis and Geus, 1933, pl. 59.

210. JERUSALEM FEATHERS
Utrecht?
1750–1800
Blue with yellow luster
Gift of Mrs. Francis P. Garvan

This type of Dutch tile is known as "Jerusalem feathers." Although generally believed to have been produced in Utrecht,[1] they are also mentioned in inventories from Rotterdam.[2] These tiles are decorated with symmetrical leafy scrolls of yellow luster outlined in blue *trek*, but the outline appears green because of the blending of blue and yellow glazes. Yellow luster, unusual in Dutch tiles, was produced from finely ground metal particles. Because such luster could not withstand firing in a high-temperature kiln, the tile's second firing was in a muffle kiln at a lower temperature; such kilns were used in the Netherlands from 1680 to 1880 usually for faience ware and only rarely for tiles. Tile 1-A turned out as intended, 2-B was partially suc-

cessful, and 2-A is decidedly a "second."
Reference: Vis coll. sale, 1927, no. 258.
Similar tiles: Korf, 1979, fig. 626.

1. De Jonge, 1971, p. 123, ill. 151b, c; Lane, 1960, p. 61.
2. W. van Traa bought De Blompot tile pottery in Rotterdam in 1843, which in the seventeenth century had belonged to the Aelmis family, and sold 250,000 tiles that year. In 1845, 469,457 tiles were sold in sixteen towns in Holland, four in Belgium, and two in Germany (which are mentioned by name). Van Traa's inventory records "blue, brown, and manganese landscapes, gilt leather, Jerusalem feathers . . . , imitations of marble (blue and brown), tortoise shell. . . ." A shortage of schooled labor forced Van Traa to close the tile pottery in 1852; the sale of tiles in stock lasted until 1873. See Hoynck, 1920, p. 190.

159

211. NAME PLAQUE
Rotterdam
Workshop of Johannes van der Wolk
1780–1800
Purple
Gift of Anthony N. B. Garvan

The clearly painted name of the workshop owner, Johannes van der Wolk, is surrounded by a wreath bound at the bottom by a bow. The leaves decorating the wreath decrease in size toward

the top, which has been cropped. This tile was once believed to be the signature for *The Battle of Ramillies* (no. 220), but its size and, more convincingly its glaze color, make this impossible. On March 19, 1784, Johannes van der Wolk bought a tile pottery with a house and yard for 12,045 guilders: 4,045 guilders cash, the rest in a note. This sum included 300 guilders for tools. He sold the pottery in 1841. Van der Wolk was elected *hoofdman* (dean) of the

master tile painters of the Guild of Saint Luke eight times: on October 10, 1787, with Jan Aelmis; kept on in October 1790; reappointed in 1793 and kept on in 1794; and reappointed in 1797, 1803, 1806, and 1807.[1]
Reference: Vis coll. sale, 1927, no. 177.

1. Hoynck, 1920, pp. 158, 158, 329; Vis and Geus, 1933, p. 87; De Jonge, 1971, p. 87.

212. SUN, MOON, AND STARS
(ROZENSTER)
Friesland
1750–1850
Blue
Gift of Mrs. Francis P. Garvan

Alternate configuration

These tiles in combination form a geometric design composed of eight-petaled rosettes. The rosettes differ in size and shape, and form varying patterns depending on the configuration of tiles within the panel: the eye may focus on the sun in the center, with moonrays on the sides and quarter-stars in the corners, or on the moon in the center with sunrays on the sides (the stars' position remains unchanged).[1]

This panel is composed of tiles made in different workshops, primarily in Friesland, during the eighteenth and nineteenth centuries. It is evident that tile 2-A, for example, is not part of the original combination: the quarter-star reveals slight variations in size and border element.
Similar tiles: Altonaer Museum, 1965, pl. XII, no. 966; Scheurleer, 1966, figs. 6a, 7a; Kaufmann, 1973, fig. 283.

1. Amsterdam, Sotheby, cat. 337, 1981, no. 106.

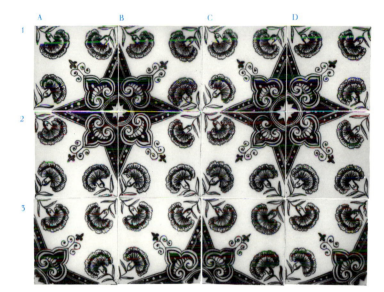

213. CARNATIONS AND STAR
c. 1800
Blue
Gift of Edward W. Bok

Each tile in this panel is decorated with a carnation in three corners and one-quarter of a four-pointed star in the fourth. Four conjoined tiles complete a star, which encloses a smaller eight-pointed white star encircled by a blue medallion. Between each two points of the larger star is an irregular heart-shaped form—reminiscent of the Chinese *ju-i* motif—extended by a double ox-head-like scroll embellished with an abstract cloverleaf. This design is found in other decorative arts and was borrowed for tiles.
Similar tiles: Scheurleer, 1966, p. 27, figs. 6b, 7b; Korf, 1979, fig. 628.

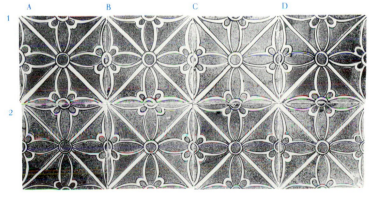

214. GEOMETRIC DESIGNS
1750–1850
Purple
Gift of Edward W. Bok

The spattered purple tiles of this panel are decorated with elongated cruciform ellipses separated by white diagonals in reserve technique.[1]
Similar tiles: Jessel, 1962, pl. 53; Elling, 1978, fig. 29.

1. P. J. Tichelaar describes this technique in Pluis, 1975, pp. 5–9.

Tile Pictures

FIG. 55 Staircase of Nieborów palace near Warsaw, decorated to the domed ceiling with blue pastoral tiles, c. 1765

1. Now in Museum Boymans–van Beuningen, Rotterdam.
2. Hoynck, 1920, pp. 39–43.
3. This has variously been interpreted as a biblical allegory; see De Goederen, 1962.
4. Victoria and Albert Museum, London; see Vis and Geus, 1933, pl. 2.
5. De Jonge, 1971, ills. 41, 42.
6. Many Aelmis sketches have been preserved in the Gemeentelijke Archiefdienst, Rotterdam. Several of the tile pictures are in the Historisch Museum der Stad Rotterdam, the Rijksmuseum, Amsterdam, and the Victoria and Albert Museum, London. See also Hoynck, 1920, pp. 176–90, 323, for Aelmis genealogy; Hoynck points out that Johannis Aelmis was elected dean (*hoofdman*) of the Guild of Saint Luke nineteen times between 1709 and 1742. After the Aelmis family, two more owners kept the workshop in full production until 1852, i.e., for 160 years in all.

The earliest tile pictures appeared in the form of corner tablets and shop signs. The oldest of the few signs known today[1] was made in Rotterdam in 1594–95 for the facade of a house owned by a sea captain and his wife, who sold tiles and majolica on the premises.[2] Both the house and the framed polychrome picture composed of twenty tiles were called *In duysent vreesen* (In thousand fears), a name readily understood by contemporaries who saw the picture—comprising a warrior, lamb, wolf, bear, griffin, and another man—as symbolic of the many dangers threatening the young Republic of the United Netherlands.[3] Another well-published sign, this one from the facade of a seed dealer in Gorinchem in the first quarter of the seventeenth century,[4] is composed of twelve polychrome tiles with ornamental tiled borders and entitled *In de 3 blompotten* (In the three flowerpots). This sign depicts three vases, each filled with five flowers, and the coats of arms of the city of Gorinchem and the Van Arkel family. Both signs were advertisements for products sold on the premises.

However, tile pictures—those with each tile carrying only a part of an overall composition as opposed to tile panels made up of many similar tiles—today are usually thought of as those embellishing interiors. They were first made in pairs, each three or four tiles wide and twelve tiles high, to be used on each side of a fireplace, replacing the earlier carved sandstone pillars after the first quarter of the seventeenth century. Some pictures were decorated with ornamentation resembling the pillars they had replaced; others showed princely figures[5] or floral still lifes. These were used inside the hearth and were eight tiles wide by twelve tiles high, the height of most fireplaces. Substituting tile pictures for paintings, however, became more and more fashionable during the eighteenth and nineteenth centuries. In Rotterdam, tile painters created floral still lifes and seascapes based on the popularity of these subjects in other mediums. Tile pictures with flower vases were made in large numbers and in different sizes in Delft, Rotterdam, Makkum, and Harlingen; many of the best were the work of the Aelmis family, from 1692 to 1787 owners of De Blompot (The Flowerpot) in Rotterdam.[6] De Blompot was then sold and continued operating until 1852, but without either the success or artistic achievement of the previous owners.

Between the late seventeenth and the early nineteenth centuries, De Blompot and other Dutch tileworks obtained important commissions for the decoration of castles and churches in Spain and Portugal,[7] where the demand was for large scenes in blue or purple. Large tile pictures were also exported to chateaux in France such as Rambouillet (1715–30) and the Trianon at Versailles (1670–87), which were decorated with tiles throughout. In Germany, two castles at Nymphenburg near Munich (1716–39) and others near Brühl (1729–48)[8] were beautified with tile pictures. Several castles in Poland were extensively decorated with tiles in the mid-eighteenth century, although the tiles served a different decorative function than in the Netherlands (fig. 9). The walls and ceiling of the grand staircase in Nieborów palace of the Radziwill princes were lined with tiles, as was the landing and an adjacent room (fig. 55 and no. 134).

While castles, palaces, and churches in western and northern Europe were being decorated with tiled walls in the French style, the residents of the countryside in northern Holland and Friesland were embellishing their houses with tile pictures of more familiar subjects.[9] Farmers preferred pictures of horses, cows, cats, or canaries (fig. 10); much admired also were floral pictures which fit inside the fireplace or else were set into walls along with plain tiles, producing an effect similar to that of a painting hung on a white plastered wall. In Holland and Friesland it remained fashionable to decorate farmhouses, especially kitchens, with such tile pictures until late in the nineteenth century.

Council chambers of town halls were occasionally adorned with tile pictures or with mantel flower pieces, and taverns frequently had entire walls enlivened with seascapes (for example, De Prins Inn in Makkum) or harbor views.

7. Simões, 1959; De Jonge, 1971, pp. 109–14.
8. De Jonge, 1971, pp. 90–98; 104–8.
9. Exceptional for the Netherlands is a tiled room in the French style designed by Adam Sybel for a house in Workum and produced by the Tichelaar works in Makkum in 1799 (now in the Fries Museum, Leeuwarden).

215. URN WITH FLOWERS
Delft or Rotterdam
1710–50
Blue and purple
Gift of Anthony N. B. Garvan

This large tile picture features a flower-filled urn resting on a pedestal, with birds and insects darting around the bouquet. Fauna, flora, and meander patterns on the vase and pedestal are purple, but the foliage and most of the surface area of the vase and pedestal are blue. Above the rim of the vase are densely packed peonies and thickly striated leaves; smaller, more delicate flora such as tulips, carnations, and fernlike foliage are more spaciously disposed in the upper section. Exotic birds and insects provide an oriental touch. This piece is related to a group of flower vase tableaux discussed in detail by De Jonge.[1] Produced mainly in Delft, these tile pictures were primarily destined for royal residences in Germany and France. The best feature a soaring, pyramidal bouquet set in an elegantly tapered, elaborately decorated vase resting on a marbleized pedestal.[2] This panel is a simplified version of this type; others include a pair of floral tile pictures in the Victoria and Albert Museum[3] and one formerly in the collection of D.H.G. Bolten in Veere, Zeeland.[4] Features this panel share with those in London include the floral arrangement and the decorated pedestal supporting the vase. The pair of birds corresponds more closely to those in the Bolten piece.
Reference: Vis coll. sale, 1927, no. 287.

1. De Jonge, 1959; De Jonge, 1971, pp. 104–8.
2. Such tableaux are found in the Rijksmuseum, Amsterdam, and in the Nationalmuseet, Copenhagen; see De Jonge, 1971, ills. 137a, b.
3. Like the Museum's panel, both examples were originally part of the Vis collection; see Victoria and Albert Museum, 1923, p. 32 pl. 132; Vis and Geus, 1933, pl. 52; De Jonge, 1971, ill. 139a.
4. De Jonge, 1971, ill. 139b.

164

216. URN WITH FLOWERS
1700–1750
Polychrome
Purchased: Edgar V. Seeler Fund

Elegantly drawn striped tulips, peonies, columbines, and unidentified flowers, leaves, and vines are contained in an urn on a pedestal. A dragonfly dives from the upper-left corner, a butterfly from the right.

165

217. PAIR OF FLOWER VASES
Friesland, Makkum?
1750–1800
Blue
Gift of Mrs. Francis P. Garvan

This pair of tile pictures features matching ornamental urns filled with bouquets of lush, distinctly outlined flowers. Heavier, fuller blossoms, such as cabbage roses, are clustered at the center of each bouquet; a curving stalk of hollyhock divides the arrangement. Marigolds, small roses, and large tulips are among the flowers which complete the composition. Playful, exotic fowl—parrots or peacocks—flank the base of the urn, following a tradition that first appeared in ornamental flower prints of the early seventeenth century, such as those by Claes Jansz Visscher (see fig. 26).

The urn rests on a concave, marbleized base containing a cartouche depicting a pastoral scene. *Reference:* Vis coll. sale, 1927, no. 111.

1-B, reverse   2-B, reverse

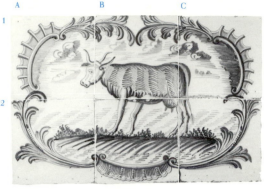

218. HORSE AND COW
Makkum, Friesland
Tichelaars Koninklijke
Makkumer Aardewerk– en
Tegelfabriek
1760–80
Blue
Gift of Mrs. Francis P. Garvan

Framed by *rocaille* cartouches, this horse and cow stand on convex patches of ground resembling plowed fields and are silhouetted against broad skies filled with windblown clouds. The scenes are executed in a simple, lively style resembling that of contemporary popular woodcuts. Fields, skies, and animals are all covered with rows of thick striations, often in alternating tones of dark- and light-blue. Tile pictures depicting bounding, prancing horses and sedentary, large-uddered cows were frequently mounted together over hearths.[1] They were complementary depictions of action and stasis, and may have denoted activity and repose on a more abstract level: the bounding horse had appeared in emblem books as the symbol of freedom, and the cow traditionally symbolized the earth.[2] In many tile pictures, the horse and cow are accompanied by a male and female farmer respectively, associating the animals with male and female behaviors (riding and milking) and with the genders themselves.[3] Allusions to gender are

not foreign to tile pictures with pastoral themes, as is evident in no. 217, which contains matching scenes of a maid milking and a gentleman fishing.

1. See Elling, 1978, fig. 121, for tile pictures *in situ.*
2. For the bounding horse associated with freedom, see Goltzius's engraving (fig. 56), and for a tile derived from this print, see Pluis, Van den Akker, and Muller, 1974, fig. 65. See also D. P. Pers, *Bellerophon of lust tot vvysheyd* (Amsterdam, 1614), which contains a bounding horse inscribed "Vryheyd, Blyheyd"; John Landwehr, *Dutch Emblem Books* (Utrecht, 1962), p. 39, fig. 8, p. 60, no. 179. Karel van Mander, "VVttbeeldinghen der Figuren," in *Het Schilder-boeck* (Haarlem, 1603–4), p. 125, states that the "cow stands for the earth." The significance of cattle in seventeenth-century Dutch prints and paintings is discussed by Joaneath Spicer, "The Origin of the Dutch Cattle Piece," in *Essays in Northern European Art Presented to Egbert Haverkamp Begemann on His Sixtieth Birthday,* edited by Anne-Marie Logan (Doornspijke, 1985), pp. 251–59.
3. Elling, 1978, figs. 122–28.

FIG. 56 Hendrik Goltzius (Dutch, 1558–1616) after Jan van der Straet (Flemish, 1523–1605)
The Wild Horse, plate from "The Royal Stable of Don Juan of Austria," 1578
Engraving
Philadelphia Museum of Art. The Charles M. Lea Collection

**219. COMMEDIA DELL'ARTE
FIGURES**
Makkum, Friesland
Tichelaars Koninklijke
Makkumer Aardewerk– en
Tegelfabriek
c. 1900
Blue
Gift of Mrs. Francis P. Garvan

An elaborate rococo frame here
serves as a proscenium for a
prancing jester. His costume
identifies him with the Italian
commedia dell'arte, although the
specific character he represents is
uncertain. The inscription in the
cartouche at the bottom of the
frame reads *Komt tot mij* (Come
to me). The second panel, with an
identical frame, is probably a
companion piece; it depicts Gilotin (Giglio, Gilles), another commedia dell'arte character, identified by his double-pointed hat
and the pipes and horns he carries. Gilotin is a seventeenth-century variant of Pierrot, or Petro-
lino.[1] The inscription in the
cartouche reads *Wie zijt gij* (Who
art thou?). That such ensembles
of tile pictures were not unusual
is attested to by the summer din-
ing room of the palace of Brühl,
West Germany; its decoration
consisted of numerous blue-and-
white tile pictures depicting Har-
lequin and Pulcinella.[2] Each tile
in these panels is individually
numbered on the reverse in the
lower-right corner to facilitate the
construction of the picture; each
tile also bears the mark of the
Tichelaar factory. A figure nearly
identical to the jester in the first
panel is depicted in a simpler,
frameless picture composed of six
rather than twenty tiles, preserved in the Fries Museum,
Leeuwarden.[3]

1. Pierre Louis Duchartre, *La
Comédie italienne* (Paris, 1924),
p. 268.
2. De Jonge, 1971, p. 97, ill. 122a.
3. Ibid., ill. 103b.

The Battle of Ramillies

The battle of Ramillies was fought around a small village in the province of Brabant on May 12 and 13, 1706. One of the most important battles of the War of the Spanish Succession (the European war which began in 1701 and ended with the treaties of Utrecht and Rastaat in 1713–14), Ramillies proved to be a major victory for the Netherlands and especially for the Duke of Marlborough, who led the defense of the English and the Dutch against the more numerous troops of Louis XIV and Spain.

This scene is a compilation of two prints by different artists, both entitled *The Battle of Ramillies.*[1] One, by Pieter Schenk (fig. 57), is a copy of an earlier print by Jan van Huchtenburg (fig. 58) after Adam Frans van der Meulen (1632–1690).[2] The foreground figures, with the exception of the soldiers grouped around the cannons in the lower right, are all borrowed from Schenk. These soldiers, as well as the figures in the middle ground and background and their landscape setting, are excerpted from a print of *The Battle of Ramillies* engraved in reverse (fig. 60) after a drawing by Jan Luyken (fig. 59). This drawing was also reused after Luyken's death to depict such battles as those of Mollwitz (1741) and Losowitz (1756) in Austria-Hungary.[3]

Although the painter of these tiles relied heavily on prints illustrating the battle, it is not certain that he intended to depict this specific event. Such a monumental tile painting, however, had to result from a special commission[4] and must have held particular meaning for its initial owner; possibly it was commissioned to commemorate a prominent figure who showed exceptional valor in battle, most likely at Ramillies.

No concrete evidence exists concerning the scene's original installation, but its place of manufacture can be determined with some certainty. The color and style of the painting, taken in conjunction with the composition and thinness of the tiles, date this work to the late eighteenth century. At this time the Rotterdam tileworks De Blompot, owned and run by the Aelmis family, was the only workshop in Holland capable of producing such a large and intricate work.[5]

1. Mrs. van Deelen of the Museum Atlas van Stolk, Rotterdam, kindly brought these two prints to the author's attention. It was general practice during this time for painters and engravers to have on hand a number of battle scenes produced previously. On obtaining a commission, the artists would adapt a scene by changing details, such as flags, and giving it the specified size by adding trees and foreground as needed. See J. F. Heijbroek, "Frederik Muller (1817–1881) en zijn prentenverzamelingen," *Bulletin van het Rijksmuseum,* vol. 29, no. 1 (1981), pp. 20–21.

2. A legend below the etching by Schenk identifies the major participants and describes the action of battle.

3. This drawing was used for an engraving *The Battle of Mollwitz* in 1741; see P. van Eeghen and J. P. van der Kellen, *Het werk van Jan en Caspar Luyken,* 2 vols. (Amsterdam, 1905), no. 270. The drawing was used again as an illustration in *De Nederlandsche Mercurius* (October 1756), p. 138, where it represented the battle at Losowitz that had taken place on the first of October of that year. C. Felius, assistant in the printroom of the Rijksuniversiteit, Leiden, kindly provided this information.

4. A battle scene on wood, metal, or canvas is not uncommon, but a battle scene as a tile painting of this size is unique.

5. See Hoynck, 1920, pp. 177–79, and Simões, 1959, p. 111.

FIG. 57 Pieter Schenk (Dutch, 1660–1718)
The Battle of Ramillies
Etching
Rijksprentenkabinet, Rijksmuseum, Amsterdam

FIG. 58 Jan van Huchtenburg
(Dutch, 1647–1733) after Adam
Frans van der Meulen (Flemish,
1632–1690)
Cavalry Engagement
Engraving
The New York Public Library

FIG. 59 Jan Luyken (Dutch, 1649–
1712)
The Battle of Ramillies, c. 1695
Ink and Wash
Prentenkabinet, Rijksuniversiteit,
Leiden

FIG. 60 After Jan Luyken
The Battle of Ramillies
Engraving
Rijksprentenkabinet,
Rijksmuseum, Amsterdam

13-D, reverse   16-P, reverse

220. THE BATTLE OF RAMILLIES

Rotterdam
De Blompot (owned by the
  Aelmis family)
1750–1800
Purple
Gift of Mrs. Francis P. Garvan

A ferocious battle rages in the foreground of this battle scene. Set behind the main action are supporting troops in formation. Although no single hero is depicted, the composition is focused on three central figures who sit high on their horses, brandishing swords and a flag. The middle figure looks over his left shoulder at the advancing cavalry. Around them, soldiers are being unhorsed and wounded as the cavalries charge one another from the sides. In the middle distance, infantrymen armed with pikes and muskets are formed into square units or deployed in firing lines.[1] Hills, meadows, and a river are visible in the background. The entire composition is framed by a dark, foliated foreground flanked by two tall trees. The painting, which covers 400 tiles,[2] has remained essentially intact, sustaining only minor losses of tiles in the sky and along the right side. Unfortunately, the signature tiles in the lower right corner are also missing. In addi-

tion to the lost tiles, there are bullet holes in tiles 10-T, 13-V, 15-D, and 16-U; shrapnel scars are present along the lower third of the painting. The scene was probably removed from its original home after 1910, the year its first recorded owner, Eelco M. Vis, started assembling his tile collection.
Reference: Vis coll. sale, 1927, no. 329.

1. Pikemen fighting in squares were common during the first half of the seventeenth century, but had virtually disappeared when Marlborough was fighting in the Low Countries, replaced by the invention of the bayonet in France in the second half of the seventeenth century. (Information kindly supplied by Capt. Edward Lee Holt, USAF [Ret.], Richmond.) Christian Beaufort-Spontin, *Harnisch und Waffe europas* (Munich, 1982), p. 117, notes that some armies began to eliminate pikemen after 1687. The pike was abolished in France by 1703, in England by 1705, in the Netherlands by 1708, and finally in Russia by 1721.
2. Vis and Geus, 1933, p. 41, state that this tile picture was composed of 384 tiles.

Corner Motifs

FIG. 61 Flemish drug pot with Italianate decoration, 16th century
Collection of D. A. Wittop Koning

FIG. 62 Italian majolica drug pot (*albarello*), probably from Tuscany, c. 1490–1500
Victoria and Albert Museum, London

1. Het Princessehof, 1981, pp. 11, 12.
2. Ibid., pp. 2, 20–21.

The corner motif is one of the most distinctive characteristics of the Dutch tile. These modest yet lively ornaments mark the boundaries of each tile, reinforcing its identity as a discrete unit within a series. Simultaneously, the motifs form clusters of four on tile panels, providing visual continuity between central images, a function necessitated both by the variation of central images from tile to tile and by the separation of the images from one another by broad expanses of white.

The corner motif took shape only gradually. During the sixteenth and early seventeenth centuries, it scarcely existed as such; lavish ornamentation on tiles remained the rule, and primary and secondary motifs were not yet strongly polarized. Decoration often took the form of two fields of equal expanse, one with the design painted directly (on a white ground), and the other done in reserve. The pattern sometimes extended diagonally over four or sixteen tiles, and the emphasis on the continuity of the overall pattern tended to obscure the boundaries of the individual tiles. Reserve fields on ornamental tile panels often featured foliage (no. 9) or rosettes (no. 18).[1]

Early pictorial tiles, such as those depicting animals (no. 46), and soldiers had identical motifs in all four corners, covering half of the expanse of the tiles, which set off the colorful image in the center of each tile. Corner motifs in early pictorial tiles thus approximated the form that became dominant slightly later in the century. After 1625 the section of the tile painted in reserve technique began to be displaced by a linear ornament painted positively in blue. It also became routine to give the tile four identical corner decorations, a change that affected the overall appearance by allowing for the opening up of white space between the corner motif and the central image, thus creating a much lighter effect. Corner motifs at this point assumed a new range of forms: the fleur-de-lis (Corner motif 17–22), leaf (Corner motif 35–37), spiral ox-head (*ossekop;* Corner motif 48–57), and cloverlike cruciform (*Heilige Drievuldigheid;* Corner motif 44–47) made their appearance in myriad variations between 1620 and 1650. Among the motifs in use during the latter half of the century, the spider's-head (*spinnekop;* Corner motif 58–61) occurred most frequently.

Although the various subjects depicted on tiles were never rigidly matched with particular corners, each image appears more frequently with certain corner motifs. Fleurs-de-lis, often with yellow bases, appear with flowers (no. 76), ox-heads with animals (no. 55), and so on. Certain corners almost always accompany framing elements, for example, the *Wan-Li* motif (here called mock-fret; Corner motif 9–14), which accompanies an assortment of round, scalloped, and bracketed frames (nos. 50, 53, 83) or a theatrical archway (no. 113).

The sources for corner motifs remain a topic of debate. It has been suggested that certain motifs, especially the ox-head, are the progeny of the negative blue forms that followed the contours of the white foliage in corners painted in reserve.[2] Other sources for corners include the Italian wares imported into the Netherlands in great numbers and the indigenous Netherlandish wares whose decoration was influenced by Italian prototypes, for example, the two-toned leaf motif (Corner motif 41–43) similar to that appearing on Italian jars decorated with blue-and-white leaf-and-vine patterns (*foglie*). Netherlanders also produced jars displaying the same type of decoration (fig.

61). Similarly, the cruciform motif, with its cluster of three round petals and flanking blue leaf forms, may have derived from a cloverlike motif occurring on Italian (fig. 62) and subsequently on Netherlandish (fig. 63) apothecary jars.

Although the first half of the seventeenth century witnessed the emergence of a wide variety of corner motifs, its latter decades were marked by consolidation. Types such as the ox-head and spider's-head continued to appear during these decades, but they gradually were reduced in size (Corner motifs 56, 58). After 1700 new forms appeared, some of which showed the influence of French decorative trends (no. 171). Another new corner motif, the carnation (Corner motif 65), was used frequently on purple tiles, whose popularity burgeoned between the mid-seventeenth and mid-eighteenth centuries (no. 136). Only with the nineteenth century, and the production once again of tiles decorated with ornamental patterns requiring a number of tiles for completion (no. 212) did tile painters begin to delete the corner motif, which for two centuries had been a nearly constant, if unobtrusive, characteristic of Dutch tiles.

175

Foliage 1–8

Mock-fret 9–16

Fleur-de-lis 17–24

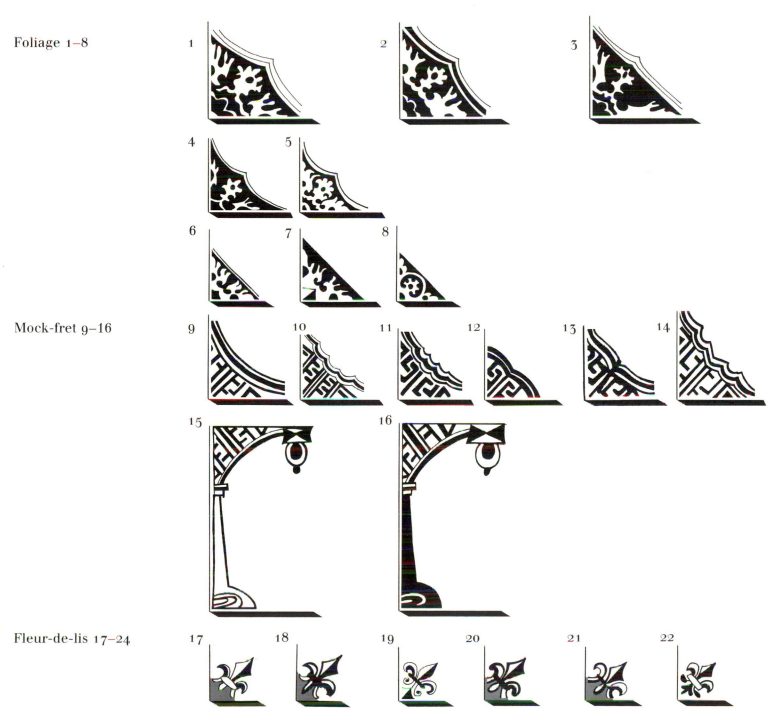

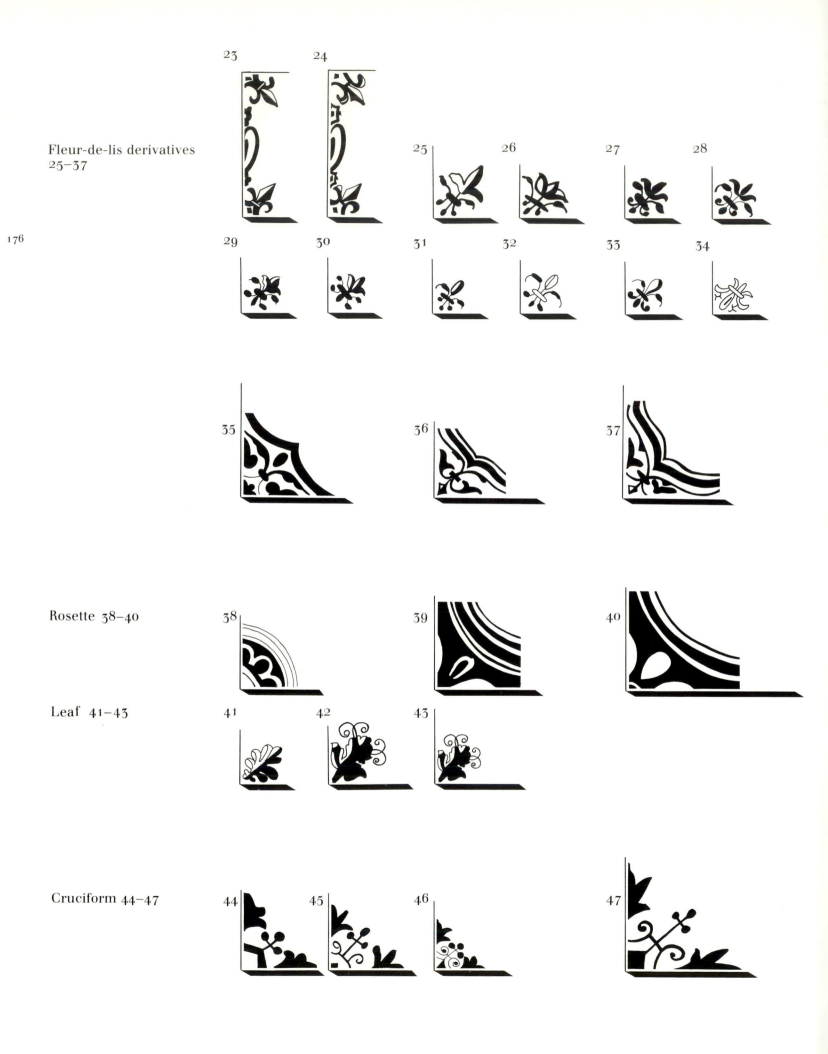

Fleur-de-lis derivatives
25–37

176

Rosette 38–40

Leaf 41–43

Cruciform 44–47

Ox–head 48–57

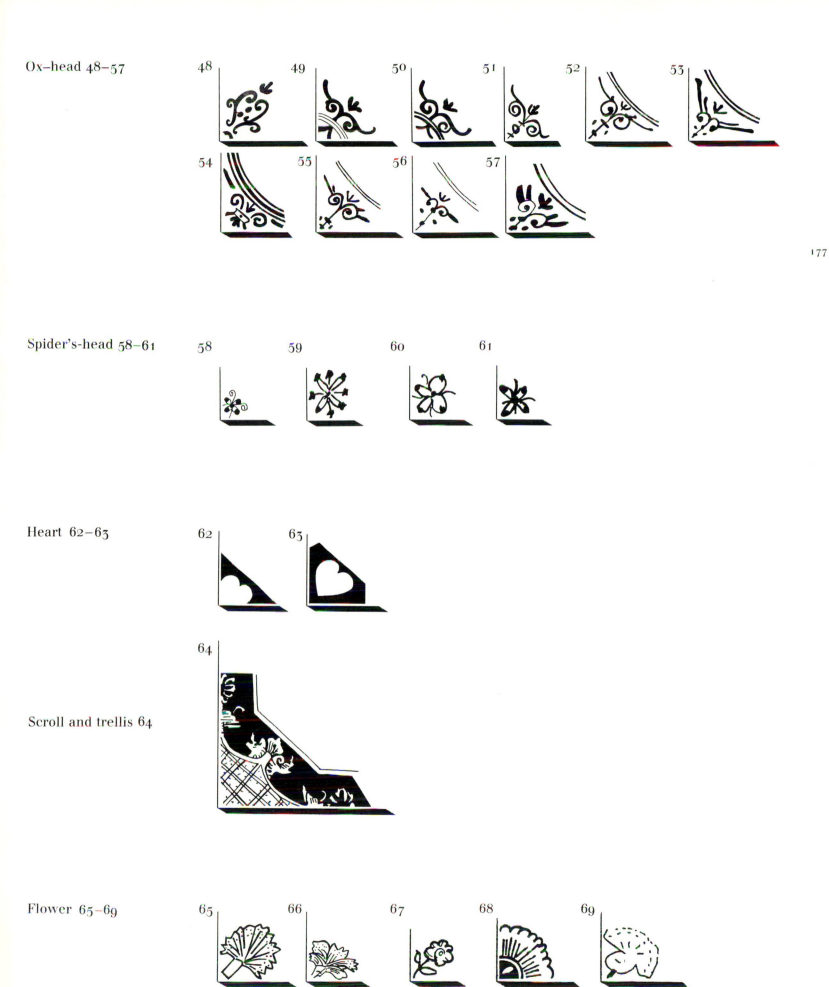

177

Spider's-head 58–61

Heart 62–63

Scroll and trellis 64

Flower 65–69

Technical Notes

Little attention has previously been focused on how tiles deteriorate and on what treatments are most suitable for the preservation of this kind of ceramic material. On a more fundamental level, there has been no analysis of the actual physical or chemical composition of Dutch tiles from the period 1550 to 1800. These two aspects of the study of Dutch tiles are explored here along with a discussion of a general conservation treatment for Dutch tiles and of a new mounting procedure for tile display.

Technical Examination

While an outline of how tiles are manufactured has been given by several authors,[1] identification of the raw materials and the components of the fired ceramics has relied on traditional assumptions about what those materials might be. There has been no attempt heretofore to characterize those components by chemical or physical analysis. Such general questions as how clays and glaze materials change with time, or more specific questions directed to whether the products of one factory can be distinguished from the wares of another—perhaps in a different location—have not been addressed from a technical viewpoint. It is possible that such questions may be resolved quite clearly by elemental or mineralogical determinations if sufficient sampling is carried out.[2]

It is clear that changes in ceramic structure in tiles from 1550 to 1800 reflect changes in the demand, volume of production, and fashion of the times, as well as technological developments in the ceramic industry in Holland during this period. Up to the early seventeenth century, tiles were characterized by thick bodies (commonly 2 centimeters thick, or slightly more)[3] from coarse red clays with numerous inclusions of varying sizes. The porosity of the ceramic bodies, presumably derived from local clay beds of either fluvial or diluvial origin, is very uneven, and indicates that screening and elaborate levigating techniques were not employed by the tilemaker at this point to improve the homogeneity of his wares. There is no evidence from the surface topography or from cross sections of tiles at this period that the surfaces were smoothed in forms by a roller. Lead-glazed floor tiles show stamped or incised designs, which are commonly filled with clay slip and covered with a thick lead glaze; in the some twenty examples in this collection, the slip is white. Most of these floor tiles have been very severely abraded, the glaze, and sometimes the body, having suffered from being too soft to withstand the wear to which it was subjected. Majolica-decorated (tin-glazed) floor tiles suffered even more abuse from wear. Clearly unsuitable in terms of their material performance as well as their cost, glazed earthenware floor tiles were abandoned by later generations of tilemakers.

The ceramic tiles that developed late in this first period of tile production (c. 1600) are covered with opaque white or off-white glazes of lead and tin oxides, and decorated with blue, green, yellow, brown and other colors in the Italian majolica tradition. These glazes are often applied very unevenly over a slip of white clay and crushed lead ore and contain many blow holes, voids, and inhomogeneities that are due to

1. See, for example, Paape, 1794; Hoynck, 1920; Berendsen et al.,1967; De Jonge, 1971, pp. 8–13; Kaufmann, 1973, pp. 10–16.
2. For general discussion of the "fingerprinting" of specific ceramic sites by elemental analyses, see I. Perlman and F. Asaro, "Pottery Analysis by Neutron Activation," *Archaeometry*, vol. 2 (1969), pp. 21–52; R. Abascal, G. Harbottle, and E. V. Sayre, "Correlation between Terra cotta Figurines and Pottery from the Valley of Mexico and Source Clays by Activation Analysis," *Archaeological Chemistry*, vol. 138 (1974), pp. 81–99; F. Widemann et al., "A Lyons Branch of the Pottery-Making Firm of Ateius of Arezzo," *Archaeometry*, vol. 17 (1975), pp. 45–59. It should be noted that complications such as similar clay sources, trade in raw materials, or subsequent weathering often obscure the "fingerprinting" of nearby sites.
3. The compendium that follows this text notes the thickness in millimeters of each tile catalogued, together with its length and width. The Munsell color of the ceramic body is recorded, as is the number of nail holes from the cutting form, or block, used to shape the tile. The data are largely the result of work by Melissa Meighan and Carol Stringari.

impurities in the glazes or overglazes, incomplete mixing, and in some cases, interactions between the glaze and the underlying ceramic body. Mechanically, tiles from this period tend to be relatively friable. Although in some cases this weakness may be caused by weathering, it is probably more often associated with incomplete firing of the ceramic, caused either by too low a final temperature or too short a "maturing" time in the kiln.

In tiles from the first half of the seventeenth century, cross sections are very frequently layered or marbled due to intentional admixtures of clays. Certainly this period produced experimentation in many factories, some of them newly established,[4] with clays other than the traditional local types that had been used for utilitarian redware, terra cotta, or brickmaking. Often the result is an uneven or incomplete mixing of a red clay (a ball, or plastic, clay with high iron content) with a grey or buff clay (a relatively nonplastic, or lean, clay, perhaps with a high calcium content). It is not unusual to observe measurable separation or gaps between these layers, nor is it uncommon to observe that the layering occurs in horizontal bands and is related to attempts to flatten the tiles, perhaps by rolling or other mechanical means as yet undocumented.

Part of the motivation for adding lean, nonplastic material to the tiles would have been to reduce warping and cracking during drying and firing and to allow thinner tiles to be manufactured. A second factor would have been to create fired bodies of a lighter or whiter color than those made from local reddish clays alone, following the fashion of the times, particularly with the growing popularity of Oriental blue and white wares that were arriving by Dutch East Indies Company boats from the Far East after 1620. A third reason for changing clay mixes may have been to obtain a better bond between the glaze and the body of the tile. The current poor adhesion of the glaze to the substrata in many tiles of this period indicates the difficulties in "fitting" glaze to body during the drying, firing, and cooling cycles of lead/tin-glazed tile manufacture. Some of these technical difficulties undoubtedly reflect the influx of new, inexperienced workshops into the field or the changeover of other ceramic manufacturers, such as brickmakers, to the rapidly expanding marketplace for tiles, where demand was exceeding supply.

The tiles from this period are still relatively thick for the most part, with numerous inclusions and uneven, large pores throughout. The hardness ranges from compact to extremely friable. It is a notable feature of the poorly mixed or wedged, heavily marbled tiles of this period that in addition to being mechanically weak, they are more prone to salt damage than tiles of any other type or period. Part of the explanation for this lies in the ready transfer of salt through large gaps and pores; part of the damage can probably be attributed to the inadequate bond between the glaze and the body that is common on such tiles and which allows salts to accumulate at the glaze/body interface and mechanically to push the glaze off with time, as the salts go through the cycles of dehydration, rehydration, and recrystallization (fig. 64). In cross section under magnification to 250×, the lead/tin glazes are usually inhomogeneous, incompletely matured or fused, and laced with voids and blowholes.[5] Cobalt blue was used more frequently for decoration than polychromy, with obvious economies for the tile manufacturers.

Toward the middle of the seventeenth century and continuing into the early eighteenth, tile manufacturers made considerable changes in ceramic processing. While it may be safe to assume that different factories adopted the changes at different rates, the production of Dutch tiles during this period was characterized in general by thinner bodies of more even whiteness (or "buffness") across the full section. The economic incentives for reducing the thickness of the tiles were strong—many more tiles could be produced with the same amount of clay, more tiles could be stacked in the kiln, and more tiles could be fired for a given amount of fuel. The tile bodies show

4. Van Dam, 1982, pp. 16–40.
5. Mixtures of lead and tin oxides with other materials—such as salt and soda—produced at this period a white "glaze," which lacked sufficient lead oxide or other fluxing or glass-forming components to create a smooth, glossy surface when fired. To overcome the matte finish of this glaze, tile-makers began to apply a thin layer of fritted lead and tin oxides, called *kwaart*. As Tichelaar points out above, this glaze development has not yet been studied closely.

6. It would appear that toward the end of this period glazes were being more carefully made, with improved selection of raw materials, pulverizing, and fritting of the various ingredients, so that the white glaze was applied only once, with no overglaze or *kwaart* required. The dating of this development, again, has not yet been determined.

7. The results were determined by d.c. emission spectroscopy at McCrone Associates, Chicago.

8. These data were from neutron activation analysis at the Phoenix reactor of the University of Michigan, with the assistance of Gary Cariveau at the Detroit Institute of Arts.

9. These XRD analyses were performed by Michael Wajda, at Dickinson College, Carlisle, Pa., Geology Department, through the courtesy of Professor Niemitz.

10. Van Dam, 1982, pp. 15–17, 83, published Delft inventories from 1621 and 1623 that mention English or Tournai earth, while Brabant earth is mentioned in an 1661 inventory. Hoynck, 1920, p. 8, cites English earth used at a Rotterdam tileworks in 1627. Hudig, 1928, pp. 73, 74, 78, found earths from Tournai, Ghent, the Rhineland, and Delft used in Amsterdam in 1684–85.

180

less numerous and smaller inclusions than in the preceding transitional period, suggesting that levigating or screening of raw clay or both were taking place. The smaller size of the pores in the tiles indicates improved mixing, milling, or blunging, and fewer of the tiles contain strong marbling or red veining. The tiles are generally thinner and flatter than those from the preceding period, showing less warping; the production of this kind of tile required an increased control over the processes of drying and firing of the ceramics. The smoothness and uniformity of the tiles, for most factories, reveal that leather-hard tiles were being rolled. The fired bodies are less friable than were earlier wares. The glazes[6] tend to be more completely fused than in earlier examples, although there are still many voids and flaws in the glazes compared to tiles of the next century or modern ones.

During the eighteenth century, tiles begin to be less carefully decorated, but the degeneration of design does not necessarily parallel a deterioration in the technical production of the ceramics. Instead, there probably was an increase in the efficiency of production, as demand diminished and required that producers make tiles more economically in order to stay in business. The tiles reached a thinness of about 8 millimeters, in many cases not much thinner than the thinnest products in the previous period. The color and porosity of the bodies tend to be quite uniform. Severe technical glaze flaws are less common than in earlier tiles, though glazes are much less refined in cross section than those of the later nineteenth century.

Two tables (figs. 65 and 66) give preliminary results of elemental analyses of tiles from the seventeenth century. Figure 65 shows that large amounts of calcium are present in the tile bodies,[7] while several samples[8] in fig. 66 can probably be distinguished as coming from different sites based on strontium, scandium, and thorium concentrations. X-ray diffraction studies of later tile samples[9] show that calcium silicates and silica are the main components of the fired bodies, although the survey is too incomplete to allow valid generalizations to be drawn about mineral composition at this point. Nonetheless, it is clear from the ceramic evidence that traditional red plastic clay materials were supplanted by a silica-rich paste with admixed calcium

FIG. 64 Photograph showing the effect of salt damage on tiles 1979-50-483–486.

from marl or other sources during the development of the tile industry in the Netherlands during the seventeenth and eighteenth centuries.[10] Further analysis, including studies of elemental composition and mineralogic features, is underway and may lead to a clear chronology of calcium-rich additions and possibly characterization of regional differences in tile manufacturing material.

FIG. 65 Major Elements in Tile Bodies (in percentage by weight)

	28-66-71	1979-50-53	1979-50-43
Silicon	25-30+	25-30+	25-30+
Calcium	20	20	20
Aluminum	7	10	8
Iron	5	4	3
Potassium	2	2	2
Sodium	2	2	1
Magnesium	2	1	1
Titanium	0.3	0.3	0.3
Lead	0.5	0.2	0.1
Manganese	0.08	0.05	0.05
Barium	0.03	0.03	0.03
Strontium	0.03	0.03	0.03
Tungsten*	0.02	0.02	0.02
Copper	0.005	0.02	0.01
Zirconium	0.02	0.01	0.01
Boron	0.01	0.008	0.008
Chromium	0.01	0.008	0.008
Nickel	0.003	0.005	0.003
Vanadium	0.002	0.002	0.002
Cobalt*	0.0007	0.001	0.0008
Gallium	0.0007	0.0001	0.0005
Beryllium	0.0005	0.0005	0.0005
Silver	<0.0005	0.005	<0.0005
Tin	0.0005	0.005	not detected

* from tungsten carbide mill?

FIG. 66 Minor and Trace Elements in Tile Bodies (sodium and iron in percentage by weight; others in parts per million by weight)

	135,1-B	134,	135,1-A	153,4-C	11,3-A	11,2-B	11,2-A	11,3-B	198,1-D	198,4-A	198,2-D	198,3-A
Sodium	1.04	0.66	0.70	0.88	0.76	0.75	0.68	0.71	1.41	0.66	1.17	1.09
Iron	1.84	2.35	2.57	2.86	2.53	2.76	3.33	1.38	3.07	1.75	2.99	1.24
Samarium	4.32	4.89	4.21	4.37	5.89	5.65	6.27	7.04	5.47	6.08	5.67	6.19
Lutetium	0.34	0.36	0.32	0.30	0.38	0.38	0.42	0.44	0.46	0.38	0.37	0.38
Uranium	2.0	1.9	1.7	1.5	2.6	2.8	3.1	2.9	2.1	2.0	2.1	2.3
Thorium	8.9	9.2	8.9	8.1	11.5	10.9	12.8	12.3	10.8	10.3	10.2	11.6
Cadmium	No	No	4.6	No	4.1	6.4	8.0	6.1	6.5	3.3	4.3	5.6
Gold	No	0.015	0.011	No	No	No	No	0.009	No	No	0.013	0.007
Barium	201	194	185	170	290	305	391	317	216	241	241	251
Neodymium	22	25	21	27	25	32	33	30	32	24	34	28
Arsenic	10.9	7.7	8.5	7.2	15.3	23.5	23.3	16.1	7.5	9.7	7.5	11.9
Bromine	26.3	7.9	9.9	29.8	16.4	28.1	18.7	17.1	54.7	5.1	16.1	23.3
Rubidium	71	75	75	74	107	97	155	109	106	83	106	102
Lanthanum	25.2	25.4	24.7	39.0	32.7	31.3	35.1	37.2	30.5	31.1	32.7	31.1
Cerium	47.5	45.2	59.3	60.5	58.4	61.6	77.6	55.4	74.0	45.7	75.1	47.5
Ytterbium	1.83	1.37	1.98	2.18	2.01	2.02	2.59	1.20	2.51	1.38	2.40	1.52
Selenium	No	No	No	0.9	No	No	No	No	No	No	No	No
Mercury	No	No	No	0.7	No	No	No	No	2.2	2.2	3.8	No
Tellurium	7.6	7.5	9.7	10.3	9.3	10.3	12.6	5.5	11.8	6.5	12.7	10.2
Chromium	56	53	74	73	64	77	85	53	85	44	85	46
Hafnium	6.5	4.2	3.8	7.2	3.6	4.0	5.1	4.4	7.7	4.5	7.9	4.9
Strontium	302	555	594	749	476	1013	755	539	719	234	656	No
Silver	No	0.75	No	No	No	No	No	No	1.4	No	No	No
Cesium	3.85	4.38	6.69	5.23	5.77	10.80	7.94	2.54	4.26	2.89	6.94	1.19
Nickel	47	No	37	No	31	48	54	No	42	No	38	No
Terbium	1.1	1.1	1.5	0.8	1.4	1.1	1.4	0.8	1.4	0.5	1.3	0.8
Scandium	6.68	7.70	9.83	9.41	9.72	10.51	12.90	4.81	11.20	5.94	10.50	5.60
Rubidium	62	70	91	111	98	155	134	48	102	75	114	61
Zinc	47	45	74	66	68	73	95	61	77	42	73	24
Tantalum	0.56	0.52	0.73	0.73	0.68	0.70	0.88	0.43	0.92	0.49	1.02	0.45
Cobalt	7.9	9.5	15.9	41	22.4	23.1	18.5	10.3	14.4	9.3	30.0	3.9
Europium	0.92	0.90	1.25	1.22	1.25	1.31	1.66	0.67	1.54	0.82	1.43	0.86
Antimony	0.5	0.4	6.4	0.9	12.2	3.9	7.1	0.5	1.0	1.4	0.4	0.2

While Dutch tiles are relatively durable glazed ceramics, they are susceptible to damage by brittle fracture, abrasion, and soluble salts. The first type of damage is characteristic of the brittle microstructure of these low-fired ceramics, which are composed of many partly sintered mineral particles in irregular arrays, often with large voids between those clusters. The second type of damage, abrasion, is due to the softness of the lead/tin glazes on the one hand and the friability of the ceramic body on the other. The third type of damage, caused by soluble salts, is the most insidious and difficult to assess. In this type of deterioration, salts accumulate behind the glazed surface, and recrystallize, presumably with increases in volume due to absorbed water and water of crystallization; the mechanical forces produced by these recrystallizing salts, in combination with chemical effects that are still poorly understood, can ultimately detach the glaze from the underlying ceramic body (see figs. 64 and 67).

182

Although a number of studies and articles have been written about salt damage,[11] reliable methods for evaluating the degree of damage and the most effective treatment to remove the salt without further deterioration have not been developed for this kind of ceramic. Moreover, while relatively few of the tiles in this collection were suffering from active damage due to salts when inspected in 1979, the possibility could not be dismissed that the potential for damage from accumulated salts existed in a latent condition, not unambiguously evident under microscopic examination, awaiting sufficiently adverse factors for the salts to be activated and erupt through the glaze surface. In order to evaluate what percentage of the collection might be expected to suffer ultimately from salt damage, a simple analytical survey—a sampling of twelve tiles from the early seventeenth to early nineteenth century—was carried out by determining how much readily soluble salt material could be expected from the tiles when they were immersed in deionized water. All of the tiles sampled contained salts in large quantities, as measured by a conductivity cell; twenty-four and forty-eight hour soaking waters contained salt concentrations sufficient to increase the conductivity of the initially nearly salt-free water by factors of 10^4 to 10^5.

A subsequent experiment identified the major soluble salts extracted in the soaking process and roughly quantified these.[12] The soaking waters from eighteen tiles dated to the mid-1600s were evaporated to dryness, and the solid residues were subjected to X-ray diffraction analysis; the major components of the recrystallized mixture were calcium sulfate dihydrate and sodium chloride, that is, plaster of Paris and common salt. The solids collected in these evaporations were weighed; 1 to 2 grams of salt were removed after three to five days of soaking, and in some cases considerably more salt was removed. Crudely averaged, the soluble salt content of the tiles sampled in this test was 0.5% by weight. Differently viewed, one out of every two hundred parts of each tile could be subject to movement or diffusion whenever water was absorbed into or removed from the ceramic body. This cannot be regarded as a stable condition for such rigid but open inorganic material, particularly if the tile is mounted for display on a nonporous support, where the primary surface for evaporation of absorbed water is the glazed surface; in this situation the salts are drawn ultimately by evaporation to the very place where they are most likely to produce degradation of the glaze decoration.

Further laboratory work was undertaken to find the safest and most efficient method of reducing these high salt contents to lower, more stable, levels without further deterioration of the tiles. A variety of soaking techniques commonly used in conservation, and several modifications of these, were tested against one another for effectiveness. The results, excluding ultrasonic cleaning techniques, are summarized in figs. 68–70. Further refinement of the most promising treatment involving

11. See Terwen, 1981, pp. 20–23, and J. A. Last, "The Desalination of Ceramics: A Review of the Foremost Methods," M.A. thesis, Queen's University, Kingston, Ontario (1979); also H. Jedrzejewska, "Removal of Soluble Salts from Stone," in *1970 New York Conference on Conservation of Stone and Wooden Objects* (London, 1970), pp. 19–34; J. Olive and C. Pearson, "The Conservation of Ceramics from Marine Archaeological Sources," in *Conservation in Archaeology and the Applied Arts* (London, 1975), pp. 63–68; R. V. Sneyers and P. J. de Henau, "The Conservation of Stone," in *The Conservation of Cultural Property* (Paris, 1968), pp. 209–35; T. Stambolov and J.R.J. van Asperen de Boer, *The Deterioration and Conservation of Porous Building Materials in Monuments* (Rome, 1972); T. Stambolov, "The Corrosive Action of Salts," *Lithoclastia*, no. 1 (1976), pp. 3–8; E. M. Winkler, *Stone: Properties, Durability in Man's Environment* (New York, 1973).

12. Much of this experimental work was performed tirelessly by Richard Kerschner. In order to use tiles of fairly uniform composition which had been exposed to roughly equivalent amounts of salt, the tiles from *The Battle of Ramillies* (no. 220) were selected for testing the relative efficacy of different desalination methods.

FIG. 67 Diagram showing the main pathways by which soluble salts from the ground, from underlying water, and from masonry can be transferred to the glazed surface of a tile. The transfer is aided by dryness and heat in the interior space, which promote evaporation of the water and precipitation of the salt at or near the tile surface. Cycling of interior humidity (from hot and dry to cold and wet) compounds the damage caused by the rehydration and dehydration of soluble salts just under the glaze.

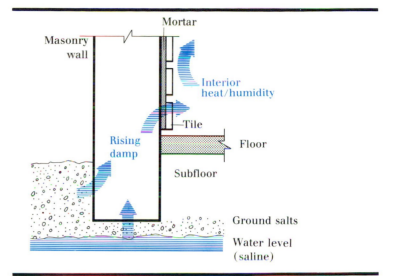

FIG. 68 The change in the logarithm of measured resistivity with time is schematically illustrated for two of the desalination methods listed in the table in fig. 70. Line B represents measurements from poulticing prior to immersion, followed by water changes once daily without further poulticing. Line C depicts measurements from water changes twice weekly and no poulticing. Line A gives the log resistivity of the deionized water used; note that these values always exceed the measured log resistivity values of the soaking water. Log resistivity = (1/log conductivity).

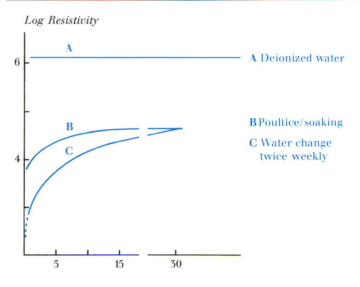

FIG. 69 Extraction rate in ppm/hr vs. time, plotted schematically for static immersion conditions at 20°C and 60°C, with daily changes of deionized water. Line A is divided in two stages: in stage 1, various readily soluble, accumulated salts are extracted rapidly at first from tiles; in stage 2, after sufficient exposure to deionized water, the tiles give off calcium almost exclusively, reflecting hydrolytic degradation of the ceramic body. At the elevated temperature (60°C), higher concentrations of salt are detected in the soaking bath, indicating that the diffusion process is temperature dependent. Line B is divided into three stages: in stage 1, high extraction rates are produced by the elevated temperature; in stage 2, predominantly calcium cations are extracted, indicating degradation of the ceramic body; in stage 3, aluminum and silicon appear in the soaking waters, suggesting alumino-silicate breakdown is occurring.

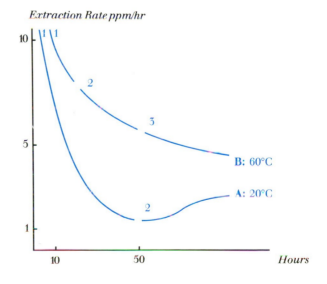

Fuller's earth poultices was developed during the course of desalination of some 1,400 tiles. In the end, the following was the procedure used for desalinating:

1. Remove all loose mortar and grout and old repair material.
2. Dampen the reverse of the tile thoroughly with deionized water.
3. Apply Fuller's earth poultice (mixed with deionized water) to the back and edges of the tile and allow to dry with the (unpoulticed) glaze side down for one to three days.
4. Dust off all loose poultice, using a scraper where necessary.
5. Immerse the tile in a tank of deionized water at room temperature, placing the tile, glaze side down, on a riser to promote convection around the tile.
6. Remove the tile from the tank after twelve to twenty-four hours of soaking and grind off as much mortar or grout as possible, keeping the tile wet with deionized water during the grinding process.
7. Scrub off all the mortar or grout under a stream of deionized water or with a stiff bristle brush in a tank.
8. Reapply the poultice, as in steps 3 and 4 above.
9. Allow to dry one to three days and then dust or scrape off the sides and back; reimmerse the tile in deionized water for twelve to twenty-four hours, monitoring the water with a conductivity cell. Repeat steps 8 and 9 until the resistivity of the deionized water reaches a fairly level value above 30,000 ohms.

From a practical viewpoint, this procedure takes advantage of two simple observations made during more than thirty-five laboratory tests and many more actual desalination treatments. First, the initial use of a poultice on a well-dampened surface with high soluble salt content (prior to any full immersion) prevents salts near the surface from being driven further inward, away from the surface, by the front of water during immersion in a tank and also can cut in half treatment time and labor. The initial and subsequent poultices provide surface layers to which the soluble salts are drawn by evaporation, and in which these salts tend to be trapped on drying, rather than on the tile itself where they would be left if there were no poultice. In other words, besides providing a much faster method of removing salts when applied at the outset, a poultice can lead to more effective removal of soluble salts during the drying phase(s) of a treatment. Second, after an initial period of soaking, which often produces very

FIG. 70 Main Desalination Methods

Static immersion at 20°C
1. "Control"—daily change of water
2. Variations in frequency of water change—hourly, every two hours, two times per day, biweekly, weekly
3. Alterations in position or elevation of tiles in soaking tanks

Electrophoresis
1. Without stirring
2. With stirring
3. Variations in voltage and amperage

Grout removal
1. Prior to soaking
2. After initial period of soaking

Immersion in 1 vol. ethanol: 3 vol. water

Wicking, prior to immersion

Poulticing with Fuller's earth
1. After initial periods of soaking
2. Prior to soaking

Heating, to 60° and 90°C
1. Without stirring
2. With stirring

high rates of soluble salt removal, the rate of soluble salt extraction depends on time- and temperature-controlled diffusion mechanisms in such a way that soaking intervals of much less than twelve hours do not appear to be very effective in removing the soluble salts situated more deeply within the ceramic matrix. It may be that there is a wetting factor (perhaps time dependent) together with ion mobility and solubility, absorption/desorption, and capillary effects due to the configuration of the pores that must combine in order to draw these salts out of the ceramic body.

This latter observation about the complexity of diffusion control was the focus of a series of tests that attempted to expose the diffusion mechanism more clearly and to evaluate critically whether water-induced structural damage occurs to a tile during desalination procedures designed to remove the danger of damage from absorbed salts. Atomic-absorption spectroscopy[13] was employed to measure the concentration of specific ions that compose the various salts (the sulfate ion and ions of sodium, chlorine, calcium, magnesium, potassium) and the major elements that compose the tile body and glaze (calcium, silicon, aluminum, sodium, magnesium, potassium, and iron from the body and lead from the glaze), which could appear in the soaking water when the tile is being degraded chemically. This analytical technique is accurate and sensitive, being able to detect elements in solution at concentrations of parts per million (ppm) or less. In combination with atomic absorption, X-ray diffraction analysis was applied to thin sections of the tiles in an effort to identify specifically which components of the ceramic might be subject to breakdown in water, or hydrolysis. While these analyses are far from complete at this point, the data indicate the following:

1. The most mobile soluble ions, the sodium and potassium cations and the chloride ion, tend to be drawn into the soaking water first.

2. Residual mortar or grout tend either to trap soluble salts or to retard the diffusion process, in either case extending the desalination soaking time.

3. Long-term soaking procedures extract a calcium-rich component (or components) of the tile body, typically at a rate between 0.1 and 0.5 ppm/hr at room temperature after one hundred hours of immersion in deionized water.

4. Raising the temperature of the soaking water results in an increase in the rate of calcium extraction and with time also causes the breakdown of a silicate or alumino-silicate in the body. Represented in a very schematic way in fig. 70, the data reveal that long-term soaking and elevated water temperatures are not advisable conditions for desalination treatments of such ceramic materials, contrary to some current conservation practices.

General Conservation/Restoration Procedures

While the technical examination and the analysis of the desalination process for Dutch tiles represent two major aspects of conservation work performed in 1984, they were only two parts in the overall treatment of the tiles, which can be divided into the following eight steps.

1. *Unmounting.* In order to remove tiles from frames or backings, nailed frames were cut open with a jeweler's saw and gently pried with a small lever in the form of a specially ground screwdriver. Many tiles or fragments were loose within the frames and could simply be lifted out of the frames; others required the softening or dissolution of adhesive before they could be detached. Protein-based adhesives (such as hide glue) were softened by applying damp paper toweling where the adhesive held the tiles to the frame. The toweling was kept damp with water that was warmed from 60° to 90° centigrade, until the adhesive softened. The less frequently encountered adhesives based on lead-white putties or on mixtures of resin and wax were softened with

13. This work was carried out admirably by Michael Wajda, with the aid of Professor R. E. Leyon, at Dickinson College.

185

organic solvents, particularly toluene or xylene or mixtures of methylene chloride, acetone, and toluene. A long, thin spatula was used to separate the tiles from the softened adhesive.

2. *Removal of old repairs, overpaint, and adhesive.* Fills or replacements of missing parts, usually made of plaster, were removed by softening with water or by scraping with a scalpel, under the binocular microscope where necessary. A very small number of the old fills were made of restorer's compo or of mortarlike materials; the former yielded in some cases, to solvent mixtures containing methylene chloride, although the typical treatment consisted of softening with water, followed by mechanical removal. Much of the overpainting contained lead-based paints that were cross-linked sufficiently to require fairly strong solvent mixtures containing methylene chloride (a commercial paint stripper that did not contain any dye was frequently employed for this task). Ethanol was applied on swabs to take up the softened paint and paint residues.

3. *Sampling.* When samples were taken from the reverse for elemental analysis, the surfaces around the sample sites were thoroughly cleared of all loose material prior to drilling. The samples for neutron activation and for emission spectroscopy were 100 milligrams. The first 2 to 3 millimeters of each drilling were discarded as being contaminated with excessive amounts of mortar and not representative of the internal composition of the ceramic.

4. *Stain removal.* Most severe stains were treated prior to desalination to reduce the likelihood of stain spreading (and worsening) during the soaking process. The chemicals that proved effective included organic solvents (acetone, alcohol, and methylene chloride) on some organic stains; a detergent formulation (based on EDTA, an anionic and a nonionic detergent); 10% EDTA in water (usually heated to 60°C); hot 10% sodium hexametaphosphate in water; and 10% oxalic acid in water (usually heated). For the most difficult stains, which usually contained iron, best results were obtained by wetting the surface of the stain with the detergent mixture for thirty seconds to five minutes, followed by application of hot oxalic acid for a similar period, then swabbing with acetone and thoroughly rinsing with ethanol. This process was repeated until the stain was sufficiently reduced, but never more than five times to avoid possible further damage to the glaze and the ceramic body; poultices of talc and deionized water were applied up to three times after the stain was reduced, in order to draw out any remaining chemicals. The goal of the stain-removal step was to minimize disfigurement or illegibility caused by staining, not to eliminate completely surface appearances that may have occurred during the "natural" aging of a tile.

5. *Desalination.* Excessive amounts of soluble salts were removed by the procedure described above. An important and intended side effect of the soaking was to wet and in many cases to soften the residual mortar or grout on the reverse and edges of the tiles and thereby to facilitate the grinding step.

6. *Grinding.* Optimal desalination rates depend on the removal of grout or mortar from the porous surfaces on the reverse and edges of the tiles. Ideally, this material should therefore be eliminated before any desalination treatment begins by dry grinding or grinding with the minimal amount of water—overwetting will cause soluble salts near the surface to be pushed into the tile interior, from which they may not be extracted as quickly as they have entered. In practice it is feasible to remove grout at an intermediate stage in the process, preferably during the first soaking, without substantial decreases in the rate of desalination. A variety of means for taking off the often large and uneven remains of grout or mortar were tried, including ultrasonic cleaning, flexible-shaft tools, and microsandblasting equipment; the easiest, fastest, and safest tool proved to be a relatively coarse and open silicon-carbide grinding wheel mounted on a variable-speed potter's wheel with Akemi polyester adhesive and sealed with a RTV silicone at the edges. The wheel was run at extremely slow speeds

(10–30 rpm's) and the tiles were kept wet. The mortar was ground to as even and thin a layer as possible without abrading any of the body of the tile itself. In terms of the simple examination of the tiles, this grinding step allowed the reverse and edges of a tile to be easily seen, so that any marks or initials on the reverse could be recorded and any evidence of manufacture, such as the intentional beveling of the edges of a tile, revealed. Grinding served the additional purpose of leveling the reverse of the tiles for subsequent mounting.

7. *Consolidation/joining.* Tests to determine an effective consolidant for loose glaze and friable edges of tile shards showed that polyvinyl butyral (PVB) solutions in xylene/ethanol provided better penetration and strength than a number of acrylic and polyvinyl acetate solutions or emulsions and that PVB appeared less adversely affected by water than other possible consolidants. In situations where the glaze was extremely poorly adhered or where the body of the ceramic was badly delaminated or powdering, the consolidant was applied prior to desalination. In joining broken fragments of tile after desalination, polyvinyl acetate AYAT—a very high molecular weight PVA—was added to the PVB solution to form a thicker adhesive layer.

8. *Fills/inpainting replacement.* Missing sections of tiles were cast in molding plaster, the adjacent edges having first been sealed with a thin coating of PVB. For very shallow losses, such as those along break lines or substantial losses of the glaze layer, either plaster or a commercial plaster repair mixture (made of very fine plaster and adhesive) were used. After being leveled with files or sandpaper, the fills were sealed with a PVB solution or an acrylic solution (Acryloid B-72) and toned or inpainted with a reversible acrylic paint to which dry pigments were often added. No attempt was made to obscure these repairs completely; in most cases they are evident, even to the untrained eye, after a few moments inspection from a distance of a meter or more. Most of these fills were toned to minimize the contrast between the plaster fill and the intact portion of the tile. This aesthetic of restoration is based on the criteria that losses should not detract from the overall appearance of a tile or an assemblage for the average viewer, yet the extent of loss should be readily apparent to anyone interested in knowing what is original and what is restored. In a very small number of cases, inpainting was carried slightly beyond simple toning, as the complexity of the design image required some completion in order for it to be read properly without the distraction of a disfiguring loss. In none of these latter instances was the inpainting carried to the point where it could deceive the interested viewer: the inpainting was left rough and not leveled by lacquering, and it was never carried beyond the area of loss or fill, leaving the original glaze surface uncovered. It seems antithetical to the interests of scholarship, conservation, and indeed art appreciation to present, in a museum display, as if it were freshly made and undamaged, a three hundred year old tile that has been cracked, badly stained, or broken.

A special variation of the foregoing restoration was introduced for the large tile picture of a battle (no. 220), in which 26 tiles were completely missing from the current configuration of 400. All the tiles were marked on the reverse consecutively from bottom to top at the factory, and the tile in the lower left corner of the current configuration (16-A) is marked 17. Clearly there was another column, numbers 1 to 16, at the left border; considerations of symmetry and framing would also argue for two additional columns on the right border, suggesting that the original picture consisted of 448 tiles. Rather than substituting painted masonite or plaster imitations for the 26 lost tiles, glazed ceramic replacements were fashioned for better durability and maintenance of the picture over a long period of time. More than one hundred test firings were necessary to produce glaze colors sufficiently close to those of the original.[14] A red ceramic body, slight variation in glaze color, irregular tile shape, lack of cutting holes, and matte glaze differentiate the replacements from the originals, leaving the restorations evident to the practiced eye after brief inspection.[15]

14. The 26 replacement tiles were made with great perseverance by Anna Maria Carmona, Moscow, Pennsylvania.

15. The 26 replacement tiles in *The Battle of Ramillies* are 1-A, 1-B, 1-D, 1-F, 1-K, 1-Y, 2-A–C, 2-E, 2-F, 2-H, 2-K, 2-M, 3-A–F, 4-C–F, 16-X, and 16-Y. Of the remaining 374 tiles, 256 were missing shards or were broken; these tiles were restored following the procedures described above. There are circular holes in four tiles—10-T, 13-V, 15-D, 16-U—most likely caused by bullets; these holes were not repaired.

Mounting

In the past, dealers and collectors of Dutch tiles have used a surprisingly large variety of materials to mount tiles for display. Supports have ranged from the thin wooden flats of cigar boxes to thick, heavy slabs of slate. Adhesives for attaching the tiles to the support have included lead-white putties, grout-cement mixtures, and concoctions of resin, filler, and/or wax. In a great many instances, these mounting materials have caused severe mechanical damage to the tiles that they were intended to protect.

In the case of this collection, almost one of every three tiles had been damaged solely by inadequately composed mounts. The most common offenders were open wooden frames with cross members, utilizing animal hide or bone glue. Breakage occurred when these flexible frames bent, warped, or cracked during handling. Some of the small edge losses and glaze chips were due to compression or percussion when the flexible supports forced adjacent edges against each other; these losses may also have been the result of shrinkage or expansion of the frames or adhesive, both of which are dimensionally unstable in the face of abrupt changes of humidity. In other cases, it was clear that impact or shock during previous handling or shipping were responsible for fracturing the tiles; on the most brittle supports—such as slate—mounted tiles were frequently broken when the support fractured on impact.

Less apparent from the obverse of many tiles was damage from adhesive failure. Water-based adhesives, especially hide and bone glues, penetrated into the porous ceramic when freshly applied. With time, these adhesives became extremely brittle, no longer moving when the support moved; consequently, when subject to movement, the adhesive layers broke at either the ceramic-adhesive interface or the adhesive-support interface. The former failure created the most losses, producing spalling of the glue-impregnated subsurfaces, additional fracture planes, and blind cracks. Both types of adhesive failure left tiles or tile fragments loose in their frames and prone to further injury or loss.

Establishing safer, more durable mounting systems for tiles[16] was a clear priority. Tests were carried out on a variety of adhesives and mounting materials, with traditional mounts included in these tests as bases for comparison. Figure 71 lists the adhesives and supports that were subjected to a series of simple empirical tests, tests designed to bring out differences in the performance of the various combinations with

16. The preliminary testing of the adhesive and mounting stems was carried out by Wendy Stayman.

FIG. 71 Main Mounting Supports and Adhesives

Support	Failure
Plywood	D,F
Plexiglass	D,B,F,S,W
Fiberglass/polyester sheet	D,F,S
Aluminum/polyethylene sandwich	B,D,F,W
Aluminum honeycomb	None

Failure key:

A Poor application characteristics
B Poor bonding surface
D Distortion, warping
F Excessive flexibility
I Inadequate bond strength
R Lack of reversibility
S Poor resistance to shock or
   impact
W Poor weight/strength ratio

Adhesive	
Rubber-based (industrial marble formulation)	A,S
Latex (industrial formulation for ceramic tile)	S
Polyester (Akemi)	A,R,S
Epoxy (Ren RP106-H953)	A,R,S
Epoxy foam (Ren RP1774/198 hardener)	A,R,S
Paraffin: rosin: plaster (1:2:2)	I,S
Microcrystalline wax	I,S
Hot-melt Ethylene vinyl acetate copolymer	I
Contact cement	R,S
Silicone RTV (Dow 732 and others)	I (exc. on Al), R
Polyvinyl acetate emulsion (Jade 403)	A,S

respect to the following criteria: appropriate bond strength and resistance to vandalism; reversibility; durability, alteration with time, staining; resistance to shock; ease of handling—weight, resistance to flexing or to dimensional change; and ease of application, including toxicity.

Plaster and cement as adhesives were eliminated from consideration in these tests when they failed even in initial preselection tests. The best traditional methods, which utilize wax or a wax mixture, also proved very unsatisfactory, showing poor bond strength and poor resistance to shock or transportation. Lack of reversibility or of shock resistance characterized several support systems suggested in the recent conservation literature. In sum, the best results for every category except reversibility were obtained for systems with aluminum honeycomb interiors—and skins of either aluminum or epoxy-fiberglass—and silicone RTV adhesives. To allow for reversibility, tile surfaces were sealed prior to bonding with silicone by an acrylic solution (Acryloid B-72) in xylene, usually applied in two to four coatings to develop a thin surface layer. Once the tile has been adhered to the support, the sealant can be softened or swelled in appropriate solvents sufficiently to release the silicone. Facilitating this solvent release was the accessibility of the silicone and acrylic, since only small dots of silicone (2 cm or less) were applied in each corner of a tile. Differences in level between tiles in any given assemblage were usually made up by simply applying thicker dots of silicone; in some instances, however, the differences in level were great enough to require small corner pads of felt to be inserted under the thinner tiles in order to build them up to the level of adjacent tiles. The undyed white felt dots were saturated with silicone prior to attachment to the support. Curiously, a similar system has been used to put heat-deflecting tiles on the NASA space shuttle.

Aluminum-skinned honeycomb panels were ultimately chosen over the fiberglass-reinforced version based on the greater ease of cutting, finishing, and cleaning, in addition to durability and resistance to flexing. For panels less than 100 centimeters in height or width, 1.6 centimeters honeycomb paneling was selected as the best solution to both adequate strength and cost of materials; larger panels were made 2.5 centimeters thick, to ensure adequate rigidity.

In the mounting procedure, one final concern of scholarly interest focused on the visibility of initials, designs, or doodles on the reverse of certain tiles. While the tile pictures were numbered at the factory for convenience of installation, some tiles in the collection have other intentional markings on the reverse. The mounts for these are provided with plexiglass windows on the rear of the panels, so that they can be easily seen. The windows were cut into the panels; the 1.2 centimeters thick plexiglass is bonded with epoxy and slightly recessed from the back surface of the mount to prevent scratching.

Summary

Analysis has confirmed that from an early period (before 1650) Dutch tiles contain unusually large amounts of calcium (20% by weight and more) and that calcium-rich materials were being added intentionally to improve the factory processing of tiles. Even after firing, the calcium-rich components of the ceramic body remain susceptible to hydrolytic attack. Degradation of these calcium-rich components must weaken the strength of the ceramic structure after repeated wettings and, in particular, the bond between glaze and body. Beyond this kind of self-destruction are the substantial problems caused by accumulated soluble salts. An expeditious method for removing potentially damaging levels of soluble salts has been devised. In this desalination method, salt-laden tiles are exposed to deionized water for minimal periods of time to reduce any further deterioration or hydrolysis of the tile body, as measured by atomic absorption and X-ray diffraction. Further work is clearly needed to explore the physical factors involved in tile deterioration and conservation treatment, particularly structural weaknesses caused by expansion and contraction of the body with wetting-drying cycles.

Compendium of Tile Data

The accession information and the physical data for each tile illustrated in the catalogue are provided in this compendium.

The first column gives the coordinate position of each tile within its panel.

The second column lists the Philadelphia Museum of Art accession number. Tile donors are identified by accession number prefix as follows:

1983–101–	Gift of Anthony N. B. Garvan
1981–77–	Gift of Anthony N. B. Garvan
1979–50–	Gift of Mrs. Francis P. Garvan
66–210–	Purchased: Edgar V. Seeler Fund
61–67–	Gift of S. Krider Kent
30–44–	Gift of Miss May Audubon Post
30–10–	Gift of Edward W. Bok
28–66–	Gift of Edward W. Bok
21–3–	Bequest of Emmeline Reed Bedell
19–	Ozeas, Ramborger, Keehmle Collection
16–	Gift of William Seltzen Rice
12–	Gift of Karl J. Freund
08–	Purchased: Joseph E. Temple Fund
97–	Bequest of Mrs. Frederick Graff

The third column gives the tile or tile fragment's average height and width respectively, in millimeters to the nearest .5 millimeter (excluding grout and fills).

The fourth column specifies the average thickness of the tile, including the glaze, but not at the "fat" edge where the glaze puddled during drying or firing.

The fifth column gives the color of the clay body based on the Munsell Color System, matched in north-facing daylight (80–100 footcandles) with a small component (less than 25%) of mixed warm and cool fluorescent light (Sylvania Lifeline: Natural F96712-N and F96712-D).

Color	Munsell values	
white	5Y	9/2, 9/1, 8.5/1
buff	7.5Y	9/2
	5Y	8.5/2
	2.5Y	9/4, 9/2, 8.5/2
yellow	5Y	9/6–9/4
	2.5Y	8.5/6, 8.5/4, 8/6
pk/or (pink/orange)	7.5YR	8/8, 8/6, 7/8, 7/6
	5YR	8/6–7/6
red	10R	5/10–5/8
	2.5YR	5/10–5/8

The sixth column lists the number of edges at specific bevel angles. The first number, in parentheses, is the number of edges; the second is the number of degrees (to the nearest 2.5°) deviation from 90°, measuring from the glaze surface. Where fewer than four edges are listed, either the absent angle is 90° or an edge is missing.

The seventh column gives the number of apparent holes in the corners of the glazed surface of the tile made by the nails in the trimming block. Where the block skipped and made two holes in a corner, only one was counted. Where five holes are noted (see panel no. 1), the fifth is in the center of the tile.

The last column offers a general statement regarding the condition of each tile, with an emphasis on breaks, losses, fills, and inpainting. "Small losses" indicates glaze and/or body losses of less than 1/8 of the total tile surface (small chips, to be expected from normal wear, are not noted). "Inpainted" indicates that an attempt has been made to reconstruct the missing portion of the design.

Tile	Accession Number	Dimensions (in mm)	Thickness (in mm)	Clay Body	Beveling of Edge (in degrees)	Nail Holes	Condition
1. Floor Tiles							
1-A	1979-50-7	141 x 144	22.5	red	(2) 10, (1) 75, (1) 5	5	1/2 glaze loss
1-B	1979-50-6	142 x 144	23.5	red	(3) 10, (1) 5	5	1/2 glaze loss
1-C	1979-50-8	142.5 x141	23	red	(1) 10, (2) 7.5, (1) 5	3	1/2 glaze loss
1-D	1979-50-11	142.5 x 144	23	red	(4) 5	4	3/4 glaze loss
2-A	1979-50-16	143 x 141	23	red	(3) 10, (1) 5	3	1/4 glaze loss
2-B	1979-50-10	142 x 144	22.5	red	(2) 10, (2) 5	5	1/8 glaze loss
2-C	1979-50-4	143 x 142	23	red	(1) 10, (3) 5	5	1/2 glaze loss
2-D	1979-50-12	143 x 141	23	red	(1) 7.5, (3) 5	2	3/4 glaze loss
3-A	1979-50-3	142 x 142	23	red	(4) 5	4	1/4 glaze loss
3-B	1979-50-5	144 x 142.5	23.5	red	(4) 5	5	1/8 glaze loss
3-C	1979-50-2	141 x 142	23.5	red	(3) 5, (1) 2.5	5	1/2 glaze loss
3-D	1979-50-9	144 x 143	23.5	red	(3) 7.5, (1) 5	5	1/2 glaze loss
4-A	1979-50-14	141 x 143	23.5	red	(1) 7.5, (3) 5	3	1/2 glaze loss
4-B	1979-50-1	143 x 141	23	red	(2) 10, (2) 5	5	1/4 glaze loss
4-C	1979-50-13	141 x 143	23	red	(1) 10, (3) 5	5	1/2 glaze loss
4-D	1979-50-15	142.5 x 141	23.5	red	(2) 7.5, (2) 5	5	1/4 glaze loss
2. Floor Tiles							
1	1979-50-22	143 x 142	21.5	red	(2) 15, (2) 10	0	
2	1979-50-20	142 x 141	22	red	(1) 12.5, (1) 10, (2) 5	0	
3. Floor Tile							
	1979-50-24	115 x 115	20	red	(1) 10, (2) 5	0	1/4 glaze loss
4. Floor Tile							
	1979-50-25	114 x 112	22	red	(1) 10, (3) 5	0	break
5. Floor Tile							
	1979-50-810	127 x 134	19.5	pk/or and buff	(1) 10, (2) 5	4	edge break
6. Floor Border Tile							
	1979-50-809	130 x 129	20.5	buff	(1) 10, (1) 7.5, (2) 5	4	1/8 loss
7. Floor Tiles							
A	1979-50-23	145 x 145.5	16	red	(1) 10, (3) 5	1	corner loss
B	1979-50-26	146 x 145	17	red	(1) 10, (3) 5	1	
8. Floor Tile							
	1979-50-19	147 x 150	17.5	red	(4) 5	4	

Tile	Accession Number	Dimensions (in mm)	Thickness (in mm)	Clay Body	Beveling of Edge (in degrees)	Nail Holes	Condition

9. Ornamental Fruit in Quatrefoils

Tile	Accession Number	Dimensions	Thickness	Clay Body	Beveling of Edge	Nail Holes	Condition
1-A	1979-50-488	135 x 136	15.5	yellow	(3) 7.5	3	small loss
1-B	30-10-48(41)	134 x 134	17	yellow	(1) 10, (1) 7.5, (2) 5	2	
1-C	1979-50-489	136 x 136.5	15	buff	(2) 10, (2) 7.5	3	small losses
1-D	1979-50-487	136 x 136	15.5	buff	(2) 10, (2) 7.5	3	
2-A	30-10-48(44)	133 x 135	16	yellow	(2) 10, (2) 7.5	2	
2-B	30-10-48(42)	133 x 134	15.5	pk/or and yellow	(3) 15, (1) 10	2	small loss
2-C	1979-50-490	135 x 135	15.5	pk/or and yellow	(3) 10, (1) 7.5	3	
2-D	30-10-48(43)	133 x 133.5	16	yellow	(2) 20, (2) 15	2	¼ loss—inpainted
3-A	1979-50-460	134 x 135	16	pk/or	(4) 10	4	⅛ loss
3-B	1979-50-459	135 x 136	15	pk/or	(3) 10, (1) 7.5	4	
3-C	1979-50-497	129 x 135	15.5	yellow	(1) 10, (2) 10, (1) 5	3	⅛ loss
3-D	1979-50-495	135 x 136	16	pk/or	(1) 15, (3) 12.5	2	⅛ loss
4-A	1979-50-462	135 x 134	14	pk/or	(3) 10, (1) 5	4	small loss
4-B	1979-50-461	136 x 136	15	buff	(1) 7.5, (3) 5	4	small loss
4-C	1979-50-498	130 x 136	16	buff	(1) 35, (1) 10, (2) 5	2	small loss
4-D	1979-50-496	133 x 127	16	yellow	(1) 35, (2) 15, (1) 10	1	small losses

10. Ornamental Fruit in Quatrefoil

Tile	Accession Number	Dimensions	Thickness	Clay Body	Beveling of Edge	Nail Holes	Condition
1-A	1979-50-458	135 x 136	14.5	marbleized pk/or and buff and red	(1) 15, (2) 10	2	
1-B	1979-50-455	136 x 136	15.5	pk/or and marbleized red	(1) 15, (3) 10	2	small loss; tone fill; corner loss
2-A	1979-50-457	135 x 135	15	marbleized pk/or and buff	(1) 15, (3) 10	2	
2-B	1979-50-456	136 x 136	15	marbleized pk/or and buff and red	(1) 10, (1) 7.5, (2) 5	2	

11. Ornamental Fruit in Quatrefoil

Tile	Accession Number	Dimensions	Thickness	Clay Body	Beveling of Edge	Nail Holes	Condition
1-B	1979-50-467	132 x 132	16	pk/or	(1) 10, (3) 5	2	
1-C	1979-50-468	132 x 131	16	pk/or	(2) 15, (1) 10, (1) 5	3	various large cracks
2-A	1979-50-465	134 x 136	16	yellow and marbleized red	(3) 5, (1) 2.5	3	
2-B	1979-50-464	134 x 133	16.5	yellow and marbleized red	(4) 5	3	
2-C	1979-50-469	132 x 132	18	pk/or	(2) 10, (1) 5	2	crack
3-A	1979-50-463	135 x 135	15	yellow and marbleized red	(1) 10, (3) 5	3	small losses
3-B	1979-50-466	133 x 134	15.5	yellow and marbleized red	(3) 5, (1) 0	4	

12. Ornamental Fruit in Quatrefoil

Tile	Accession Number	Dimensions	Thickness	Clay Body	Beveling of Edge	Nail Holes	Condition
1-A	1983-101-127	133 x 134	13.5	pk/or	(4) 15	3	
1-B	1983-101-129	134 x 134	14.5	pk/or and buff	(4) 15	2	
2-A	1983-101-126	134 x 135	14	mixed buff and pk/or	(4) 15	3	small losses corner loss
2-B	1983-101-128	134 x 135	16	mixed buff and pk/or	(4) 10	3	⅛ loss

13. Ornamental Fruit in Quatrefoils (Pompadour)

Tile	Accession Number	Dimensions	Thickness	Clay Body	Beveling of Edge	Nail Holes	Condition
1-A	1979-50-493	131 x 131	16	pk/or	(4) 7.5	3	
1-B	1979-50-492	137 x 138	16.5	pk/or and buff	(1) 7.5, (3) 5	2	
2-A	1979-50-494	139 x 139	16	pk/or	(1) 10, (2) 5, (1) 2.5	2	
2-B	1979-50-491	135 x 137	15	pk/or and buff	(2) 10, (2) 7.5	2	corner loss

14. Ornamental Fruit in Quatrefoils (Pompadour)

Tile	Accession Number	Dimensions	Thickness	Clay Body	Beveling of Edge	Nail Holes	Condition
1-A	1979-50-479	129 x 128	14	pk/or	(1) 5	4	small losses
1-B	1979-50-480	133 x 132	13	pk/or and buff	(2) 5	4	small losses
2-A	1979-50-481	131 x 129	13.5	pk/or and buff	(1) 10, (1) 5	4	small losses
2-B	1979-50-482	132 x 130	14	pk/or and buff		4	small losses

15. Ornamental Flower Vases in Quatrefoils (Pompadour)

Tile	Accession Number	Dimensions	Thickness	Clay Body	Beveling of Edge	Nail Holes	Condition
1-A	1979-50-403	134.5 x 135.5	15.5	yellow	(1) 10, (3) 5	4	
1-B	1979-50-438	133 x 133	16	pk/or	(3) 15, (1) 10	4	⅛ loss
1-C	1979-50-405	134 x 134	15	pk/or	(4) 10	2	loss
1-D	1979-50-449	132 x 132.5	16	pk/or	(1) 15, (3) 10	4	small losses
1-E	1979-50-446	133 x 133	15.5	pk/or	(3) 15, (1) 10	4	
2-A	1979-50-447	135 x 135	14	pk/or	(1) 15, (2) 10, (1) 5	2	⅛ loss
2-B	1979-50-437	131.5 x 132	16	marbleized pk/or and red	(3) 15, (1) 10	4	small losses

Tile	Accession Number	Dimensions (in mm)	Thickness (in mm)	Clay Body	Beveling of Edge (in degrees)	Nail Holes	Condition
2-C	1979-50-440	135 x 135	14	pk/or	(2) 15, (2) 10	2	small losses
2-D	1979-50-445	134 x 135	15	pk/or	(1) 15, (3) 10	2	
2-E	1979-50-404	134 x 133	15	yellow	(1) 12.5, (3) 10	2	¼ loss
3-A	1979-50-443	135 x 135	14.5	pk/or	(2) 15, (2) 10	2	small losses
3-B	1979-50-450	132.5 x 133	16	pk/or	(1) 20, (1) 15, (2) 10	4	⅛ loss
3-C	1979-50-444	135 x 136	14	pk/or	(3) 10, (1) 5	2	
3-D	1979-50-406	134 x 136	14.5	yellow and marbleized red	(4) 10	2	⅛ loss
3-E	1979-50-435	135 x 135	14	pk/or	(2) 10, (2) 5	2	⅛ loss
4-A	1979-50-442	133 x 132	16	pk/or	(1) 15, (3) 10	4	¼ loss
4-B	1979-50-436	132 x 132	15.5	buff and marbleized pk/or	(1) 15, (3) 10	4	small losses
4-C	1979-50-448	132 x 133	16	pk/or	(4) 10	2	⅛ loss
4-D	1979-50-439	135 x 135	14	buff	(1) 15, (2) 10, (1) 5	2	¼ loss
4-E	1979-50-441	133 x 133	16	buff and marbleized pk/or	(4) 10	2	

16. Ornamental Flower Vase in Quatrefoil (Pompadour)

	Accession Number	Dimensions (in mm)	Thickness (in mm)	Clay Body	Beveling of Edge (in degrees)	Nail Holes	Condition
	1979-50-396	138 x 137	15.5	yellow	(1) 10, (1) 7.5, (2) 5	4	

17. Ornamental Flower Vase in Quatrefoil (Pompadour)

	Accession Number	Dimensions (in mm)	Thickness (in mm)	Clay Body	Beveling of Edge (in degrees)	Nail Holes	Condition
	1979-50-397	136 x 137.5	15	pk/or	(2) 10, (2) 5	2	

18. Ornamental Flower Vases with Rosettes

Tile	Accession Number	Dimensions (in mm)	Thickness (in mm)	Clay Body	Beveling of Edge (in degrees)	Nail Holes	Condition
1-A	1979-50-422	136 x 135	14.5	pk/or	(2) 15, (2) 10	2	small losses
1-B	1979-50-378	135 x 132	15	pk/or	(2) 10, (1) 7.5, (1) 5	2	
1-C	1979-50-425	133 x 133	15.5	pk/or	(2) 15, (1) 12.5, (1) 10	2	
1-D	1979-50-433	134 x 133	15.5	pk/or	(3) 10, (1) 5	2	small losses
2-A	1979-50-432	134 x 134	16	pk/or	(3) 15, (1) 10	2	small losses
2-B	1979-50-377	135 x 135	14.5	pk/or	(2) 12.5, (2) 10	2	
2-C	1979-50-427	132 x 132	16	pk/or and yellow	(4) 15	2	
2-D	1979-50-424	135 x 135	16	pk/or	(2) 12.5, (2) 10	2	
3-A	1979-50-386	128 x 130	16	pk/or	(2) 10, (2) 5	2	
3-B	1979-50-376	134 x 134	15	pk/or	(1) 15, (2) 12.5, (1) 10	2	
3-C	1979-50-375	134 x 134	15.5	buff	(3) 10, (1) 7.5	2	
3-D	1979-50-429	134 x 133	15	pk/or	(4) 15	2	
4-A	1979-50-420	133 x 135	16	pk/or	(1) 10, (2) 5	2	
4-B	1979-50-383	131 x 130	15	yellow	(4) 10	2	
4-C	1979-50-385	130 x 131	15	pk/or	(4) 10	2	corner loss
4-D	1979-50-419	136 x 136	16.5	pk/or	(4) 5	3	
5-A	1979-50-379	132 x 132	16	pk/or and yellow	(2) 12.5, (2) 10	2	small losses
5-B	1979-50-428	132 x 131	14	pk/or	(2) 20, (2) 15	4	
5-C	1979-50-434	133 x 132	14	buff	(1) 12.5, (2) 10, (1) 5	4	small losses
5-D	1979-50-426	135 x 135	16	yellow	(2) 10, (2) 5	2	small losses
6-A	1979-50-382	133 x 132	14	buff	(3) 10, (1) 5	2	small losses
6-B	1979-50-430	132 x 132	16.5	buff	(2) 15, (2) 10	2	
6-C	1979-50-421	132 x 135	16	pk/or and yellow	(2) 15, (2) 10	2	
6-D	1979-50-384	129 x 131	16	pk/or and buff	(3) 15, (1) 10	3	corner loss
7-A	1979-50-431	134 x 133	14.5	pk/or	(2) 12.5, (2) 10	2	2 corner losses
7-B	1979-50-423	134 x 136	16.5	yellow	(1) 12.5, (2) 10, (1) 7.5	2	corner loss
7-C	1979-50-381	131 x 132	17	pk/or and red	(1) 12.5, (3) 10	2	small losses
7-D	1979-50-380	133 x 135	16.5	buff	(1) 20, (3) 15	2	small losses

19. Ornamental Flower Vases in Diamonds

Tile	Accession Number	Dimensions (in mm)	Thickness (in mm)	Clay Body	Beveling of Edge (in degrees)	Nail Holes	Condition
1-A	30-10-48(21)	137 x 137	15.5	pk/or and buff	(4) 10	2	
1-B	1979-50-395	135 x 135	16.5	yellow	(2) 10, (2) 5	2	
1-C	1979-50-401	130 x 131	15	pk/or and buff	(3) 15, (1) 5	3	
2-A	1979-50-399	132 x 131	15.5	pk/or and buff	(2) 15, (2) 10	2	
2-B	1979-50-402	130 x 135	15	pk/or and marbleized red	(1) 10, (2) 7.5	2	
2-C	1979-50-400	135 x 136	14.5	yellow	(4) 10	2	
3-A	30-10-48(23)	135 x 135	13.5	pk/or and buff	(4) 5	2	
3-B	30-10-48(19)	137 x 137	14	pk/or and buff	(4) 10	2	
3-C	30-10-48(24)	132 x 133	12	pk/or and marbleized buff	(4) 10	6	

20. Ornamental Flower Vases in Diamonds

Tile	Accession Number	Dimensions (in mm)	Thickness (in mm)	Clay Body	Beveling of Edge (in degrees)	Nail Holes	Condition
1-A	1979-50-389	135 x 136	15.5	buff	(4) 10	4	
1-B	1979-50-390	138 x 134	16.5	pk/or and buff	(1) 45, (3) 10	4	
2-A	1979-50-387	136 x 134	15.5	pk/or and buff	(1) 15, (2) 12.5, (1) 7.5	4	
2-B	1979-50-388	137 x 136	15.5	pk/or and marbleized buff	(1) 15, (2) 10, (1) 5	4	small loss

Tile	Accession Number	Dimensions (in mm)	Thickness (in mm)	Clay Body	Beveling of Edge (in degrees)	Nail Holes	Condition

21. Ornamental Flower Vases in Diamonds

Tile	Accession Number	Dimensions	Thickness	Clay Body	Beveling of Edge	Nail Holes	Condition
1-A	1979-50-392	131 x 132	13.5	pk/or	(3) 7.5, (1)	2	
1-B	1979-50-391	131 x 135	14	pk/or and marbleized red and buff	(1), (3) 10	2	small loss
2-A	1979-50-394	135 x 134	14	pk/or	(2) 12.5, (2) 10	2	
2-B	1979-50-393	131 x 133	14	pk/or	(3) 12.5, (1) 10	2	

22. Ornamental Flower Vases in Diamonds

Tile	Accession Number	Dimensions	Thickness	Clay Body	Beveling of Edge	Nail Holes	Condition
1-A	30-10-48(12)	130 x 130	15	pk/or	(1) 15, (1) 12.5, (1) 10, (1) 5	4	
1-B	30-10-48(14)	127 x 128	14	pk/or and red	(4) 15	4	
1-C	30-10-48(16)	128 x 127.5	14.5	pk/or	(2) 20, (2) 15	4	small corner and other losses
1-D	30-10-48(13)	126 x 128	15	pk/or and red	(1) 20, (3) 15	4	
2-A	30-10-48(10)	126 x 128	14.5	pk/or	(3) 15, (1) 10	4	
2-B	30-10-48(18)	127 x 126	13.5	pk/or and red	(3) 17.5, (1) 15	4	
2-C	30-10-48(15)	127 x 127.5	14.5	pk/or and red	(2) 15, (2) 12.5	4	small losses
2-D	30-10-48(17)	127 x 126	14	pk/or	(1) 20, (1) 15, (1) 10, (1) 5	4	small losses

23. Ornamental Flower Vases in Diamonds

Tile	Accession Number	Dimensions	Thickness	Clay Body	Beveling of Edge	Nail Holes	Condition
1	30-10-48(11)	128 x 129	13.5	marbleized pk/or and red	(3) 10, (1) 5	4	
2	30-10-48(20)	129 x 130	14	red	(1) 7.5, (3) 5	4	

24. Ornamental Flower Vase in Diamond

Tile	Accession Number	Dimensions	Thickness	Clay Body	Beveling of Edge	Nail Holes	Condition
	30-10-48(22)	130.5 x 132	14	buff	(4) 15	3	corner loss

25. Ornamental Floral Border Tile

Tile	Accession Number	Dimensions	Thickness	Clay Body	Beveling of Edge	Nail Holes	Condition
	1979-50-822	63 x 135	14	pk/or and red	(1) 7.5, (3) 5	2	

26. Ornamental Floral Border Tile

Tile	Accession Number	Dimensions	Thickness	Clay Body	Beveling of Edge	Nail Holes	Condition
	1979-50-307	66 x 135	15.5	buff and marbleized red	(1) 10, (3) 5	2	

27. Star Tulips

Tile	Accession Number	Dimensions	Thickness	Clay Body	Beveling of Edge	Nail Holes	Condition
1-A	1979-50-515	135 x 135	15.5	pk/or	(1) 50, (3) 10	2	
1-B	1979-50-522	133 x 134	15	pk/or and red	(1) 15, (3) 12.5	2	
1-C	1979-50-526	136 x 135	16	pk/or and buff	(2) 10, (2) 7.5	2	corner loss
1-D	1979-50-530	134 x 135	15.5	pk/or and buff	(2) 12.5, (2) 10	2	
2-A	1979-50-517	134 x 134	15	pk/or and red	(2) 15, (2) 10	2	
2-B	1979-50-521	135 x 135	15	pk/or	(1) 45, (1) 12.5, (2) 10	2	
2-C	1979-50-523	136 x 131	15.5	pk/or	(2) 10, (2) 7.5	2	
2-D	1979-50-528	133 x 134	16	pk/or	(1) 10, (3) 7.5	2	
3-A	1979-50-518	135 x 134	15.5	pk/or and buff	(1) 10, (3) 7.5	2	small losses
3-B	1979-50-520	137 x 137	15	pk/or and buff	(1) 15, (2) 10, (1) 7.5	2	
3-C	1979-50-524	136 x 137	16	pk/or and buff	(3) 10, (1) 5	2	
3-D	1979-50-529	136 x 136	15	pk/or	(4) 7.5	2	corner loss; inpainted
4-A	1979-50-516	133 x 134	15.5	pk/or and red and buff	(3) 10, (1) 7.5	2	small losses
4-B	30-10-48(40)	133 x 134	15.5	buff	(1) 7.5, (3) 5	4	small losses
4-C	1979-50-525	135 x 136	16	pk/or	(3) 12.5, (1) 7.5	2	
4-D	1979-50-527	136 x 135	15.5	pk/or	(3) 12.5, (1) 7.5	2	small losses

28. Star Tulips

Tile	Accession Number	Dimensions	Thickness	Clay Body	Beveling of Edge	Nail Holes	Condition
1-A	1979-50-478	133 x 133	16	pk/or and buff	(2) 15, (1) 12.5, (1) 10	2	
1-B	1979-50-476	132 x 132	16.5	pk/or and yellow	(1) 15, (1) 12.5, (2) 10	2	
2-A	1979-50-477	134 x 135	16.5	pk/or and buff	(2) 15, (2) 12.5	2	
2-B	1979-50-475	132 x 132	16.5	pk/or	(4) 15	2	

Tile	Accession Number	Dimensions (in mm)	Thickness (in mm)	Clay Body	Beveling of Edge (in degrees)	Nail Holes	Condition

29. Star Tulips

Tile	Accession Number	Dimensions (in mm)	Thickness (in mm)	Clay Body	Beveling of Edge (in degrees)	Nail Holes	Condition
1-A	1979-50-502	131 x 132	16	pk/or	(4) 10	3	⅛ loss
1-B	1979-50-511	132 x 131	15.5	pk/or	(3) 10, (1) 5	3	small loss
1-C	1979-50-510	132 x 132	14.5	pk/or	(4) 10	4	small loss
1-D	1979-50-506	135 x 136	15.5	pk/or and buff	(3) 10, (1) 5	4	
2-A	1979-50-501	133 x 133	15.5	pk/or	(4) 10	4	small loss
2-B	1979-50-509	131 x 132	15	pk/or and red	(2) 12.5, (2) 10	4	
2-C	1979-50-505	132 x 132	15.5	pk/or	(2) 10, (2) 7.5	3	
2-D	1979-50-514	132 x 132	15.5	pk/or and buff	(2) 12.5, (2) 10	4	
3-A	1979-50-500	134 x 134	15	pk/or and red	(2) 10, (2) 7.5	4	small loss
3-B	1979-50-504	132 x 132.5	16	pk/or	(1) 12.5, (3) 10	4	
3-C	1979-50-508	132 x 133	14.5	pk/or	(4) 10	4	
3-D	1979-50-513	132 x 132	15	pk/or	(2) 10, (2) 7.5	4	small loss
4-A	1979-50-499	133 x 132	16	pk/or and yellow	(2) 10, (2) 7.5	3	edge broken; small losses
4-B	1979-50-503	133 x 133	15.5	pk/or	(3) 10, (1) 7.5	4	small loss
4-C	1979-50-507	131 x 132	15	pk/or	(4) 10	4	small losses
4-D	1979-50-512	132 x 133	15.5	pk/or and red	(3) 10, (1) 7.5	4	small loss

30. Star Tulips

Tile	Accession Number	Dimensions (in mm)	Thickness (in mm)	Clay Body	Beveling of Edge (in degrees)	Nail Holes	Condition
1-A	30-10-48(39)	130 x 130	15.5	pk/or	(2) 15, (2) 12.5	2	small loss
1-B	30-10-48(38)	131 x 131	17	pk/or	(1) 15, (3) 10	2	small loss
1-C	1979-50-519	135 x 135	15	pk/or	(1) 10, (1) 7.5, (2) 5	2	
2-A	30-10-48(34)	130 x 130	16	yellow	(3) 15, (1) 10	2	
2-B	30-10-48(36)	131 x 131	15.5	pk/or	(1) 15, (1) 12.5, (2) 10	1	small losses; corner loss
2-C	30-10-48(35a)	130 x 132	15	pk/or	(3) 15, (1) 10	2	

31. Star Tulips

Tile	Accession Number	Dimensions (in mm)	Thickness (in mm)	Clay Body	Beveling of Edge (in degrees)	Nail Holes	Condition
1-A	1979-50-471	134 x 133	15	pk/or and red	(1) 10, (2) 7.5, (1) 5	4	
1-B	1979-50-472	133 x 133	15	pk/or	(1) 10, (1) 7.5, (2) 5	4	
2-A	1979-50-473	133 x 134	14.5	pk/or and buff and red	(4) 10	4	
2-B	1979-50-474	133 x 133	14.5	pk/or and buff	(3) 10, (1) 7.5	4	

32. Star Tulips

Tile	Accession Number	Dimensions (in mm)	Thickness (in mm)	Clay Body	Beveling of Edge (in degrees)	Nail Holes	Condition
1-A	1979-50-451	130 x 131	15.5	pk/or	(3) 10, (1) 7.5	4	small loss
1-B	1979-50-453	129 x 131	16.5	pk/or and red	(2) 12.5, (1) 10, (1) 5	4	small loss
2-A	1979-50-454	130 x 130	16	pk/or	(4) 10	4	
2-B	1979-50-452	132 x 130	16.5	pk/or and red	(1) 15, (3) 10	4	

33. Star Tulips

Tile	Accession Number	Dimensions (in mm)	Thickness (in mm)	Clay Body	Beveling of Edge (in degrees)	Nail Holes	Condition
A	30-10-48(37)	131 x 131	15	pk/or	(3) 10, (1) 5	3	
B	30-10-48(35)	134 x 133.5	17	pk/or	(4) 10	2	small loss

34. Grapes and Pomegranates

Tile	Accession Number	Dimensions (in mm)	Thickness (in mm)	Clay Body	Beveling of Edge (in degrees)	Nail Holes	Condition
1-A	1979-50-543	129 x 126.5	14	pk/or	(1) 15, (1) 10	2	small loss
1-B	1979-50-558	131 x 132	13	pk/or	(4) 5	3	
1-C	1979-50-540	131 x 131	12.5	pk/or	(1) 10, (3) 5	3	
1-D	1979-50-557	132 x 132	15	pk/or	(1) 15, (3) 10	2	
2-A	1979-50-559	133 x 132	14.5	pk/or	(4) 10	2	small loss
2-B	1979-50-541	132 x 133	14.5	pk/or	(2) 12.5, (2) 10	2	
2-C	1979-50-556	131 x 131	12.5	pk/or	(4) 10	3	
2-D	1979-50-542	131 x 130	12.5	pk/or	(3) 10, (1) 5	3	

35. Grapes and Pomegranates

Tile	Accession Number	Dimensions (in mm)	Thickness (in mm)	Clay Body	Beveling of Edge (in degrees)	Nail Holes	Condition
1-A	30-10-48(30)	133.5 x 134	16	pk/or	(4) 5	4	
1-B	30-10-48(9)	132 x 131	14	pk/or	(1) 15, (3) 10	3	
1-C	30-10-48(32)	135 x 134	14	pk/or	(2) 15, (1) 5	3	
1-D	30-10-48(6)	131 x 132	15	yellow	(2) 12.5, (2) 10	2	
2-A	30-10-48(8)	133 x 135	15.5	buff	(1) 10, (3) 5	2	corner loss
2-B	30-10-48(31)	134 x 133	15	pk/or and red	(4) 5	2	
2-C	30-10-48(5)	136 x 136	15.5	pk/or	(2) 10, (2) 5	1	small loss
2-D	30-10-48(29)	135 x 135	14	marbleized pk/or and red	(1) 7.5, (3) 5	2	
3-A	1979-50-536	135 x 134	18	yellow	(4) 10	3	small loss
3-B	30-10-48(1)	133 x 134	16	yellow	(3) 12.5, (1) 10	2	
3-C	1979-50-538	133 x 134	16	pk/or	(1) 15, (3) 10	3	small loss
3-D	30-10-48(2)	137 x 137	15.5	pk/or	(4) 5	2	corner loss
4-A	30-10-48(3)	134 x 134	16	pk/or	(1) 10, (2) 7.5	4	small loss

Tile	Accession Number	Dimensions (in mm)	Thickness (in mm)	Clay Body	Beveling of Edge (in degrees)	Nail Holes	Condition
4-B	1979-50-537	132 x 132	16.5	pk/or	(1) 10	4	
4-C	1979-50-555	133 x 134.5	16	pk/or	(1) 15, (3) 10	2	corner loss
4-D	1979-50-553	135 x 137	18	yellow	(2) 10, (2) 7.5	3	

36. Pomegranates

Tile	Accession Number	Dimensions (in mm)	Thickness (in mm)	Clay Body	Beveling of Edge (in degrees)	Nail Holes	Condition
1-A	1979-50-534	136 x 135	16	pk/or		4	⅛ loss; toned fills
1-B	1979-50-532	136 x 136	17.5	yellow	(4) 5	3	small losses; toned fills
2-A	1979-50-533	136 x 136	17	buff		3	⅛ loss; toned fills
2-B	1979-50-535	135 x 130	16.5	pk/or and yellow		3	small losses; toned fills; edge broken

37. Grapes and Pomegranates

Tile	Accession Number	Dimensions (in mm)	Thickness (in mm)	Clay Body	Beveling of Edge (in degrees)	Nail Holes	Condition
	1979-50-552	134 x 126	15.5	pk/or	(3) 10	3	small losses; corner loss; edge broken

38. Grapes and Pomegranates

Tile	Accession Number	Dimensions (in mm)	Thickness (in mm)	Clay Body	Beveling of Edge (in degrees)	Nail Holes	Condition
1-A	1979-50-576	133 x 133	15.5	pk/or	(1) 15, (3) 10	3	
1-B	1979-50-571	132 x 132	15	buff	(4) 10	3	corner loss
1-C	1979-50-567	130 x 132	15	pk/or	(1) 15, (2) 10, (1) 5	3	
1-D	1979-50-565	132 x 132	14.5	buff	(1) 15, (3) 10	3	
2-A	1979-50-566	131 x 131.5	15	buff	(2) 10, (2) 5	3	
2-B	1979-50-575	132 x 133	15	buff	(4) 10	3	small losses
2-C	1979-50-573	133 x 132	15	pk/or and buff	(2) 15, (2) 10	3	
2-D	1979-50-572	132 x 132.5	15.5	buff	(4) 10	2	corner loss
3-A	1979-50-574	132 x 133.5	15	pk/or and buff	(1) 15, (3) 10	3	small losses
3-B	1979-50-569	132 x 132.5	14.5	buff	(3) 10, (1) 5	2	corner and small losses
3-C	1979-50-570	133 x 132	15	pk/or	(4) 10	3	small losses
3-D	1979-50-562	133 x 132	15	pk/or	(1) 12.5, (3) 10	3	corner losses

39. Grapes and Pomegranates

Tile	Accession Number	Dimensions (in mm)	Thickness (in mm)	Clay Body	Beveling of Edge (in degrees)	Nail Holes	Condition
1-A	1979-50-546	134 x 133.5	14.5	buff	(1) 15, (2) 10, (1) 5	3	small loss; toned fill
1-B	1979-50-547	132 x 132	15	yellow	(4) 10	4	small losses
2-A	1979-50-544	132 x 132	14	pk/or and yellow	(4) 10	4	corner loss
2-B	1979-50-545	132 x 132	15	pk/or	(1) 15, (1) 12.5, (1) 10, (1) 5	4	small loss

40. Grape and Pomegranate Border Tile

Tile	Accession Number	Dimensions (in mm)	Thickness (in mm)	Clay Body	Beveling of Edge (in degrees)	Nail Holes	Condition
	1979-50-560	63 x 133.5	18	buff	(2) 7.5, (2) 5	3	small corner loss

41. Grapes and Pomegranates

Tile	Accession Number	Dimensions (in mm)	Thickness (in mm)	Clay Body	Beveling of Edge (in degrees)	Nail Holes	Condition
1-A	1979-50-549	133 x 133.5	14.5	pk/or	(2) 10, (2) 5	2	small corner loss
1-B	1979-50-550	132 x 132.5	14.5	marbleized pk/or and red	(1) 10, (3) 5	2	small corner loss
2-A	1979-50-548	132 x 132	14	pk/or and yellow	(4) 5	2	
2-B	1979-50-551	131 x 133	14	pk/or	(2) 10, (2) 5	2	

42. Animals and Hunter in Roundels

Tile	Accession Number	Dimensions (in mm)	Thickness (in mm)	Clay Body	Beveling of Edge (in degrees)	Nail Holes	Condition
1-A	1983-101-5	114 x 113	14	yellow	(2) 7.5, (2) 5	2	
1-B	1983-101-4	113 x 114	14	pk/or and buff	(2) 10, (2) 7.5	2	corner loss
2-A	1983-101-7	113 x 114.5	14	pk/or and buff	(2) 10, (2) 7.5	2	
2-B	1983-101-6	114 x 116	14	pk/or	(4) 7.5	2	

43. Animal Border Tiles

Tile	Accession Number	Dimensions (in mm)	Thickness (in mm)	Clay Body	Beveling of Edge (in degrees)	Nail Holes	Condition
A	1983-101-1	88 x 89	13.5	pk/or	(3) 10, (1) 5	2	
B	1983-101-2	86 x 86.5	14	pk/or	(1) 10, (2) 7.5, (1) 5	2	
C	1983-101-3	87.5 x 88	14	pk/or	(4) 15	2	

Tile	Accession Number	Dimensions (in mm)	Thickness (in mm)	Clay Body	Beveling of Edge (in degrees)	Nail Holes	Condition

44. Cow Border Tile

Tile	Accession Number	Dimensions (in mm)	Thickness (in mm)	Clay Body	Beveling of Edge (in degrees)	Nail Holes	Condition
	1979-50-71	79 x 134	15.5	buff	(4) 5	2	

45. Bear Border Tile

Tile	Accession Number	Dimensions (in mm)	Thickness (in mm)	Clay Body	Beveling of Edge (in degrees)	Nail Holes	Condition
	1979-50-72	92 x 133	15	buff and marbleized red	(2) 15, (2) 10	3	

46. Animals in Diamonds

Tile	Accession Number	Dimensions (in mm)	Thickness (in mm)	Clay Body	Beveling of Edge (in degrees)	Nail Holes	Condition
1-A	1979-50-42	133 x 132	15	buff	(2) 15, (2) 10	3	2 breaks; ¼ loss—inpainted
1-B	1979-50-36	131 x 133	15	pk/or and buff	(1) 20, (2) 15, (1) 10	3	small loss
1-C	1979-50-57	133 x 132	15	pk/or and buff	(1) 10, (3) 5	0	
1-D	1979-50-43	131 x 131	14.5	pk/or and buff	(2) 10, (2) 5	1	break; ⅛ loss—inpainted
2-A	1979-50-55	131 x 130	14	yellow	(4) 10	2	break; ⅛ loss—inpainted
2-B	1979-50-38	130 x 131	14	pk/or	(3) 15, (1) 10	2	small losses
2-C	1979-50-37	133 x 132	15	red	(1) 25, (1) 20, (2) 15	2	⅛ loss—inpainted
2-D	1979-50-44	132 x 132	15	pk/or	(4) 10	3	break; small loss—inpainted
3-A	1979-50-35	132 x 132	15.5	red	(3) 15, (1) 10	2	⅛ loss—inpainted
3-B	1979-50-56	132 x 133	15	pk/or	(4) 10	2	¼ loss—inpainted
3-C	1979-50-45	131 x 131	14	pk/or and yellow	(3) 10, (1) 5	1	break; small loss—inpainted
3-D	1979-50-58	130 x 131	15	pk/or	(3) 10, (1) 5	2	break; ⅛ loss—inpainted

47. Hound in Diamond

Tile	Accession Number	Dimensions (in mm)	Thickness (in mm)	Clay Body	Beveling of Edge (in degrees)	Nail Holes	Condition
	1979-50-33	139 x 139	15	pk/or and yellow	(2) 10, (1) 7.5, (1) 5	2	

48. Animals and Man in Diamonds

Tile	Accession Number	Dimensions (in mm)	Thickness (in mm)	Clay Body	Beveling of Edge (in degrees)	Nail Holes	Condition
1-A	1979-50-41	134 x 135	15	pk/or	(4) 10	3	small losses
1-B	1979-50-52	131 x 132	16	pk/or and buff	(2) 10, (2) 5	2	small losses
1-C	1979-50-32	136 x 136	15.5	buff	(1) 15, (1) 12.5, (2) 10	3	
1-D	1979-50-54	130 x 132	15	buff	(4) 10	2	⅛ loss
2-A	1979-50-40	132 x 133	15	pk/or and buff	(3) 5	3	
2-B	1979-50-53	130 x 131	15	buff	(3) 10, (1) 5	4	small losses
2-C	1979-50-31	134 x 135.5	16	buff	(1) 15, (3) 10	3	
2-D	1979-50-34	135 x 134	16	buff	(2) 10, (2) 5	3	
3-A	1979-50-128	134 x 135	16	pk/or and buff	(4) 15	3	
3-B	1979-50-39	136 x 137	16	buff	(2) 30, (1) 10, (1) 7.5	4	small losses; edge broken
3-C	1979-50-173	130 x 132	16	pk/or	(3) 5	2	small losses
3-D	12-112	130 x 131	14.5	pk/or and buff	(4) 10	2	¼ loss

49. Animals and Hunter in Diamonds

Tile	Accession Number	Dimensions (in mm)	Thickness (in mm)	Clay Body	Beveling of Edge (in degrees)	Nail Holes	Condition
1-A	1979-50-192	111 x 111	14	pk/or	(3) 10, (1) 5	2	small loss
1-B	1979-50-51	112 x 111	15	pk/or	(4) 10	2	
2-A	1979-50-50	111 x 113	14.5	pk/or	(4) 10	2	
2-B	1979-50-129	114 x 112	14	pk/or	(1) 12.5, (3) 10	2	

50. Dog and Fox in Roundels

Tile	Accession Number	Dimensions (in mm)	Thickness (in mm)	Clay Body	Beveling of Edge (in degrees)	Nail Holes	Condition
A	1979-50-75	130 x 130	11	pk/or	(2) 10, (2) 5	2	
B	1979-50-76	128 x 129	11.5	pk/or and marbleized red		2	edges broken

51. Animals and Birds in Scalloped Roundels

Tile	Accession Number	Dimensions (in mm)	Thickness (in mm)	Clay Body	Beveling of Edge (in degrees)	Nail Holes	Condition
1-A	1979-50-131	135 x 136	15.5	pk/or	(2) 12.5, (2) 10	3	
1-B	1979-50-130	136 x 137	15	pk/or	(1) 15, (3) 10	4	small losses
2-A	1979-50-62	134 x 135	16	pk/or	(1) 17.5, (3) 15	2	
2-B	1979-50-60	136 x 135	15.5	pk/or	(1) 10, (3) 5	4	small losses

Tile	Accession Number	Dimensions (in mm)	Thickness (in mm)	Clay Body	Beveling of Edge (in degrees)	Nail Holes	Condition
3-A	1979-50-59	135.5 x 135.5	15	pk/or	(2) 10, (2) 7.5	2	small losses
3-B	1979-50-74	135 x 135	15.5	pk/or	(3) 10, (1) 7.5	2	
4-A	1979-50-73	136 x 134	17	pk/or	(4) 15	2	small losses
4-B	1979-50-61	136.5 x 137	16	pk/or	(4) 5	4	

52. Animals in Scalloped Roundels

Tile	Accession Number	Dimensions (in mm)	Thickness (in mm)	Clay Body	Beveling of Edge (in degrees)	Nail Holes	Condition
1-A	30-10-47(94)	134 x 135	11.5	pk/or	(2) 10, (2) 5	4	
1-B	30-10-47(86)	133 x 134	11	pk/or	(2) 10, (2) 5	4	
1-C	30-10-47(83)	133 x 132	12.5	pk/or	(1) 15, (3) 10	4	small losses
2-A	30-10-47(85)	134 x 134	12	pk/or	(4) 5	4	small losses
2-B	30-10-47(84)	134 x 133	12.5	pk/or and yellow	(3) 5	4	
2-C	30-10-47(90)	131 x 131	11.5	white	(2) 5	4	small losses

53. Canine in Scalloped Roundel

Tile	Accession Number	Dimensions (in mm)	Thickness (in mm)	Clay Body	Beveling of Edge (in degrees)	Nail Holes	Condition
	30-10-47(87)	127 x 128	11.5	pk/or	(1) 12.5, (3) 10	2	small corner loss

54. Animals

Tile	Accession Number	Dimensions (in mm)	Thickness (in mm)	Clay Body	Beveling of Edge (in degrees)	Nail Holes	Condition
A	30-10-47(44)	129 x 129.5	12	pk/or	(2) 10, (2) 5	2	corner loss
B	30-10-47(43)	133 x 134	15	pk/or	(3) 10, (1) 5	3	small losses
C	30-10-47(37)	125 x 127	13	pk/or	(4) 5	2	
D	30-10-47(41)	126.5 x 129	13	pk/or	(2) 10, (2) 5	2	corner losses

55. Animals

Tile	Accession Number	Dimensions (in mm)	Thickness (in mm)	Clay Body	Beveling of Edge (in degrees)	Nail Holes	Condition
1-A	1979-50-48	129 x 129	14.5	pk/or	(3) 5	4	corner and other losses
1-B	1979-50-49	130 x 130.5	14	pk/or	(1) 10, (3) 5	3	corner and other losses; toned fills
1-C	1979-50-27	131 x 131.5	14	pk/or	(4) 10	4	small losses; toned fills
1-D	1979-50-30	129 x 130	14.5	pk/or	(2) 12.5, (1) 10, (1) 7.5	3	corner and other losses; toned fills
1-E	1983-101-9	133 x 131	15	pk/or	(1) 10, (3) 5	4	⅛ loss
2-A	1979-50-46	131 x 130.5	15	pk/or	(3) 5	4	small losses
2-B	1979-50-47	131 x 130	12	pk/or	(2) 15, (2) 10	3	3 small losses; toned fills
2-C	1979-50-29	128 x 130	14	pk/or	(3) 5	3	loss; bottom edge broken; toned fill
2-D	1983-101-10	128 x 130	12.5	pk/or	(1) 15, (2) 10, (1) 5	4	small losses
2-E	1979-50-28	129 x 131.5	16	pk/or	(1) 5	3	⅛ corner loss; toned fill

56. Animals in Bracketed Frames

Tile	Accession Number	Dimensions (in mm)	Thickness (in mm)	Clay Body	Beveling of Edge (in degrees)	Nail Holes	Condition
1-A	1979-50-68	130 x 130	12	pk/or	(1) 10, (1) 7.5, (2) 5	3	⅛ loss
1-B	1979-50-70	131 x 131.5	12	pk/or		3	
2-A	1979-50-69	131.5 x 131.5	14	pk/or	(4) 10	4	small losses
2-B	1979-50-67	130 x 130	12	pk/or and red	(1) 10, (3) 5	3	small losses
3-B	28-66-163	130.5 x 127.5	11.5	pk/or and yellow	(1), (1) 7.5, (2) 5	4	break; loss inpainted

57. Horse

Tile	Accession Number	Dimensions (in mm)	Thickness (in mm)	Clay Body	Beveling of Edge (in degrees)	Nail Holes	Condition
	28-66-73	129 x 128	10	yellow		2	break

58. Dogs in Roundels

Tile	Accession Number	Dimensions (in mm)	Thickness (in mm)	Clay Body	Beveling of Edge (in degrees)	Nail Holes	Condition
1-A	1979-50-66	129 x 130	9	pk/or	(4) 10	1	
1-B	1979-50-63	130 x 130.5	7.5	buff	(1) 15, (2) 10, (1) 5	1	
2-A	1979-50-64	128 x 130	9	yellow	(3) 10, (1) 7.5	2	corner losses
2-B	1979-50-65	129 x 131	8.5	buff	(1) 12.5, (3) 10	1	

59. Birds in Chinese Gardens

Tile	Accession Number	Dimensions (in mm)	Thickness (in mm)	Clay Body	Beveling of Edge (in degrees)	Nail Holes	Condition
A	1979-50-816	131 x 131	13	pk/or and yellow	(2) 7.5, (2) 5	3	small loss— inpainted
B	1979-50-817	133 x 132	13.5	pk/or	(1) 15, (2) 10, (1) 5	1	corner loss— inpainted

Tile	Accession Number	Dimensions (in mm)	Thickness (in mm)	Clay Body	Beveling of Edge (in degrees)	Nail Holes	Condition
60. Duck and Butterfly in Roundels							
A	1983-101-11	128 x 123	11	yellow	(1) 7.5, (2) 5	2	broken edge
B	1983-101-8	129 x 129	12	yellow	(1) 10, (2) 7.5, (1) 5	1	small loss; toned fill
61. Parrots and Roosters							
1-A	1983-101-22	127 x 127.5	11	pk/or	(1) 10, (3) 7.5	4	
1-B	1983-101-23	125 x 126	11.5	pk/or and marbleized red	(4) 5	4	
2-A	1983-101-24	126 x 127	10	pk/or and marbleized red	(4) 5	4	
2-B	1983-101-21	126 x 124	10	pk/or	(2) 10, (2) 7.5	4	
62. Birds							
1-A	1981-77-37	127 x 128.5	11	pk/or	(4) 10	3	small corner loss
1-B	1979-50-123	131 x 132	14	pk/or and red	(1) 10, (1) 7.5, (1) 5	4	⅛ loss
1-C	30-44-5L	132 x 130	15	pk/or	(1) 10, (3) 5	4	small losses
2-A	1979-50-120	130 x 130	11	pk/or	(3) 10, (1) 5	2	small losses
2-B	1979-50-122	133 x 133	14	pk/or	(1) 10, (1) 7.5, (2) 5	4	⅛ loss
2-C	1979-50-121	132 x 132	15.5	pk/or and marbleized red	(4) 5	4	⅛ loss
63. Birds on Branches							
1-A	1983-101-18	125 x 126	11	yellow	(1) 15, (3) 10	2	small loss
1-B	1983-101-15	127 x 126	10.5	yellow	(1) 10, (2) 5	1	corner loss
1-C	1983-101-19	126 x 126	10.5	pk/or and yellow	(3) 15, (1) 7.5	0	
2-A	1983-101-13	124 x 124.5	10	pk/or	(3) 5	0	crack
2-B	1983-101-20	126 x 127	10	yellow	(3) 10, (1) 5	2	small corner loss
2-C	1983-101-16	126 x 126	10.5	yellow	(4) 15	1	small loss
64. Birds on Branches							
A	1983-101-12	127 x 128	11	pk/or and yellow	(3) 10, (1) 5	3	
B	1983-101-17	128 x 129	11.5	pk/or and yellow	(2) 10, (2) 7.5	2	small losses
C	1983-101-14	128 x 129	11	yellow	(4) 7.5	2	corner loss
65. Birds and Flowers in Roundels							
1-A	1983-101-28	130 x 130	12	pk/or	(1) 15, (3) 10	4	small corner loss
1-B	1981-77-65	129 x 129	11.5	pk/or	(2) 10, (2) 5	4	small corner loss
1-C	1981-77-60	130 x 130	11	pk/or	(4) 10	4	
1-D	1981-77-64	129 x 130	12	pk/or	(1) 12.5, (3) 10	4	
2-A	1981-77-62	128 x 130	11	pk/or	(4) 10	4	
2-B	1981-77-68	130 x 130	11.5	pk/or	(1) 15, (1) 12.5, (2) 5	4	
2-C	1983-101-27	130 x 130	11.5	pk/or	(1) 15, (3) 10	3	small losses
2-D	1981-77-61	130 x 130	11.5	pk/or	(1) 15, (1) 12.5, (2) 10	4	
3-A	1979-50-297	131 x 132	11.5	pk/or	(3) 10, (1) 5	4	very small corner loss
3-B	1983-101-25	129 x 129	12.5	pk/or	(1) 20, (3) 15	4	small losses
3-C	1983-101-26	128 x 130	12	pk/or	(4) 15	3	small losses— inpainted
3-D	1981-77-67	130.5 x 131	12.5	pk/or	(2) 12.5, (2) 10	4	
4-A	1979-50-298	132 x 131	10.5	buff	(1) 15, (1) 10, (2) 5	4	
4-B	1981-77-63	130 x 130	11.5	pk/or	(3) 10, (1) 5	4	
4-C	1981-77-70	129 x 129	11.5	pk/or and buff	(4) 10	4	small losses
4-D	1981-77-59	129 x 129	12	yellow	(2) 10, (1) 5	4	
5-A	1983-101-29	129 x 129	12	pk/or	(4) 10	4	
5-B	1979-50-296	132 x 132	12	pk/or	(2) 5	2	small losses
5-C	1981-77-66	130 x 130	11	pk/or	(3) 10, (1) 5	4	
5-D	1979-50-295	131 x 131	12	pk/or	(3) 10, (1) 5	3	small corner loss
66. Birds							
1-A	1979-50-117	130 x 131.5	12.5	pk/or	(1) 15, (3) 10	2	⅛ loss; toned fill
1-B	1979-50-127	128 x 130	11.5	buff	(3) 10	2	bottom edge broken
1-C	1979-50-116	131 x 119	13	pk/or	(1) 15, (1) 12.5, (1) 10, (1) 5	1	right edge cut; small loss
2-A	1979-50-125	129 x 130	13	pk/or	(1) 10, (2) 5	3	small losses

Tile	Accession Number	Dimensions (in mm)	Thickness (in mm)	Clay Body	Beveling of Edge (in degrees)	Nail Holes	Condition
2-C	1979-50-119	132 x 118	13	pk/or	(1) 12.5, (1) 10, (2) 7.5	2	right edge cut
3-A	1979-50-118	129 x 128	10.5	red	(2) 20, (1) 12.5, (1) 10	2	corner loss; toned fill
3-B	1979-50-124	131 x 130	11.5	yellow	(1) 10, (3) 5	2	
3-C	1979-50-126	131 x 121	11	yellow	(4) 5	1	left edge cut

67. Birds

Tile	Accession Number	Dimensions (in mm)	Thickness (in mm)	Clay Body	Beveling of Edge (in degrees)	Nail Holes	Condition
1-A	28-66-91	128.5 x 128	12	pk/or	(2) 12.5, (2) 10	1	loss; toned fill
1-B	30-44-5H	128 x 128	12.5	pk/or	(1) 12.5, (2) 10, (1) 7.5	4	loss; toned fill
1-C	28-66-90	128 x 130	12.5	pk/or	(1) 15, (2) 12.5, (1) 10	2	small losses
2-A	28-66-179	127.5 x 127	11	pk/or	(3) 12.5, (1) 5	1	⅛ loss; toned fill
2-B	28-66-92	128 x 128	11	yellow	(1) 20, (1) 17.5, (1) 7.5, (1) 5	2	2 breaks; toned fill
2-C	28-66-178	129 x 129	11.5	pk/or	(1) 10, (3) 7.5	2	bottom edge broken

68. Parrot

Tile	Accession Number	Dimensions (in mm)	Thickness (in mm)	Clay Body	Beveling of Edge (in degrees)	Nail Holes	Condition
	30-44-5J	128 x 128	11	pk/or and red	(3) 10, (1) 5	2	2 corner losses

69. Goose

Tile	Accession Number	Dimensions (in mm)	Thickness (in mm)	Clay Body	Beveling of Edge (in degrees)	Nail Holes	Condition
	28-66-87	132 x 133	12	pk/or	(1) 15, (3) 10	3	3 breaks; ⅛ loss; toned fill

70. Butterfly

Tile	Accession Number	Dimensions (in mm)	Thickness (in mm)	Clay Body	Beveling of Edge (in degrees)	Nail Holes	Condition
	28-66-89	127 x 126	9	pk/or	(1) 10, (3) 5	0	⅛ loss; toned fill

71. Swan

Tile	Accession Number	Dimensions (in mm)	Thickness (in mm)	Clay Body	Beveling of Edge (in degrees)	Nail Holes	Condition
	1981-77-42	128 x 129.5	7.5	yellow	(1) 10, (3) 5	2	break

72. Flowers in Landscapes

Tile	Accession Number	Dimensions (in mm)	Thickness (in mm)	Clay Body	Beveling of Edge (in degrees)	Nail Holes	Condition
A	28-66-83	134 x 135	15	pk/or	(3) 10	2	¼ loss
B	28-66-80	133 x 133	14.5	pk/or	(3) 15, (1) 10	2	¼ loss

73. Tulips

Tile	Accession Number	Dimensions (in mm)	Thickness (in mm)	Clay Body	Beveling of Edge (in degrees)	Nail Holes	Condition
1-A	1979-50-224	137 x 136	15	buff	(1) 7.5, (2) 5, (1) 2.5	3	small losses
1-B	1979-50-225	138 x 140	15.5	pk/or	(2) 10, (2) 5	3	
1-C	1979-50-230	131 x 133	15	yellow	(1) 7.5, (3) 5	3	
1-D	1979-50-228	131 x 133	15.5	pk/or and buff	(1) 10, (3) 5	3	
2-A	1979-50-223	136 x 136	15	pk/or	(3) 10, (1) 5	3	small losses
2-B	1979-50-226	135 x 137	15.5	pk/or and yellow	(1) 10, (3) 5	3	
2-C	1979-50-229	131 x 133	15	yellow	(1) 10, (2) 5	3	
2-D	1979-50-227	133 x 134	15.5	buff	(1) 7.5, (2) 5	3	
3-A	1979-50-233	130 x 132	14.5	pk/or	(1) 5	2	
3-B	1979-50-231	132 x 132	13.5	pk/or and red	(1) 15, (3) 5	3	
3-C	1979-50-232	132 x 133	13	pk/or	(1) 15, (3) 10	3	
3-D	1979-50-234	132 x 131	12.5	pk/or	(1) 10, (3) 5	3	
4-A	1979-50-273	135 x 135	16.5	pk/or	(3) 10, (1) 5	2	small losses
4-B	1979-50-271	136 x 136	16.5	yellow	(2) 15, (2) 10	2	
4-C	1979-50-237	136 x 136	17.5	yellow	(1) 15, (2) 10, (1) 7.5	1	⅛ loss; toned fill
4-D	1979-50-235	134 x 134	17.5	yellow	(1) 10, (3) 5	2	⅛ loss; toned fills
5-A	1979-50-238	131 x 131	16	yellow	(3) 10	2	¼ loss; toned fills
5-B	1979-50-274	136 x 136	17	buff	(4) 10	2	
5-C	1979-50-272	136 x 136	17	yellow	(4) 10	2	small losses
5-D	1979-50-236	135 x 135	16	buff and some red	(2) 5	2	

74. Tulips

Tile	Accession Number	Dimensions (in mm)	Thickness (in mm)	Clay Body	Beveling of Edge (in degrees)	Nail Holes	Condition
1-A	1979-50-242	134 x 134	13	pk/or	(4) 10	3	⅛ loss; toned fills
1-B	1979-50-241	133 x 135	12.5	pk/or and yellow	(2) 10, (2) 15	4	small losses; toned fills
2-A	1979-50-240	131 x 132	15	pk/or	(2) 5	2	⅛ loss; toned fill
2-B	1979-50-239	133 x 133	15	pk/or and yellow		2	small losses; toned fills

Tile	Accession Number	Dimensions (in mm)	Thickness (in mm)	Clay Body	Beveling of Edge (in degrees)	Nail Holes	Condition

75. Flowers and Dragonfly

Tile	Accession Number	Dimensions (in mm)	Thickness (in mm)	Clay Body	Beveling of Edge (in degrees)	Nail Holes	Condition
A	28-66-82	130.5 x 132	13.5	pk/or	(1) 10, (1) 7.5, (2) 5	2	⅛ loss; toned fill
B	28-66-81	131.5 x 131	13.5	pk/or	(1) 7.5, (2) 5	2	⅛ loss; break; toned fills
C	28-66-78	131 x 131	13	red	(1) 10, (3) 5	2	¼ loss; 2 breaks; toned fills
D	28-66-79	130 x 130	13.5	pk/or and marbleized red	(2) 10, (1) 5	2	break; small losses; toned fills

76. Flowers

Tile	Accession Number	Dimensions (in mm)	Thickness (in mm)	Clay Body	Beveling of Edge (in degrees)	Nail Holes	Condition
1-A	1979-50-300	132 x 134	14.5	pk/or and red	(3) 10, (1) 7.5	3	
1-B	1979-50-299	127 x 129	12.5	yellow	(2) 10, (2) 5	2	
1-C	1979-50-255	130 x 131	10	pk/or	(4) 10	2	
2-A	1979-50-256	130 x 130	13	pk/or and buff	(1) 15, (1) 12.5, (1) 10, (1) 5	4	
2-B	1979-50-257	128.5 x 130	11.5	pk/or and buff	(3) 15, (1) 10	3	
2-C	1979-50-302	128 x 127	11.5	pk/or and buff	(1) 10, (2) 7.5, (1) 5	2	
3-A	1979-50-254	132 x 133	13	buff and red	(3) 5	2	
3-B	1979-50-301	132 x 130	11.5	pk/or	(3) 5	4	small corner loss
3-C	1979-50-253	133 x 134	13.5	buff and yellow	(1) 10, (2) 5	3	
4-A	1979-50-252	134 x 134	13.5	buff and red		4	
4-B	1979-50-258	129 x 129	11	pk/or and buff	(1) 7.5, (3) 5	4	
4-C	1979-50-251	134 x 133	14.5	buff and red	(4) 5	3	small losses

77. Flowers

Tile	Accession Number	Dimensions (in mm)	Thickness (in mm)	Clay Body	Beveling of Edge (in degrees)	Nail Holes	Condition
1-A	1979-50-309	128 x 128	10.5	pk/or and yellow	(1) 15, (3) 10	2	small losses
1-B	1979-50-322	130.5 x 131	13.5	pk/or	(4) 5	2	small loss
1-C	1979-50-314	128 x 127	10	pk/or	(1) 10, (3) 5	2	
1-D	1979-50-323	128 x 129	10	pk/or and red	(1) 15, (1) 10, (1) 7.5, (1) 5	2	2 breaks
2-A	1979-50-313	131 x 131	13.5	pk/or	(1) 7.5, (3) 5	2	
2-B	1979-50-320	129 x 130	10	pk/or	(1) 15, (3) 10	2	
2-C	1979-50-315	131 x 132	14	pk/or	(1) 10, (3) 5	2	small losses
2-D	1979-50-312	134 x 133	13	pk/or and buff	(4) 10	3	small loss
3-A	1979-50-318	132 x 132	14	pk/or	(2) 10, (2) 5	2	
3-B	1979-50-317	129 x 128	10	pk/or	(1) 20, (3) 10	2	
3-C	1979-50-319	129 x 128	10.5	buff	(2) 12.5, (1) 10, (1) 7.5	2	
3-D	1979-50-316	130 x 131	13	pk/or	(1) 10, (3) 5	2	small losses
4-A	1979-50-311	132 x 133	15	pk/or	(1) 10, (1) 7.5, (2) 5	2	small losses
4-B	1979-50-321	131 x 131	13.5	pk/or	(3) 7.5, (1) 5	2	
4-C	1979-50-310	131 x 132	14	pk/or	(1) 12.5, (1) 10, (2) 5	2	
4-D	1979-50-324	129 x 129	9	pk/or	(3) 10, (1) 5	2	

78. Flowers

Tile	Accession Number	Dimensions (in mm)	Thickness (in mm)	Clay Body	Beveling of Edge (in degrees)	Nail Holes	Condition
1-A	1979-50-248	129 x 130	11.5	pk/or and yellow	(3) 10, (1) 5	2	
1-B	1979-50-250	130 x 129	14.5	pk/or	(2) 10, (2) 5	3	
2-A	1979-50-247	131 x 130	12	pk/or	(4) 5	2	
2-B	1979-50-249	130.5 x 131	14.5	pk/or and yellow	(4) 5	2	

79. Flowers in Scalloped Frames

Tile	Accession Number	Dimensions (in mm)	Thickness (in mm)	Clay Body	Beveling of Edge (in degrees)	Nail Holes	Condition
1-A	1983-101-116	129.5 x 128	12.5	pk/or	(1) 10, (2) 5	4	edge broken
1-B	1983-101-114	128 x 129	12	pk/or	(3) 5, (1) 2.5	3	
2-A	1983-101-115	129 x 129	12	pk/or and red	(4) 10	3	
2-B	1983-101-113	130 x 130	12	red	(2) 10, (2) 5	3	

80. Flowers

Tile	Accession Number	Dimensions (in mm)	Thickness (in mm)	Clay Body	Beveling of Edge (in degrees)	Nail Holes	Condition
1-A	1979-50-243	134 x 134	14.5	pk/or	(1) 15, (1) 12.5, (2) 10	2	small loss
1-B	1979-50-244	133 x 133	14.5	pk/or	(1) 15, (2) 10, (1) 5	2	small loss
2-A	1979-50-246	132 x 131	13	pk/or	(3) 15, (1) 10	2	corner loss
2-B	1979-50-245	134 x 134	15	pk/or	(3) 15, (1) 10	3	

81. Flowers

Tile	Accession Number	Dimensions (in mm)	Thickness (in mm)	Clay Body	Beveling of Edge (in degrees)	Nail Holes	Condition
1-A	1979-50-262	127 x 127	11	yellow	(2) 10	3	small losses; toned fills
1-B	1979-50-260	127 x 128	12	yellow	(4) 10	2	small losses; toned fills

Tile	Accession Number	Dimensions (in mm)	Thickness (in mm)	Clay Body	Beveling of Edge (in degrees)	Nail Holes	Condition
2-A	1979-50-259	128 x 127	12	pk/or	(4) 10	2	small losses; toned fills
2-B	1979-50-261	126 x 125	10	buff		1	small losses; toned fills

82. Triple Tulips in Bracketed Frames

Tile	Accession Number	Dimensions (in mm)	Thickness (in mm)	Clay Body	Beveling of Edge (in degrees)	Nail Holes	Condition
1-A	30-10-47 (126)	131 x 132	13.5	pk/or and yellow	(2) 15, (1) 10, (1) 5	3	small losses
1-B	30-10-47 (130)	129 x 128	13	pk/or and buff	(1) 20, (3) 10	2	small losses
1-C	30-10-47 (133)	132 x 132	13	pk/or	(1) 15, (1) 12.5, (2) 10	3	
1-D	30-10-47 (129)	131 x 132	13	pk/or and yellow	(3) 15, (1) 12.5	3	small loss
2-A	30-10-47 (131)	131 x 130.5	13.5	pk/or and red	(1) 15, (3) 10	3	
2-B	30-10-47 (132)	131.5 x 131.5	13	pk/or and buff	(1) 15, (2) 10, (1) 5	3	small losses
2-C	30-10-47 (125a)	132 x 130	13	buff	(1) 15, (1) 12.5, (1) 7.5, (1) 10	3	small losses
2-D	30-10-47 (125)	131 x 132	13	pk/or and yellow	(1) 15, (2) 10, (1) 5	2	small losses
3-A	30-10-47 (129a)	132 x 130	13	pk/or and yellow	(1) 12.5, (3) 10	3	2 breaks
3-B	30-10-47 (134)	127 x 128.5	13.5	pk/or and buff	(4) 10	2	small losses
3-C	30-10-47 (128)	129 x 128	13.5	pk/or and yellow	(2) 15, (1) 12.5, (1) 10	2	small losses
3-D	30-10-47 (126a)	132 x 133	13	pk/or	(2) 15, (1) 12.5, (1) 7.5	3	

83. Triple Tulips in Bracketed Frames

Tile	Accession Number	Dimensions (in mm)	Thickness (in mm)	Clay Body	Beveling of Edge (in degrees)	Nail Holes	Condition
1-A	1979-50-284	128 x 128	11	pk/or and yellow	(4) 5	2	
1-B	1979-50-283	129 x 128	11	yellow	(1) 20, (1) 15, (2) 10	2	small losses; 2 corners inpainted
2-A	1979-50-286	129 x 127	12	pk/or and yellow	(2) 10, (1) 5	2	right side broken; ⅛ loss; 2 corners inpainted
2-B	1979-50-285	130 x 129	11	yellow and marbleized orange	(1) 20, (3) 10	2	small corner loss

84. Triple Tulips in Bracketed Frames

Tile	Accession Number	Dimensions (in mm)	Thickness (in mm)	Clay Body	Beveling of Edge (in degrees)	Nail Holes	Condition
1-A	1979-50-288	130 x 130	13.5	marbleized pk/or and red	(2) 10, (2) 5	2	
1-B	1979-50-287	130 x 133	14	pk/or	(1) 10, (2) 5	3	
2-A	1979-50-282	129 x 129	12	pk/or	(1) 20, (1) 15, (2) 10	4	
2-B	1979-50-279	132 x 131	13	pk/or	(3) 15, (1) 5	2	small loss
3-A	1979-50-280	131 x 131	12.5	pk/or	(4) 15	4	small loss
3-B	1979-50-281	129 x 130	12	pk/or	(1) 20, (3) 15	3	small loss
4-A	1979-50-290	133 x 131	12	pk/or	(2) 10, (2) 5	3	
4-B	1979-50-289	131 x 131.5	12	pk/or	(1) 20, (3) 15	2	small loss

86. Triple Tulip in Scalloped Roundel

Tile	Accession Number	Dimensions (in mm)	Thickness (in mm)	Clay Body	Beveling of Edge (in degrees)	Nail Holes	Condition
	1979-50-305	126.5 x 128.5	11	buff	(1) 15, (3) 5	4	small corner loss

87. Triple Tulips

Tile	Accession Number	Dimensions (in mm)	Thickness (in mm)	Clay Body	Beveling of Edge (in degrees)	Nail Holes	Condition
1-A	1979-50-345	129 x 130	11	pk/or	(1) 10, (3) 5	2	
1-B	1979-50-342	134 x 133	15	pk/or and red	(4) 10	2	⅛ loss
1-C	1979-50-347	132 x 130	15	pk/or	(1) 45, (1) 12.5, (1) 10, (1) 7.5	2	small losses
1-D	1979-50-348	130 x 130	11	pk/or	(2) 10, (2) 5	2	
2-A	1979-50-344	132 x 132	13.5	pk/or	(4) 10	2	
2-B	1979-50-351	130 x 129	11.5	yellow	(3) 5	2	
2-C	1979-50-354	126 x 125	11.5	pk/or	(4) 5	2	
2-D	1979-50-352	132 x 132	14	yellow	(1) 10, (1) 7.5, (2) 5	2	small losses
3-A	1979-50-341	133 x 133	13.5	pk/or	(1) 12.5, (3) 10	2	small losses
3-B	1979-50-356	129 x 129	11	pk/or	(3) 10, (1) 5	3	corner loss
3-C	1979-50-355	129 x 131	12	pk/or	(4) 5	3	corner and other small losses
3-D	1979-50-346	131 x 131	13	pk/or	(1) 12.5, (3) 10	2	
4-A	1979-50-353	129 x 128	11	pk/or	(2) 10, (2) 7.5	4	
4-B	1979-50-350	127 x 127	11	pk/or	(1) 10, (2) 7.5, (1) 5	2	
4-C	1979-50-343	132 x 126	12.5	buff	(3) 10, (1) 5	2	small losses; edge loss
4-D	1979-50-349	128 x 129	11	pk/or	(3) 10, (1) 7.5	1	

88. Triple Tulips

Tile	Accession Number	Dimensions (in mm)	Thickness (in mm)	Clay Body	Beveling of Edge (in degrees)	Nail Holes	Condition
A	1979-50-292	131 x 130	14.5	pk/or	(1) 12.5, (2) 10, (1) 5	3	
B	1979-50-293	129 x 130	14	pk/or	(1) 15, (3) 10	4	
C	1979-50-291	130 x 131	14	pk/or	(3) 10, (1) 5	3	⅛ loss

Tile	Accession Number	Dimensions (in mm)	Thickness (in mm)	Clay Body	Beveling of Edge (in degrees)	Nail Holes	Condition

89. Flowers in Ovals

Tile	Accession Number	Dimensions (in mm)	Thickness (in mm)	Clay Body	Beveling of Edge (in degrees)	Nail Holes	Condition
1-A	1979-50-264	133 x 132	14.5	pk/or and yellow	(4) 5	3	
1-B	1979-50-263	130 x 132	14	pk/or and yellow	(4) 5	3	
2-A	1979-50-266	130 x 129	15	buff, pk/or, and marbleized red	(3) 10, (1) 15	4	
2-B	1979-50-265	130 x 130	11	pk/or and buff	(4) 5	2	

90. Tulips in Diamonds

Tile	Accession Number	Dimensions (in mm)	Thickness (in mm)	Clay Body	Beveling of Edge (in degrees)	Nail Holes	Condition
1-A	1979-50-278	128 x 129	11.5	pk/or	(4) 10	3	
1-B	1979-50-277	129 x 128	11.5	pk/or	(1) 15, (2) 10, (1) 5	4	
2-A	1979-50-275	127 x 128	13	pk/or	(3) 10, (1) 5	3	
2-B	1979-50-276	127 x 128	14	pk/or	(1) 15, (3) 10	3	

91. Composite Flowering Bulbs in Diamonds

Tile	Accession Number	Dimensions (in mm)	Thickness (in mm)	Clay Body	Beveling of Edge (in degrees)	Nail Holes	Condition
1-A	1979-50-364	129 x 130	11	pk/or	(4) 10	2	
1-B	1979-50-365	128 x 129	12	pk/or and yellow	(2) 10, (2) 5	2	
1-C	1979-50-358	130 x 131	12	pk/or and yellow	(4) 15	4	
1-D	1979-50-357	130 x 129	11.5	pk/or and yellow	(4) 5	2	small corner losses
2-A	1979-50-362	127 x 127	11	yellow	(2) 15, (2) 10	2	
2-B	1979-50-363	128 x 128	11	yellow	(3) 12.5, (1) 10	2	
2-C	1979-50-369	127 x 130	11	pk/or and yellow	(1) 10, (3) 5	2	small corner loss
2-D	1979-50-359	127 x 127	11.5	pk/or	(4) 5	2	
3-A	1979-50-367	126 x 128	11.5	pk/or	(4) 10	2	small corner loss
3-B	1979-50-361	128 x 128	11.5	pk/or	(2) 10, (2) 5	2	
3-C	1979-50-366	126 x 127	11.5	pk/or and yellow	(2) 10, (2) 5	2	
3-D	1979-50-360	126 x 126	11.5	pk/or	(1) 12.5, (3) 10	2	

92. Flowering Bulbs in Diamonds

Tile	Accession Number	Dimensions (in mm)	Thickness (in mm)	Clay Body	Beveling of Edge (in degrees)	Nail Holes	Condition
1-A	1979-50-337	129 x 129	14	red	(1) 10, (2) 7.5, (1) 5	4	
1-B	1979-50-340	132 x 131	14	red	(2) 10, (2) 5	4	
1-C	1979-50-334	129 x 131	14	red	(2) 10, (1) 7.5, (1) 5	4	
1-D	1979-50-325	131 x 131	14.5	pk/or and red	(2) 10, (2) 5	4	
2-A	1979-50-333	132 x 132	14	pk/or and red	(1) 7.5, (3) 5	4	
2-B	1979-50-332	132 x 132	13.5	red	(1) 10, (3) 5	4	
2-C	1979-50-330	130 x 130	14	red	(4) 10	4	
2-D	1979-50-339	129 x 129	13.5	pk/or and red	(1) 10, (3) 5	4	
3-A	1979-50-329	128 x 129	13.5	red	(2) 7.5, (2) 5	4	
3-B	1979-50-336	130 x 132	14.5	pk/or and red	(1) 10, (3) 5	4	
3-C	1979-50-331	131 x 131	14	red	(1) 10, (3) 5	4	
3-D	1979-50-327	129 x 130	14	red	(3) 10, (1) 5	4	small loss
4-A	1979-50-328	128 x 129	13.5	red	(2) 7.5, (2) 5	4	
4-B	1979-50-326	129 x 129	14	red	(3) 10, (1) 5	4	
4-C	1979-50-338	129 x 129	13.5	red	(1) 10, (1) 7.5, (2) 5	4	
4-D	1979-50-335	128.5 x 129.5	14.5	pk/or and red	(1) 7.5, (3) 5	4	

93. Flowering Shrubs in Diamonds

Tile	Accession Number	Dimensions (in mm)	Thickness (in mm)	Clay Body	Beveling of Edge (in degrees)	Nail Holes	Condition
1-A	1979-50-267	130 x 127	16	yellow	(2) 15, (2) 10	4	
1-B	1979-50-268	130 x 131.5	17	buff	(1) 15, (3) 12.5	4	
2-A	1979-50-270	130 x 131	16	buff and marbleized pk/or	(1) 20, (3) 10	4	
2-B	1979-50-269	129 x 129	17	pk/or and yellow	(2) 17.5, (2) 15	4	

94. Flower Vase

Tile	Accession Number	Dimensions (in mm)	Thickness (in mm)	Clay Body	Beveling of Edge (in degrees)	Nail Holes	Condition
	28-66-128	133 x 132	11	pk/or	(2) 15, (1) 12.5	4	break; small losses

95. Flower Vases in Bracketed Frames

Tile	Accession Number	Dimensions (in mm)	Thickness (in mm)	Clay Body	Beveling of Edge (in degrees)	Nail Holes	Condition
1-A	1983-101-120	130 x 130.5	12	yellow and orange	(1) 12.5, (3) 10	2	
1-B	1983-101-119	130.5 x 132	12	yellow and orange	(3) 10, (1) 7.5	2	
2-A	1983-101-118	131.5 x 134	12.5	yellow and orange	(4) 10	3	
2-B	1983-101-117	129.5 x 131	12	yellow-orange	(3) 10, (1) 7.5	2	

96. Flower Vases

Tile	Accession Number	Dimensions (in mm)	Thickness (in mm)	Clay Body	Beveling of Edge (in degrees)	Nail Holes	Condition
1-A	1979-50-408	127 x 132	11	pk/or	(2) 10, (1) 5	4	bottom edge broken
1-B	1979-50-407	132 x 132	13	yellow	(3) 5	4	
2-A	1979-50-409	130 x 130	12	pk/or	(3) 7.5, (1) 5	4	small losses
2-B	1979-50-410	131 x 132	13	pk/or	(3) 5	4	
3-A	30-44-59	132 x 131	17.5	red	(1) 10, (1) 7.5, (1) 5	4	small loss

Tile	Accession Number	Dimensions (in mm)	Thickness (in mm)	Clay Body	Beveling of Edge (in degrees)	Nail Holes	Condition
3-B	1979-50-593	130 x 131	15.5	pk/or	(1) 7.5, (3) 5	4	
4-A	1979-50-412	132 x 132	12	pk/or	(1) 15, (1) 12.5, (2) 10	4	1/8 loss
4-B	1979-50-413	132 x 131	16	yellow	(3) 10	4	small glaze losses
5-A	1979-50-414	127 x 129	13	pk/or	(1) 15, (3) 10	2	1/8 loss
5-B	1979-50-411	131 x 124	13	pk/or	(1) 15, (1) 10, (1) 5	2	small losses

97. Flower Vases in Diamonds

Tile	Accession Number	Dimensions (in mm)	Thickness (in mm)	Clay Body	Beveling of Edge (in degrees)	Nail Holes	Condition
1-A	1979-50-418	130 x 129.5	13	pk/or	(4) 10	4	
1-B	1979-50-371	131 x 130	12.5	pk/or and buff	(2) 10, (1) 7.5, (1) 5	4	corner loss
1-C	1979-50-373	130 x 130	13	pk/or and buff	(1) 10, (2) 5, (1) 2.5	4	small losses; corner loss
1-D	1979-50-372	129 x 130	12.5	pk/or	(3) 10, (1) 5	3	
2-A	1979-50-415	129 x 129.5	13	pk/or	(3) 10, (1) 7.5	4	
2-B	1979-50-374	128 x 130	12.5	pk/or	(1) 10, (3) 5	4	small losses
2-C	1979-50-416	130 x 130	14	pk/or		3	
2-D	1979-50-417	130 x 129	13	pk/or	(1) 20, (1) 12.5, (2) 10	4	

98. Flower Vase

Tile	Accession Number	Dimensions (in mm)	Thickness (in mm)	Clay Body	Beveling of Edge (in degrees)	Nail Holes	Condition
	28-66-162	128.5 x 128	12	pk/or	(3) 10, (1) 5	2	break

99. Fruit Compotes

Tile	Accession Number	Dimensions (in mm)	Thickness (in mm)	Clay Body	Beveling of Edge (in degrees)	Nail Holes	Condition
1-A	1979-50-607	127 x 126	16	red	filled	4	small losses; toned fills
1-B	1979-50-605	126 x 125	15.5	pk/or	(1) 15, (1) 10	3	1/8 loss; toned fills
2-A	1979-50-608	126 x 125	16	red	filled	3	small losses; toned fills
2-B	1979-50-606	126 x 125	15.5	red	filled	4	1/4 loss; toned fills

100. Fruit Compotes

Tile	Accession Number	Dimensions (in mm)	Thickness (in mm)	Clay Body	Beveling of Edge (in degrees)	Nail Holes	Condition
1-A	1979-50-601	132 x 134	14	pk/or	(3) 10, (1) 5	3	small losses
1-B	30-10-48 (26)	132 x 132	14	pk/or and marbleized yellow	(4) 10	3	
1-C	30-10-48 (25)	129 x 130	12.5	pk/or and yellow	(1) 25, (2) 20, (1) 12.5	3	
2-A	1979-50-604	135 x 134	14.5	pk/or	(2) 5	2	
2-B	1979-50-603	132 x 133	12	pk/or and buff	(1) 12.5, (3) 10	3	
2-C	1979-50-602	131 x 131	12.5	buff	(1) 10, (2) 5	3	small losses

101. Fruit Compotes

Tile	Accession Number	Dimensions (in mm)	Thickness (in mm)	Clay Body	Beveling of Edge (in degrees)	Nail Holes	Condition
1-A	30-10-48 (28)	134 x 133	13.5	pk/or and marbleized red	(4) 10	2	small losses; toned fills
1-B	1979-50-599	130 x 130	13.5	pk/or	(3) 10, (1) 5	4	small losses; toned fills
1-C	30-10-48 (27)	135 x 134	13	pk/or and marbleized red	(1) 15, (1) 12.5, (2) 10	2	small losses; toned fills
2-A	1979-50-597	130 x 131	14.5	red	(1) 15, (1) 12.5, (2) 10	1	1/4 loss; toned fills
2-B	1979-50-598	127 x 127	14	red	(4) 5	4	small losses; toned fills
2-C	1979-50-600	130.5 x 131	14.5	pk/or	(4) 7.5	2	1/4 loss; toned fills

102. Fruit Compotes

Tile	Accession Number	Dimensions (in mm)	Thickness (in mm)	Clay Body	Beveling of Edge (in degrees)	Nail Holes	Condition
A	1979-50-595	133 x 132	12.5	pk/or	(4) 15	3	
B	1979-50-594	131 x 132	14.5	pk/or	(4) 10	4	
C	30-10-47 (74)	131 x 131	10.5	pk/or and buff	(4) 15	2	

103. Fruit Compote

Tile	Accession Number	Dimensions (in mm)	Thickness (in mm)	Clay Body	Beveling of Edge (in degrees)	Nail Holes	Condition
	1979-50-596	126 x 126	11	pk/or	(2) 10, (2) 5	2	

104. Fruit and Vegetables

Tile	Accession Number	Dimensions (in mm)	Thickness (in mm)	Clay Body	Beveling of Edge (in degrees)	Nail Holes	Condition
1-A	1979-50-614	125 x 126	9	yellow	(4) 5	2	
1-B	1979-50-623	125 x 125.5	9	yellow	(3) 5	1	
1-C	1979-50-617	126 x 126	9	yellow	(2) 7.5, (2) 5	1	
1-D	1979-50-621	125 x 126	8.5	yellow	(3) 5	2	
2-A	1979-50-618	127 x 126	9	yellow	(1) 10, (2) 5	2	2 breaks
2-B	1979-50-625	127 x 128	9.5	yellow	(3) 5	2	

Tile	Accession Number	Dimensions (in mm)	Thickness (in mm)	Clay Body	Beveling of Edge (in degrees)	Nail Holes	Condition
2-C	1979-50-627	126 x 125	9	yellow	(3) 5	1	
2-D	1979-50-616	127 x 126	9	yellow	(3) 10, (1) 5	2	
3-A	1979-50-624	126 x 126	9	buff	(4) 5	2	
3-B	1979-50-620	126 x 126	9	yellow	(4) 5	2	
3-C	1979-50-626	128.5 x 128.5	8.5	yellow	(4) 5	2	
3-D	1979-50-615	126 x 126	8.5	yellow	(1) 10, (2) 5	2	break; ⅛ loss; toned fill
4-A	1979-50-628	125 x 126	8.5	yellow	(1) 2.5, (3) 5	2	corner loss
4-B	1979-50-619	128 x 128	9.5	buff	(4) 5	1	3 breaks; small losses—inpainted
4-C	1979-50-629	126 x 125	9	yellow	(4) 5	2	break
4-D	1979-50-622	126 x 126	8.5	yellow	(3) 5	2	

105. Fruit Clusters

Tile	Accession Number	Dimensions (in mm)	Thickness (in mm)	Clay Body	Beveling of Edge (in degrees)	Nail Holes	Condition
1-A	1979-50-582	126 x 125	11	pk/or	(2) 10, (2) 5	2	
1-B	1979-50-577	126.5 x 125	12.5	buff	(1) 15, (1) 10, (2) 5	2	
1-C	1979-50-585	127.5 x 127.5	13	pk/or	(2) 10, (2) 5	2	
1-D	1979-50-591	128 x 127	11	pk/or	(1) 10, (3) 5	2	
2-A	1979-50-581	124 x 124	13.5	pk/or	(2) 15, (2) 10	1	small loss
2-B	1979-50-587	126 x 126	12.5	pk/or	(1) 15, (1) 10, (2) 5	1	small loss
2-C	1979-50-590	126 x 126	12	yellow	(1) 15, (3) 10	2	
2-D	1979-50-583	125 x 125	12.5	pk/or	(2) 10, (2) 5	2	
3-A	1979-50-580	127 x 127	12.5	buff	(4) 10	2	
3-B	1979-50-584	126 x 127.5	12.5	pk/or	(1) 15, (2) 10, (1) 7.5	2	
3-C	1979-50-588	125 x 126	12.5	pk/or	(4) 15	2	
3-D	1979-50-589	127 x 128	13.5	pk/or	(2) 10, (2) 5	2	small corner loss
4-A	1979-50-592	126 x 127	11.5	pk/or	(1) 10, (3) 5	2	small loss
4-B	1979-50-586	126 x 127	11	pk/or	(1) 35, (1) 10, (1) 5	2	
4-C	1979-50-579	126 x 126	11	pk/or	(2) 10, (2) 5	2	corner loss
4-D	1979-50-578	127 x 125.5	12.5	pk/or	(2) 15, (2) 10	1	small corner loss

106. Fruit

Tile	Accession Number	Dimensions (in mm)	Thickness (in mm)	Clay Body	Beveling of Edge (in degrees)	Nail Holes	Condition
1-A	1979-50-611	127 x 127.5	9.5	yellow	(4) 5	0	
1-B	1979-50-612	125 x 128	11	pk/or and buff	(2) 10, (2) 5	3	
2-A	1979-50-609	124 x 125	10	pk/or and buff	(4) 5	2	
2-B	1979-50-610	124 x 126	10	pk/or and buff	(1) 10, (3) 5	2	small losses

107. Fruit Bowl

Tile	Accession Number	Dimensions (in mm)	Thickness (in mm)	Clay Body	Beveling of Edge (in degrees)	Nail Holes	Condition
	1979-50-613	128.5 x 129	9	buff	(2) 10, (2) 5	2	

108. Fruit Basket

Tile	Accession Number	Dimensions (in mm)	Thickness (in mm)	Clay Body	Beveling of Edge (in degrees)	Nail Holes	Condition
	1979-50-723	122 x 122	7.5	pk/or	(2) 10, (2) 5	2	

109. Villagers (Pilgrim Tiles)

Tile	Accession Number	Dimensions (in mm)	Thickness (in mm)	Clay Body	Beveling of Edge (in degrees)	Nail Holes	Condition
1-A	1979-50-153	135 x 136	14.5	pk/or and buff	(2) 20, (2) 15	4	very small loss; toned fill
1-B	1979-50-155	135 x 135	14	pk/or	(3) 125, (1) 10	4	small losses; toned fills
1-C	1979-50-150	136 x 137	14	pk/or and buff	(2) 20, (2) 15	4	⅛ loss; toned fills
1-D	1979-50-151	136 x 136	14	pk/or	(4) 15	4	small loss; toned fills
2-A	1979-50-152	135 x 136	13.5	pk/or	(2) 15, (2) 10	4	small losses; toned fills
2-B	1070-50-156	136 x 136	14	pk/or and buff	(3) 20, (1) 15	3	small loss; toned fill
2-C	1979-50-158	136 x 139	14	pk/or and buff	(2) 20, (2) 15	3	¼ loss; toned fills
2-D	1979-50-157	134 x 134	14	pk/or	(2) 15, (2) 10	1	¼ loss; toned fills

110. Scenes from Daily Life

Tile	Accession Number	Dimensions (in mm)	Thickness (in mm)	Clay Body	Beveling of Edge (in degrees)	Nail Holes	Condition
1-A	1979-50-140	127 x 131	11	pk/or	(1) 25, (3) 10	2	bottom edge lost
1-B	1979-50-161	131 x 131	11	pk/or	(2) 15, (2) 10	4	
1-C	1979-50-163	136 x 135	13	pk/or	(3) 10, (1) 5	4	break; small losses; toned fills
1-D	1070-50-162	131 x 131.5	11.5	pk/or	(1) 15, (2) 12.5, (1) 10	4	3 breaks; small loss; toned fill
2-A	1979-50-159	130 x 131	11.5	pk/or	(3) 10, (1) 5	4	small loss; toned fill

Tile	Accession Number	Dimensions (in mm)	Thickness (in mm)	Clay Body	Beveling of Edge (in degrees)	Nail Holes	Condition
2-B	1979-50-114	130 x 130	12	pk/or	(2) 10, (2) 10	4	break
2-C	1979-50-115	131 x 132	11.5	pk/or	(2) 15, (2) 10	4	2 breaks
2-D	1979-50-164	130 x 131	12	pk/or	(3) 15, (1) 10	4	
3-A	1979-50-169	131 x 131	11.5	pk/or	(1) 15, (2) 10, (1) 5	4	small loss; toned fill
3-B	1979-50-166	136 x 134	12.5	pk/or	(2) 10, (2) 5	4	
3-C	1979-50-167	131 x 131	10.5	pk/or	(2) 10, (2) 5	4	
3-D	1979-50-139	129 x 129	13	pk/or	(2) 10, (2) 5	4	
4-A	1979-50-160	132 x 133	11.5	pk/or	(2) 15, (2) 10	4	
4-B	1979-50-165	132 x 133	11.5	pk/or and buff	(2) 10, (2) 5	4	small losses; toned fills
4-C	1979-50-168	131 x 132	11	pk/or	(1) 12.5, (3) 10	4	small losses; toned fills
4-D	1979-50-172	135 x 134	11.5	pk/or and yellow	(1) 10, (3) 7.5	4	small loss; toned fill
5-A	1979-50-142	128 x 130	12	pk/or	(2) 10, (2) 5	2	
5-B	1979-50-170	132 x 131	11.5	pk/or	(4) 10	4	
5-C	1979-50-171	131 x 131	11	pk/or	(1) 15, (3) 10	4	small loss; toned fill
5-D	1979-50-141	128 x 129	11	yellow	(1) 15, (1) 12.5, (1) 10, (1) 5	2	

111. Town Crier, Skater, and Fisherman

A	1979-50-144	131 x 132.5	12.5	pk/or and yellow	(3) 10, (1) 5	4	small losses
B	1979-50-143	130 x 130	14	pk/or	(3) 15, (1) 10	3	corner losses
C	1981-77-51	128 x 129	12	yellow	(2) 10	2	

112. Drinker, Musicians, and Peddler

1-A	28-66-86	126 x 132	8	pk/or	(1) 7.5	3	3 breaks
1-B	28-66-85	126 x 130	13	pk/or	(3) 10	3	edge cut
2-A	28-66-180	130 x 132	13	pk/or	(3) 7.5, (1) 5	2	
2-B	28-66-84	127 x 132	11.5	pk/or and buff	(4) 10	3	

113. Figures in Archways

A	1979-50-149	129 x 129	11	pk/or	(4) 10	2	
B	1979-50-212	127 x 128	11	pk/or	(2) 10, (2) 5	2	
C	1979-50-211	129 x 123	10	pk/or	(3) 5	2	left edge cut

114. Town Crier

	1979-50-132	129 x 130	13	pk/or	(1) 10, (3) 5	4	

115. Ladies and Men

1-A	1979-50-133	131 x 131	10.5	buff and marbleized pk/or	(1) 15, (1) 10, (1) 7.5, (1) 5	4	small loss; toned fill
1-B	1979-50-145	132 x 131	12	pk/or	(1) 15, (2) 12.5, (1) 10	1	⅛ loss; toned fill
1-C	1979-50-146	131 x 131.5	12	pk/or	(2) 15, (2) 10	4	⅛ loss; toned fills
2-A	1979-50-134	131 x 132	12.5	pk/or	(1) 10, (1) 7.5, (2) 5	2	small loss; toned fill
2-B	1979-50-147	127 x 130.5	12	pk/or	(2) 15, (1) 10	3	bottom edge broken; toned fill
2-C	1979-50-148	120 x 130	12	pk/or	(1) 15, (1) 10, (1) 7.5	3	bottom edge broken; toned fill

116. Figures

A	30-10-47 (15)	132 x 131	12.5	pk/or and red		3	corner loss
B	30-10-47 (12)	130 x 132	12.5	red	(4) 10	2	small corner loss
C	30-10-47 (8)	130 x 130	13	pk/or and red	(2) 10	2	corner loss

117. Elegant Pairs

1-A	1979-50-135	130 x 130	9	yellow	(2) 10, (1) 5	2	
1-B	1979-50-136	129 x 130	9.5	pk/or and buff	(1) 10, (1) 7.5, (2) 5	2	
2-A	1979-50-137	130 x 129	10.5	yellow	(1) 10, (3) 5	2	small loss; toned fill
2-B	1979-50-138	130 x 129	9.5	pk/or and buff	(1) 15, (1) 12.5, (1) 7.5, (1) 5	2	small losses; toned fills

Tile	Accession Number	Dimensions (in mm)	Thickness (in mm)	Clay Body	Beveling of Edge (in degrees)	Nail Holes	Condition

118. Hunter

Tile	Accession Number	Dimensions (in mm)	Thickness (in mm)	Clay Body	Beveling of Edge (in degrees)	Nail Holes	Condition
	28-66-181	130 x 130	11.5	yellow	(3) 15, (1) 10	1	3 breaks; ¼ loss; toned fills

119. Fisherman and Horseback Rider

Tile	Accession Number	Dimensions (in mm)	Thickness (in mm)	Clay Body	Beveling of Edge (in degrees)	Nail Holes	Condition
A	28-66-112	127 x 126	10	pk/or	(1) 10, (2) 5	1	4 breaks; ¼ loss; toned fill
B	28-66-157	125 x 125	9.5	pk/or	(1) 15, (3) 10	2	small losses; 3 breaks; toned fills

120. Acrobat

Tile	Accession Number	Dimensions (in mm)	Thickness (in mm)	Clay Body	Beveling of Edge (in degrees)	Nail Holes	Condition
	1979-50-154	129 x 130	8.5	buff	(2) 15, (2) 10	3	small losses; toned fills

121. Acrobats

Tile	Accession Number	Dimensions (in mm)	Thickness (in mm)	Clay Body	Beveling of Edge (in degrees)	Nail Holes	Condition
A	1983-101-122	132 x 131	8	yellow	(2) 5, (1) 2.5	2	
B	1983-101-123	131 x 130.5	8	yellow	(1) 10, (3) 5	2	

122. Portrait in Oval Frame

Tile	Accession Number	Dimensions (in mm)	Thickness (in mm)	Clay Body	Beveling of Edge (in degrees)	Nail Holes	Condition
	1983-101-125	131 x 130.5	8.5	pk/or	(3) 10, (1) 7.5	4	

123. Putti Playing a Guessing Game

Tile	Accession Number	Dimensions (in mm)	Thickness (in mm)	Clay Body	Beveling of Edge (in degrees)	Nail Holes	Condition
	1981-77-34	132 x 133	15.5	pk/or	(1) 15, (2) 12.5, (1) 10	2	small losses; 2 toned fills— inpainted

124. Cupid in an Archway

Tile	Accession Number	Dimensions (in mm)	Thickness (in mm)	Clay Body	Beveling of Edge (in degrees)	Nail Holes	Condition
	1979-50-728	127.5 x 128.5	13	buff and marbleized pk/or	(4) 10	3	

125. Bacchus

Tile	Accession Number	Dimensions (in mm)	Thickness (in mm)	Clay Body	Beveling of Edge (in degrees)	Nail Holes	Condition
	1981-77-36	129 x 128	13	pk/or	(3) 7.5, (1) 5	3	2 breaks

126. Cupids Playing

Tile	Accession Number	Dimensions (in mm)	Thickness (in mm)	Clay Body	Beveling of Edge (in degrees)	Nail Holes	Condition
1-A	1979-50-726	128 x 129	11	pk/or	(4) 7.5	2	
1-B	1979-50-727	128 x 128	10.5	pk/or	(2) 10, (2) 5	2	
2-A	1979-50-724	128 x 128	11	pk/or and yellow	(1) 7.5, (3) 5	2	
2-B	1979-50-725	128 x 126	11	pk/or	(3) 10, (1) 7.5	2	

127. Putto Playing Music

Tile	Accession Number	Dimensions (in mm)	Thickness (in mm)	Clay Body	Beveling of Edge (in degrees)	Nail Holes	Condition
	1983-101-30	127 x 127	11.5	pk/or	(4) 15	2	

128. Musical Angels

Tile	Accession Number	Dimensions (in mm)	Thickness (in mm)	Clay Body	Beveling of Edge (in degrees)	Nail Holes	Condition
	28-66-164	132 x 132	10	yellow	(4) 10	0	4 breaks; toned fills

129. Children's Games

Tile	Accession Number	Dimensions (in mm)	Thickness (in mm)	Clay Body	Beveling of Edge (in degrees)	Nail Holes	Condition
1-A	1983-101-62	131 x 131	8	buff	(4) 5	2	
1-B	1983-101-33	131 x 131	7.5	yellow	(2) 10, (2) 5	3	
1-C	1983-101-47	130 x 130	8	pk/or	(2) 10, (1) 7.5, (1) 5	2	small losses; toned fills
1-D	1983-101-34	132 x 132	8.5	yellow	(1) 7.5, (3) 5	3	
1-E	1983-101-46	132.5 x 132.5	8	yellow	(4) 5	3	
1-F	1983-101-32	132 x 132	7.5	yellow	(4) 5	2	
1-G	1983-101-58	129 x 128	8	pk/or	(4) 10	2	
1-H	1983-101-48	130 x 130	7.5	pk/or	(3) 10, (1) 5	2	
2-A	1983-101-40	132 x 132	8	pk/or and yellow	(1) 10, (3) 7.5	2	
2-B	1983-101-41	131 x 131	7.5	pk/or and buff	(1) 10, (2) 5	3	
2-C	1983-101-42	132 x 132	8.5	yellow	(1) 10, (3) 5	2	
2-D	1983-101-35	130 x 130	7.5	pk/or	(1) 5	2	

Tile	Accession Number	Dimensions (in mm)	Thickness (in mm)	Clay Body	Beveling of Edge (in degrees)	Nail Holes	Condition
2-E	1983-101-43	132 x 132.5	8	yellow	(4) 10	6	
2-F	1983-101-44	132 x 131.5	8	yellow	(4) 5	1	
2-G	1983-101-45	130 x 131	8	buff	(2) 50, (2) 5	3	
2-H	1983-101-37	130 x 131	8.5	buff	(4) 10	3	
3-A	1983-101-88	127 x 132	7.5	yellow	(2) 10, (2) 5	2	
3-B	1983-101-49	133 x 132	8	yellow	(4) 5	3	
3-C	1983-101-50	131 x 132	8	buff	(4) 5	2	
3-D	1983-101-51	133 x 130.5	8	yellow	(1) 60, (1) 10, (2) 5	3	
3-E	1983-101-83	131.5 x 134	7.5	pk/or	(1) 10, (3) 5	2	
3-F	1983-101-53	134 x 129	8	yellow	(2) 20, (2) 10	3	
3-G	1983-101-54	132.5 x 131	8	buff and yellow	(1) 50, (1) 7.5, (2) 5	3	
3-H	1983-101-55	132 x 131.5	8	buff	(1) 10, (2) 7.5, (1) 5	3	
4-A	1983-101-56	129 x 130	8.5	pk/or and buff	(3) 10, (1) 5	1	small loss; toned fill
4-B	1983-101-57	131 x 132	8	yellow	(1) 15, (1) 10, (2) 5	3	
4-C	1983-101-73	131 x 132	7	pk/or	(3) 10, (1) 5	3	
4-D	1983-101-59	131 x 131	8	buff	(3) 10, (1) 5	3	
4-E	1983-101-52	131 x 130	8	pk/or	(3) 10, (1) 15	4	
4-F	1983-101-39	130 x 130	8	yellow	(4) 5	3	small loss; toned fill
4-G	1983-101-78	132 x 133.5	8	pk/or	(4) 5	3	small loss; toned fill
4-H	1983-101-63	130 x 126	8	pk/or	(1) 15, (3) 10	3	right edge broken
5-A	1983-101-64	131 x 132	8.5	pk/or	(1) 7.5, (3) 5	1	small loss; toned fill
5-B	1983-101-65	128 x 129	9	pk/or and yellow	(1) 10, (3) 5	2	small losses; toned fills
5-C	1983-101-66	131 x 130	8	pk/or	(1) 10, (3) 5	2	
5-D	1983-101-67	132 x 133	8	yellow	(1) 10, (3) 5	2	
5-E	1983-101-68	131 x 131	8	buff	(3) 5	2	
5-F	1983-101-69	133 x 133	8	pk/or	(3) 5	5	
5-G	1983-101-36	128 x 132	8	yellow	(1) 10, (3) 5	1	small losses; toned fills
5-H	1983-101-71	131 x 132.5	8	pk/or	(4) 5	3	
6-A	1983-101-72	129 x 127	8.5	buff	(4) 10	2	small loss; toned fill
6-B	1983-101-61	128 x 128	8	pk/or and buff	(2) 15, (2) 12.5	2	small loss; toned fill
6-C	1983-101-74	129 x 130	8	yellow	(4) 10	2	
6-D	1983-101-75	130 x 130	8	yellow	(1) 10, (3) 5	2	
6-E	1983-101-76	133 x 132.5	8	buff	(4) 5	3	
6-F	1983-101-77	132 x 133	8.5	pk/or	(4) 5	2	
6-G	1983-101-70	131 x 131	8	buff	(3) 10, (1) 5	3	
6-H	1983-101-79	131 x 132	8	pk/or	(1) 10, (1) 7.5, (2) 5	3	
7-A	1983-101-80	132 x 132	8	yellow	(4) 7.5	2	
7-B	1983-101-81	132 x 131	8.5	yellow	(1) 5	3	
7-C	1983-101-82	132 x 131	7.5	yellow	(1) 15, (2) 10, (1) 5	6	
7-D	1983-101-91	132 x 133	8	pk/or and buff	(3) 5	2	
7-E	1983-101-84	127 x 126	10	pk/or	(4) 5	2	
7-F	1983-101-85	133 x 132	8	buff		2	
7-G	1983-101-86	132 x 132	8	yellow	(4) 5	3	
7-H	1983-101-87	131 x 132	8	yellow	(1) 7.5, (1) 5	3	
8-A	1983-101-89	129 x 131	7.5	pk/or	(3) 5	3	
8-B	1983-101-90	129 x 129	8	pk/or	(1) 15, (3) 10	2	
8-C	1983-101-38	128 x 129	8.5	buff	(4) 10	3	
8-D	1983-101-60	127 x 126	8	pk/or and yellow	(4) 10	4	
8-E	1983-101-92	129 x 129	8	buff	(3) 10, (1) 5	1	small loss; toned fill
8-F	1983-101-93	132 x 132	8	yellow		3	
8-G	1983-101-94	133 x 131	7.5	pk/or and yellow	(3) 7.5, (1) 5	2	
8-H	1983-101-95	129 x 130	7.5	yellow	(4) 10	1	⅛ loss; toned fills

130. Boy Spinning a Peg Top

Tile	Accession Number	Dimensions (in mm)	Thickness (in mm)	Clay Body	Beveling of Edge (in degrees)	Nail Holes	Condition
	28-66-176	126 x 127	12.5	pk/or	(3) 5	3	

131. Boys Romping

Tile	Accession Number	Dimensions (in mm)	Thickness (in mm)	Clay Body	Beveling of Edge (in degrees)	Nail Holes	Condition
1-A	28-66-120	131 x 130	8	yellow	(1) 10, (2) 5, (1) 25	3	break
1-B	28-66-116	130 x 132	8.5	yellow	(1) 10, (3) 7.5	4	break; corner loss
1-C	28-66-122	126 x 128	8.5	buff	(3) 7.5	1	2 breaks; toned fills
2-A	28-66-119	125 x 130	7.5	pk/or and buff	(4) 5	3	2 breaks; toned fill
2-B	28-66-117	129 x 130	8	buff	(3) 5	2	break; corner loss
2-C	28-66-121	129 x 129	8.5	yellow	(1) 10, (3) 7.5	3	break; toned fill

Tile	Accession Number	Dimensions (in mm)	Thickness (in mm)	Clay Body	Beveling of Edge (in degrees)	Nail Holes	Condition

132. Boy Urinating

Tile	Accession Number	Dimensions (in mm)	Thickness (in mm)	Clay Body	Beveling of Edge (in degrees)	Nail Holes	Condition
	28-66-111	129 x 127	8.5	buff	(1) 15, (3) 10	3	2 breaks

133. Shepherds and Shepherdesses in Landscapes

Tile	Accession Number	Dimensions (in mm)	Thickness (in mm)	Clay Body	Beveling of Edge (in degrees)	Nail Holes	Condition
1-A	1979-50-644	133 x 131	10.5	pk/or	(1) 7.5, (3) 5	0	corner loss; right edge broken
1-B	1979-50-645	130 x 130	10	buff	(3) 10	0	small losses
1-C	1979-50-655	131 x 131	10.5	pk/or	(1) 10, (3) 5	0	
1-D	1979-50-646	131 x 132	11	pk/or	(1) 10, (3) 5	0	small losses
2-A	1979-50-648	131 x 131	12	pk/or and buff	(1) 10, (3) 5	0	small losses
2-B	1979-50-650	130 x 130	11.5	pk/or and buff	(1) 15, (3) 10	3	
2-C	1979-50-649	128 x 129	11	yellow	(1) 10, (3) 5	1	small losses; toned fills
2-D	1979-50-651	132 x 132	10	pk/or	(4) 10	0	
3-A	1979-50-652	132 x 131	11	pk/or	(4) 5	1	small losses
3-B	1979-50-653	131 x 130	12.5	yellow	(2) 10, (2) 5	4	
3-C	1979-50-659	131 x 131	11	pk/or	(1) 10, (3) 5	0	small losses; toned fills
3-D	1979-50-654	130 x 132	11	buff	(3) 7.5	0	corner loss; toned fill
4-A	1979-50-658	131 x 133	11.5	yellow	(4) 5	0	small losses
4-B	1979-50-656	130 x 130	12	pk/or	(4) 5	0	⅛ loss
4-C	1979-50-657	127.5 x 132.5	11.5	pk/or	(1) 25, (3) 5	0	small losses
4-D	1979-50-647	131 x 134	11	pk/or	(2) 5	0	⅛ loss; toned fills

134. Shepherds and Shepherdesses in Landscapes

Tile	Accession Number	Dimensions (in mm)	Thickness (in mm)	Clay Body	Beveling of Edge (in degrees)	Nail Holes	Condition
A	1979-50-640	130 x 130	11.5	pk/or and yellow	(1) 15, (1) 10	0	
B	1979-50-643	130 x 130	11.5	pk/or	(4) 10	0	
C	28-66-129	131 x 132	10.5	pk/or	(2) 10, (2) 5	0	3 breaks; toned fills
D	1979-50-642	132 x 133	11.5	pk/or	(3) 10, (1) 5	1	
E	1979-50-641	132 x 134	12	pk/or	(3) 5	0	

135. Shepherds and Shepherdesses in Landscapes

Tile	Accession Number	Dimensions (in mm)	Thickness (in mm)	Clay Body	Beveling of Edge (in degrees)	Nail Holes	Condition
A	28-66-130	129 x 130	8	buff	(3) 5	1	2 breaks; small losses—inpainted; toned fill
B	28-66-127	127 x 127	10	yellow	(1) 20, (3) 10	2	break

136. Shepherds and Shepherdesses in Landscapes

Tile	Accession Number	Dimensions (in mm)	Thickness (in mm)	Clay Body	Beveling of Edge (in degrees)	Nail Holes	Condition
1-A	1979-50-213	129 x 127	8	pk/or and yellow		2	2 breaks
1-B	1979-50-216	128 x 129	7.5	yellow	(3) 10, (1) 5	2	
2-A	1979-50-214	128 x 129	7	yellow	(1) 10, (3) 5	0	break; loss—inpainting
2-B	1979-50-215	128 x 130	8	buff	(4) 5	2	

137. Shepherds and Shepherdesses in Landscapes

Tile	Accession Number	Dimensions (in mm)	Thickness (in mm)	Clay Body	Beveling of Edge (in degrees)	Nail Holes	Condition
1-A	1979-50-217	131 x 129	8	buff	(4) 10	2	
1-B	1979-50-219	124 x 131	8	buff	(3) 10	2	small loss
2-A	1979-50-220	132 x 130	8	buff	(4) 5	2	
2-B	1979-50-218	130 x 130	8.5	yellow	(4) 5	2	

138. Shepherds in Landscapes

Tile	Accession Number	Dimensions (in mm)	Thickness (in mm)	Clay Body	Beveling of Edge (in degrees)	Nail Holes	Condition
A	1981-77-40	127 x 126	8.5	yellow	(2) 50, (1) 10, (1) 5	2	break; edge broken
B	1981-77-41	127 x 124	8	buff	(1) 20, (2) 15	1	left edge broken; ⅛ loss; toned fills

139. Shepherds and Shepherdess in Landscapes

Tile	Accession Number	Dimensions (in mm)	Thickness (in mm)	Clay Body	Beveling of Edge (in degrees)	Nail Holes	Condition
A	1979-50-222	130 x 130	8	buff	(3) 5	0	
B	1979-50-221	129 x 130	7.5	yellow	(1) 15, (1) 10, (2) 2.5	0	

Tile	Accession Number	Dimensions (in mm)	Thickness (in mm)	Clay Body	Beveling of Edge (in degrees)	Nail Holes	Condition

140. Portraits of Frederik Hendrik and William III

Tile	Accession Number	Dimensions (in mm)	Thickness (in mm)	Clay Body	Beveling of Edge (in degrees)	Nail Holes	Condition
A	1979-50-824	126 x 126	11	buff	(3) 10, (1) 5	0	⅛ loss; corner loss
B	1979-50-823	128 x 127	11.5	buff	(3) 15, (1) 10	0	

141. The Sacrifice of Isaac

Tile	Accession Number	Dimensions (in mm)	Thickness (in mm)	Clay Body	Beveling of Edge (in degrees)	Nail Holes	Condition
	28-66-158	127 x 127.5	8.5	yellow	(3) 5	1	¼ loss; 3 breaks toned fill

142. Moses Receiving the Ten Commandments

Tile	Accession Number	Dimensions (in mm)	Thickness (in mm)	Clay Body	Beveling of Edge (in degrees)	Nail Holes	Condition
	1979-50-96	130 x 130	9	yellow	(3) 5	2	3 breaks; corner loss—inpainted

143. The Resurrection

Tile	Accession Number	Dimensions (in mm)	Thickness (in mm)	Clay Body	Beveling of Edge (in degrees)	Nail Holes	Condition
	08-253	129 x 131	7.5	yellow	(3) 5	2	

144. Scenes from the New Testament

Tile	Accession Number	Dimensions (in mm)	Thickness (in mm)	Clay Body	Beveling of Edge (in degrees)	Nail Holes	Condition
1-A	19-147	130 x 130	8	pk/or	(1) 10, (3) 5	2	
1-B	16-299	129 x 129.5	8.5	yellow	(1) 10, (2) 5	2	corner loss
2-A	16-298	129 x 129.5	8.5	yellow	(1) 10, (3) 5	2	
2-B	19-146	129 x 130	7.5	pk/or and yellow	(2) 10, (1) 7.5, (1) 5	2	

145. Scenes from the Old Testament

Tile	Accession Number	Dimensions (in mm)	Thickness (in mm)	Clay Body	Beveling of Edge (in degrees)	Nail Holes	Condition
A	1979-50-100	129 x 129	8.5	buff	(1) 5	1	small loss; toned fill
B	1979-50-99	128 x 127	8	pk/or and light-yellow		2	

146. Scenes from the Old and New Testaments

Tile	Accession Number	Dimensions (in mm)	Thickness (in mm)	Clay Body	Beveling of Edge (in degrees)	Nail Holes	Condition
A	21-3-193	123 x 118	8	yellow	(1) 50, (1) 45	0	all edges cut
B	21-3-190	122 x 111	8	yellow	(1) 50, (1) 40	0	all edges cut
C	21-3-194	122 x 114	8	yellow	(2) 40	1	all edges cut
D	21-3-189	122 x 111	7.5	buff	(1) 60, (1) 50	0	small loss; toned fill; all edges cut

147. Scenes from the Old and New Testaments

Tile	Accession Number	Dimensions (in mm)	Thickness (in mm)	Clay Body	Beveling of Edge (in degrees)	Nail Holes	Condition
1-A	1979-50-108	130 x 132	8	yellow	(1) 15, (1) 10, (2) 5	2	small losses
1-B	1979-50-104	128 x 130	8	buff	(1) 50, (2) 15, (1) 10	2	corner and other small losses
1-C	1979-50-105	129 x 131	8	yellow	(1) 15, (1) 10, (2) 5	2	
1-D	97-716-2	128 x 127	8	buff	(1) 10, (3) 5	2	break
2-A	1979-50-113	130 x 131	8	yellow	(1) 10, (3) 5	1	
2-B	1979-50-109	129 x 130	7.5	buff	(1) 50, (3) 10	2	small corner loss
2-C	1979-50-107	130 x 131.5	8.5	buff	(2) 5	2	
2-D	97-716-3	129 x 128	8	pk/or	(2) 15, (1) 10, (1) 5	2	
3-A	1979-50-112	132 x 130	8	yellow	(4) 10	2	break
3-B	97-716-12	128 x 129	8.5	buff	(3) 5	1	
3-C	97-716-15	129.5 x 128	8.5	buff	(1) 10, (3) 5	2	
3-D	1979-50-88	129 x 129	7.5	yellow	(1) 25, (1) 20	1	
4-A	97-716-9	130 x 128	8	yellow	(2) 50, (1) 10, (1) 5	1	small losses
4-B	97-716-5	127.5 x 125	8	yellow	(3) 10, (1) 5	2	losses
4-C	97-716-19	130 x 127	8.5	buff	(1) 50, (1) 35, (1) 10, (1) 5	1	
4-D	1979-50-103	128 x 126	8	yellow	(3) 15, (1) 5	2	

148. Scenes from the Old and New Testaments and the Apocrypha

Tile	Accession Number	Dimensions (in mm)	Thickness (in mm)	Clay Body	Beveling of Edge (in degrees)	Nail Holes	Condition
1-A	1979-50-80	127 x 128	8	yellow	(1) 10, (3) 5	2	
1-B	1979-50-78	128 x 128.5	8	yellow	(3) 10, (1) 5	1	small losses; toned fills
1-C	1979-50-93	130 x 130	9.5	yellow	(1) 10, (1) 7.5, (2) 5	1	break
1-D	1979-50-94	130 x 130	8	yellow	(1) 10, (1) 5	2	
1-E	97-716-1	129.5 x 126	8.5	yellow	(1) 45, (2) 10, (1) 5	2	
2-A	97-716-11	129 x 128	8.5	yellow	(3) 10, (1) 5	2	
2-B	1979-50-77	128 x 128	9	yellow	(1) 10, (3) 5	0	

Tile	Accession Number	Dimensions (in mm)	Thickness (in mm)	Clay Body	Beveling of Edge (in degrees)	Nail Holes	Condition
2-C	1979-50-101	129 x 132	8	yellow	(2) 10, (1) 5	1	break; small losses— inpainted; toned fill
2-D	1979-50-95	130 x 131	9	yellow	(4) 5	1	
2-E	1979-50-79	131 x 131	9	yellow	(4) 5	2	
3-A	1979-50-81	128 x 126	8	yellow	(1) 30, (3) 10	2	small loss
3-B	97-716-13	127 x 127	9	yellow	(2) 10, (1) 5	2	
3-C	1979-50-106	126 x 129	7.5	yellow	(2) 35, (1) 30, (1) 10	2	small losses
3-D	1979-50-102	127 x 131	8.5	yellow	(1) 15, (2) 10	2	small losses— inpainted; toned fill
3-E	1979-50-85	127 x 129	7.5	yellow	(1) 30, (3) 25	0	2 breaks
4-A	1979-50-84	128 x 126	7.5	buff	(1) 12.5, (2) 10, (1) 5	2	
4-B	1979-50-82	127.5 x 126.5	8	yellow	(3) 10, (1) 5	2	
4-C	1979-50-111	128 x 127	8	yellow	(1) 45, (3) 25	1	
4-D	97-716-8	130 x 126	7.5	yellow	(3) 10, (1) 5	0	
4-E	97-716-16	129 x 126	8	yellow	(1) 35, (2) 30, (1) 10	1	small loss
5-A	97-716-6	124 x 124	8	yellow	(1) 30, (2) 25, (1) 20	0	
5-B	1979-50-83	127 x 127	8	yellow	(2) 20, (2) 15	2	
5-C	1979-50-110	130 x 132	8	yellow and pk/or	(1) 40, (3) 15	2	small loss— inpainted
5-D	97-716-17	129 x 128	8	yellow and pk/or	(1) 45, (3) 20	3	
5-E	97-716-4	127 x 127	7.5	yellow	(3) 15, (1) 5	1	

149. Scenes from the New Testament

Tile	Accession Number	Dimensions (in mm)	Thickness (in mm)	Clay Body	Beveling of Edge (in degrees)	Nail Holes	Condition
A	1979-50-97	130 x 130	8	pk/or and yellow	(4) 10	2	
B	1979-50-98	130 x 130	8	pk/or and yellow	(2) 10, (1) 7.5, (1) 5	1	

150. Jesus on the Road to Emmaus

Tile	Accession Number	Dimensions (in mm)	Thickness (in mm)	Clay Body	Beveling of Edge (in degrees)	Nail Holes	Condition
	97-716-20	128.5 x 129	8	yellow	(3) 10, (1) 5	2	bottom edge cut

151. Scenes from the Old and New Testaments

Tile	Accession Number	Dimensions (in mm)	Thickness (in mm)	Clay Body	Beveling of Edge (in degrees)	Nail Holes	Condition
1-A	1979-50-91	128 x 127	7	white	(4) 5	2	
1-B	1979-50-90	128 x 129	7.5	white		2	
1-C	1979-50-92	126 x 129	7	white	(2) 5	2	
2-A	1979-50-87	130 x 128	7.5	white	(4) 10	2	
2-B	1979-50-86	127 x 130	8	buff	(2) 10, (1) 5	0	
2-C	1979-50-89	127 x 129	7	white and buff	(4) 5	1	

152. Pikeman and Musketeer

Tile	Accession Number	Dimensions (in mm)	Thickness (in mm)	Clay Body	Beveling of Edge (in degrees)	Nail Holes	Condition
A	1981-77-39	131.5 x 131	15.5	pk/or (slight marbling)	(2) 15, (1) 12.5, (1) 10	1	small losses— inpainted; small corner loss
B	1981-77-38	131 x 133	15	pk/or (slight marbling)	(2) 15, (1) 10, (1) 7.5	2	small losses— inpainted

153. Roman Soldiers and Saracen Bowmen

Tile	Accession Number	Dimensions (in mm)	Thickness (in mm)	Clay Body	Beveling of Edge (in degrees)	Nail Holes	Condition
A	1983-101-104	131 x 130	14	pk/or	(4) 10	4	
B	1983-101-107	130 x 130	14	pk/or	(4) 10	4	corner losses
C	1983-101-110	130 x 131	14	pk/or	(2) 15, (2) 10	4	
D	1983-101-105	128 x 130	14.5	pk/or and red	(4) 15	4	small losses
E	1983-101-111	130 x 130	13.5	pk/or	(3) 10, (1) 5	4	
F	1983-101-109	130 x 131	14.5	pk/or	(2) 12.5, (2) 10	4	small losses
G	1983-101-112	120 x 128	14.5	pk/or	(2) 15, (1) 10	4	bottom edge loss; toned fill
H	1983-101-106	130 x 130	14	pk/or	(2) 10, (2) 5	4	small losses

154. Soldiers

Tile	Accession Number	Dimensions (in mm)	Thickness (in mm)	Clay Body	Beveling of Edge (in degrees)	Nail Holes	Condition
1-A	1983-101-100	129 x 128	12	pk/or and yellow	(1) 10	2	
1-B	1983-101-101	130 x 130	12	pk/or and red	(1) 10, (3) 5	1	
2-A	1983-101-103	128 x 128	11	pk/or		3	
2-B	1983-101-102	130 x 130	12	pk/or and yellow	(1) 15, (3) 10	2	

155. Pikemen and Musketeers

Tile	Accession Number	Dimensions (in mm)	Thickness (in mm)	Clay Body	Beveling of Edge (in degrees)	Nail Holes	Condition
1-A	1981-77-47	131 x 130	12	pk/or	(1) 15, (3) 10	4	break
1-B	1981-77-48	130 x 124	11	pk/or	(1) 15, (2) 10	4	left edge broken
1-C	1981-77-52	130 x 130	11.5	pk/or and marbleized red	(2) 15, (1) 10	4	small losses; ¼ loss reverse
1-D	1981-77-43	130 x 125	11.5	pk/or and marbleized red	(2) 15, (2) 10	4	small losses

Tile	Accession Number	Dimensions (in mm)	Thickness (in mm)	Clay Body	Beveling of Edge (in degrees)	Nail Holes	Condition
1-E	1981-77-45	131 x 131	11.5	pk/or	(1) 15, (3) 10	4	small losses
1-F	1981-77-55	130 x 131	10.5	pk/or	(3) 15, (1) 10	4	
1-G	1981-77-44	132 x 131	10.5	pk/or	(4) 10	4	small loss
2-A	1981-77-54	126 x 130	11.5	pk/or	(3) 10, (1) 5	4	small losses
2-B	1981-77-50	130 x 131	11.5	pk/or	(2) 15, (2) 10	4	small losses
2-C	1981-77-58	131 x 130	11	pk/or	(2) 15, (2) 10	4	small losses
2-D	1981-77-49	129 x 130.5	11	pk/or	(1) 20, (1) 15, (2) 10	4	
2-E	1981-77-46	132 x 132	12	pk/or	(3) 15, (1) 10	4	⅛ loss; toned fill
2-F	1981-77-57	130 x 130	11	yellow	(2) 15, (2) 10	4	
2-G	1981-77-53	131 x 131	11	pk/or	(1) 20, (1) 15, (2) 10	4	small losses

156. Pikemen and Musketeers

Tile	Accession Number	Dimensions	Thickness	Clay Body	Beveling of Edge	Nail Holes	Condition
1-A	1979-50-185	130 x 129.5	12.5	pk/or and red	(3) 10, (1) 5	3	
1-B	1979-50-186	126 x 128	12.5	pk/or	(4) 5	3	
2-A	1979-50-184	130 x 131	12.5	pk/or	(3) 10, (1) 5	3	
2-B	1979-50-183	126 x 126	12	pk/or	(3) 5, (1) 10	4	

157. Pikemen and Saracen Bowman

Tile	Accession Number	Dimensions	Thickness	Clay Body	Beveling of Edge	Nail Holes	Condition
1-A	1979-50-193	131 x 132	14.5	pk/or and buff	(2) 10, (2) 5	4	
1-B	1979-50-196	131 x 131	15	pk/or and buff	(1) 10, (3) 5	4	small loss; toned fill; break
2-A	1979-50-195	133 x 133	15.5	pk/or and buff	(2) 5	4	
2-B	1979-50-194	132 x 132	15	pk/or and buff	(4) 10	3	small loss; toned fill

158. Pikeman

Tile	Accession Number	Dimensions	Thickness	Clay Body	Beveling of Edge	Nail Holes	Condition
	1979-50-187	132.5 x 132	14.5	pk/or	(1) 12.5, (3) 10	3	

159. Pikemen and Musketeers

Tile	Accession Number	Dimensions	Thickness	Clay Body	Beveling of Edge	Nail Holes	Condition
1-A	1979-50-191	127 x 129	11.5	pk/or	(1) 15, (2) 12.5, (1) 10	2	
1-B	1979-50-209	129 x 130	12	yellow	(1) 10, (1) 5	4	small loss
1-C	1979-50-203	127 x 127	11.5	pk/or and yellow	(4) 10	2	
1-D	1979-50-205	127 x 126	12	pk/or and yellow	(3) 15, (1) 12.5	2	
2-A	1979-50-206	126 x 127	11.5	pk/or	(4) 10	2	
2-B	1979-50-189	127 x 128	12.5	pk/or	(1) 15, (1) 12.5, (2) 10	2	
2-C	1979-50-201	128 x 129	11.5	pk/or	(1) 15, (3) 10	2	
2-D	1979-50-204	126 x 127	12	pk/or and buff	(1) 15, (2) 12.5, (1) 5	2	
3-A	1979-50-208	127 x 129	11.5	pk/or	(2) 10, (2) 7.5	1	small loss
3-B	50-10-47(10)	129 x 131	11.5	pk/or and buff	(1) 7.5, (3) 5	3	small losses
3-C	1979-50-190	128 x 128	12.5	pk/or	(2) 10, (2) 7.5	2	
3-D	1979-50-188	127 x 128	12	pk/or and red	(2) 12.5, (2) 10	2	

160. Marksman, Musketeer, and Pikeman

Tile	Accession Number	Dimensions	Thickness	Clay Body	Beveling of Edge	Nail Holes	Condition
A	1981-77-197	132 x 131	13	pk/or	(4) 20	2	corner loss
B	1981-77-198	127.5 x 129	14.5	pk/or	(1) 20, (1) 15, (1) 12.5, (1) 10	4	corner and other small losses
C	1981-77-56	130.5 x 130	12.5	yellow	(4) 5	2	

161. Musketeers and Pikemen

Tile	Accession Number	Dimensions	Thickness	Clay Body	Beveling of Edge	Nail Holes	Condition
1-A	1979-50-202	127 x 129	12.5	pk/or and yellow	(1) 15, (2) 10, (1) 5	4	
1-B	1979-50-210	130 x 128.5	12.5	pk/or and yellow	(4) 10	4	
2-A	1979-50-199	126 x 127	13.5	pk/or	(4) 5	3	
2-B	1979-50-200	129 x 129	12.5	pk/or	(3) 10, (1) 5	4	

162. Cavalry

Tile	Accession Number	Dimensions	Thickness	Clay Body	Beveling of Edge	Nail Holes	Condition
1-A	1981-77-25	130 x 130	11	pk/or and yellow	(1) 10, (3) 7.5	2	small losses
1-B	1981-77-17	131 x 132	12	yellow	(2) 5, (2) 2.5	2	
1-C	1981-77-15	130 x 131	12	pk/or	(4) 5	2	
1-D	1981-77-13	129 x 130	12	yellow	(4) 5	1	small losses
2-A	1981-77-16	130 x 130	11.5	pk/or	(4) 5	1	
2-B	1981-77-23	130 x 130	10.5	pk/or	(4) 5	2	
2-C	1981-77-28	129 x 129	11.5	pk/or	(1) 10, (2) 7.5, (1) 5	2	
2-D	1981-77-18	129 x 130	11	pk/or	(1) 10, (3) 5	2	
3-A	1981-77-21	130 x 130	11.5	pk/or	(1) 10, (1) 7.5, (2) 5	0	
3-B	1981-77-20	130 x 130	12	yellow	(4) 5	2	
3-C	1981-77-22	128 x 128	11.5	pk/or	(3) 10, (1) 5	2	break
3-D	1981-77-24	132 x 131	12	pk/or	(1) 10, (3) 5	2	corner loss
4-A	1981-77-14	129 x 130	11.5	yellow	(1) 10, (2) 5, (1) 2.5	1	
4-B	1981-77-26	130 x 131	11	pk/or and yellow	(2) 10, (2) 5	2	

Tile	Accession Number	Dimensions (in mm)	Thickness (in mm)	Clay Body	Beveling of Edge (in degrees)	Nail Holes	Condition
4-C	1981-77-27	130 x 130	11.5	pk/or and yellow	(4) 5	2	
4-D	1981-77-19	130 x 131	11.5	yellow	(3) 5	2	

163. Dragoon

	Accession Number	Dimensions (in mm)	Thickness (in mm)	Clay Body	Beveling of Edge (in degrees)	Nail Holes	Condition
	30-10-47(26)	128 x 127.5	12	pk/or	(1) 15, (3) 10	3	

164. Cavalry

Tile	Accession Number	Dimensions (in mm)	Thickness (in mm)	Clay Body	Beveling of Edge (in degrees)	Nail Holes	Condition
1-A	1983-101-98	130 x 130	9.5	yellow	(2) 5	2	
1-B	1983-101-99	130 x 130	10.5	yellow	(1) 5	1	small corner loss; toned fill
1-C	1983-101-96	131 x 131	10.5	pk/or and yellow	(2) 7.5	1	
1-D	1983-101-97	129 x 129	11.5	yellow	(1) 10, (2) 5	1	
2-A	1979-50-174	131 x 130	10.5	pk/or and buff		2	
2-B	1979-50-177	128 x 129	10.5	buff and yellow		2	
2-C	1979-50-175	130 x 130	11	buff	(2) 7.5, (1) 5	1	small corner loss; toned fill
2-D	1979-50-180	130 x 130	10	buff	(3) 5	2	small losses
3-A	1979-50-181	131 x 131	11	buff	(2) 10, (2) 5	1	small corner loss
3-B	1979-50-176	130 x 130	11	buff	(2) 5	1	
3-C	1979-50-179	131 x 131	11.5	buff	(2) 5	2	
3-D	1979-50-178	130 x 130	12	buff		2	small losses

165. Saracen Horseman

	Accession Number	Dimensions (in mm)	Thickness (in mm)	Clay Body	Beveling of Edge (in degrees)	Nail Holes	Condition
	1979-50-182	128 x 128	10.5	yellow	(4) 5	2	

166. Drawbridge, Well, and Ruin

Tile	Accession Number	Dimensions (in mm)	Thickness (in mm)	Clay Body	Beveling of Edge (in degrees)	Nail Holes	Condition
A	28-66-75	126 x 125	10	yellow	(1) 15, (1) 10, (2) 5	2	⅛ loss
B	28-66-74	126 x 126	10.5	pk/or	(1) 15, (2) 10, (1) 5	3	break; small losses; toned fills
C	28-66-76	127 x 127	10	pk/or	(4) 10	2	¼ loss; toned fill

167. Harbor Scene

	Accession Number	Dimensions (in mm)	Thickness (in mm)	Clay Body	Beveling of Edge (in degrees)	Nail Holes	Condition
	1979-50-639	128 x 128	8	buff and yellow	(2) 10, (2) 5	0	small losses; corner loss

168. Waterscape

Tile	Accession Number	Dimensions (in mm)	Thickness (in mm)	Clay Body	Beveling of Edge (in degrees)	Nail Holes	Condition
A	1979-50-638	127 x 127	10	pk/or and buff	(3) 5, (1) 2.5	2	corner loss

169. Water Scenes

Tile	Accession Number	Dimensions (in mm)	Thickness (in mm)	Clay Body	Beveling of Edge (in degrees)	Nail Holes	Condition
A	1979-50-633	128 x 127	8.5	yellow	(2) 10, (2) 5	4	
B	1979-50-631	128.5 x 130	9	pk/or	(4) 5	4	
C	1979-50-632	128.5 x 129	8	yellow	(4) 2.5	2	
D	61-67-7	129 x 128	8	pk/or	(2) 15, (1) 10	0	corner loss; toned fill
E	61-67-6	129 x 131.5	8	pk/or	(2) 15, (2) 5	1	
F	61-67-5	130 x 132	8	pk/or	(1) 10, (2) 15, (1) 10	2	
G	1979-50-630	130 x 130	9	yellow	(1) 10, (2) 5	3	
H	30-10-47(60)	128 x 126	8	pk/or	(1) 5, (3) 5	2	bottom edge broken; corner loss

170. Harbor Views

Tile	Accession Number	Dimensions (in mm)	Thickness (in mm)	Clay Body	Beveling of Edge (in degrees)	Nail Holes	Condition
1-A	28-66-167	127 x 129.5	7.5	yellow	(4) 5	2	break; 2 small losses—inpainted
1-B	28-66-165	129 x 129	8	yellow	(2) 20, (1) 5	3	3 breaks; small losses—inpainted
1-C	28-66-168	127 x 127.5	7.5	yellow	(1) 15, (3) 10	3	break—inpainted
1-D	28-66-166	130 x 130	8	yellow	(1) 25, (1) 15, (2) 10	0	break; 2 corner losses—inpainted
2-A	28-66-169	129 x 129	8.5	yellow	(2) 10, (1) 5	1	⅛ loss; 3 breaks—inpainted
2-B	28-66-171	130 x 131	8	buff	(3) 10, (1) 5	2	10 breaks; small losses—inpainted

Tile	Accession Number	Dimensions (in mm)	Thickness (in mm)	Clay Body	Beveling of Edge (in degrees)	Nail Holes	Condition
2-C	28-66-172	130 x 127.5	8	buff	(2) 15, (2) 10	2	3 breaks; small losses—inpainted
2-D	28-66-170	127.5 x 125	8	yellow	(1) 15, (1) 10, (1) 5	1	4 breaks; ⅛ loss—inpainted

171. Waterscapes

Tile	Accession Number	Dimensions (in mm)	Thickness (in mm)	Clay Body	Beveling of Edge (in degrees)	Nail Holes	Condition
1-A	1979-50-666	128 x 130	7.5	pk/or and yellow	(2) 10, (1) 7.5, (1) 5	3	2 breaks
1-B	1979-50-660	127 x 129	7.5	yellow	(1) 10, (1) 10, (2) 5	0	left edge cut
1-C	1979-50-664	128 x 132	7.5	yellow	(3) 15, (1) 12.5	2	
1-D	1979-50-663	127 x 129	7.5	yellow	(1) 17.5, (1) 15, (2) 10	1	
1-E	1979-50-662	125 x 131	7.5	yellow	(2) 12.5, (2) 10	1	
2-A	1979-50-674	127 x 128	7.5	yellow	(1) 10	0	
2-B	1979-50-668	131 x 128	7.5	yellow	(3) 10, (1) 7.5	2	
2-C	1979-50-661	130 x 130	8	yellow	(4) 10	1	
2-D	1979-50-669	127 x 130.5	7.5	yellow	(4) 5	2	
2-E	1979-50-665	129 x 129	7.5	yellow	(1) 15, (1) 10	0	
3-A	1979-50-670	130 x 130	7.5	yellow	(1) 25, (3) 5	2	
3-B	1979-50-672	127 x 127	8	yellow	(2) 10, (2) 7.5	0	
3-C	1979-50-671	128 x 128	8	yellow	(2) 10, (1) 7.5	0	
3-D	1979-50-667	130 x 128	7.5	yellow	(4) 75	0	
3-E	1979-50-673	127 x 130	7.5	yellow	(4) 7.5	0	

172. Landscapes

Tile	Accession Number	Dimensions (in mm)	Thickness (in mm)	Clay Body	Beveling of Edge (in degrees)	Nail Holes	Condition
1-A	1979-50-637	127 x 127	8.5	pk/or	(4) 10	2	
1-B	1983-101-162	129 x 129	8	pk/or and buff	(1) 10, (2) 5	2	
1-C	1983-101-163	127.5 x 127.5	9	pk/or	(3) 10, (1) 5	2	break
2-A	1983-101-161	127 x 129	9	pk/or and yellow	(1) 10, (2) 5, (1) 7.5	2	
2-B	1979-50-636	127 x 126	8.5	yellow	(1) 10, (2) 7.5, (1) 5	2	
2-C	1983-101-164	127 x 127	8	yellow	(4) 5	2	
3-A	1979-50-634	129 x 128	9	yellow	(2) 10, (2) 5	2	2 breaks—inpainting
3-B	1979-50-635	127 x 127	8.5	yellow	(3) 10, (1) 5	2	
3-C	1983-101-160	128.5 x 130	8	pk/or and yellow	(2) 15, (2) 12.5	2	

173. Country Scenes

Tile	Accession Number	Dimensions (in mm)	Thickness (in mm)	Clay Body	Beveling of Edge (in degrees)	Nail Holes	Condition
A	1983-101-158	129 x 130	8	pk/or and buff	(4) 30	2	
B	1983-101-157	128 x 128	8	buff	(1) 35	2	small corner loss
C	1983-101-159	128.5 x 124	8	buff	(4) 10	1	

174. Water and Country Scenes

Tile	Accession Number	Dimensions (in mm)	Thickness (in mm)	Clay Body	Beveling of Edge (in degrees)	Nail Holes	Condition
1-A	1983-101-166	131 x 131.5	8	pk/or and yellow	(1) 15, (3) 10	1	break
1-B	1983-101-165	128 x 129	8	pk/or and yellow	(3) 10, (1) 7.5	0	
2-A	1983-101-167	129 x 129.5	8	yellow	(4) 10	0	
2-B	1983-101-168	129 x 130	8	pk/or and yellow	(1) 10, (3) 5	0	

175. Sailboat

Tile	Accession Number	Dimensions (in mm)	Thickness (in mm)	Clay Body	Beveling of Edge (in degrees)	Nail Holes	Condition
	1981-77-35	133.5 x 132	13.5	pk/or	(1) 10, (1) 5	2	

176. Men-of-War and Sloops

Tile	Accession Number	Dimensions (in mm)	Thickness (in mm)	Clay Body	Beveling of Edge (in degrees)	Nail Holes	Condition
A	1979-50-677	129 x 132	13.5	pk/or	(2) 10, (2) 5	2	bottom edge lost
B	1979-50-675	130 x 130	12.5	pk/or and buff	(1) 15, (3) 10	3	corner missing; toned fill
C	1979-50-678	130 x 131.5	12	pk/or and buff	(1) 10, (3) 5	4	small losses
D	1979-50-676	129 x 129	11	pk/or	(3) 10	2	

177. Men-of-War, Frigates, Flutes, and a Herring Buss

Tile	Accession Number	Dimensions (in mm)	Thickness (in mm)	Clay Body	Beveling of Edge (in degrees)	Nail Holes	Condition
1-A	1979-50-686	129 x 129.5	11.5	buff	(1) 10, (3) 5	2	
1-B	1983-101-188	128 x 129	12	yellow	(1) 10, (1) 7.5, (2) 5	2	
1-C	1979-50-683	127.5 x 129	11	pk/or	(4) 5	2	corner loss
1-D	1979-50-685	128 x 129	11	yellow	(1) 10, (3) 5	2	
2-A	1979-50-684	129.5 x 129	11	buff	(1) 35, (1) 10, (2) 5	2	
2-B	1983-101-189	129 x 128.5	11.5	pk/or	(1) 10, (2) 7.5, (1) 5	2	
2-C	1983-101-193	130 x 130	11.5	buff	(1) 15, (1) 10, (2) 5	2	
2-D	1983-101-194	127 x 128	11	yellow	(1) 15, (2) 10, (1) 5	2	
3-A	1983-101-185	130 x 130	11.5	pk/or	(1) 15, (3) 10	2	
3-B	1983-101-186	129.5 x 130	11	yellow	(1) 12.5, (3) 10	2	
3-C	1983-101-183	128 x 128	12	pk/or	(4) 5	2	
3-D	1983-101-191	130.5 x 128	11.5	pk/or	(1) 20, (2) 10, (1) 5	2	
4-A	1983-101-187	129 x 127.5	11.5	pk/or	(2) 10, (2) 5	2	
4-B	1983-101-192	127.5 x 129	11	pk/or	(1) 10, (3) 5	2	

Tile	Accession Number	Dimensions (in mm)	Thickness (in mm)	Clay Body	Beveling of Edge (in degrees)	Nail Holes	Condition
4-C	1983-101-190	128 x 129	11	pk/or and yellow	(2) 10, (2) 5	2	
4-D	1983-101-184	129 x 129	12	yellow	(1) 7.5, (3) 5	2	

178. Sailing Ships

Tile	Accession Number	Dimensions (in mm)	Thickness (in mm)	Clay Body	Beveling of Edge (in degrees)	Nail Holes	Condition
A	1981-77-30	128 x 131	11	pk/or	(2) 20, (1) 15	2	edge and other losses; toned fills
B	1981-77-31	130 x 130	11	yellow	(1) 50, (3) 25	2	
C	1981-77-32	131 x 130	10	yellow	(1) 25, (3) 20	1	corner and other losses; toned fills
D	1981-77-2	128 x 129	10	yellow	(4) 20	2	
E	1981-77-1	130 x 129	11	pk/or and buff	(3) 20, (1) 15	2	corner loss
F	1981-77-4	130 x 130	11	pk/or	(1) 15, (1) 12.5, (2) 10	2	break; toned fills
G	1981-77-3	125 x 126	11.5	yellow	(1) 15, (3) 10	2	small losses; toned fills
H	1981-77-29	128 x 130	10.5	pk/or	(1) 25, (2) 20	2	break; edge and other losses; toned fills

179. Pinks

Tile	Accession Number	Dimensions (in mm)	Thickness (in mm)	Clay Body	Beveling of Edge (in degrees)	Nail Holes	Condition
A	1979-50-679	130 x 130	11.5	buff and yellow	(3) 5	2	
B	1979-50-680	128 x 128	12	buff		2	small corner loss
C	1979-50-681	128.5 x 128	11.5	yellow	(4) 5	2	
D	1979-50-682	127 x 126	11.5	buff	(2) 5	2	small corner loss

180. Fishing Fleet

Tile	Accession Number	Dimensions (in mm)	Thickness (in mm)	Clay Body	Beveling of Edge (in degrees)	Nail Holes	Condition
A	28-66-97	126 x 127	10.5	pk/or	(1) 15, (2) 12.5, (1) 10	2	break
B	28-66-174	125 x 126	10.5	pk/or	(4) 10	2	break; small losses; toned fills
C	28-66-173	127 x 126	11	pk/or	(1) 12.5, (3) 10	1	small losses

181. Coastal Vessels

Tile	Accession Number	Dimensions (in mm)	Thickness (in mm)	Clay Body	Beveling of Edge (in degrees)	Nail Holes	Condition
A	28-66-95	127 x 103	10	yellow	(1) 10, (3) 5	2	filed right edge; break
B	28-66-93	128 x 126	10.5	buff	(1) 10, (3) 5	3	break; small losses
C	28-66-100	128 x 129	10.5	yellow	(3) 5	2	break
D	28-66-99	128 x 128	10	buff	(3) 10, (1) 5	2	1/8 loss
E	28-66-98	129 x 128	10.5	yellow	(3) 10, (1) 7.5	3	break; 1/8 loss
F	28-66-94	127.5 x 129	9.5	yellow	(1) 10, (3) 5	3	break; small losses
G	28-66-96	128 x 124	10.5	yellow	(1) 30, (1) 15, (2) 5	4	left edge cut

182. Sea Creatures

Tile	Accession Number	Dimensions (in mm)	Thickness (in mm)	Clay Body	Beveling of Edge (in degrees)	Nail Holes	Condition
A	1983-101-181	127 x 128	11.5	pk/or	(2) 12.5, (2) 10	3	small losses
B	1983-101-180	128.5 x 128.5	11.5	yellow	(2) 10, (2) 5	2	
C	1983-101-182	127 x 128	11	pk/or and yellow	(3) 15, (1) 10	3	

183. Arion Playing the Lyre

Tile	Accession Number	Dimensions (in mm)	Thickness (in mm)	Clay Body	Beveling of Edge (in degrees)	Nail Holes	Condition
	1983-101-31	130 x 129	12	yellow	(1) 15, (3) 10	4	corner loss

184. Triton

Tile	Accession Number	Dimensions (in mm)	Thickness (in mm)	Clay Body	Beveling of Edge (in degrees)	Nail Holes	Condition
	1981-77-83	131 x 130	14.5	pk/or	(2) 17.5, (1) 15, (1) 7.5	3	

185. Whale

Tile	Accession Number	Dimensions (in mm)	Thickness (in mm)	Clay Body	Beveling of Edge (in degrees)	Nail Holes	Condition
A	1983-101-195a	135 x 133.5	14	pk/or	(1) 10, (2) 7.5, (1) 5	4	
B	1983-101-195b	134 x 136.5	14.5	pk/or	(4) 15	4	

185. Dolphin

Tile	Accession Number	Dimensions (in mm)	Thickness (in mm)	Clay Body	Beveling of Edge (in degrees)	Nail Holes	Condition
A	1983-101-169a	131 x 131	12.5	pk/or	(1) 5, (3) 2.5	4	1/8 glaze loss; toned fill
B	1983-101-169b	130.5 x 129.5	13.5	pk/or	(4) 15	4	toned fill

Tile	Accession Number	Dimensions (in mm)	Thickness (in mm)	Clay Body	Beveling of Edge (in degrees)	Nail Holes	Condition
186. Sea Creatures							
A	1979-50-707	128 x 128.5	10.5	pk/or	(2) 10, (2) 5	2	
B	1979-50-708	128 x 128	12	pk/or	(2) 10, (2) 5	2	
C	1979-50-709	129 x 127	11	pk/or	(1) 10, (2) 5	2	
D	1979-50-710	126 x 127	12	pk/or and marbleized yellow	(2) 10, (2) 5	2	
E	1979-50-711	126 x 127	12	pk/or	(2) 10, (2) 5	2	
F	1979-50-712	126 x 125.5	11.5	pk/or	(1) 10, (3) 5	2	
G	1979-50-715	127 x 127	11.5	pk/or	(1) 10, (2) 5	2	
H	1979-50-716	127 x 128	11	pk/or	(2) 5	2	
I	1979-50-717	128 x 129	10.5	pk/or	(3) 10, (1) 5	2	
J	1979-50-718	128 x 127	10.5	pk/or	(1) 10, (1) 7.5, (2) 5	2	
K	1979-50-713	127 x 126	11	pk/or	(1) 10, (3) 5	2	
L	1979-50-714	128 x 127	11	pk/or	(2) 10, (2) 5	2	
M	1979-50-719	127 x 128	10.5	pk/or	(2) 10, (2) 5	2	
N	1979-50-720	125 x 126	11	pk/or	(2) 2.5	2	
O	1979-50-721	128 x 127	12	pk/or	(1) 7.5, (3) 5	2	
P	1979-50-722	127 x 127	11.5	pk/or	(4) 5	2	
Q	1979-50-702	126 x 127	10.5	pk/or and red	(3) 10, (1) 7.5	2	
R	1979-50-700	125 x 125.5	9.5	pk/or	(4) 10	2	small corner loss
187. Merman and Venus							
A	1979-50-699	126 x 126	9.5	pk/or and red	(3) 15, (1) 40	4	
B	1979-50-701	126 x 126.5	9	pk/or	(1) 15, (2) 10, (1) 5	2	
188. Sea Creatures							
A	1979-50-691	129 x 131	11.5	pk/or	(1) 10, (3) 5	2	corner loss
B	1979-50-692	131 x 132.5	11.5	pk/or	(4) 5	2	small losses
C	1979-50-693	131 x 132	12.5	pk/or	(1) 7.5, (3) 5	2	⅛ loss; edges
D	1979-50-694	129 x 129	12	yellow	(1) 7.5, (3) 5	2	bottom edge broken
189. Neptune							
	1983-101-124	128 x 129	11.5	yellow	(4) 5	2	
190. Fish							
A	1983-101-171	127 x 129.5	9	buff	(1) 15, (2) 10, (1) 5	2	small loss; toned fill
B	1983-101-170	129.5 x 129.5	10	yellow	(1) 15, (2) 10, (1) 5	0	small loss; toned fill
C	1983-101-172	129 x 129	8.5	yellow	(4) 5	2	small loss; toned fill
D	1983-101-173	128 x 128	9	yellow	(3) 10, (1) 5	3	small losses
191. Merman and Mermaid							
A	1979-50-687	131 x 132	9.5	yellow	(1) 7.5, (3) 5	0	
B	1979-50-688	132 x 131.5	8.5	pk/or and yellow	(2) 5	2	
192. Fortuna and Venus							
A	1979-50-690	125 x 126	11.5	pk/or and yellow	(4) 5	3	small losses; toned fill
B	1979-50-689	124 x 127	11	pk/or	(1) 7.5, (2) 5, (1) 2.5	2	small losses
193. Sea Creatures							
A	1979-50-706	130 x 130	11	pk/or	(4) 5	2	
B	1979-50-705	128 x 130	11	pk/or	(4) 5	2	
C	1979-50-704	129 x 129	11	pk/or	(4) 5	2	
D	1979-50-695	128 x 130	11	pk/or	(2) 5	2	
E	1979-50-703	131 x 132	11.5	pk/or	(1) 7.5, (3) 5	2	
F	1979-50-697	130 x 129	11	pk/or	(1) 10, (3) 5	3	⅛ loss
G	1979-50-696	131 x 131	11	pk/or	(4) 5	2	small losses
H	1979-50-698	131 x 131	11	pk/or	(3) 5	2	
194. Sea Creatures							
A	1983-101-176	128 x 126	10.5	yellow	(1) 15, (1) 12.5, (2) 5	2	
B	1983-101-178	128 x 130	11.5	yellow	(1) 10, (3) 5	2	

Tile	Accession Number	Dimensions (in mm)	Thickness (in mm)	Clay Body	Beveling of Edge (in degrees)	Nail Holes	Condition
C	1983-101-175	129 x 130	11	yellow	(3) 10, (1) 5	2	
D	1983-101-177	125 x 127.5	11	yellow	(2) 5	2	
E	1983-101-174	129 x 129	11.5	yellow	(4) 5	2	
F	1983-101-179	130 x 129.5	10.5	pk/or and yellow	(4) 5	2	

195. Sea Creatures

Tile	Accession Number	Dimensions	Thickness	Clay Body	Beveling of Edge	Nail Holes	Condition
A	1981-77-5	128 x 128	10.5	yellow	(1) 15, (2) 12.5, (1) 10	2	
B	1981-77-6	131 x 130	10.5	pk/or and yellow	(1) 15, (2) 12.5, (1) 5	2	
C	1981-77-7	129 x 129	11	pk/or	(3) 10, (1) 5	3	
D	1981-77-8	129 x 128	11	yellow	(1) 10, (1) 7.5, (2) 5	2	

196. Sea Creatures

Tile	Accession Number	Dimensions	Thickness	Clay Body	Beveling of Edge	Nail Holes	Condition
A	28-66-107	129 x 130	9.5	yellow	(2) 12.5, (1) 10, (1) 5	4	break
B	28-66-104	128 x 128	10.5	yellow	(3) 10, (1) 5	4	4 breaks; small losses; 2 toned fills
C	28-66-102	127 x 129	9.5	yellow	(3) 10, (1) 5	3	2 breaks; small losses; toned fills
D	28-66-106	127 x 128	11	yellow	(4) 5	3	4 breaks; small losses; toned fills
E	28-66-108	127 x 127	10	yellow	(1) 10, (3) 5	4	break; small losses
F	28-66-101	128 x 128	10.5	buff	(3) 10, (1) 5	4	break
G	28-66-103	128 x 128	10	buff	(1) 12.5, (2) 10, (1) 5	4	4 breaks; small loss— inpainted
H	28-66-182	127 x 129	10	yellow	(1) 12.5, (1) 10, (2) 7.5	3	
I	28-66-105	127 x 127	11	yellow	(2) 10, (1) 5	1	small losses

197. Ornamental Landscapes, Fruit, and Flowers with Aigrette Wreaths

Tile	Accession Number	Dimensions	Thickness	Clay Body	Beveling of Edge	Nail Holes	Condition
1-A	1983-101-130	128 x 127	10	pk/or	(3) 10, (1) 5	1	small loss
1-B	1983-101-131	127.5 x 127	9.5	pk/or	(4) 5	2	
1-C	1983-101-132	127.5 x 127.5	10	pk/or	(1) 12.5, (3) 10	2	
1-D	1983-101-133	125 x 126	10	pk/or	(4) 5	2	small losses
1-E	1983-101-134	126 x 126	10	pk/or	(4) 5	1	
2-A	1983-101-135	127 x 127	10	pk/or	(1) 10, (3) 5	0	
2-B	1983-101-136	127 x 126	9.5	pk/or	(1) 10, (1) 7.5, (2) 5	2	
2-C	1983-101-137	125 x 126	10	pk/or	(1) 10, (2) 7.5, (1) 5	1	
2-D	1983-101-138	125 x 126	9.5	pk/or	(1) 10, (3) 5	1	
2-E	1983-101-139	126 x 127	10	pk/or	(4) 5	1	
3-A	1983-101-140	125 x 126	10	pk/or	(2) 10, (2) 5	2	
3-B	1983-101-152	126 x 126	9.5	pk/or	(1) 10, (3) 5	2	
3-C	1983-101-142	126 x 125	9.5	pk/or	(2) 10, (2) 7.5	2	small losses
3-D	1983-101-143	125 x 125	9.5	pk/or	(2) 10, (2) 5	2	
3-E	1983-101-144	125 x 125	9.5	pk/or	(1) 10, (3) 5	1	small losses
4-A	1983-101-145	126 x 126	10	pk/or	(4) 10	2	
4-B	1983-101-146	125 x 127	9.5	pk/or	(2) 10, (2) 5	1	small losses
4-C	1983-101-147	127 x 127	10	pk/or	(4) 10	2	
4-D	1983-101-148	126.5 x 126	9.5	pk/or	(1) 10, (2) 7.5, (1) 5	2	
4-E	1983-101-149	125 x 126	9.5	pk/or	(4) 5	2	
5-A	1983-101-150	127.5 x 127	11	pk/or	(1) 15, (2) 12.5, (1) 10	0	
5-B	1983-101-151	128 x 127	10	pk/or	(2) 15, (1) 10, (1) 5	0	
5-C	1983-101-141	125 x 125	10.5	pk/or and yellow	(3) 10, (1) 5	1	
5-D	1983-101-153	126 x 125	9.5	pk/or	(1) 7.5, (3) 5	1	
5-E	1983-101-154	126 x 125.5	10	pk/or	(4) 10	1	

198. Ornamental Stars, Cruciforms, Fleurs-de-lis

Tile	Accession Number	Dimensions	Thickness	Clay Body	Beveling of Edge	Nail Holes	Condition
1-A	1979-50-783	133 x 133	12	pk/or	(2) 15, (2) 10	4	
1-B	1979-50-778	131 x 131	13	pk/or	(1) 15, (1) 10, (2) 5	4	
1-C	1979-50-785	130 x 130	13	pk/or	(1) 15, (1) 12.5, (2) 10	4	small corner loss
1-D	1979-50-729	130 x 130	12	pk/or	(1) 12.5, (1) 15, (1) 20, (1) 15	4	
2-A	1979-50-777	133 x 134	12.5	pk/or	(3) 10, (1) 15	4	small losses
2-B	1979-50-776	130 x 130	12	pk/or	(3) 15, (1) 10	4	small losses
2-C	1979-50-781	131 x 133	13	pk/or	(2) 15, (2) 10	4	
2-D	1979-50-731	130 x 131	13	pk/or	(1) 12.5, (1) 10, (2) 15	4	small corner loss
3-A	1979-50-732	131 x 131	13.5	pk/or	(2) 20, (1) 15, (1) 5	4	small losses
3-B	1979-50-775	130 x 129.5	13	pk/or	(1) 20, (2) 15, (1) 5	4	
3-C	1979-50-780	130 x 131	12	pk/or	(3) 15, (1) 10	4	
3-D	1979-50-787	133 x 132	12	pk/or	(3) 10, (1) 5	4	
4-A	1979-50-730	134 x 134	11.5	pk/or	(2) 5, (1) 7.5, (1) 10	4	
4-B	1979-50-774	131 x 131	13	pk/or	(2) 15, (2) 10	4	small losses
4-C	1979-50-788	130 x 130	13	pk/or	(3) 15, (1) 10	4	

Tile	Accession Number	Dimensions (in mm)	Thickness (in mm)	Clay Body	Beveling of Edge (in degrees)	Nail Holes	Condition
4-D	1979-50-784	132 x 132	12	pk/or	(2) 15, (2) 10, (1) 5	4	small losses
5-A	1979-50-779	133 x 132.5	13	pk/or	(1) 10, (2) 5, (1) 15	3	break; toned fill
5-B	1979-50-773	130 x 131	12	pk/or	(3) 15, (1) 10	4	
5-C	1979-50-786	132 x 131	12.5	pk/or	(3) 15, (1) 10	4	small losses
5-D	1979-50-782	131 x 131	12.5	pk/or	(1) 15, (2) 10, (1) 5	4	

199. Ornamental Stars, Cruciforms, and Fleurs-de-lis

Tile	Accession Number	Dimensions (in mm)	Thickness (in mm)	Clay Body	Beveling of Edge (in degrees)	Nail Holes	Condition
1-A	1979-50-768	130 x 129	13	pk/or	(3) 10, (1) 7.5	4	corner loss
1-B	1979-50-767	131 x 130	13	pk/or	(3) 10, (1) 7.5	3	small corner loss—inpainted
1-C	1979-50-771	132 x 132	13	pk/or	(1) 10, (3) 5	4	corner loss
1-D	1979-50-765	130 x 130	13	pk/or	(4) 10	4	small loss
2-A	1979-50-770	132 x 131	13	pk/or	(1) 15, (2) 10, (1) 12.5	4	
2-B	1979-50-766	130 x 129	13.5	pk/or	(1) 1.5, (3) 10	4	
2-C	1979-50-759	131 x 130	12.5	pk/or	(4) 10	4	
2-D	1979-50-769	132 x 131	12.5	pk/or and buff	(3) (10)	4	
3-A	1979-50-763	130 x 129	13.5	pk/or and buff	(1) 10, (3) 7.5	2	
3-B	1979-50-762	130 x 130	14	pk/or and buff	(1) 7.5, (3) 5	3	
3-C	1979-50-757	132 x 131	15	pk/or	(4) 10	3	
3-D	1979-50-761	130 x 130	14	pk/or and red	(1) 15, (2) 12.5, (1) 10	4	
4-A	1979-50-772	130 x 125	14	pk/or	(1) 15, (3) 10	4	small corner loss
4-B	1979-50-758	132 x 131	15	pk/or and red	(3) 15, (1) 10	4	small losses
4-C	1979-50-760	134 x 133	11.5	pk/or and buff	(3) 10, (1) 7.5	4	
4-D	1979-50-764	134 x 134	12	buff and red	(1) 15, (1) 12.5, (2) 10	4	break

200. Ornamental

Tile	Accession Number	Dimensions (in mm)	Thickness (in mm)	Clay Body	Beveling of Edge (in degrees)	Nail Holes	Condition
1-A	1979-50-741	131 x 132	15	pk/or	(2) 10, (2) 5	4	
1-B	1979-50-743	132 x 132	15	pk/or	(1) 20, (2) 10, (1) 5	4	
1-C	1979-50-755	131 x 132	15.5	pk/or	(2) 10, (2) 5	4	
1-D	1979-50-751	131 x 133	15.5	pk/or	(3) 10, (1) 5	4	
2-A	1979-50-746	132 x 133.5	15	pk/or	(3) 5	4	
2-B	1979-50-748	133 x 133	15	pk/or	(4) 5	4	
2-C	1979-50-753	132 x 133	15	pk/or	(4) 10	4	
2-D	1979-50-742	133 x 132	15	pk/or	(3) 10, (1) 5	4	

201. Ornamental

Tile	Accession Number	Dimensions (in mm)	Thickness (in mm)	Clay Body	Beveling of Edge (in degrees)	Nail Holes	Condition
1-A	1979-50-754	132 x 132	11.5	pk/or	(1) 10, (3) 5	2	
1-B	1979-50-747	134 x 136	12.5	pk/or and yellow	(1) 10, (3) 5	2	
1-C	1979-50-744	135 x 134	13.5	pk/or and yellow	(3) 10, (1) 5	2	
1-D	1979-50-749	132 x 134	14	yellow	(2) 40, (2) 5	2	
2-A	1979-50-745	134 x 134	13	pk/or and yellow	(3) 10, (1) 7.5	2	
2-B	1979-50-756	136 x 135	12	pk/or and yellow	(1) 15, (3) 10	2	large corner loss
2-C	1979-50-752	132 x 134.5	14	pk/or and yellow	(1) 30, (1) 15, (1) 10, (1) 5	2	corner loss
2-D	1979-50-750	132 x 135	16	yellow	(1) 40, (2) 10, (1) 5	2	

202. Ornamental

Tile	Accession Number	Dimensions (in mm)	Thickness (in mm)	Clay Body	Beveling of Edge (in degrees)	Nail Holes	Condition
1-A	1979-50-734	131 x 132.5	13	pk/or	(4) 10	2	
1-B	1979-50-736	131 x 131	12.5	pk/or	(3) 10, (1) 5	2	small losses
2-A	1979-50-733	130 x 131	12.5	pk/or	(4) 10	2	
2-B	1979-50-735	130 x 132	13	pk/or	(3) 12.5, (1) 10	2	

203. Ornamental

Tile	Accession Number	Dimensions (in mm)	Thickness (in mm)	Clay Body	Beveling of Edge (in degrees)	Nail Holes	Condition
1-A	1979-50-740	130 x 130	13	pk/or	(1) 15, (3) 10	2	
1-B	1979-50-739	130 x 131	14.5	pk/or	(1) 15, (1) 12.5, (2) 10	2	
2-A	1979-50-738	130 x 131	13	pk/or	(4) 15	4	
2-B	1979-50-737	131 x 132	13	pk/or and marbleized red	(1) 15, (1) 12.5, (2) 10	4	

204. Fleurs-de-lis

Tile	Accession Number	Dimensions (in mm)	Thickness (in mm)	Clay Body	Beveling of Edge (in degrees)	Nail Holes	Condition
1-A	1979-50-805	134 x 135	16	pk/or	(1) 7.5, (1) 5	4	
1-B	1979-50-807	134 x 134	15.5	pk/or	(4) 5	4	
2-A	1979-50-808	135 x 135	16	pk/or	(1) 10, (2) 7.5, (1) 5	4	
2-B	1979-50-806	134 x 135	15	pk/or	(4) 10	4	

205. Acanthus Leaves (Palmette)

Tile	Accession Number	Dimensions (in mm)	Thickness (in mm)	Clay Body	Beveling of Edge (in degrees)	Nail Holes	Condition
1-A	1979-50-803	128 x 130	11	pk/or and yellow	(3) 7.5, (1) 5	5	
1-B	1979-50-801	130 x 130	11	pk/or	(3) 7.5, (1) 5	3	
2-A	1979-50-802	129 x 130	11	pk/or	(4) 5	2	
2-B	1979-50-804	130 x 130	11	pk/or	(1) 12.5, (2) 10, (1) 7.5	2	

Tile	Accession Number	Dimensions (in mm)	Thickness (in mm)	Clay Body	Beveling of Edge (in degrees)	Nail Holes	Condition
206. Stylized Vines							
1-A	1979-50-815	131 x 134	16	pk/or and red	(3) 10	4	small losses
1-B	1979-50-813	133 x 133	17	pk/or	(2) 10, (2) 5	3	⅛ loss; toned fill
2-A	1979-50-812	135 x 135	17	buff	(2) 10, (2) 5	4	small losses
2-B	1979-50-814	133 x 132	16.5	pk/or and red	(4) 10	4	discolored glaze
207. Plant Forms and Chinese Scroll							
1-A	1979-50-818	130 x 130	13.5	pk/or	(1) 20, (1) 12.5, (2) 10	3	small loss
1-B	1979-50-821	132 x 131	14	pk/or	(1) 10, (3) 5	4	
2-A	1979-50-820	135 x 134	14.5	pk/or	(2) 10, (1) 7.5, (1) 5	3	small loss
2-B	1979-50-819	132 x 131	14.5	pk/or	(3) 15, (1) 10	4	corner loss
208. Tortoise Shell							
A	1970-50-791	129 x 127.5	12	pk/or	(2) 10, (1) 7.5, (1) 5	0	small losses—inpainted
B	1979-50-790	130 x 131	11	pk/or	(4) 10	2	small losses—inpainted
C	1979-50-792	131 x 130	10.5	pk/or	(1) 7.5, (3) 5	0	small losses—inpainted
D	1979-50-789	128 x 124	9.5	pk/or	(1) 10, (3) 5	0	small losses—inpainted
209. Marbleized							
1-A	1981-77-10	128 x 130	13	pk/or	(1) 10, (2) 7.5, (1) 5	2	small losses—inpainted
1-B	1981-77-12	128 x 128	13	pk/or	(4) 5	2	small losses—inpainted
2-A	1981-77-9	128 x 129	12	pk/or and buff	(3) 7.5, (1) 5	1	⅛ loss—inpainted
2-B	1981-77-11	128 x 127	13.5	pk/or and buff	(2) 7.5, (2) 5	0	small losses—inpainted
210. Jerusalem Feathers							
1-A	1979-50-794	126 x 127	8	yellow and buff	(2) 10, (2) 5	2	losses—inpainted
1-B	1979-50-795	127 x 127	8	yellow	(3) 10, (1) 7.5	2	
2-A	1979-50-796	131 x 130	7.5	buff	(2) 10, (2) 5	2	7 breaks; ¼ loss—inpainted
2-B	1979-50-793	128.5 x 129	8	buff	(3) 10, (1) 5	2	break
211. Name Plaque							
	1981-77-71	117 x 128	7.5	yellow	(1) 10, (1) 5	2	top edge lost; toned fill
212. Sun, Moon, and Stars (Rozenster)							
1-A	1979-50-797	129 x 128.5	9	yellow	(1) 10, (1) 5	3	small and corner losses
1-B	1979-50-798	127 x 127	9.5	yellow	(1) 10, (3) 5	2	small and corner losses
2-A	1979-50-799	128 x 128	8	yellow	(3) 10, (1) 7.5	0	corner loss—inpainted
2-B	1979-50-800	129 x 129.5	9	yellow	(1) 10, (2) 5	3	small and corner losses
213. Carnations and Star							
1-A	28-66-147	129 x 130	7.5	pk/or and buff	(4) 10	3	
1-B	28-66-148	128.5 x 129	8	pk/or and buff	(1) 15, (2) 12.5, (1) 10	3	
1-C	28-66-143	129 x 130	7.5	pk/or and buff	(3) 15, (1) 10	3	
1-D	28-66-151	129.5 x 129.5	8	pk/or and buff	(2) 15, (2) 10	3	
2-A	28-66-145	128 x 128	7.5	pk/or and buff	(4) 5	3	
2-B	28-66-140	129 x 128	7.5	pk/or and buff	(4) 10	3	break
2-C	28-66-141	128 x 130	7.5	pk/or and buff	(4) 10	3	
2-D	28-66-144	129 x 129	7.5	pk/or and buff	(3) 15, (1) 10	3	
3-A	28-66-150	129 x 129	7.5	pk/or and buff	(1) 12.5, (3) 10	3	
3-B	28-66-149	128 x 129	7.5	pk/or and buff	(4) 10	3	
3-C	28-66-142	130 x 130	7.5	pk/or and buff	(4) 10	4	
3-D	28-66-146	127 x 128.5	8	buff	(1) 15, (1) 12.5, (2) 10	2	

Tile	Accession Number	Dimensions (in mm)	Thickness (in mm)	Clay Body	Beveling of Edge (in degrees)	Nail Holes	Condition

214. Geometric Designs

Tile	Accession Number	Dimensions (in mm)	Thickness (in mm)	Clay Body	Beveling of Edge (in degrees)	Nail Holes	Condition
1-A	28-66-132	128 x 28	9	yellow	(3) 5	2	3 breaks; small loss—inpainted
1-B	28-66-133	128.5 x 128	8.5	yellow	(2) 15, (2) 10	2	2 breaks
1-C	28-66-135	128 x 127	8.5	yellow	(1) 10	1	2 breaks; corner loss—inpainted
1-D	28-66-137	123 x 106	8.5	buff	(1) 10, (1) 5	0	½ loss; break—inpainted
2-A	28-66-134	100 x 126	8	yellow	(1) 5	0	½ loss; 2 breaks—inpainted
2-B	28-66-131	127.5 x 128	9	yellow	(1) 10, (3) 5	2	break
2-C	28-66-138	127 x 127	8.5	buff	(4) 5	2	break
2-D	28-66-136	127 x 127	8.5	yellow	(2) 5	2	½ loss; 2 breaks—inpainted

215. Urn with Flowers

Tile	Accession Number	Dimensions (in mm)	Thickness (in mm)	Clay Body	Beveling of Edge (in degrees)	Nail Holes	Condition
1-A	1983-101-121a	130 x 130	7.5	buff	(4) 10	3	2 breaks—inpainted
1-B	1983-101-121b	129 x 129.5	7.5	buff	(4) 10	3	2 breaks—inpainted
1-C	1983-101-121c	130 x 130	8	buff	(4) 15	3	3 breaks—inpainted
1-D	1983-101-121d	129 x 129	7.5	buff	(4) 12.5	3	break; loss—inpainted
2-A	1983-101-121e	129 x 129	7.5	buff	(1) 15, (2) 10, (1) 5	3	3 breaks—inpainted
2-B	1983-101-121f	129 x 129.5	7.5	buff	(1) 20, (3) 10	3	break—inpainted
2-C	1983-101-121g	130 x 130	7.5	buff	(1) 15, (2) 10, (1) 5	3	2 breaks—inpainted
2-D	1983-101-121h	130.5 x 130	7.5	buff	(1) 15, (2) 10, (1) 5	3	break—inpainted
3-A	1983-101-121i	130 x 130	7.5	buff	(1) 15, (1) 10, (2) 5	3	5 breaks—inpainted
3-B	1983-101-121j	129.5 x 129.5	7.5	buff	(3) 10, (1) 5	2	5 breaks—inpainted
3-C	1983-101-121k	130 x 130	7.5	buff	(1) 15, (2) 10, (1) 5	1	2 breaks—inpainted
3-D	1983-101-121l	131 x 131	7.5	buff	(1) 15, (3) 10	3	2 breaks—inpainted
4-A	1983-101-121m	130 x 131	7.5	buff	(4) 10	2	2 breaks—inpainted
4-B	1983-101-121n	129 x 129	7.5	buff	(2) 15, (2) 10	3	break—inpainted
4-C	1983-101-121o	129 x 130	7.5	buff	(2) 15, (2) 10	2	break—inpainted
4-D	1983-101-121p	130 x 130	7.5	buff	(1) 15, (1) 10, (2) 5	2	small loss; 5 breaks—inpainted
5-A	1983-101-121q	131 x 129	7.5	buff	(4) 10	2	4 breaks; small loss—inpainted
5-B	1983-101-121r	130.5 x 130	7.5	buff	(1) 15, (2) 10, (1) 5	2	small loss—inpainted
5-C	1983-101-121s	129 x 128.5	7	buff	(2) 15, (2) 10	2	
5-D	1983-101-121t	129.5 x 129	7.5	buff	(1) 15, (3) 10	3	3 breaks—inpainted
6-A	1983-101-121u	128 x 130	7	buff	(1) 15, (3) 10	3	2 breaks—inpainted
6-B	1983-101-121v	130 x 130	7.5	buff	(4) 10	3	break—inpainted
6-C	1983-101-121w	130 x 130	7	buff	(3) 15, (1) 10	3	2 breaks—inpainted
6-D	1983-101-121x	129 x 129	7.5	buff	(2) 15, (2) 10	3	break—inpainted
7-A	1983-101-121y	129 x 129	7.5	buff	(1) 15, (3) 10	3	break—inpainted
7-B	1983-101-121z	130 x 130	7	buff	(1) 20, (2) 15, (1) 5	3	break—inpainted
7-C	1983-101-121aa	129 x 129.5	7	buff	(2) 15, (2) 10	3	break—inpainted
7-D	1983-101-121bb	130 x 129.5	7	buff	(1) 15, (2) 10, (1) 5	2	2 breaks—inpainted
8-A	1983-101-121cc	129 x 130	7	buff	(2) 15, (2) 12.5	2	

Tile	Accession Number	Dimensions (in mm)	Thickness (in mm)	Clay Body	Beveling of Edge (in degrees)	Nail Holes	Condition
8-B	1983-101-121dd	129 x 130	7	buff	(1) 20, (3) 10	3	break—inpainted
8-C	1983-101-121ee	129 x 129	7	buff	(1) 15, (3) 10	2	break—inpainted
8-D	1983-101-121ff	129 x 130	7	buff	(1) 15, (3) 10	3	break—inpainted
9-A	1983-101-121gg	129 x 129	7	buff	(2) 15, (2) 10	3	break; ⅛ loss
9-B	1983-101-121hh	129.5 x 129.5	7	buff	(4) 10	3	2 breaks—inpainted
9-C	1983-101-121ii	129.5 x 130	7	buff	(2) 15, (2) 10	3	2 breaks—inpainted
9-D	1983-101-121jj	129 x 129	7	buff	(1) 15, (3) 10	2	break; small loss—inpainted

216. Urn with Flowers

Tile	Accession Number	Dimensions (in mm)	Thickness (in mm)	Clay Body	Beveling of Edge (in degrees)	Nail Holes	Condition
1-A	66-209-1a	126 x 126.5	8.5	yellow	(3) 10, (1) 7.5	3	
1-B	66-209-1b	127 x 127	8	yellow	(3) 10, (1) 5	3	
1-C	66-209-1c	127 x 126.5	7.5	yellow	(1) 15, (3) 10	3	break
2-A	66-209-1d	127 x 127	7.5	yellow	(2) 15, (2) 10	3	break
2-B	66-209-1e	127 x 127	7.5	yellow	(4) 10	2	
2-C	66-209-1f	126 x 126	7.5	yellow	(3) 10, (1) 7.5	3	
3-A	66-209-1g	128 x 127	7.5	yellow	(1) 15, (3) 10	3	
3-B	66-209-1h	127 x 127	7.5	yellow	(4) 10	3	2 breaks; small loss—inpainted
3-C	66-209-1i	127 x 126.5	7.5	yellow	(1) 15, (2) 10, (1) 5	3	
4-A	66-209-1j	127 x 127	7.5	yellow	(3) 10, (1) 5	3	
4-B	66-209-1k	128 x 127	7.5	pk/or	(3) 10, (1) 5	3	
4-C	66-209-1l	128 x 127	8	pk/or	(3) 10, (1) 7.5	3	

217. Flower Vase (left)

Tile	Accession Number	Dimensions (in mm)	Thickness (in mm)	Clay Body	Beveling of Edge (in degrees)	Nail Holes	Condition
1-A	1979-50-830a	131 x 130	8.5	yellow	(3) 15, (1) 10	2	
1-B	1979-50-830b	129.5 x 131	8.5	yellow	(4) 10	2	
1-C	1979-50-830c	129.5 x 130.5	9	yellow	(1) 20, (2) 15, (1) 10	1	small corner loss
1-D	1979-50-830d	130.5 x 129	8.5	yellow	(3) 15, (1) 10	2	break
2-A	1979-50-830e	131 x 128	8.5	yellow	(1) 15, (2) 10, (1) 5	2	break
2-B	1979-50-830f	130 x 129.5	8.5	yellow	(1) 20, (2) 15, (1) 12.5	2	
2-C	1979-50-830g	130 × 129.5	8.5	yellow	(1) 10, (1) 15, (1) 10, (1) 5	2	
2-D	1979-50-830h	129 x 130	8.5	yellow	(2) 15, (2) 10	2	
3-A	1979-50-830i	129.5 x 130	8.5	yellow	(1) 15, (2) 10, (1) 5	2	
3-B	1979-50-830j	130 x 128.5	8.5	yellow	(1) 15, (2) 10, (1) 5	3	
3-C	1979-50-830k	130 x 130.5	8.5	yellow	(2) 15, (2) 10	2	break
3-D	1979-50-830l	131 x 130	8.5	yellow	(2) 15, (1) 10, (1) 5	2	
4-A	1979-50-830m	129 x 129	8.5	yellow	(2) 15, (2) 10	2	
4-B	1979-50-830n	130 x 129	8.5	yellow	(1) 15, (3) 10	2	4 breaks
4-C	1979-50-830o	129.5 x 130	8.5	yellow	(4) 5	2	
4-D	1979-50-830p	131 x 129.5	8.5	yellow	(1) 20, (2) 15, (1) 10	2	
5-A	1979-50-830q	129 x 130	8.5	yellow	(1) 15, (2) 10, (1) 5	3	break
5-B	1979-50-830r	130 x 129.5	8.5	yellow	(1) 15, (3) 10	2	
5-C	1979-50-830s	130 x 129	8.5	yellow	(1) 20, (1) 15, (2) 10	2	
5-D	1979-50-830t	130 x 130	8.5	yellow	(4) 20	2	
6-A	1979-50-830u	129 x 130	8.5	yellow	(2) 15, (2) 10	2	
6-B	1979-50-830v	129 x 130	8.5	yellow	(3) 20, (1) 15	2	
6-C	1979-50-830w	130 x 130	8.5	yellow	(2) 20, (2) 15	2	2 breaks
6-D	1979-50-830x	130 x 131	8.5	yellow	(3) 15, (1) 10	2	

217. Flower Vase (right)

Tile	Accession Number	Dimensions (in mm)	Thickness (in mm)	Clay Body	Beveling of Edge (in degrees)	Nail Holes	Condition
1-A	1979-50-831a	128 x 130	8	yellow	(3) 10, (1) 5	3	
1-B	1979-50-831b	129 x 130	8	yellow	(2) 15, (1) 10, (1) 5	2	corner loss; toned fill
1-C	1979-50-831c	130 x 130	8	buff	(3) 15, (1) 12.5	2	
1-D	1979-50-831d	129 x 130	8	yellow	(1) 15	2	
2-A	1979-50-831e	130 x 130	8	yellow	(2) 15, (2) 12.5	2	break; toned fill
2-B	1979-50-831f	130 x 130	8	yellow	(4) 15	2	
2-C	1979-50-831g	130 x 130	8.5	yellow	(2) 10, (2) 7.5	2	
2-D	1979-50-831h	130 x 130	8.5	yellow	(3) 10, (1) 5	2	
3-A	1979-50-831i	130 x 130	8.5	yellow	(4) 15	2	break
3-B	1979-50-831j	130 x 129	8.5	yellow	(4) 10	2	
3-C	1979-50-831k	129 x 130	8.5	yellow	(1) 7.5, (3) 5	2	
3-D	1979-50-831l	129 x 129.5	8	buff and yellow	(1) 12.5, (3) 10	1	2 breaks; corner loss; toned fill

Tile	Accession Number	Dimensions (in mm)	Thickness (in mm)	Clay Body	Beveling of Edge (in degrees)	Nail Holes	Condition
4-A	1979-50-831m	129 × 130	8	buff	(3) 15, (1) 10	2	
4-B	1979-50-831n	130 x 130	8.5	pk/or and buff	(1) 20, (2) 15, (1) 10	2	2 breaks; toned fill—inpainted
4-C	1979-50-831o	130 x 130	8	pk/or and buff	(1) 20, (2) 15, (1) 10	2	
4-D	1979-50-831p	130 x 129	8	pk/or and buff	(4) 15	2	
5-A	1979-50-831q	130 x 130	8.5	buff	(3) 15, (1) 10	2	
5-B	1979-50-831r	129 x 130.5	8.5	yellow	(1) 20, (2) 15, (1) 10	2	
5-C	1979-50-831s	128 x 129	8	yellow	(1) 25, (1) 17.5, (2) 15	2	
5-D	1979-50-831t	127 x 127	8	yellow	(2) 15, (2) 10	2	
6-A	1979-50-831u	129 x 130	8	buff	(2) 17.5, (2) 15	2	break
6-B	1979-50-831v	129 x 130	8	buff	(1) 20, (3) 15	2	break
6-C	1979-50-831w	130 x 129	8	buff and yellow	(2) 15, (2) 10	2	
6-D	1979-50-831x	130 x 129	8	buff and yellow	(1) 20, (3) 15	2	

218. Horse

Tile	Accession Number	Dimensions (in mm)	Thickness (in mm)	Clay Body	Beveling of Edge (in degrees)	Nail Holes	Condition
1-A	1979-50-826a	127 x 128	8	buff	(4) 5	2	small loss
1-B	1979-50-826b	128 x 129	8	buff	(4) 10	2	small losses
1-C	1979-50-826c	129 x 129	8	buff	(1) 7.5, (2) 5	2	
2-A	1979-50-826d	128 x 129	8	buff	(1) 7.5, (3) 5	2	break
2-B	1979-50-826e	130 x 129	8	buff	(4) 5	2	
2-C	1979-50-826f	129 x 127	8	buff	(1) 10, (3) 5	2	

218. Cow

Tile	Accession Number	Dimensions (in mm)	Thickness (in mm)	Clay Body	Beveling of Edge (in degrees)	Nail Holes	Condition
1-A	1979-50-827a	129 x 129	8.5	buff	(4) 5	2	break; small loss; toned fill
1-B	1979-50-827b	128 x 128.5	8	buff	(4) 5	2	small loss
1-C	1979-50-827c	127 x 128.5	8	buff	(2) 10, (2) 5	2	small loss
2-A	1979-50-827d	129 x 128.5	8	buff	(1) 10, (3) 5	2	
2-B	1979-50-827e	130 x 128	8.5	buff	(4) 5	2	break; small loss; toned fill
2-C	1979-50-827f	128 x 127	7.5	buff	(3) 10, (1) 5	2	

219. Commedia dell'Arte Figure (top)

Tile	Accession Number	Dimensions (in mm)	Thickness (in mm)	Clay Body	Beveling of Edge (in degrees)	Nail Holes	Condition
1-A	1979-50-829a	130 x 130	8	buff	(1) 10, (3) 5	0	2 breaks
1-B	1979-50-829b	129 x 130	8	buff	(2) 10, (2) 5	0	3 breaks; ¼ loss—inpainted
1-C	1979-50-829c	130 x 130.5	8.5	buff	(1) 12.5, (1) 10, (2) 5	0	break
1-D	1979-50-829d	129 x 129	8	buff	(2) 10, (2) 5	0	2 breaks
1-E	1979-50-829e	129 x 129	8	buff	(3) 5	0	break
2-A	1979-50-829f	129 x 131	8	buff	(1) 15, (2) 10, (1) 5	0	2 breaks; small loss; toned fill
2-B	1979-50-829g	129 x 130	8	buff	(1) 10, (3) 5	0	
2-C	1979-50-829h	129 x 129	8.5	buff	(1) 15, (3) 10	0	
2-D	1979-50-829i	129 x 130	8.5	buff	(2) 10, (2) 5	0	
2-E	1979-50-829j	129 x 130	8.5	buff	(2) 15, (2) 10	0	break; small loss
3-A	1979-50-829k	129 x 129	8	buff	(4) 10	0	
3-B	1979-50-829l	131 x 131	8.5	buff	(1) 15, (2) 10, (1) 5	0	corner loss
3-C	1979-50-829m	130 x 130	8.5	buff	(1) 15, (3) 10	0	
3-D	1979-50-829n	129 x 129	8	buff	(1) 15, (3) 5	0	
3-E	1979-50-829o	128 x 129	8	buff	(4) 10	0	
4-A	1979-50-829p	129 x 131	8	buff	(4) 10	0	break; small loss
4-B	1979-50-829q	130 x 129.5	8.5	buff	(2) 10, (2) 5	0	2 breaks
4-C	1979-50-829r	131 x 129	8	buff	(4) 10	0	break
4-D	1979-50-829s	129 x 130	8	buff	(3) 10, (1) 5	0	
4-E	1979-50-829t	128 x 129	8	buff	(1) 10, (3) 5	0	

219. Commedia dell'Arte Figure (bottom)

Tile	Accession Number	Dimensions (in mm)	Thickness (in mm)	Clay Body	Beveling of Edge (in degrees)	Nail Holes	Condition
1-A	1979-50-828a	129 x 130	8	buff	(1) 10, (3) 5	0	3 breaks
1-B	1979-50-828b	131 x 131	8.5	buff	(4) 5	0	4 breaks; small loss; toned fill
1-C	1979-50-828c	130 x 130	8	buff	(2) 10, (1) 5	0	3 breaks; small loss; toned fill
1-D	1979-50-828d	129 x 130	8.5	buff	(2) 10, (2) 5	0	
1-E	1979-50-828e	130 x 130	8	buff	(4) 5	0	break
2-A	1979-50-828f	130 x 129	8.5	buff	(4) 5	0	break
2-B	1979-50-828g	129 x 130	8.5	buff	(3) 5	0	2 breaks; small loss—inpainted
2-C	1979-50-828h	131 x 131	8.5	buff	(2) 10, (2) 5	0	
2-D	1979-50-828i	129 x 130	8.5	buff	(3) 10, (1) 5	0	
2-E	1979-50-828j	131 x 130	8.5	buff	(1) 15, (2) 10, (1) 5	0	
3-A	1979-50-828k	129 x 130	8.5	buff	(1) 10, (3) 5	1	2 breaks

Tile	Accession Number	Dimensions (in mm)	Thickness (in mm)	Clay Body	Beveling of Edge (in degrees)	Nail Holes	Condition
3-B	1979-50-828l	129 x 130	8.5	buff	(1) 10, (2) 5	0	
3-C	1979-50-828m	130 x 129	8	buff	(3) 5	0	3 breaks; small losses—inpainted
3-D	1979-50-828n	130 x 130	8.5	buff	(4) 5	0	
3-E	1979-50-828o	130 x 130	8	buff	(1) 10, (3) 5	0	
4-A	1979-50-828p	130 x 130	8	buff	(3) 5	0	
4-B	1979-50-828q	130 x 131	8	buff	(4) 5	0	
4-C	1979-50-828r	130 x 129	8.5	buff	(1) 15, (2) 10, (1) 5	0	
4-D	1979-50-828s	130 x 129	8	buff	(1) 15, (2) 10, (1) 5	0	
4-E	1979-50-828t	130 x 130	8.5	buff	(3) 5	0	2 breaks

220. The Battle of Ramillies

The 400 tiles in this panel (accession number 1979-50-152) range in height from 127 to 130 mm and in width from 128 to 131 mm, with a dimensional mode of 130 by 130 mm; the thickness range is from 7 to 8 mm, with a mode of 8 mm. The clay body of the tiles varies from buff to yellow. The edges bevel from 5 to 15°, with a mode of 10°, and the number of nail holes varies from 0 to 4, with a mode of 4.

Bibliography

(with abbreviations of frequently cited sources)

224

GENERAL

Bartsch, Adam von. *Le Peintre graveur.* 21 vols. Vienna, 1803–21.

Blunt, Wilfrid. *Tulipomania.* London, 1970.

Box, C. R. *The Dutch Seaborne Empire: 1600–1800.* New York, 1965.

Braudel, Fernand. *Civilization and Capitalism, 15th–18th Century.* Vol. 1, *The Structures of Everyday Life: The Limits of the Possible.* Vol. 2, *The Wheels of Commerce.* Translated by Siân Reynolds. New York, 1982.

Briels, J. *Zuid Nederlandse immigratie, 1572–1630.* Haarlem, 1978.

Brugmans, H. *Het huiselijk en maatschappelijk leven onzer voorouders.* 2 vols. Amsterdam, 1931.

Cats, Jacob. *Sinne- en minnebeelden.* Amsterdam, 1622.
———. *Houwelyck.* Amsterdam, 1625.

De la Court, 1662
De la Court, Pieter. *Interest van Holland ofte gronden van Hollands welvaren.* Amsterdam, 1662. Translated as *The True Interest and Political Maxims of the Republick of Holland and West-Friesland.* London, 1702.

Geyl, Pieter. *The Netherlands in the Seventeenth Century.* Pt. 1, *1609–1648.* New York, 1961.

De Groot and Vorstman, 1980
De Groot, Irene, and Vorstman, Robert. *Sailing Ships: Prints by the Dutch Masters from the Sixteenth to the Nineteenth Century.* Translated by Michael Hoyle. Maarssen, 1980.

Hollstein, 1949–
Hollstein, F.W.H. *Dutch and Flemish Etchings, Engravings, and Woodcuts, c. 1450–1700.* Vols. 1– . Amsterdam, 1949– .

Hoogewerff, G. J. *De geschiedenis van de St. Lucasgilden in Nederland.* Amsterdam, 1947.

De Jongh, E. *Zinne- en minnebeelden in de schilderkunst van de zeventiende eeuw.* Amsterdam, 1967.

Van Mander, Karel. *Leven der doorluchtige Nederlandsche en Hoogduytsche schilders.* Amsterdam, 1617.

Meyer, 1962
Meyer, Maurits de. *De volks- en kinderprent in de Nederlanden van de 15ᵉ tot de 20ᵉ eeuw.* Antwerp, 1962.

Montias, John Michael. *Artists and Artisans in Delft: A Socio-Economic Study of the Seventeenth Century.* Princeton, N.J., 1982.

Netherlands Bicentennial Committee. *The Dutch Republic in the Days of John Adams: 1775–1795.* Traveling exhibition, 1976–77. Circulated by the Smithsonian Traveling Exhibition Service.

The Pierpont Morgan Library, New York. *William & Mary and Their House.* New York, 1979.

Preston, 1974
Preston, Rupert. *The Seventeenth Century Marine Painters of the Netherlands.* Leigh-on-Sea, 1974.

Regin, 1976
Regin, Deric. *Traders, Artists, Burghers: A Cultural History of Amsterdam in the Seventeenth Century.* Assen, 1976.

Rijksmuseum, Rijksprentenkabinet, Amsterdam. *Catchpennyprints: Dutch Popular- and Childrenprints.* July 10–October 3, 1976. Catalogue by C. F. van Veen.

Ripa, Cesare. *Baroque and Rococo Pictorial Imagery.* Reprint of *Iconologia,* 1758–60. Edited and translated by Edward A. Maser. New York, 1971.

Scheller, R. W. "Nieuwe gegevens over het St. Lukasgilde te Delft in de zestiende eeuw." *Nederlands Kunsthistorisch Jaarboek,* vol. 23 (1972), pp. 41–48.

Skelton, 1952
Skelton, R. A. *Decorative Printed Maps of the Fifteenth to Seventeenth Centuries.* New York, 1952.

Thornton, Peter. *Seventeenth-Century Interior Decoration in England, France and Holland.* New Haven, 1978.

Van Veen, C. F. *Dutch Catchpenny Prints: Three Centuries of Pictorial Broadsides for Children.* The Hague, 1971.

Visscher, Roemer. *Sinnepoppen.* Amsterdam, 1614.

Volker, T. *Porcelain and the Dutch East India Company as Recorded in the Dagh-Registers of Batavia Castle, Those of Hirado and Deshima and Other Contemporary Papers, 1602–1682.* Leiden, 1954.

De Vries, Jan. *The Dutch Rural Economy in the Golden Age, 1500–1700.* New Haven, 1974.

Van de Waal, 1952
Van de Waal, H. *Drie eeuwen Vaderlandsche geschied-uitbeelding 1500–1800: Een iconologische studie.* 2 vols. The Hague, 1952.

Zumthor, Paul. *Daily Life in Rembrandt's Holland.* New York, 1963.

225

Altonaer Museum, 1965
Altonaer Museum, Hamburg. *Fliesen: Sammlung Johann Keller, München.* June–August 1965.

Amsterdam, Christie's. *Dutch Tiles, Delft and Glass, Asiatic and European Ceramics, Art Nouveau and Art Déco.* October 23–24, 1979.

———. *Dutch Delft from the Collection of the Late A. Vromen Jr.* October 24, 1979.

———. *Dutch Tiles, Delft and Glass, Asiatic and European Ceramics, Art Nouveau and Art Déco.* March 25–26, 1980.

———. *Fine Dutch Tiles from the Property of the Estate of the Late Mabel Brady Garvan, Including Tiles from the Eelco M. Vis Sale, New York, 1927 and from Various Other Properties and European Ceramics, Including Delft.* June 11, 1980.

———. *Hollandse tegels, Delfts aardewerk en glas, Europese ceramiek, Art Nouveau en Art Déco.* October 21–23, 1980.

Amsterdam, Christie's, 1981
Amsterdam, Christie's. *Een belangrijke particuliere collectie Nederlandse tegels.* October 13, 1981.

———. *Hollandse tegels, Europese ceramiek, Delfts aardewerk, glas, Art Nouveau en Art Déco.* May 13–14, 1982.

———. *Special Collectors Sale Including Dutch Tiles, Early (Pedal and Motor-cycle) Lamps, Textiles, Mechanical Music, Toys, Dolls and Model Cars . . . .* November 30, 1982.

———. *Fine European Ceramics, Glass, Dutch Delftware, Art Nouveau and Art Déco . . . .* October 27, 1983.

Amsterdam, Kunstveilingen Sotheby Mak van Waay B. V. *Hollandse tegels de collectie van de Heer F. Leerink.* Pt. 1, *Bijbelse voorstellingen.* Pt. 2, *Dierfiguren.* Cat. 321. November 18, 1980.

Amsterdam, Sotheby, cat. 327, 1981
Amsterdam, Kunstveilingen Sotheby Mak van Waay B. V. *Hollandse tegels de collectie van de Heer F. Leerink.* Pt. 3, *Landschappen.* Pt. 4, *De menselijke figuur.* Pt. 5, Schepen. Cat. 327. April 28, 1981.

Amsterdam, Sotheby, cat. 337, 1981
Amsterdam, Kunstveilingen Sotheby Mak van Waay B. V. *Hollandse tegels de collectie*

van de Heer F. Leerink. Pt. 6, *Mythologische onderwerpen en zeewezens.* Pt. 7, *Ornamenten.* Cat. 337. November 18, 1981.

Amsterdam, Sotheby, cat. 349, 1982
Amsterdam, Kunstveilingen Sotheby Mak van Waay B. V. *Hollandse tegels de collectie van wijlen de Heer F. Leerink.* Pt. 8, *Vogels.* Pt. 9, *Bloemen.* Cat. 349. May 13, 1982.

———. *Tegels, Chinese en Japanse ceramiek, Aziatische kunst, ethnografica, sculptures, wapens en oude kunstnijverheid.* Cat. 357 B–D. November 10–11, 1982.

Anthonisen, B. "Waarom Mozes hoorns heeft!" *Tegel,* vol. 7 (1978–79), pp. 10–12.

Barber, Edwin Atlee. *Tin Enameled Pottery: Maiolica, Delft and Other Stanniferous Faience.* Philadelphia, 1906.

Baumann, Hans Gottfried. "Een tegelvondst in Hamburg." *Tegel,* vol. 10 (1982), pp. 34–37.

Berendsen et al., 1967
Berendsen, Anne, et al. *Tiles: A General History.* Translated by Janet Seligman. London, 1967.

Van den Bergh, A. J., and Dirkzwager, N. "Een spotprent op tegels." *Tegel,* vol. 8 (1980), pp. 2–5.

Bodenheim, F. "Loodglazuuraardewerk uit het eind van de 16de en het begin van de 17de eeuw." *Oud-Holland,* vol. 49 no. 5 (1932), pp. 229–36.

Bolwerk, P.B.M. "Een nieuwe methode voor het opplakken van tegels." *Tegel,* vol. 10 (1982), pp. 38–40.

De Bruyn, Astrid. "De Hollandse schouw in de 17de eeuw." *Spiegel Historiael,* vol. 11, no. 4 (April 1976), pp. 248–49.

Bureau van de Rijksinspecteur voor Roerende Monumenten, The Hague. *Kunst in het Klein: De schoonheid van oude tegels.* No. 3. N.d.

Van der Burgh, A.H.H. "Aanteekeningen betreffende de oudste Delftsche plateelbakkers." *Oud-Holland,* vol. 21 (1903), pp. 22–50.

Caiger-Smith, Alan. *Tin-Glaze Pottery in Europe and the Islamic World: The Tradition of 1000 Years in Maiolica, Faience and Delftware.* London, 1973.

Cohen, Arnold. "Traditional Dutch Tilemaking." *Ceramics Monthly,* vol. 24, no. 9 (November 1976), pp. 40–44.

Cooper-Hewitt Museum, New York. *Tiles in the Collection of the Cooper-Hewitt Museum.* Washington, D.C., 1980.

Van Dam, Jan Daniel. "Tegelverzamelaars in Nederland." *Jaarboek het Fries Genootschap,* vol. 61 (1981), pp. 109–18.

Van Dam, 1982, *Geleyersgoet*
Van Dam, Jan Daniel. *Geleyersgoet en Hollants porceleyn: Ontwikkelingen in de Nederlandse aardewerkindustrie 1560–1660. Mededelingenblad Nederlandse Vereniging van Vrienden van de Ceramiek,* no. 108 (1982), pp. 2–92.

Dronkers, F. S. "Tegelbakkerij te Hasselt." *Tegel* (1972), pp. 3–6.

Dubbe, 1972
Dubbe, B. "Daar waar de keizer te voet gaat: Bijdrage tot de iconografie van de Nederlandse wandtegel." *Antiek,* vol. 7, no. 4 (November 1972), pp. 303–17.

"Eenmaal andermaal . . . De veilingbijlage van *Antiek.*" *Antiek,* vol. 15, no. 2 (August–September 1980), insert, pp. 1–2.

Elhorst, J.H.W. "Tegeltapijten in de Buitenkerk van Kampen." *Tegel,* vol. 8 (1980), pp. 16–19.

Elling, 1978
Elling, Gertrud, and Elling, Wilhelm. *Fliesen und Fliesenbilder in Westmünsterland.* Vreden, 1978.

Von Falke, Otto. "Holländische Fayencebilder." *Pantheon,* vol. 19 (January–June 1937), pp. 154–58.

Forrer, 1901
Forrer, Robert R. *Geschichte der Europäischen Fliesen-Keramik vom Mittelalter bis zum Jahre 1900.* Strasbourg, 1901.

Fries Museum, 1971–72
Fries Museum, Leeuwarden. *Antwerps plateel. Mededelingenblad Vrieden van de Nederlandse Ceramiek,* nos. 62–63 (1971), pp. 2–80. Catalogue of an exhibition held December 18, 1971–January 29, 1972. Introduction by Dingeman Korf. Text by Herbert Jan Hijmersma.

Gallois, H. C. "Over Rotterdamsche tegels." *Mededeelingen van den Dienst voor Kunsten en Wetenschappen der Gemeente 's Gravenhage* (April 1919), pp. 18–25.

Van Gelder, H. E. "Het grote tegeltableau der Collectie Loudon." *Bulletin van het*

Rijksmuseum, vol. 4, no. 4 (1956), pp. 96–101.

——, and Jansen, Beatrice. *Aardewerk en porselein in de Nederlandse musea.* Zeist, 1965.

Gemeentemuseum, The Hague. *Nederlands aardewerk 1500–1800.* August 6–October 2, 1949. Catalogue by Beatrice Jansen.

Geus, 1919–21

Geus, Commer de. "Tegels en tegeltableaux." *Oude Kunst,* vol. 4 (1919), pp. 154–61, 258–66; vol. 5 (1919–20), pp. 94–100; vol. 6 (1920–21), pp. 127–36.

Geus, 1921

Geus, Commer de. "The History of the Dutch Wall Tile, as Exemplified in the Vis Collection." *The Connoisseur,* vol. 61, no. 242 (October 1921), pp. 64–72.

Geus, 1922

Geus, Commer de. "The History of the Dutch Wall Tile as Exemplified in the Vis Collection: Some Further Types." *The Connoisseur,* vol. 63, no. 250 (June 1922), pp. 75–83.

——. "The History of the Dutch Wall Tile, as Exemplified in the Vis Collection: Composite Decorations." *The Connoisseur,* vol. 65, no. 260 (April 1923), pp. 210–16, 219.

Geus, 1931

Geus, Commer de. *Oud-Nederlandsche tegels: Bijdrage tot de kennis van de Nederlandsche ceramiek, naar aanleiding van de collectie Arthur Isaac in het Rijksmuseum te A'dam.* Amsterdam, 1931.

De Goederen, 1962

De Goederen, G. "In duijsent vreesen?" *Vrienden van de Nederlandse Ceramiek,* no. 27 (June 1962), pp. 14–24; no. 30 (March 1963), pp. 37–38.

Groneman, A. "De 16e-eeuwse tegelvloeren in het kasteel der Nassau's te Breda en enige andere producten van oud-nederlandse majolicanijverheid; een nieuwe toeschrijving aan Guido Andries." *Vrienden van de Nederlandse Ceramiek,* no. 16 (September 1959), pp. 1–25, 30–32.

De Haan, Johan. "Tegelfragmenten met afwijkende hoekmotieven." *Tegel,* vol. 7 (1978–79), pp. 24–25.

Hanekuijk, D. "Olifanten op tegels." *Tegel,* vol. 11 (1983), pp. 2–15.

Havard, Henry. *Histoire de la faïence de Delft.* 2 vols. Paris, 1878.

——. *La Céramique hollandaise: Histoire des faïences de Delft, Haarlem, Rotterdam, Arnheim, Utrecht etc. . . . 2 vols.* Amsterdam, 1909.

Heger, H.-J. R. "Bijbeltegels uit Neurenberg." *Tegel,* vol. 8 (1980), pp. 8–11.

Van Helden, R.C.P. "De komeet van 1664." *Tegel,* vol. 9 (1981), pp. 2–3.

Hetjens-Museum, Deutsches Keramikmuseum, Düsseldorf. *Niederländische Fliesen 16.–19. Jahrhundert: Sammlung Albert Poensgen.* Autumn 1983.

Hijmersma, Herbert Jan. "Majolica in de zuidelijke Nederlanden." *Spiegel Historiael,* vol. 10, no. 9 (September 1975), pp. 501–3.

Hijmersma, 1975

Hijmersma, Herbert Jan. "De verbreiding van de majolica in West-Europa." *Spiegel Historiael,* vol. 10, no. 10 (October 1975), pp. 564–65.

Hijmersma, 1977

Hijmersma, Herbert Jan. "Guido di Savino and Other Antwerp Potters of the Sixteenth Century." *The Connoisseur,* vol. 195, no. 786 (August 1977), pp. 264–71.

"Holland's Golden Age: Decorative Arts." *Museum News: The Toledo Museum of Art,* n.s., vol. 1, no. 3 (Autumn 1957), pp. 19–22.

Holthuis, Muller, and Smeenk, 1971

Holthuis, L. B.; Muller, H. E.; and Smeenk, C. "Vogels op Nederlandse 17de eeuwse tegels naar gravures van Adriaen Collaert en iets over Leguatia gigantea." *Bulletin Museum Boymans–van Beuningen,* vol. 21, no. 1 (1971), pp. 3–19.

Honey, William Bowyer. "Dutch Pottery and Glass." *The Burlington Magazine,* vol. 81, no. 477 (December 1942), pp. 295–300.

——. *European Ceramic Art from the End of the Middle Ages to about 1815.* 2 vols. London, 1949–52.

Hoynck, 1920

Hoynck van Papendrecht, A. *De Rotterdamsche plateel- en tegelbakkers en hun product 1590–1851: Bijdrage tot de geschiedenis der oude Noord-Nederlandsche majolika.* Rotterdam, 1920.

Hudig, Ferrand W. "Een Amsterdamsche tegelbakkerij." *Oud-Holland,* vol. 43 (1926), pp. 73–79.

——. "Wapengoet en porceleyn." *Oud-Holland,* vol. 43 (1926), pp. 162–81.

——. "Amsterdamsche aardewerkvondsten, I." *Oud-Holland,* vol. 45 (1928), pp. 61–83.

Hudig, 1929

Hudig, Ferrand W. *Delfter Fayence.* Berlin, 1929.

Huijg, Adriaan. *De Bijbel op tegels.* Boxtel, 1978.

Jessel, 1962

Jessel, Hans Werner. *Fliesen Bilderbuch.* Flensburg, [c. 1962].

De Jonge, 1947

De Jonge, C. H. *Oud-Nederlandsche majolica en Delftsch aardewerk.* Amsterdam, 1947.

——. "Hollandse tegelkamers in Duitse en Franse kastelen uit de eerste helft van de 18e eeuwe." *Nederlands Kunsthistorisch Jaarboek,* vol. 10 (1959), pp. 125–209.

——. *"Westraven" 1661–1961: Van pannen en estriken tot tegels en plastieken.* Utrecht, 1961.

——. "Delft-ware at Vught: The Fentener van Vlissingen Collection." *Apollo,* n.s., vol. 80, no. 33 (November 1964), pp. 384–89.

——. *Delfts aardewerk.* Rotterdam, 1965.

De Jonge, 1966

De Jonge, C. H. "Een 17e eeuwse Hollandse tegelvloer in het kasteel Beauregard bij Blois." *Vrienden van de Nederlandse Ceramiek,* no. 43 (June 1966), pp. 3–45, 50–51.

——. "Een particuliere verzameling Delfts aardewerk." *Vrienden van de Nederlandse Ceramiek,* no. 48 (September 1967), pp. 3–73, 76–77.

De Jonge, 1971

De Jonge, C. H. *Dutch Tiles.* Translated by P. S. Falla. London, 1971.

Kaufmann, 1973

Kaufmann, Gerhard. *Bemalte Wandfliesen: Kulturgeschichte, Technik und Dekoration der Fliesen in Mitteleuropa.* Munich, 1973.

"Het kerstverhaal op tegels." *Tegel,* vol. 9 (1981), pp. 4–8.

De Kleyn, J. "Over aardewerk met sgraffito of slib-krasversiering en aanverwante technieken." *Vrienden van de Nederlandse Ceramiek,* no. 33 (December 1963), pp. 6–20, 51.

Knipping, 1961
Knipping, John B. "De voorstellingswereld van de Nederlandse wandtegels." *Vrienden van de Nederlandse Ceramiek,* no. 24 (October 1961), pp. 1–25, 35–37.

Knipping, 1962
Knipping, John B. "De voorstellingswereld van de Nederlandse wandtegels: 3. Ikonografie van de tegels der verzameling 'Van Teijen' te Monnikendam." *Vrienden van de Nederlandse Ceramiek,* no. 25 (January 1962), pp. 17–37, 39–41.

Knochenhauer, Paul F. *Niederländische Fliesen-Ornamente.* Berlin, 1886.

Korf, 1957
Korf, Dingeman. "Ovaaltjes." *Vrienden van de Nederlandse Ceramiek,* no. 8 (1957), pp. 14–15.

———. " 'Haarlemse tegels.' " *Vrienden van de Nederlandse Ceramiek,* no. 10 (January 1958), pp. 12–16, 22.

———. "Spiegeltegels." *Vrienden van de Nederlandse Ceramiek,* no. 11 (April 1958), pp. 11–12.

———. "Ovaaltegels." *Vrienden van de Nederlandse Ceramiek,* no. 12 (July 1958), pp. 20–22, 25–26.

Korf, 1958, "De Drietulp"
Korf, Dingeman. "De Drietulp." *Vrienden van de Nederlandse Ceramiek,* no. 13 (December 1958), pp. 15–18, 24.

———. "Tegels in het interieur." *Vrienden van de Nederlandse Ceramiek,* no. 17 (December 1959), pp. 19–22, 34.

———. *Tegels.* Bussum, 1959.

Korf, 1961
Korf, Dingeman. "Kwadraattegels." *Vrienden van de Nederlandse Ceramiek,* no. 21 (January 1961), pp. 16–18, 24.

———. *Nederlandse majolica.* Bussum, 1963.

———. "Recente vondsten van Nederlandse majolica." Pts. 1–8. *Vrienden van de Nederlandse Ceramiek,* no. 36 (September 1964), pp. 1–5, 50; no. 39 (June 1965), pp. 25–31, 45; no. 45 (December 1966), pp. 5–10, 30; no. 51 (June 1968), pp. 10–20, 43; no. 53 (December 1968), pp. 1–9, 31; no. 60 (1970), pp. 26–35, 42; nos. 66–67 (1972), pp. 3–18, 92; nos. 69–70 (1973), pp. 2–7, 60–61.

———. *Dutch Tiles.* Translated by Marieke Clarke. New York, 1964.

———. "Wat doen we met onze tegels." *Antiek,* vol. 1, no. 4 (1966), pp. 10–14.

Korf, 1968
Korf, Dingeman. *Haarlemse majolica- en tegelbakkers. Vrienden van de Nederlandse Ceramiek,* no. 50 (March 1968), pp. 3–32.

———. "We verzamelen tegels." *Antiek,* vol. 2, no. 8 (1968), pp. 366–73.

Korf, 1969
Korf, Dingeman. *De tegelverzameling Nanne Ottema in het Gemeentelijk Museum het Princessehof te Leeuwarden. Vrienden van de Nederlandse Ceramiek,* nos. 56–57 (1969), pp. 3–83.

———. "Majolicaschotelgoed en -tegels met religieuze opschriften." *Antiek,* vol. 5, no. 10 (May 1971), pp. 601–12.

Korf, 1976
Korf, Dingeman. "Merkwaardige majolicavondsten bij Haarlem." *Antiek,* vol. 10, no. 8 (March 1976), pp. 769–89.

Korf, 1979
Korf, Dingeman. *Tegels.* 7th rev. ed. Haarlem, 1979.

Kühnast, Gerd. "Die Kellinghusener Fayencefliesen." *Tegel* (1972), pp. 11–16.

———. "De tien jaar na Hallig Hooge." *Tegel,* vol. 7 (1978–79), pp. 26–28.

Landzaat, F. H. "Een ontdekking." *Tegel,* vol. 10 (1982), pp. 29–33.

Lane, Arthur. "Delftse tegels uit Hampton Court en Daniel Marot's werkzaamheid aldaar." *Bulletin van het Rijksmuseum,* vol. 57, no. 1 (1959), pp. 12–21.

Lane, 1960
Lane, Arthur. *A Guide to the Collection of Tiles: Victoria and Albert Museum.* 2d ed. London, 1960.

Langseth-Christensen, Lillian. "The Willet-Holthuysen Kitchen." *Gourmet,* vol. 39, no. 11 (November 1979), pp. 42–43, 74–78.

Lasch, Bernd. "Netherlandish Faience at Düsseldorf." *The Burlington Magazine,* vol. 58, no. 339 (June 1931), pp. 301–3.

Van Lemmen, 1980
Van Lemmen, Hans. "Hollandse negentiende eeuwse 'six inch' tegels in Engeland en Schotland." *Tegel,* vol. 8 (1980), pp. 24–27.

Van Loo, J. "Schilderssportretten op tegels." *Vrienden van de Nederlandse Ceramiek,* no. 45 (December 1966), pp. 16–21, 30–31.

———. "De 'Vrienden-vitrine' voor de eerste maal in gebruik." *Tegel,* vol. 8 (1980), pp. 28–32.

———. "Over wederdopers en klein-formaat portrettegels." *Tegel,* vol. 10 (1982), pp. 2–11.

Van Luttervelt, R. "Nederlandse tegeltableaux te New-York." *Bulletin van den Nederlandse Oudheidkundige,* vol. 6, no. 3 (1950), pp. 146–48.

Marggraf, Rainer. "Tegeltableaus met huisdieren uit huizen in het Graafschap Benthiem." *Tegel,* vol. 6 (1977), pp. 10–29.

Matusz, J. *Delfts aardewerk.* Translated by H. J. Bergmans. Amerongen, 1977.

Meyer, Hellmuth, and Meyer-Küpper, Ursula. "Allegorien der Elemente auf Fliesen." *Mededelingenblad Nederlandse Vereniging van Vrienden van de Ceramiek,* no. 105 (1982), pp. 15–19.

———. "Eine Serie von Schiffsfliesen mit Medaillons." *Mededelingenblad Nederlandse Vereniging van Vrienden van de Ceramiek,* no. 105 (1982), pp. 11–14.

Musées Royaux d'Art et d'Histoire, Brussels. *Faïences hollandaises, XVIIe–XVIIIe–début XIXe.* 2 vols. Anvers, 1956–58. Catalogue by J. Helbig.

Neurdenburg, Elisabeth. *Oud aardewerk toegelicht aan de verzamelingen in het Nederlandsch Museum voor Geschiedenis en Kunst te Amsterdam.* Amsterdam, 1917.

Neurdenburg, 1923, *Old Dutch Pottery*
Neurdenburg, Elisabeth. *Old Dutch Pottery and Tiles.* Translated by Bernard Rackham. New York, 1923.

———. "Twee Rotterdamsche tegeltableaux." *Rotterdamsch Jaarboekje,* 3rd ser., vol. 1 (1923), pp. 62–65.

———. *Oude Nederlandsche majolica en tegels Delftsch aardewerk.* Amsterdam, 1944.

Nicaise, H. "Les Origines italiennes des faïenceries d'Anvers et des Pays-Bas au XVIe siècle." *Bulletin de l'Institut Historique Belge de Rome,* vol. 14 (1934), pp. 109–29.

Noon, Mary A. "Renaissance and Post-Renaissance Tiles of Spain and the Netherlands." *Chronicle of the Museum for the Arts of Decoration of Cooper Union,* vol. 1, no. 2 (April 1936), pp. 36–51.

Ormsbee, Thomas Hamilton. "Delft Tiles, Their Variety and Imitations." *American Collector,* vol. 11, no. 8 (September 1942), pp. 8–9, 19.

———. "An 18th Century Trade Scene on Tiles." *American Collector,* vol. 13, no. 11 (December 1944), p. 5.

Ottema, 1920
Ottema, Nanne. *Friesche majolica.* N.p., 1920.

———. "De opkomst van het Majolica-Bedrijf in de noordelijke Nederlanden." *Oud-Holland,* vol. 42 (1925), pp. 237–62.

———. "Tegelschilders." *Historia: Maandschrift voor Geschiedenis,* vol. 9 (1949), pp. 199–205.

Paape, 1794
Paape, Gerrit. *De plateelbakker of Delftsch aardewerkmaker.* Dordrecht, 1794.

Peelen, Ida C. E. "Afbeeldingen op Delftsch aardewerk, ontleend aan prenten." *Oud-Holland,* vol. 34 (1916), pp. 232–35.

Peelen, 1922
Peelen, Ida C. E. *Rijks-Museum "Huis Lambert van Meerten" te Delft.* Delft, 1922.

Pennsylvania Museum, Philadelphia. *Exhibition of Tiles.* 1915. Introduction by Edwin Atlee Barber.

Philippe, L. *Les Carreaux plombés du Château de Treffort et de Saint-Martin-le-Chatel.* Bourg, 1914.

Philippen, 1932
Philippen, L.J.M. "Oud Antwerpsch plateelwerk." In Museum de Gulden Spoor, Antwerp, *Gedenkboek Frans Claes* (Antwerp, 1932), pp. 243–57.

———. *De Oud-Antwerpsche majolica.* Brussels, 1938.

Piccolpasso, Cipriano. *The Three Books of the Potter's Art . . . .* Translated by Bernard Rackham. London, 1934.

Pitter, H. "Gesigneerde bijbeltegels." *Tegel,* vol. 9 (1981), pp. 16–19.

Pluis, Jan. *Tegels met bijbelse voorstellingen.* Zutphen, 1967.

Pluis, 1975
Pluis, Jan. "Nederlandse gesprenkelde tegels met een geschilderde voorstelling." *Tegel,* vol. 5 (1975), pp. 5–29.

———. "Bijbeltegels van G. D.

Graaf." *Tegel,* vol. 7 (1978–79), pp. 20–23.

———. "De keeshond op tegeltableaus." *Tegel,* no. 7 (1978–79), pp. 2–6.

Pluis, 1979
Pluis, Jan. *Kinderspelen op tegels.* Assen, 1979.

———. "Twee bijzondere Harlinger kinderspeltegels." *Tegel,* vol. 8 (1980), pp. 20–23.

———. "Kanariekooitableaus." *Tegel,* vol. 11 (1983), pp. 16–41.

Pluis, Van den Akker, and Muller, 1974
Pluis, Jan; Van den Akker, Minze; and Muller, H. E. *Dieren op tegels. Mededelingenblad Vrienden van de Nederlandse Ceramiek,* nos. 75–76 (1974), pp. 2–128.

Het Princessehof, 1980
Gemeentelijk Museum het Princessehof, Leeuwarden. *Schepen op tegels.* Summer 1980. Catalogue by Jan Daniel van Dam.

Het Princessehof, 1981
Gemeentelijk Museum het Princessehof, Leeuwarden. *Het ornament op Nederlandse tegels: 1560–1625.* Summer 1981. Catalogue by Jan Daniel van Dam.

Het Princessehof, 1982
Gemeentelijk Museum het Princessehof, Leeuwarden. *De Nederlandse tegel in kleur.* Leeuwarden, 1982. Catalogue by Jan Daniel van Dam.

Rackham, Bernard. "Early Dutch Maiolica and Its English Kindred." *The Burlington Magazine,* vol. 33, no. 187 (October 1918), pp. 116–23.

———. *Early Netherlands Maiolica, with Special Reference to the Tiles at the Vyne in Hampshire.* London, 1926.

———. *Italian Maiolica.* London, [c. 1952].

Ray, 1973
Ray, Anthony. *English Delftware Tiles.* London, 1973.

De Ree, G.J.M. "Een 18e eeuws tegeltransport." *Tegel,* vol. 8 (1980), pp. 12–15.

———. "Plavuizen van Johannis J. Cramer en Andries Piers." *Tegel,* vol. 8 (1980), pp. 6–7.

———. "Tegels gevonden in Delft." *Tegel,* vol. 9 (1981), pp. 24–25.

Renaud, 1958
Renaud, J.G.N. "Middeleeuwse vloertegels." *Vrienden van de Nederlandse Ceramiek,* no. 12 (July 1958), pp. 6–13, 24.

———. "Nieuwe vondsten van aardewerk met ornament in

slib-krastechniek." *Vrienden van de Nederlandse Ceramiek,* no. 34 (March 1964), pp. 1–7, 40.

Rijksmuseum, Amsterdam. *Delfts aardewerk.* Amsterdam, 1955. Catalogue by Marie-Anne Heukensfeldt Jansen.

———. *Majolica.* Amsterdam, 1961. Catalogue by Marie-Anne Heukensfeldt Jansen.

Rijksmuseum Zuiderzeemuseum, Enkhuizen. *De verzameling tegels in het Rijksmuseum "Zuiderzeemuseum" te Enkhuizen.* Enkhuizen, 1966. Catalogue by D. F. Lunsingh Scheurleer.

Rust, W. J. "Bijbelse tegels." *Vrienden van de Nederlandse Ceramiek,* no. 40 (September 1965), pp. 1–10, 32.

Scavizzi, Giuseppe. *Maiolica, Delft and Faïence.* Translated by Peter Locke. London, 1970.

Scheurleer, 1966
Scheurleer, D. F. Lunsingh. "Een modellenboek voor tegels." *Antiek,* vol. 1, no. 4 (1966), pp. 19–29.

Scheurleer, 1969
Scheurleer, D. F. Lunsingh. "Tegels met zeventiende-eeuwse Oranjevorsten." *Antiek,* vol. 3, no. 6 (January 1969), pp. 327–36.

———. "Nederlandse tegels in het Couven-Museum te Aken." *Antiek,* vol. 4, no. 1 (1969), pp. 10–18.

———. "Invloed en navolging van het Chinese Wan Li- en Overgangsporselein op Noord-Nederlandse majolica." *Vrienden van de Nederlandse Ceramiek,* no. 60 (1970), pp. 7–21, 40–41.

Scheurleer, 1970
Scheurleer, D. F. Lunsingh. *Zeewezens op tegels.* Lochem, 1970.

———. *Delfts blauw.* Bussum, 1975.

Schoubye, Sigurd. *Hollandske vaegfliser.* Copenhagen, 1963.

Simões, 1959
Simões, J. M. Dos Santos. *Carreaux céramiques hollandaise au Portugal et en Espagne.* The Hague, 1959.

Stahl, S. "Ein Handstein des 17. Jahrhunderts aus Buxtehude." *Tegel,* vols. 3–4 (1973–74), pp. 31–40.

———. "Het herkennen van tegels van een aantal duitse fayencefabrieken uit de 18e eeuw." *Tegel,* vols. 3–4 (1973–74), pp. 14–30.

Stedelijk Museum de Lakenhal, Leiden. *Tegelschouw: Tegels uit eigen bezit.* December 23, 1970–February 7, 1971. Catalogue by Ingrid W. L. Moerman.

————. *Geleend goed: Tegel collectie G. de Goederen.* December 12, 1980–January 25, 1981. Catalogue by Ingrid W. L. Moerman.

Stedelijk Museum Vanderkelen-Mertens, Leuven. *Tegels.* Leuven, 1982. Catalogue by P. Demuynck.

Stettner, 1982
Stettner, Heinrich. "Slingerende vuurkorven aan palen." *Tegel,* vol. 10 (1982), pp. 12–27.

Stichting Tichelaars, Historisch Bezit, Makkum. *Makkum aardewerk.* Makkum, 1970.

"Symposium Antwerps plateel." *Mededelingenblad Vrienden van de Nederlandse Ceramiek,* nos. 66–67 (1972), pp. 37–52.

Tegelmuseum, 1972
Tegelmuseum It Noflik Sté, Otterlo. *Bijbelse voorstellingen op tegels en Fries aardewerk.* September 24–October 30, 1972. Catalogue by Jan Pluis and Minze van den Akker.

————. *Kinderspelen op tegels.* April 1–June 15, 1979. Catalogue by Jan Pluis and Minze van den Akker. Also shown at Altonaer Museum, Norddeutsches Landesmuseum, Hamburg, July 4–September 2, 1979; Nationalmuseet, Copenhagen, September 14–November 11, 1979; Gemeentelijk Museum het Princessehof, Leeuwarden, November 23, 1979–January 13, 1980.

Tegelmuseum, 1979
Tegelmuseum It Noflik Sté, Otterlo. *Tegel allerlei.* September 1979. Catalogue by N. Dirkzwager.

Terwen, P. A. "Ontzouten van tegels." *Tegel,* vol. 9 (1981), pp. 20–23.

Tichelaar, J. P. *"De Friese fabrieken." Vrienden van de Nederlandse Ceramiek,* no. 19 (June 1960), pp. 1–34.

————, and Tichelaar, P. J. *200 Jahre friesische Fayencen.* Catalogue of an exhibition held at Kreismuseum, Zons, March 24–June 19, 1977.

Tønder Museum, Tønder. *Fliseesamlingen i Tønder Museum: Katalogus van de tegelkollektie.* Rev. ed. Tønder, 1982. Catalogue by Sigurd Schoubye.

Victoria and Albert Museum, 1923
Victoria and Albert Museum, London. *Dutch Tiles: The Van den Bergh Gift.* London, 1923. Catalogue by Bernard Rackham.

Vis coll. sale, 1927
New York, American Art Association, Inc. *Dutch Tiles of the XV–XVIII Century: Collection of Eelco M. Vis. . . .* November 9–10, 1927.

Vis and Geus, 1926
Vis, Eelco M., and de Geus, Commer. *Altholländische Fliesen.* Vol. 1. Leipzig, 1926.

Vis and Geus, 1933
Vis, Eelco M., and de Geus, Commer. *Altholländische Fliesen.* Vol. 2. Leipzig, 1933. Text by Ferrand W. Hudig.

Vis and Geus, 1978
Vis, Eelco M., and de Geus, Commer. *Altholländische Fliesen.* 1926, 1933. 2 vols. Reprint, with revisions by D. F. Lunsingh Scheurleer. Stuttgart, 1978.

Vroegh, G. "Een interessant geschenk voor Dirk Kooyman." *Tegel,* vol. 6 (1977), pp. 2–3.

Wadsworth, B. M. "Old Delft Tiles." *School Arts Magazine,* vol. 29 (February 1930), pp. 333–39.

Wassenbergh, 1968
Wassenbergh, A. "Grauda of Gesina of . . . ? Harlingse tegels en hun ontwerpers." *Antiek,* vol. 3 (1968), pp. 198–213.

Wires, E. Stanley. "Some Dutch and English Tiles in American Collections." *Antiques,* vol. 51, no. 4 (April 1947), pp. 238–40.

Zijlstra, Jan. "Fries 'Bergs' Aardewerk." *Tegel* (1972), p. 9.

Zijp, R. P. "Bijbeltegels." In Rijksmuseum het Catharijneconvent, Utrecht, *Vroomheid per dozijn* (April 3–August 15, 1982), pp. 43–46.

229